# Concepts and Theories of Human Development

**ADDISON-WESLEY
PUBLISHING COMPANY**

Reading, Massachusetts • Menlo Park, California
London • Amsterdam • Don Mills, Ontario • Sydney

# Concepts and Theories of Human Development

**RICHARD M. LERNER**
Eastern Michigan University

ISBN 0-201-04342-4
ABCDEFGHIJ-MA-79876

To
Sam Goldfarb,
Sam Korn,
and
Sam Karson

# Preface

In this text I have attempted to provide the student with a general introduction to core concepts and major theories in developmental psychology. An integration is made of such concepts and theories, along with their philosophical bases, within a framework that presents divergent points of view about these ideas. However, the Organismic, Interactionist developmental viewpoint is clearly given major emphasis. While discussions of the views and research of learning-oriented developmentalists, for example, are presented and evaluated, as is the work of particular ethological writers, these positions are contrasted with the Organismic developmental notions of such theorists as Piaget, Werner, Schneirla, Kohlberg, and Thomas. The work of these latter theorists is representative of an orientation to developmental psychology which is viewed as being the most tenable and useful conceptual synthesis currently available. In essence then, the text attempts to integrate and evaluate core concepts, major theories, and research in developmental psychology from an Organismic, Interactionist perspective.

The format of this text stands in contrast to most other human development texts which primarily emphasize research findings. Of course, I believe that such "facts" are necessary for students. But the meaning of such information, and indeed what we actually consider to be factual, is constantly altered in the face of empirical advances and new theoretical integrations. Hence, I believe that students will appreciate and assimilate the facts of development if they are acquainted with the "meanings" attached to these facts by developmental psychologists. For this reason, and because of historical trends within the field which have now come to stress the primacy of theoretical integration, I have written this book to emphasize such integrations. Students are still given "facts," but first they are given some bases for interpreting the possible "meanings" of these facts.

Three interrelated bases for understanding human development are offered. First, the Mechanistic and the Organismic philosophies of science are shown to provide both contrasting views of "humans" and alternative approaches to the major conceptual issues of psychological development. Second, various ways of formulating these issues (the nature-nurture and the continuity-discontinuity controversies) are discussed, and recent empirical research and debate about them are evaluated. For instance, the relevance of the nature-nurture controversy to concerns about the sources of racial differences in IQ scores is indicated. Similarly, the relation between the continuity-discontinuity issue and debates about the ontogenetic (and phylogenetic) generalizability of laws of learning and of life-span changes in intellectual functioning is discussed. Finally, ways are described in which the core conceptual issues of development may provide a basis for understanding the formulation of the major types of theoretical points of view in developmental psychology. The Stage, Differential, Ipsative, and Learning approaches are discussed, and major theories and research within each approach are introduced. Thus the Stage approaches of Piaget, Kohlberg, and Freud, the Differential theoretical formulations of Erikson, the differential empirical work of Kagan and Moss, and the life-span, multivariate, sequential research approaches of Schaie, Baltes, and Nesselroade are presented. In addition, the Ipsative research, involved in the New York Longitudinal Study, of Thomas, Chess, Birch, Hertzig, and Korn, and the Learning-oriented work of Bijou and Baer and of Mischel is evaluated. Finally, the interrelation of developmental theory and research is presented along with a discussion of its social relevance.

While it is of course possible to provide the student with an integration of theory and fact by combining numerous readings and lecture materials, such a combination would not provide the student with what I consider to be a major asset of this book, which is the organization and integration of this material within what I hope is a convincing and useful framework from which to understand human development. This Organismic, Interactionist point of view, interrelated with its conceptual alternatives, permits an introduction to the study of developmental psychology that is, in my opinion, both pedagogically appropriate and more closely aligned with current emphases in the discipline than is any other single treatment.

During the course of writing the text, my ideas have been challenged and honed by the numerous colleagues with whom I have discussed the material and who have read various portions of several drafts of the book. Specifically, I would like to thank John Knapp, Joseph Fitzgerald, Samuel Karson, Henry Orloff, and Stuart Karabenick, all of Eastern Michigan University, and the many reviewers provided by the publisher. In addition, I am in great debt to the people who provided my training: Harry Beilin, Samuel Messick, Joseph Church, Elizabeth Gellert, and of course, Sam Korn. The diverse contributions of these people have sharpened my ideas, strengthened my arguments, and improved my presentation. Any limitations that remain stem totally from me. I am also grateful to Cathy Gendron for her excellent drawings of psychologists. I am also indebted to the hundreds of students who have listened semester after semester to lectures that attempted to present the material contained in this book and who have read and used various drafts of this book as their course text. Here I would especially like to thank Michael Karson for his thorough work and useful criticisms. My students' enthusiasm, comments, and interactions with me—and likewise the lack of these things—have led to substantial alterations in the format and style of presentation of various text sections.

*Ypsilanti, Michigan*                                                                                          R.M.L.
*January 1976*

# Contents

1   Human Development: Facts or Theory?   1

Students and Basic Courses in Sciences: Facts versus Theory   2
The Changing Place of Theory in Developmental Psychology   5
Philosophy, Theory, and Research   6
The Trouble with Textbooks   11
This Text's Approach   11
Cattell's Inductive-Hypothetico-Deductive Model   12
The Organismic Position   15
Summary   17

2   The Organismic and the Unity-of-Science Philosophies   19

Core Conceptual Issues of Developmental Psychology   21
The Unity-of-Science Position   23
The Organismic Position   30
Sources of Development   34
The Role of the Organism's Action   37
Unity-of-Science—Organismic Compromises   38
Summary   44

3   The Nature-Nurture Controversy: Implications of the Question, How?   47

Some Philosophical Roots of the Nature-Nurture Issue   48
The Nature-Nurture Controversy in Psychology   49
Toward a Resolution of the Nature-Nurture Controversy   50
The Nature and Nurture of Intelligence   67
Summary   80

4   The Nature-Nurture Controversy: An Interactionist Position   85

The Notion of Homology Rejected   86
Behavioral Stereotypy versus Behavioral Plasticity   89
Concepts Representing Development   94
The Critical-Periods Hypothesis   98
Instinct: Innate Behavior   100
Circular Functions and Self-Stimulation in Development   102
Some Issues in the Development of Perception   104
Summary   108

5   The Continuity-Discontinuity Issue   111

The Contributions of Heinz Werner   113
The Orthogenetic Principle   116
The Phylogeny of Learning: Continuity or Discontinuity?   122
The Stability-Instability Issue   127
Summary   132

6   Theories of Development: An Overview   135

The Stage-Theory View of Development   136
The Differential Approach to Development   141
The Ipsative Approach to Development   148
Summary   153

7   Stage Theories of Development   157

Piaget's Organismic Developmental Theory of Cognition   158

ix

Kohlberg's Stage Theory of the Development of Moral Reasoning 174
Freud's Stage Theory of Psychosexual Development 184
Summary 192

8  The Differential Approach 195

Erikson's Stage and Differential Theory of Psychosocial Development 196
The Kagan and Moss Study of Birth to Maturity 209
Schaie's General Developmental Model 215
Summary 222

9  The Ipsative Approach 225

The New York Longitudinal Study 228
Summary 249

10  The Learning Approach 253

What Is Learning? 254
Types of Learning 258
Characteristics of the Learning Approach 269
An Evaluation of the Learning Approach 273
Conclusions 276
Bowers' Analysis of Situations, Persons, and Interactions 277
Summary 278

11  Research and Social Implications 281

Facets of Research 282
Some Social Implications 298
Summary 303

References 307

Index 315

# 1
## Human Development: Facts or Theory?

## Students and Basic Courses in Sciences: Facts versus Theory

"Well, I've learned a lot of facts, but what do they all *mean*?"

A typical comment from a college student? I believe so. Many undergraduates feel that many college courses are concerned only with the memorization of facts. It is generally believed, by students and professors alike, that facts (perhaps crammed into one's head the night before an exam) are usually soon forgotten. On the other hand, general concepts are retained for a much longer time. Still, many basic college courses ask the student to deal with a lot of facts.

Certainly with today's explosion of scientific research, there are more facts to know than ever before. Thus, to get an overview of a field like child or developmental psychology a student must become acquainted with such information. Yet, as more and more data are being collected each year, rapid clarifications, refinements, and advancements are made in factual knowledge (see Ghiselli, 1974).

For example, before the work of Fantz and his colleagues (e.g., Fantz, 1958; Fantz, Ordy, and Udelf, 1962), it was believed that a newborn infant's visual world is comprised of blurry images, either because of incomplete maturation of the visual system or because of too few appropriate visual experiences. However, Fantz was able to de-

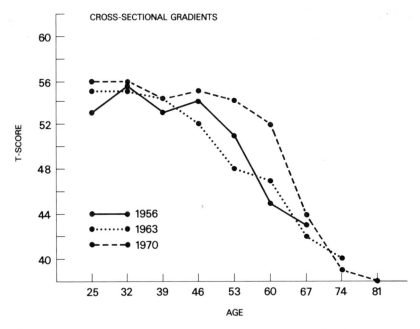

**Fig. 1.1** Age changes in intellectual ability, as revealed by conventional, cross-sectional research techniques. Note the *decreases* in intellectual ability that occur with increases in age. *Source:* K. W. Schaie, G. V. Labouvie, and B. U. Buech, "Generational and Cohort-Specific Differences in Adult Cognitive Functioning: A Fourteen-Year Study of Independent Samples," *Developmental Psychology* **9** (1973). Copyright 1973 by the American Psychological Association. Reprinted by permission.

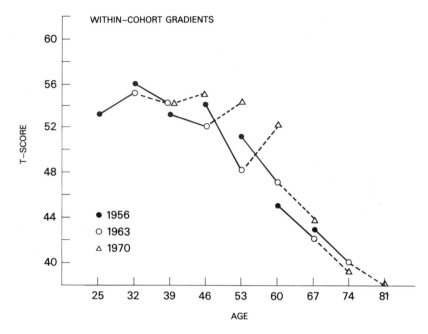

**Fig. 1.2** Age changes in intellectual ability, as revealed by new, cross-sequential, within-cohort research techniques. Note the *increases* in intellectual ability that occur between some age levels. *Source:* Schaie, Labouvie, and Buech (1973). Copyright 1973 by the American Psychological Association. Reprinted by permission.

monstrate that even in the first few weeks of life infants are capable of accommodating for near visual stimulation and also of seeing patterns. Thus, the "fact" that infants can see only diffuse light and dark stimulation and not patterns was found not to be a "fact" at all. Through use of the methods he devised, Fantz was able to clarify, refine, and advance our factual knowledge of infants' visual perception.

Similarly, other such "facts" about psychological development have fallen by the wayside in the face of new research findings. For instance, for many decades a basic "fact" of intellectual development concerned the decreases in functions that were assumed to characterize the later years of life. It was held that as people progressed from adulthood through old age there was an accelerating decline in their mental functioning (e.g., see Horn, 1970; Schaie, Labouvie, and Buech, 1973). These decrements were supposed to represent a certain "fact" of psychological development and functioning across the life span, as shown by the data in Fig. 1.1. Yet, due to Schaie and his colleagues (e.g., Nesselroade, Schaie, and Baltes, 1972; Schaie, 1965; Schaie, Labouvie, and Buech, 1973; Schaie and Strother, 1968), new techniques for the measurement of age changes in intellectual development and functioning across the life span have been devised. The application of these techniques in several studies has indicated that there may not be a general decline in intellectual functioning throughout the later years after all! Rather, as illustrated in Fig. 1.2, the results of some of these studies (e.g., Schaie, Labouvie, and Buech, 1973) indicate that for *some* measures of intellectual functioning there is no age-associated decrease. In fact, for some measures there seems to be an *increase*. Thus, through the application of new measurement designs, Schaie and his associates were able to demonstrate that a long-held "fact" about cognitive development across the human life span was not a "fact" after all.

Numerous other examples to illustrate the impermanence of facts might be offered. The idea that adolescence is a developmental period invariantly characterized by storm and stress had to be largely discarded in the face of new empirical evidence about the characteristics of adolescent behavior supplied by Douvan and Adelson (1966); similarly, the alleged "fact" that adolescents and their parents are on opposite sides of a generation gap had to be revised in light of the findings of several studies of such family members (e.g., Lerner, 1975; Lerner, Karson, Meisels, and Knapp, 1975; Weinstock and Lerner, 1972). Thus we should recognize the point that in an active science such as developmental psychology the status of our knowledge will rapidly and continually be altered. It is possible—perhaps even likely—then, that what is a "fact" when a particular student begins a basic course may no longer be a "fact" by the end of it.

I do not intend to be simply irreverent about the role of facts in science. Facts are of course absolutely essential in any active scientific enterprise. But, to paraphrase Ludwig von Bertalanffy (1933), a biologist noted for his important theoretical contributions to that science, a collection of data no more makes a science than does a heap of bricks make a house!

What then builds the bricks of a science into a house? I believe it is a science's conceptual issues. An illustration will clarify my position. Certainly the listings in a telephone directory are facts. But a knowledge of the names in the phone book would certainly be, to quote Bob Dylan, "useless and pointless knowledge!" However, if one could relate this data to some conceptual framework, then perhaps some meaning could be provided. Let us suppose that I have a hypothesis, perhaps derived from some theory in social psychology, which predicts that a person with a particular ethnic background would tend to live in a neighborhood with other people having that same ethnic background. To test my hypothesis I spread out a large street map of the city and cut out each name and address in the phone book and place it on the appropriate place on the map. After a while a pattern begins to emerge. People with Italian-sounding names seem to cluster in one area, people with Irish-sounding names in another area, and people with Jewish-sounding names in yet another. This example not only supports a hypothesis but illustrates the important point that a conceptual orientation provides a way of organizing a seemingly meaningless or obscure body of data into a meaningful and perhaps important body of factual knowledge.

We see, then, a major function of theory—to integrate existing facts, to organize them in such a way as to give them meaning. Developmental psychologists may often have numerous facts available to them—for example, facts relating to children's thinking at various ages in their lives. The results of empirical studies might indicate that young children tend to use relatively general, global, and concrete categories to organize their thinking, while older children use more differentiated, specific, and abstract categories. For instance, the younger child might label all furry, four-legged creatures as "doggies," while the older child might have different labels (e.g., "dogs," "cats," and "horses"), might have a shared, superordinate label ("animals"), and might in addition recognize that all these creatures share the common, but abstract, quality of "life." While such facts are interesting in and of themselves, their meaning is not obvious; and certainly the implications of such facts for more general psychological development and functioning are not clear. Thus, when a person such as Jean Piaget offers a theory of development of thought which allows such facts to be integrated and understood, and moreover specifies the empirically testable implications of such theoretical integrations for other areas of psychological development, the importance is obvious. Such theories are useful to developmental psychology because they integrate existing factual knowledge, as well as further advance our knowledge.

The point, then, is that while facts are important, they alone do not make a science. The development of science, I would argue, relies in addition on the advancement of theory. As a survey of the history of developmental psychology bears witness (Looft, 1972), the science of psychological development has itself evolved through an increasing emphasis on theory and conceptual integration. Let us see how.

## The Changing Place of Theory in Developmental Psychology

As we have seen, theory—as opposed to the mere collection of facts—plays a seemingly crucial, dual role in science: it serves as an integrator of existing facts *and* as a basis for the derivation of new facts. Yet this central importance of theory in developmental psychology has not always been recognized.

In the early part of this century, scientists engaged in the study of psychological development apparently viewed their role as *describers* of behavioral and physical development. For example, they carefully observed and described how children ate and slept, how language developed in the "average" child, and how physical growth proceeded (see Gesell, 1929, 1946). However, the broad theoretical meanings of such developments were essentially ignored. Thus, through the early 1930s, developmental psychology was relatively unconcerned with either general theoretical issues or broad organizing principles. Rather, the discipline was comprised of psychologists interested essentially in the collection of theoretically unrelated facts. These facts described typical behaviors or physical characteristics to be expected from specific groups of children of certain ages. In other words, developmental psychology was concerned with description and cataloguing of *normative* data; there was relatively little concern for theoretical explanation.

However, Bronfenbrenner (1963), in a review of the development of the field, concluded that from the 1930s to the early 1960s there was a progressive shift from studies involving the mere collection of data toward those concerned with more abstract psychological processes and behavioral constructs. Looking at the nature of developmental psychology in 1963, Bronfenbrenner thus stated that "first and foremost, the gathering of data for data's sake seems to have lost favor. The major concern in today's developmental research is clearly with inferred processes and constructs" (p. 527).

In a similar, but more recent, review of the status of contemporary developmental psychology, Looft (1972) reports a continuation of the trends reported by Bronfenbrenner. Looft's review, like Bronfenbrenner's, was based on an analysis of various handbooks of developmental psychology written from the 1930s through the time of his review. Each handbook sought to reflect the current content of developmental psychology to other scientists in the discipline. Looft found that developmental psychology in

1931 was largely descriptive. Thus, consistent with Bronfenbrenner's conclusion, he found that developmental psychologists devoted their time essentially to the collection of normative facts. A shift toward more general, integrative concerns was seen by 1946. Bronfenbrenner contended that this trend continued to enlarge through 1963, and Looft saw this increasing emphasis continuing through 1972. Hence, as the editor of the 1970 handbook pointed out: "The major contemporary empirical and theoretical emphases in the field of developmental psychology, however, seem to be on *explanations* of the psychological changes that occur, the mechanisms and processes accounting for growth and development" (Mussen, 1970, p. vii).

Thus, while facts alone have their place, an understanding of the meaning and implications of facts cannot be achieved without theory; and since facts will inevitably change and be modified in the face of new empirical advances, an understanding of the potential meaning and implications of any facts—through the understanding of theory—becomes of enhanced importance.

Yet while the scientific status of theory per se and the need and roles for theory remain essentially invariant, we cannot ignore research. If there were no research, then, of course, theories would be useless exercises. If there were no way to test a given theoretical integration, the formulation would be scientifically useless. Although we will discuss the role of research in developmental psychology at length in Chapter 11, as well as at other points throughout the book, it is appropriate to indicate here some of the important interrelations that exist between research and theory. Research is often done in order to try to answer the questions raised by the science. Such issue-based research results in data, as does all research. A theory may exist or can be devised to integrate a science's facts—the first role of a theory—and to lead to the generation of new facts—the second role of a theory. Someone, however, may think that these same facts can be integrated in another way—that is, with another theory. From such differences, theoretical arguments (polemics) come about. Yet, because each different theory attaches different meanings to the same facts, research is done in order to clarify the differing theoretical interpretations. And even if such theoretical differences did not exist, research would be done in order to see if ideas derived from the theory (i.e., hypotheses) could be shown to be empirically supported. In either case research is needed to show either the integrative usefulness of a theory or its usefulness in leading to new facts. Thus, while in the abstract theory and research are inextricably bound, some concrete interrelational problems exist.

Because of the complexity and abstractness of many of the controversies of a science, the interrelation of research and issues is often not evident or unequivocal. A common complaint of many people working in science is that there seems to be a widening gap between theory and research. Although there is some truth in this statement, I suggest that if one looks at the relation between research and theory at another, more basic level, an interrelation may be seen.

## Philosophy, Theory, and Research

Everything a scientist does rests upon:
1. *assumptions* about the nature of the subject matter;
2. preferences for the *topic* of study within the subject matter; and
3. preferences for the *methods* of study.

Many psychologists are interested in studying how human behavior develops. If I assume, for purposes of illustration, that all behavioral development can be regarded as the acquisition of a series of responses, then I would look for the stimuli in the person's environment that evoke these responses. Consistent with point 1, I would be assuming that even complex adult behaviors could be understood on the basis of these stimulation-producing responding relationships, and my job as a scientist would be to tease out the basic stimulus-response relations. Accordingly, and in terms of point 2, the topics that my work would bear upon could perhaps be best subsumed by the terms *learning* or *conditioning*. Moreover, as suggested by point 3, the methods I employed would be those involved with classical or operant conditioning. I would probably prefer not to study topics such as "alterations in the balance among the id, ego, and superego in determining changes in the development of people's object relations" or "the need for the development of a sense of trust in the first year of life in order for healthy personality development to proceed." Accordingly, the methods used to study these topics (e.g., clinical interviews, retrospective verbal reports) would not rank very high on my method preference list.

Now, if someone asked me how my work related to general issues in psychological development, I could point out that all scientific research, no matter what topic it bears on, is underlain by a particular philosophy of science or of *human beings*. Continuing with our above illustration, one could ask where my assumption—that behavioral development can be viewed as the cumulative acquisition of responses—came from. Couldn't other assumptions be made, for example that there is something inborn (innate) in human beings which serves to shape their behavioral development? The answer to both of the above questions is yes. The point here is that the particular assumptions I make are determined by the philosophical view I hold toward the nature of human development.

Before psychology became a science, people were philosophizing about how human beings come to be the way they are. Philosophical camps ("schools") formed to represent the different points of view. As we will see in Chapter 3, one such school argued that human beings come into the world with some inborn capacities, while another group maintained that all behavioral development can be accounted for by environmental and therefore empirical phenomena (phenomena that can be observed). This latter viewpoint played a central role in shaping a prevalent viewpoint in modern psychology—the environmentalist, or behaviorist, viewpoint. Thus, because of one's commitment to this philosophical-theoretical position, one would make the assumption that the nature of behavioral development is comprised of environmentally determined, response-acquisition phenomena.

These assertions lead to a second response to the question of how my work is related to general conceptual issues in development. We have seen how research is underlain by theory and, more primarily, by a philosophy of science or of humanity. Therefore, my work *would be* related to general conceptual issues in that it would lead to a determination of the tenability (the defensibility) of my position. As I continued to work from a particular point of view one would be able eventually to see how well this viewpoint accounted for the phenomena of behavioral development. I would be able to see if my research, based as it is on an underlying philosophical premise, continued to suffice in accounting for these phenomena. Ultimately what I would be able to learn is whether the variables I was studying were capable of explaining behavioral development, or whether other variables necessarily seemed to enter into the picture. For example, I would come to learn whether the exclusive study of the functioning of environmentally based variables, stimuli and responses, is capable of explaining behavioral development. If I found this not to be the case—I found, for example, that hereditary mechanisms seem to play a crucial role—then I would be forced either to give up my initial philosophical-theoretical position and adopt another one, or to revise my position so that it would be able to account for the functioning of these other variables in terms consistent with the original philosophical-theoretical position.

In a third way the outcome of my research work can be seen to have general theoretical relevancy. This third way, however, can be indirect, and its relevancy to general issues or theory may not even be intended. For example, someone else, by chance, might be able to use the facts that another researcher has found. However, to explain this third way more completely, let us consider some of the reasons scientists might conduct a research study.

## Some Reasons for Doing Research

The reasons that particular psychologists conduct particular studies may be very idiosyncratic and, in general, quite diverse. However, three reasons illustrate ways in which the outcome of research can have conceptual relevancy.

First, a person may be interested in illuminating some theoretical controversy. For instance, there may be an observed phenomenon that is accounted for by two different theoretical positions. In adolescent development, for example, it is typically found that there is a marked increase in the importance (saliency) of the peer group. Why does this occur? Both Anna Freud (1969) and Erik Erikson (1968) have devised theories. Consistent with the work of her father, Sigmund, Anna Freud takes what is termed a *psychosexual* position and ties this occurrence primarily to a biological change in the person (i.e., the emergence of a genital drive). Erikson, however, diverges somewhat from strict psychoanalytic (i.e., Freudian) theory and explains this occurrence in what he terms a *psychosocial* position, by specifying some possible relations between the developing person and his or her society.

Which theory is best able to account for empirical facts? This question constantly arises in the course of scientific inquiry. A clever researcher may be able to devise a study that would put the two different interpretations to a so-called *critical,* or *crucial, test*—a study whose results would provide support for one theoretical position and nonsupport for the other. If the results came out one way, theory A would be supported; if they came out in an opposite way, theory B would be supported.

It is important to note, however, that whether a scientist can perform a crucial test of two theories or only of specific competing hypotheses derived from these theories is itself a controversial issue. According to Hempel (1966), a philosopher of science, two hypotheses derived from two different theories can be neither proved nor disproved in any absolute sense. Hempel argues that this is true even if many tests of these two hypotheses are performed by the most sophisticated researchers using the most careful and extensive methods available to them and if all test outcomes result in completely favorable results for one hypothesis and completely unfavorable results for the other. Such results would not establish any absolute, conclusive validity for the former hypothesis, but rather only relatively strong support for it. It is always possible that future tests of the two hypotheses would result in favorable outcomes for the previously unfavored hypothesis and in unfavorable outcomes for the previously favored interpretation. In addition, it is also possible that if other hypotheses had been derived from the two different theories, then tests of these two new competing hypotheses would result in favorable outcomes for the theory that was not supported when the first set of derived hypotheses was tested. Thus, as Hempel argues, in an absolutely strict sense a crucial test is impossible in science.

But the results of testing two competing theoretical positions may be "crucial" (and extremely useful) in a less strict sense. Results of tests of two rival positions can indicate that one theory is relatively untenable, while the other position is relatively tenable. Because tests of the latter theory have resulted in favorable outcomes, and therefore it appears more tenable, it may be considered more *useful*. That is, the theory appears best able to account for existing facts. Because of the theory's demonstrated usefulness, it might play a more prominent role in any further work in the field. However, even construing crucial tests in a relatively unstrict way, they are few and far between in psychology. Still, they remain an important and potentially extremely useful impetus for research.

A second reason for doing research is to derive testable ideas—hypotheses—from a theory. Such deductions are made in order to see if they can be empirically supported through research. A researcher would start by saying that if his or her theory is appropriate in making the statements that it does, then certain things should necessarily also be the case. Let us say, for example, that I have a theory that says that as children develop, the conceptual categories they can actively use to designate certain classes of things in their environment become more differentiated with time. For instance, I might suspect that no matter what animal I showed to a two-and-a-half-year old, the child would respond by saying "doggie." I might also suspect that if I looked at a somewhat older child, say a six-year old, I would see the ability not only to correctly classify different animals (dogs, cats, elephants), but also the ability to classify different types of dogs correctly (collies, German shepherds, poodles). Thus, in accordance with my theory, I might hypothesize (predict) that as the children I study increase in age, their ability to correctly classify different animals correctly will also increase. If my theory is defensible, then my hypothesis, deduced from my theory, should be supported by the results of my study.

By testing deductions, the researcher can provide support or refutation for his or her theory. Research based on such *deductive reasoning* is an important component of scientific thinking, and it will be discussed in further detail below.

However, we have said that there is a third way that research can be found relevant to theory. Sometimes a researcher may conduct a study just to find out what exists. A person may have no theoretical issue in mind but may be interested only in describing the characteristics of a certain phenomenon or aspect of behavior development or in seeing what will be the behavioral result of a certain manipulation. For example, let us say that a person wonders what reasons five-year olds and fifteen-year olds might offer to explain why a person should not steal from friends. He or she might then ask groups of five- and fifteen-year olds to give their reason for not stealing from friends. The results might be that five-year-olds' reasons seem to be rather concrete and reflect a fear of punishment and an orientation to be obedient. A five-year-old might say you should not steal because your friend will hit you or your mother will punish you for doing something she says is wrong. The reasons of the fifteen-year-olds might be more abstract and reflect the notion that stealing from a friend violates implicit rules of mutual trust and respect or that as a member of society one implicitly has to respect the rights of other members. The researcher reports the information and thus adds additional facts to the literature of the science.

Although the researcher may not intend to relate his or her facts to any theories, the theoretical relevancy of the facts can be found after the research is done. In attempting to ascertain the validity of a particular theory, someone may be able to use the facts as a test of that theory. Thus, the facts reported in the above example could, after their communication, be seen to fit into a theoretical formulation. In fact, Lawrence Kohlberg (1963) has formulated a theory of moral development which could incorporate the hypothesized findings (see Chapter 7 for a detailed presentation).

In sum, although a fact may be presently loose—not related to a theory—this does not exclude the possibility that at some later time it may be seen as being related to or consistent with a general concept. Many facts not initially intended to be directly related to a theory do find their way into one. This is done through another major type of scientific thinking process: *inductive reasoning*. In this process a scientist will first start with sets of facts and then try to find some conceptual formulation to organize and hopefully explain them. Thus, a scientist using such reasoning proceeds from observed facts to integrative concepts or theories. We will find it necessary to discuss inductive reasoning again below.

In the various ways outlined above, the outcome of *all* research does bear on general conceptual and theoretical issues of a science. Although a researcher's reasons for undertaking the study of a topic may not relate to these general considerations, it is important to be aware of this perspective if only to gain an appreciation of the cumulative and dynamic aspects of a science such as developmental psychology. With this perspective a student will be able to see several things:

1.   Why some people study one topic while others investigate another. Differences in underlying philosophies of science and/or of humanity lead to differences in the assumptions a scientist makes about the nature of the subject matter. As we have seen, this leads scientists to look at different things about development and hence to investigate different topics.

2.   Why abstract, theoretical debates occur. When scientists assume a particular philosophical or theoretical point of view, they become committed to it; they attempt to defend it, to show its tenability. They will attempt to justify their position through logic and empirical research. Hence, because of commitments to different theoretical points of view, one scientist may interpret a given fact one way, while another scientist interprets it another way.

3.   Why an understanding of these theoretical concepts is crucial for an adequate understanding and appreciation of the research, data, and facts of a science. In sum, if students are given this conceptual perspective, they will know not only some implications of the results of one or a few research studies, but also the meaning and relevancy of research as it bears on the general concepts of a science.

## The Trouble with Textbooks

Unfortunately, it seems that many students do not develop this orientation and apprecia-tion in many basic courses in a science. Some students report that studying a textbook for such a course is like studying the telephone directory. Why may this often be the case?

Numerous child-psychology textbooks capably and clearly describe the dimen-sions and characteristics of a child's development. They also do a good job of acquaint-ing the reader with the presumed or known processes underlying development. Thus, authors of these texts present to the reader summaries of both the appropriate empirical research and the prevalent theoretical notions of child development (for example those of Piaget, Erikson, Freud, Bijou, and Baer). However, these theoretical accounts are necessarily somewhat limited. A full explication of any of these theorist's ideas would, and have, filled books of their own. However, for the reasons discussed in the preced-ing section, I feel a greater emphasis needs to be put on theory and concepts.

Most survey texts do not have as their main purpose the conveyance of either theory by itself or, more primarily, theory joined with the core conceptual issues involved in the study of human development. Rather, these texts emphasize research findings and empirical generalizations based on these findings. The point here is one of emphasis; most texts certainly do not exclude discussions of theories, but they do not spend most of their time on them. While most current texts do an outstanding job of presenting empirical results and trends in these findings, such a presentation does not directly provide the student with an integrative conceptual framework with which to view the field. Since the instructor often does not have the time to supply this framework, many students, after reading such a text, have the feeling of having interacted with a large mass of complex and often, for them, disjointed information. Although some digest and perhaps retain much of this information, many still struggle to understand what it all means.

Because of this situation, I believe that many incipient developmental psychologists are lost. Never realizing the intellectual excitement that the instructor feels, because he or she is well aware of both empirical trends and the conceptual implications of the research findings, the student may become turned off by a delineation of the details of particular studies; thus in failing to see the whole picture, the student does not under-stand the overall importance of the things he or she does learn about the subject.

## This Text's Approach

How do I think this book represents a significant departure from the typical text that you might read in an introductory science course?

First and foremost, I must admit that I am biased. I have certain beliefs about how best to teach and to try to understand a science; I believe that one should approach a science from a conceptual, theoretical, and deductively oriented point of view.

As suggested above, there are two major ways one can go about studying the phenomena of a science: inductively or deductively. The characteristics and uses of these processes are complex, and although a full explication of these topics is beyond the purposes of the present discussion, a brief overview will suffice for our purposes. A more detailed, but still introductory, presentation of these topics can be found in Hempel (1966).

If one follows the inductive method, one starts with facts. A scientist will first look at some set of data. Then, in an attempt to integrate these facts, the scientist will try to devise some general principles. In other words, one first focuses on facts and then tries to formulate concepts that will integrate them. Although the inductive approach is certainly a valid, important, and useful way of studying the phenomena of a science, it has been argued that this approach can lead to the compiling of a "heap of bricks" rather than a "house." This approach can lead to much data being collected without any a priori reason, that is, without any preceding, explicit theoretical rationale. Many facts might be gathered, but their general significance, if any, might be unknown or difficult to ascertain. As an alternative I elect to take a deductive approach. I prefer to begin my own scientific research from the theoretical end of the data-theory continuum.

A theory can be defined as a group of statements (for example, concepts, principles) which integrates existing facts and leads to the generation of new ones. Hempel (1966) suggests that a theory explains empirical uniformities that have been previously discovered and usually also predicts new regularities of similar kinds. To be consistent with its definition, then, I would use theory in the following way within the deductive approach:

1.  In order to be considered sound and tenable, my theory should be able to integrate existing facts. That is, it should be able to account for established empirical findings that bear on the content of my theory.
2.  Moreover, I should be able to devise some statements, based on my theory, which if found to be supported by research would, in turn, provide support for my theory (and if found false would provide nonsupport, or refutation, for it). Put in more formal terms, I should be able to generate *testable hypotheses* from my theory. My hypotheses will usually take the form of "if . . . then . . . " propositions, that is, "if my theory is appropriate in saying so and so, then such and such should be the case." In essence, I would be reasoning that if my theory were useful, then my deduction from it should be supported by the outcome of my research.
3.  I would then put my deduction to an *empirical test,* for example by doing an experiment or a correlational study. If the results yield the predicted findings, then this new fact, arrived at through deductive reasoning, will be appropriately placed within my theoretical system. This fact will be a brick added to my house rather than piled onto my heap.

In sum, by emphasizing a deductive, theoretical perspective I can see how well my facts fit together into a cohesive, understandable whole. Moreover, I can see what sort of information is needed to fill in gaps in my theory or to clarify or refine it. The facts I derive from my deductive approach will not be useless or random. Rather, they will contribute to my theoretical edifice. My deductively arrived-at fact will support, clarify, or refute my theoretical position.

## Cattell's Inductive-Hypothetico-Deductive Model

Of course, as a scientist functions in his or her day-in-day-out endeavors, such idealized deductive, theoretical reasonings may not occur, and in fact such sharp

Raymond B. Cattell

textbook divisions between inductive and deductive reasoning are typically not maintained (Cattell, 1966). Rather, as the scientist attempts to establish "general laws which can be empirically tested and which lead to deductions extending our theoretical understanding and practical control" (Cattell, 1966, p. 11), and thus tries to fulfill the function of science, both inductive and deductive reasoning may typically be used. As indicated above, there may be several reasons for doing a particular research study, and at different times the same scientist may do a particular study for any of these reasons. Thus, as pointed out by Raymond B. Cattell—one of the leading psychologists ever to contribute to the science—research, as it occurs in the real world, may have as its starting point other than deductively derived hypotheses. Rather, its initial impetus may be the noticing of a curious empirical phenomenon or regularity (Cattell, 1966). Thus we have drawn a distinction between induction and deduction in order to emphasize the point of view that science best advances when facts are gathered with at least an eventual eye toward integration with theory, yet this distinction may not necessarily characterize the scientific reasoning of the real-life practicing research psychologist. As Cattell argues, all scientists should work toward formulating general principles from which testable deductions are derived. However, this endeavor does not necessarily have to begin with a hypothesis. As we have seen, it may begin with mere interesting observations of empirical reality obtained while the scientist is working in the general theoretical atmosphere. From this empirical observation the researcher might induce that this fact is representative of some more general regularity, and as a consequence formulate a hypothesis about the validity of this induction. Then he or she might deduce what empirical consequences would have to be obtained in order for the hypothesis to be confirmed and accordingly make another, higher-order empirical observation, and the whole process would start anew.

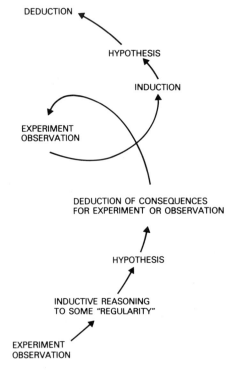

DEDUCTION

HYPOTHESIS

INDUCTION

EXPERIMENT
OBSERVATION

DEDUCTION OF CONSEQUENCES
FOR EXPERIMENT OR OBSERVATION

HYPOTHESIS

INDUCTIVE REASONING
TO SOME "REGULARITY"

EXPERIMENT
OBSERVATION

**Fig. 1.3** Cattell's notion of the inductive-hypothetico-deductive spiral. *Source:* Raymond C. Cattell (ed.), *Handbook of Multivariate Experimental Psychology,* Diagram 1.1, p. 16. Copyright 1966 by Rand McNally & Company, Chicago. Reprinted by permission of Rand McNally College Publishing Company.

What we see then is that in actuality the method that perhaps best characterizes the reasoning of the practicing scientist is neither purely deductive nor purely inductive. Rather, it may be what Cattell terms *inductive-hypothetico-deductive* in nature, as illustrated in Fig. 1.3. This method begins with some empirical observation, which in turn serves as the basis for the induction of some empirical regularity. This induction needs to be subjected to empirical verification, however, in order to ascertain its validity; accordingly, a hypothesis is derived from the induction, and the empirical consequents of this hypothesis are deduced and tested. The result of this test is, of course, another empirical observation, which is seen to continue the inductive-hypothetico-deductive spiral again.

In sum, then, although the conceptual distinction between the inductive and the deductive methods of scientific reasoning is a valid one, we must recognize that in actuality the practicing research scientist often uses both techniques. Yet it still remains the case that *inevitably* deductions from general organizing principles must eventually be drawn and tested in order for theory, and hence understanding, to be advanced. It is for this ultimate reason that we prefer and emphasize the deductive approach to science. Thus,the first way in which this book will depart from others is that (aside from having an *admittedly* biased author) the primary orientation will be conceptual and theoretical.

To do this, I will first acquaint you with the two basic philosophies of science underlying the conceptual issues of developmental psychology. We will then turn our attention to the conceptual issues themselves—the nature-nurture issue, the subordinate problems of instinct and the critical-periods hypothesis, and the continuity-discontinuity issue along with the interrelated problem of stability-instability. After this we will consider three general theoretical approaches to child development—the stage, the differential, and the ipsative—which are inclusive of the developmental approaches. We will interrelate the core conceptual issues with these three developmental theoretical approaches and another theoretical approach, which I term the *Learning approach,* and see how the former bear on the latter. We will then summarize major theoretical positions within each approach. For example, when presenting the stage theory approach to developmental psychology we will consider the work of Piaget, of Kohlberg, and of Freud.

Throughout these presentations the major emphasis will be on concepts and theory. However, this does not mean that research studies will be ignored. Research will be integrated into these conceptual discussions throughout the book, and Chapter 11 will be devoted to a presentation of the research and social implications of concepts and theories of human development. However, rather than attempt to review all research literature bearing on a particular issue, we will discuss one or two studies that illustrate, clarify, or refine the issues.

## The Organismic Position

It will become clear to the reader that I have a preferred theoretical orientation toward human development, which is termed the *organismic* position. I believe that this point of view presents a successful theoretical integration of psychological development. Although extended presentations of this viewpoint will be offered throughout this book, a brief overview of the organismic position is appropriate to present here.

What is a person? What sort of changes characterize a person as he or she develops? Where do these changes come from? How do they relate to human development? Questions such as these are inevitably involved in any theoretical consideration of psychological development and the organismic theoretical perspective has its own specific answers. Essentially, it asserts that human beings are active rather than passive and that among the changes characterizing human development are those involving the quality of psychological functioning. It is clear that in a general sense the only sources of behavior are a person's genetic inheritance (nature) and environmental experience (nurture), and thus another component of the organismic position is that human behavioral development is derived from interactions among these two sources.

The specific basic components of the organismic position can be summarized as follows:

1.   Development is characterized in part by a series of *qualitative changes* in the processes underlying development. For instance, processes involved with a person's perceptual, motivational, or cognitive development undergo changes in kind, or type

(quality), rather than just in amount, frequency, magnitude, or duration (quantity). This point of view does not deny that there are some aspects of a person that remain the same across life; rather, it asserts that human development is a synthesis between qualitative changes and processes and variables that remain the same.

2.   The *laws* that govern the functioning of these qualitative changes are related both to an organism's heredity and to its environment. Hempel (1966) defines a law as a statement asserting some invariant characteristic about a phenomenon or process; we will also grant the status of law to statements that hold only approximately, with certain qualifications or only under certain specifiable conditions, or with a given level of probability.

3.   These two sets of factors (heredity and environment) *interact* to account for behavioral development. Logically there are several possible ways that heredity and environment can be related to each other. First, it is possible that either heredity or environment might act alone as a source of behavioral development; second, it may be the case that the contribution of heredity is added to the contribution of the environment; third, heredity and environment may relate to each other in a multiplicative, or interactionist, manner. This last possibility is the one that adherents of the organismic position adopt (see a full explanation in Chapter 3).

4.   The mode of interaction between heredity and environmental variables involves the action of the environment on the organism's characteristics (e.g., a person's unfolding maturational processes, body build, temperament), and the action of the organism on aspects of its environment (for example, parents or teachers). Thus, a crucial and central component of the organismic position is that people themselves play an active, contributory role in their own development. The person does not merely wait while the environment acts to govern his or her development. Rather, in addition to being shaped by the environment, people act to shape their own world, to play an active, contributory role in their own development. Hence, contrary to the position espoused by such theorists as Skinner (1956) and Bijou and Baer (1961), who maintain that behavioral development is essentially totally controlled by the environment, organismically oriented developmentalists consider the role of the person's own activity as a central source of development. Hence, just as much as the environment and its agents (e.g., parents) influence the child, the child's own characteristics influence these environmental agents (see Bell, 1968; Erikson, 1964; Lerner, Karabenick, and Meisels, 1975; Schneirla, 1957; Thomas, Chess, Birch, Hertzig, and Korn, 1963).

A major goal of this book will be to expand and clarify the organismic position and to detail how it provides a theoretical framework with which to view psychological development. We will see how this point of view allows an interrelation and understanding of the nature-nurture, continuity-discontinuity, and critical-periods issues to be made. Furthermore, I believe that most of the major theoretical points of view in human development can be characterized as organismic. Thus, an understanding of the organismic position will allow one to integrate the major conceptual issues with the major theoretical approaches in the field. For example, although Piaget presents a theory of cognitive development, Thomas of the development of temperament-environment interrelations, Erikson of psychosocial development, Kohlberg of moral-reasoning development, and Schneirla and Hebb in part of perceptual development, all offer ideas that may appropriately be subsumed within the organismic point of view.

However, as suggested above, there is a major theoretical approach to human development that is conceptually opposed to the organismic position. This point of view can be named in various ways: the unity of science, the mechanistic, the learning, the environmentalist, or the situationalist position. In Chapter 2 we will see how the philosophical bases of these two orientations differ. In addition, in Chapter 10 we will present an overview and an evaluation of the latter approach. Although I admittedly favor the organismic point of view, I will present both for consideration and leave it to you to decide which is best able to integrate and account for the phenomena of psychological development.

In sum, we will proceed from philosophy of science to concepts, theories, and eventually to research-derived facts about child development.

## Summary

In this introductory chapter I have attempted to present my rationale for writing this book, an indication of my viewpoint toward scientific inquiry, and some of the things that I hope you will know when you have finished studying this book. The major point has been that facts alone are not enough to make a science; one needs to deal with integrative concepts and theories in order to appropriately understand and appreciate the facts of a science. In addition, a review of the history of developmental psychology in this century indicates that there has been an increasing emphasis on integrative concepts and theories of development as the science of psychological development has evolved.

We have seen that all scientific endeavors are underlain by philosophical assumptions about the nature of the subject matter under study, and that these assumptions lead the scientist to both topical and methodological preferences. Because one elects to make certain assumptions and to exclude others, one's research is related to general conceptual issues in that it will eventually lead to a determination of the appropriateness of one's initial assumptions. We have argued that all research can in some way and at some potential time be found to have theoretical relevance. This relevance can be found after the research has been conducted through an inductive reasoning process, that is, a process of starting with collected facts and moving towards general, integrative concepts.

Although the inductive process is certainly a valid approach to science, I have argued for a deductive emphasis. I opt for starting with general concepts or theories and then deducing hypotheses that should find empirical support if, in fact, my theory is appropriate and useful. By testing these hypotheses I obtain facts that can readily be integrated within my theoretical edifice. Of course, we recognize that the practicing research developmental psychologist often uses both deductive and inductive reasoning; but we choose to stress the deductive component of this inductive-hypothetico-deductive reasoning process in order to emphasize the point that deductions from general principles must be made and tested in order for theory and understanding of development to advance.

I also introduced my bias toward what I term the organismic position. This theoretical approach views human development as arising from an interaction between nature and nurture, as being characterized in part by qualitative changes, and as involving the contribution of a person's own behavior to his or her own development. I have suggested that this approach represents a framework for integrating the core concepts of human development along with most of the major theoretical approaches to the field. It is, however, necessary to contrast the organismic point of view with the other major conceptual approach to human development—the mechanistic, unity of science point of view. Although this comparison will be made at various points throughout this book, a consideration of the philosophical basis of each position will be the burden of Chapter 2.

# 2

## The Organismic and the Unity-of-Science Philosophies

In this chapter we will consider the two philosophies of science that highlight the basic, underlying philosophical controversies in human development. We will first consider the definition and objective of developmental psychology, which will then allow us to formulate the core issues that must be addressed in attempting to understand development. Then we will be able to see how the two philosophies of science offer contrasting views about these most basic issues.

Developmental psychology studies similarities and differences in psychological functioning across the life span. For example, a developmental psychologist might study how the thought processes of a one-, two-, five-, and ten-year-old are similar, and how they differ. Another possible topic might be how one's personality changes from childhood through adolescence and into adulthood and later life. When we study if, how, and why psychological functioning stays the same or changes across the life span, we are studying psychological development.

Developmental psychology is a branch of the general science of psychology. Like the science of which it is a part, and in fact like all sciences, developmental psychology has as its goal the discovery of what is true about its subject matter (Kaufmann, 1968). Thus, developmental psychology is concerned with finding out the truth about the similarities and differences of psychological functioning over the course of life. For instance, a developmental psychologist concerned with studying thought processes would want to know what, if anything, stays the same or changes in a child's thought processes as the child develops. What are the phenomena and processes that accurately characterize the development of thought? Do they stay the same across a person's life, or do they undergo change? If change characterizes development, then what brings it about?

Referring again to the work of Raymond B. Cattell, we may see how some of his research is concerned with ascertaining the factors involved in an important aspect of the individual's psychological functioning across the life span—personality. Cattell does this through application of a rather complex mathematical technique termed *factor analysis* (a technique we will have reason to deal with again, in Chapter 6). He has found that among adults there exist sixteen personality factors, or traits—such as warmth, intelligence, emotional stability, dominance, shyness, and shrewdness. Cattell also sought to discover whether there is similarity or difference in the factors that characterize adults and adolescents. After considerable research he found that there was an important difference in the personalities of adolescents and adults—among adolescents there were only fourteen factors involved in personality. Although there was considerable overlap, some of the factors present among adults were not seen among adolescents, and some of the factors seen among adolescents were not present among adults. For instance, one factor involved in adolescent personality and not found in adult personality, labeled Factor D by Cattell (Cattell, Eber, and Tatsuoka, 1970), involves complacent, deliberate, inactive behavior on the one hand, or attention-getting, excitable, overactive behavior on the other; with this adolescent personality factor we see indicated a teenager who is either an excitable show-off or rather stodgy and undemonstrative. With this example we see that Cattell found that what was true for the adolescent was not necessarily true for the adult. He thus found that in reality there was both similarity and difference in the age-associated factors of personality.

We see that Cattell's research was developmental—it attempted to discern similarities and differences in personality across the life span. Moreover, the research well illustrated the objective of developmental psychology in its attempt to discover what was really the case, what was true, about an important aspect of personality development.

In finding that the variables involved in a portion of psychological functioning change across the life span, Cattell also raised another question: What brings this change about? What is the basis, or source, of developmental change? What determines whether there will be development? In fact, these same questions may be raised even when there is similarity in psychological functioning between two points in development. After all, whether or not behavior stays the same or changes across the life span, it must be assumed that there is some reason, some determinant, of its doing so (Kaufmann, 1968). Whenever we see behavior at any point in the life span we may inquire into its source.

What we are formulating, then, is a basis for recognizing the basic questions that must be addressed in any consideration of psychological development. We are seeing that a statement of the definition and objective of developmental psychology soon leads us toward a recognition of certain inevitable questions—or conceptual issues—that must be addressed. We see that one issue is whether there is similarity or change in the development of a given psychological function across the life span. However, another issue is raised, more basic than the above. Whether or not we see similarity or difference in psychological functioning across the life span, it is obvious that this behavior—no matter how it is described—has a cause. The most basic issue we must address, then, is what is the basis, the source, of psychological functioning across the life span? Simply put, how does development come about?

In summary, we may say that the goal of developmental psychology is to know the truth about development. It is to know what development really is and what determines it. Viewing the goal of developmental psychology from this perspective brings into focus the two conceptual issues most central to any consideration of psychological development.

## Core Conceptual Issues of Developmental Psychology

The concern with what the source of development is and where the laws of development lie raises the perennial and most basic issue in developmental psychology: *the nature-nurture controversy.* The basic crux of the issue is where the determining sources (the laws) of behavioral development are to be found. What are the variables, the processes, involved in determining the course of psychological development? Are the variables involved in development most closely linked to nature (for example, genetic inheritance) or to nurture (for example, factors related solely to environmental variables, such as learning)? Put in its most extreme form, the nature-nurture issue would revolve around the question of whether nature variables alone or nurture variables alone account for behavioral development.

The nature-nurture controversy has reared its head in many forms throughout the history of psychology. It has sometimes been called the heredity-environment, the nativist-empiricist, the maturation-learning, the innate-acquired, or the preformed-epigenetic controversy. Yet, the basic thrust of the issue remains the same: To what extent do things built into the organism's system, through, for example, heredity or a maturational ground plan, determine its development and psychological functioning? and concomitantly, What is the role the environment plays in providing a source of psychological development?

Intelligence, personality, and perception have been among the various psychological topics in the history of psychology, around which the polemics of the nature-nurture controversy have swirled. William Sheldon (1940, 1942), for instance, proposed a nature-oriented "constitutional" theory linking body build with temperament/personality, while other writers (Lerner, 1969; Lerner and Korn, 1972; McCandless, 1967; Walker, 1962) have offered nurture-oriented social-learning interpretations of physique-behavior associations. The Gestalt school of psychology offered a nature (nativist) conception of perceptual processes, while Hebb (1949), among others, proposed a nurture (empiricist) view of perceptual phenomena. Some authors (e.g., Jensen, 1969) have implied that much of the behavior subsumed under the term *intelligence* is primarily hereditarily determined, while other authors (e.g., Anastasi, 1958) have maintained that no psychological function is ever inherited as such, and environmental factors always have to be taken into account. Although the precise details of the issues involved in these controversies will be explained in Chapter 3, it should be evident that psychologists have resolved in no final way the problem of where the determining sources of behavioral development lie. The nature-nurture issue remains a continuing controversy in developmental psychology and also provides the conceptual basis for the other core developmental problems.

Thus, the second central conceptual issue derives from the first. Given that there are laws determining development, and that these laws may lie within the realm of nature or nurture, how do they function and apply? Do the same laws account for development in all species of animal (across the so-called evolutionary, or phylogenetic, scale) or are different laws needed to account for the behavioral development of different species? Similarly, can the same laws explain the behavior of an individual member of a species throughout the course of its life span (across the ontogenetic span) or may different laws be needed to account for behavior at different points in the life span of humans? Let us say, for example, that a psychologist accounts for certain aspects of a 3-year-old child's behavior through the use of a single law, e.g., "only responses followed by a reward will continue to be part of a child's response repertoire." If the psychologist finds that this same law can account for this behavior throughout the child's life span, then such an instance would be termed *continuity*. However, if another law is needed to account for this behavior at other points in the child's ontogeny, then this would be an instance of *discontinuity*.

This then is the continuity-discontinuity issue. If the same laws govern behavior across the evolutionary scale (phylogeny) or the life span of human beings (ontogeny), this would be termed continuity. However, if new laws are needed at different points in either phylogeny or ontogeny to account for psychological development, this would be termed discontinuity. Although the continuity-discontinuity controversy was originally viewed as an empirical issue, writers such as Werner (1957) and Langer (1969) emphasize that the issue is clearly theoretical and logical. Whether there is psychological continuity or discontinuity between behaviors depends on whether the behaviors are theoretically believed to involve the same function or two different functions. For example, whether babbling is held to be continuous with speech depends upon whether babbling is held to be a precursory, undifferentiated, global type of utterance that later differentiates to become speech. Similarly, crawling would be held to be discontinuous with walking if one theorized that the motor skills necessary for walking emerge independent of the motor skills necessary for crawling. Thus, as we will see, whether one views development as being continuous or discontinuous rests on one's adoption of a particular theoretical orientation and, in terms of our present discussion, a particular philosophy of science.

In the history of biological and psychological sciences two different philosophies of science have come to present major conceptual forces underlying the nature-nurture and continuity-discontinuity conceptual controversies. These two positions may be termed the *unity-of-science* viewpoint and the *organismic* viewpoint. (A third philosophical orientation, *vitalism,* preceding but superseded by the organismic position, Bertalanffy, 1933, will not be dealt with here.)

## The Unity-of-Science Position

In the unity-of-science viewpoint, psychology is viewed as a branch of natural science. Hence, this view holds that the phenomena of psychology are not unique in nature but rather are controlled by the laws that govern all events and phenomena in the natural world. The position thus holds that there are basic and common laws that govern all things in the universe. Neither biology, psychology, sociology, nor any science for that matter really has its own special laws; rather, in a basic sense, all sciences and more importantly all events and phenomena in the real world are controlled by a common set of principles. The phenomena, or events, that all sciences study can, it is believed, be uniformly subsumed (unified) and understood by one common set of natural science principles (see Harris, 1957).

As summarized by Anderson, this philosophical position states that "the workings of our minds and bodies, and of all the animate or inanimate matter of which we have any detailed knowledge, are assumed to be controlled by the same set of fundamental laws, which except under certain extreme conditions we feel we know pretty well" (1972, p. 393). Simply, the initial assumption of this position is that the events of all sciences can be uniformly understood by the same one set of laws.

Proponents of this viewpoint hold that physics and chemistry are the basic natural sciences; they thus believe that the laws of these two disciplines are the one set of fundamental laws alluded to by Anderson (1972). It is the laws of chemistry and physics—the rules that depict the mechanisms by which atoms and molecules function—that are the basic, fundamental laws of the real world. Everything involves atoms and molecules; nothing in the natural world exists that is not basically made up of these things. If one understands the mechanisms by which atoms and molecules combine and function, then one understands the laws basic to everything. The mechanics of chemistry and physics becomes then the ultimate laws of all events.

Thus, these basic laws that govern all natural events and phenomena, whether organic or inorganic, are held to apply to all levels of phenomenal analysis. Consistent with Nagel (1957), we define a *level* as a state of organization of matter, or life, phenomena. For example, chemistry, with its particular set of concepts and principles, represents one level of organization, while psychology, with its own set of terms, represents another. One can describe the behavior of a person at its own level or in terms of the principles of another level. We can try to study how children at various age levels develop the ability to perform in certain situations (e.g., classroom tests) by attempting to discern the psychological factors involved in such behavior; alternatively, these very same behaviors may be described and studied at another level. The children's performance certainly involves the functioning of their muscles and nervous systems. Therefore, we may attempt to describe and understand their classroom test performance by reference to the functioning of their physiological systems, a lower level (in the sense of underlying the behavioral level) of analysis. Ultimately, of course, the functioning of their physiological systems involves the functioning of the atoms and molecules that form the basic matter of living, organic material. We can then seek to understand psychological functioning by reference to the mechanisms of physics and chemistry. These mechanisms represent the most fundamental level of analysis that can be reached, and since this level is invariably involved in any other level of analysis, we can certainly seek to understand psychology by reference to chemistry and physics. These basic physical laws are just as applicable to physiology as they are to psychology, or for that matter to any other events or phenomena in the natural world. Everything—living or nonliving—is made up of chemicals and molecules.Ultimately then, if we understand the rules by which atoms and molecules function, we can understand the components of all things in the natural world. All we must do to understand biology, psychology, sociology, or the movement of the stars is to bring each down to its most basic constituent elements, to the most fundamental level of analysis: the physical-chemical level. The events and phenomena of all sciences—of everything in the natural world—may be uniformly understood through the mechanisms involved in atoms and molecules.

Hence, proponents of this unity viewpoint do not seek to explain the phenomena of psychology per se; this is not the appropriate level of analysis. Rather, they hope to reduce these phenomena of psychological functioning to the basic, fundamental level of analysis, the laws of chemistry and physics. The basic point of this unity-of-science-position, then, is thus *reductionism*: reduce the phenomena of a given (higher, or molar) level to the elemental, fundamental (lower, or molecular) units that comprise it. It is believed that there is nothing special about the complex pattern of events we call psychological functioning. In the final analysis these events involve the functioning of the very same atoms and molecules that are involved in the workings of a liver, a kidney, or a shooting star. Thus, like everything else, psychological phenomena are governed by the laws of chemistry and physics and, upon appropriate reduction, the phenomena of psychology may be understood in terms of these laws. From this standpoint then, if we knew enough about chemistry and physics we could eliminate the science of psychology completely. As pointed out by Bolles, this reductionistic assumption involves "the doctrine that all natural events have physical causes, and that if we knew enough about physical and mechanical systems we would then be able to explain, at least in principle, all natural phenomena" (1967, p. 5).

Reductionism directly implies a continuity position. No new laws are needed to explain the phenomena of a given level of study; rather, the same exact laws apply at all levels. Since natural phenomena at any and all levels can be reduced to the phenomena of the fundamental physical-chemical level, these same laws are continuously applicable to all levels of phenomena. Since no new, additional, or different laws are needed to account for or to understand the phenomena that may be thought to characterize any particular level, continuity, by definition, exists. As we have seen, psychology may be reduced to chemistry-physics *because* the latter level is invariably present in anything that exists.

What this means then is that the "real" laws governing any and all events in the world are really the laws of chemistry and physics. In essence, the unity-of-science position holds that in the final analysis one must inevitably deal with certain basic, fundamental laws in order to completely, accurately, and ultimately understand any and all living and nonliving matter in the natural world. And, as Anderson has commented, once this concept is accepted,

It seems inevitable to go on uncritically to what appears at first sight to be an obvious corollary of reductionism: that if everything obeys the same fundamental laws, then the only scientists who are studying anything really fundamental are those who are working on those laws. In practice, that amounts to some astrophysicists, some elementary particle physicists, some logicians and other mathematicians, and few others (1972, p. 393).

Because of the belief that reductionism will lead to fundamental knowledge and because of the associated postulation of continuity in the laws and mechanisms that are involved in an appropriate consideration of natural phenomena, two events may ultimately occur. First, the phenomena in the world labeled psychological would no longer be a focus of scientific concern; these phenomena are not fundamental—they must be reduced to be appropriately understood. Second, the people in the world labeled psychologists would no longer be necessary; these people are not studying the fundamental phenomena of the natural world.

What would replace psychology, and in fact all sciences other than the "fundamental" ones, would be a consideration of the basic mechanisms of the physical-chemical level of analysis. To understand every event and phenomenon in the natural world one must understand the mechanisms of physics and chemistry. This statement highlights another major attribute of the unity-of-science position. Adherents of this position conceptualize the functioning of the components (the atoms and molecules) of the most fundamental level of analysis within the framework of a machine model. As we have seen, according to this mechanistic model, biological or psychological phenomena are only seemingly complicated constellations of physical and chemical processes. In principle, once we know the mechanisms of physical and chemical functioning, we would then know all we have to know about the world. In other words, because the fundamental level of analysis functions mechanistically, then all the world is seen as functioning mechanistically. Thus, although several different meanings of the term *mechanism* have been used by philosophers and scientists, we shall conceive of the mechanistic position as connoting an interpretation (through reductionism) of psychological phenomena in physical and chemical terms (Bertalanffy, 1933).

Since physics and chemistry are machinelike sciences, in order to move from one level of analysis to another all that must be done is to specify the mechanism by which the basic elements of physics and chemistry combine. Since the molecular (physical-chemical) laws apply at the molar (psychological) level, it is necessary only to discern

LEVEL 2          (Oranges)

LEVEL 1          (Oranges)

**Fig. 2.1**  Unity-of-science position: Each level is comprised of the same basic elements.

the mechanisms by which these molecular elements are quantitatively added. In other words, to go to a higher level, all that one must do is add these elements to what was present at the lower level. If, for example, a rat was made up of ten oranges, all that would be necessary for moving up to the human level would be to add, for instance, another sixteen oranges. Thus, the only difference between levels is a quantitative one, a difference in amount, size, magnitude, etc.

The unity-of-science position is diagramatically illustrated in Fig. 2.1. Two levels of analysis are represented; level 1, for example, could be the biological level and level 2 the psychological level. Both are comprised of the same basic thing, in this case oranges. To move from one level to another all that one must do is add more oranges. Thus between the two levels there is a continuity in the basic elements that make up each level; said another way, each level can be reduced to the same basic elements.

In summary, adherents of a unit-of-science position view psychology as a branch of natural science. They seek to reduce the phenomena of psychology to the mechanical laws of physics and chemistry because of their belief that these laws continuously apply at all phenomenal levels. Thus the basic characteristics of the unity-of-science position are as follows:

1.  It is a *natural-science* viewpoint.
2.  It is a *reductionist* viewpoint.
3.  It is a *continuity* viewpoint.
4.  It is a *mechanistic* viewpoint.
5.  It is a *quantitative* viewpoint.
6.  It is an *additive* viewpoint.

In psychology this position has been translated into various theoretical viewpoints, of which the works of Skinner (1938), Bijou and Baer (1961), and Gewirtz (1961) are representative. These authors try to formulate the determining mechanisms of human behavioral development into a natural-science model (Bijou and Baer, 1961). They attempt to discern the empirical (observable) and quantifiable parameters of environmental stimulation which fit this model (Gewirtz and Stingle, 1968). Viewing behavior as the quantitative addition of discrete elements that combine, analogously, in the mechanical manner of chemistry and physics, it is appropriate that such theorists look to the environment for the source of human behavior/personality development. A machine is passive until extrinsic energy activates it. Human beings, viewed as a machine, are also passive until environmental stimulation causes them to act. Their behavioral development becomes just the historical, "mechanical mirror" (Langer, 1969) of environmental stimulation.

Thus, those committed to a unity-of-science position would, in their psychological theorizing, try to explain behavioral development in terms of the principles of learning— that is, of classical and operant conditioning (e.g., Bijou and Baer, 1961; Gewirtz and Stingle, 1968). If human beings are passive, they must await stimulation from the environment in order to act, or more accurately, *to respond.* How does such stimulation bring human behavior under control? Unity-of-science–learning theorists would suggest that the principles of classical (respondent) learning and of operant (instrumental) learning can explain it. The former set of principles can account for stimulation-produced responding $(S{\rightarrow}R)$, while the latter can account for response-produced stimulation $(R{\rightarrow}S)$. Since these two broad types of learning are totally inclusive of the types of learning occurring in the natural world, they should be able to account for the acquisition of all responses in all organisms. Thus, unity-of-science–learning theorists deal with the generic human being—the general case of humanity. The laws of learning are ubiquitous in their applicability to all human behavior and, for that matter, to the behavior of all organisms (see Skinner, 1938).

The point of the present discussion is to make clear the general nature of the translation of the unity-of-science reductionistic, mechanistic, philosophical position into the psychological theoretical position of such learning-approach psychologists as Bijou and Baer (1961). To such psychologists all behavioral functioning is a consequence of stimulation. To understand behavior at any and all points in development, all one must do is understand the laws by which a person's responses come to be under the control of environmental stimulation. Now, psychologists functioning from this viewpoint believe that there are two sets of laws that describe and explain how responses come under environmental-stimulation control: those of classical and operant conditioning. Since all behavior is ultimately controlled by the stimulus world, and since this world exerts its control through the functioning of a fundamental set of laws of learning (those of classical and operant conditioning), then all behavior may be understood by reducing it to these same, basic laws of stimulus-response relations. All behavior—whether of two different species of animals (rats and humans) or of two differently aged groups of children (five- and fifteen-year-olds)—is comprised of the same basic stimulus-response elements and these same basic elements are also always associated on the basis of the same laws. Hence, seemingly complex behavior may be understood by reducing it to the same basic constituent elements that comprise any and all behavior. And since all behavior may be so reduced, the same laws must therefore be applicable to explain behavior at any (animal or age) level at which it occurs. Hence, continuity in the laws of learning, in the rules that account for behavioral functioning, is another aspect of the learning approach.

Thus, all that one must know in order to completely understand behavioral functioning and development is the mechanisms by which stimuli in the person's world come to control that person's behavior at all points in the life span. Once these mechanisms are known, one can reduce behavior at one point in life and at another point in life to common constituent elements. In turn, since the same elements comprise behavior at each level, one can account for any differences in behavior between points in the life span merely by reference to the quantitative difference in the stimulus-response relations in the person's behavior repertoire. If behavior is comprised totally of the stimulus-response relations a person has acquired over the course of life as a function of classical and operant conditioning, then the difference between behavior at any two points in life could only be a quantitative difference in the number of associations acquired. One could move from lower to higher levels of behavior analysis simply by adding on the similarly acquired stimulus-response associations.

By this point, then, the way in which the unity-of-science philosophy becomes translated into a psychological theoretical view of development should be clear (see Chapter 10 for a full explication). Although the unity-of-science position is an abstract philosophical view of the nature of the real world, the position is not without its influence in science in general, and in psychology in particular. In fact, in providing the learning approach to psychology, the unity-of-science position presents us with what we will see to be an influential philosophical/psychological view of the nature of humanity. Of course, while influential, the position has had important criticisms leveled against it. In fact, one may view the other major philosophy of science discussed in this chapter—the organismic position—as a culmination of the objections raised about the assumptions and the assertions of the unity-of-science position. Hence, as a means of transition to our discussion of the organismic position, let us first consider some of the important problems of the unity-of-science position.

## Problems of the Unity-of-Science Position

We have seen that the core conceptual basis of the unity-of-science position is reductionism. We have also seen that the belief in reductionism is predicated on the assertion that since all matter is comprised of basic (physical-chemical) components, the only appropriate and necessary approach to investigating the fundamental laws of the natural world is to study these basic components. Hence, the unity-of-science-adherent asserts that to understand any and all levels of phenomena in the real world, these higher levels must be reduced to the laws of the fundamental, constituent level. However, Anderson, in describing the reductionistic component of the unity-of-science position, also sees the viewpoint as advancing an argument containing a logical error.

The main fallacy in this kind of thinking is that the reductionist hypothesis does not by any means imply a "constructionist" one: The ability to reduce everything to simply fundamental laws does not imply the ability to start from those laws and reconstruct the universe. In fact, the more the elementary particle physicists tell us about the nature of the fundamental laws, the less relevance they seem to have to the very real problems of the rest of science, much less to those of society (1972, p. 393).

But why does the ability to reduce from a higher, seemingly more complex, level of analysis to the lower not necessarily imply the reverse? Why does such reductionistic ability not imply that one can move from the lower to the higher levels—and thereby construct the universe—simply by adding more of the same constituent elements onto what already exists at a lower level? Why, when we attempt to do this, and when we concomitantly learn more and more about the fundamental level, do we seem to be missing an understanding of the important problems and phenomena of the higher levels? Why does the reductionist fail when attempting to also be a constructionist? Again we may turn to Anderson.

The constructionist hypothesis breaks down when confronted with the twin difficulties of scale and complexity. The behavior of large and complex aggregates of elementary particles, it turns out, is not to be understood in terms of a simple extrapolation of the properties of a few particles. Instead, *at each level of complexity entirely new properties appear,* and the understanding of the new behaviors requires research which I think is as fundamental in its nature any any other. That is, it seems to me that one may array the sciences roughly linearly in a hierarchy, according to the idea: The elementary entities of science X obey the laws of science Y.

| X | Y |
| --- | --- |
| Solid-state or many-body physics | Elementary particle physics |
| Chemistry | Many-body physics |
| Molecular biology | Chemistry |
| Cell biology | Molecular biology |
| • | • |
| • | • |
| • | • |
| Psychology | Physiology |
| Social sciences | Psychology |

But this hierarchy does not imply that science X is "just applied Y." *At each stage entirely new laws, concepts, and generalizations are necessary,* requiring inspiration and creativity to just as great a degree as in the previous one. Psychology is not applied biology, nor is biology applied chemistry (Anderson, 1972, p. 393; ital. added).

What Anderson is thus saying is that the constructionist hypothesis fails because, simply, "more is different." In other words, as one studies levels higher and higher in complexity, one is concomitantly seeing that new, qualitatively different characteristics come about—or emerge—at each of these levels. The new characteristics are not present at the lower, fundamental level and therefore not understandable by reduction to the lower level. One cannot move from higher to lower level (and back again) merely by adding or subtracting more of the same, because as one combines more of the same into a higher level of complexity, there is present in this combination a quality that is not present in the less complex constituent elements as they exist in isolation. Thus, the reductionist, unity-of-science position fails because reductionism does not mean constructionism, and in turn, constructionism fails because of the presence of qualitatively new properties emerging and characterizing each higher level of analysis.

However, reductionism fails for other reasons as well. Reductionism is predicated on the belief that reference to the constituent elements comprising all matter can suffice in accounting for the nature of phenomena at all levels of analysis. However, we have seen this continuity assumption is weak. If qualitatively different, new phenomena characterize each higher level of analysis, then by definition continuity does not exist. If something new does exist, this clearly means that *just* the same thing as existed before does not exist. One may not explain all natural phenomena by reference to one common set of continuously applicable, fundamental laws. In other words, shortcomings of the reductionistic, unity-of-science position also involve the inadequacy of its continuity assumption, and thus this philosophical position is unable to explain all natural phenomena through reduction to one set of fundamental laws. Reductionism cannot be used to successfully explain all levels of phenomena in the natural world, because

This conception appears to ignore the additional fact that once the behavior has been explained physiologically, the physiology still remains to be explained (cf. Skinner, 1950). Furthermore, if physiology in turn is to be explained by biochemistry and it by physics, how physics is to be explained poses an enduring problem because there are no sciences left. In short, this type of explanation leads to a finite regression with one science left unexplained—unless, of course, it is self-explanatory; no one is likely to admit that of physics (Eacker, 1972, p. 559).

We see, then, that there are many problems with the unity-of-science position. It fails to suffice in accounting for the nature of the phenomena present at all levels of analysis because at each different level of analysis there exist qualitatively new, and hence discontinuous, phenomena. Hence, one should perhaps resort to a point of view that emphasizes these phenomena. What is being alluded to then is the fact that the very objections raised about the unity-of-science position seem, in their explication, to suggest the necessary characteristics for a point of view that would successfully counter the position. Specifically, mechanistic constructionism fails because of new phenomena emerging to characterize higher levels of analysis; hence, the first component of a successful alternative position would be positing emergence and qualitative discontinuity as characterizing developmental changes. The notion of emergence would be introduced to counter the problems of reductionism, while the idea of qualitative discontinuity would be raised to address the inability of a constructionist position to account for all phenomena present at all stages. In essence, a developing organism would be viewed as a creature passing through qualitatively different stages of development, stages made different because of the presence of new (and hence lawfully distinct) phenomena emerging to characterize that portion of the life span.

These alternative views of the nature of differences between levels of analysis, or between portions of the ontogeny of the organism, are represented in the organismic philosophy of science. Let us consider then the ways in which this second position offers a viable, opposing view of the nature of the world.

## The Organismic Position

Adherents of the organismic philosophy of science (e.g., Bertalanffy, 1933; Schneirla, 1957) reject the reductionism of unity of science and maintain that at each new level of phenomenal organization there is an *emergence* of new phenomena that cannot be reduced to lower levels of organization. They hold that one cannot appropriately make a quantitative reduction to a lower organizational level and hope to understand all phenomena at the higher organizational level. This inability to reduce occurs because at each higher organizational level something new comes about, or emerges. Thus, a change in quality and not merely in quantity characterizes the differences between one level of analysis and another. If one reduces to the lower level then one will eliminate the opportunity of dealing with the new characteristic that actually is the essential characteristic of the higher level, the attribute that defines the difference between the lower and higher levels. For example, going from one animal level to another, or from one stage of human life to another, would be analogous to changing from an orange into a motorcycle. How many oranges comprise a motorcycle? Obviously this is a ludicrous question, because here we have a change in kind, type, quality, rather than merely in amount, magnitude, or quantity.

The above argument—the irreducibility of a latter form to an earlier one—is the essence of the *epigenetic viewpoint.* One cannot reduce a qualitative change, something new, to a precursory form. Epigenesis denotes that at each higher level of complexity there emerges a new characteristic, one that simply was not present at the lower organizational level and thus whose presence is what establishes a new level as just that—a stage of organization qualitatively different from a preceding one. Thus, according to Gottlieb (1970, p. 111), epigenesis connotes that patterns of behavioral activity and sensitivity are not immediately evident in the initial stages of development. Since development is characterized by these qualitative emergences, then by definition the various new behavioral capacities that develop are not actually present until they do in fact emerge.

The doctrine of epigenesis thus asserts that development is characterized by qualitative emergences. New things come about in development. Newness means just that—something not present before, either in smaller form or even in precursory form. Simply, then, epigenesis asserts that development is represented by the emergence of characteristics at each new stage of development that were not present in any precursory form previous to their emergence.

Thus, as indicated above, the presence of qualitatively new characteristics at each higher stage indicates that reduction to lower levels is inappropriate if full understanding of the new stage is sought. A one-year-old's behavior may perhaps be understood by reference to relatively simple stimulus-response, reflexlike associations; yet when the child reaches about two years of age there may emerge a new symbolic function— language (as an example of the ability to represent physical reality through use of nonphysical symbols). Thus, as one consequence of this representational ability the child may now show behaviors (e.g., being able to imitate some person or event long after that thing is actually viewed) that may best be understood by reference to this emergent symbolic ability; trying to reduce this two-year-old's behavior to the functioning shown at one year of age would be inappropriate because the representational ability that enables one to account for the two-year-old's behavior was simply not present at the earlier age. Thus an antireductionist view is maintained, because the qualitative change that depicts a higher stage of development cannot be understood, since it does not exist, at the lower level. Because the nature of what exists changes from stage to stage and there is qualitative change from stage to stage, there cannot be continuity between stages. New things—variables, processes, and/or laws—represent the differences between stages; hence such qualitative change means that discontinuity characterizes differences between stages. The differences are in *what* exists and

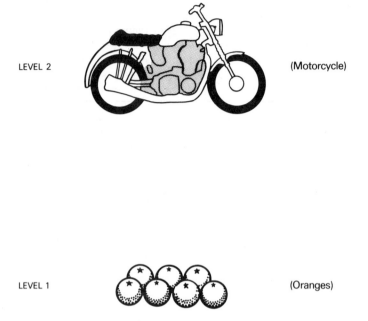

LEVEL 2                                                                    (Motorcycle)

LEVEL 1                                                                    (Oranges)

**Fig. 2.2**  Organismic position: Qualitative discontinuity exists between levels.

not just in *how much* exists. Thus, to the organismic thinker, laws of the psychological level of analysis are unique in nature—they are not merely reducible to the laws of physics and chemistry. Similarly, each different phyletic or ontogenetic level is viewed as qualitatively discontinuous from every other.

This aspect of the organismic position is represented in Fig. 2.2, which shows qualitative discontinuity between the two represented levels. One cannot reduce one level to another, because something new has emerged at the higher level. Although level 1 is comprised of oranges, level 2 is a motorcycle. One cannot hope to understand the functioning of a motorcycle through even an intensive study of oranges!

We have not yet seen on what basis the organismic viewpoint asserts that qualitative discontinuity characterizes development. How do organismic thinkers explain their assertion that epigenesis—qualitative discontinuity—represents differences between levels?

Organismic thinkers would be in agreement with an idea borrowed from Gestalt psychology that the whole (the organism) is more than the sum of its parts. That is, a human organism is more than a liver added to two kidneys, added to one spinal cord, and to one brain, and to one heart, etc. They would reject the additive assumption underlying the unity-of-science position and instead maintain that a multiplicative type of combination would be more accurate. They would argue that organisms as organized systems show in the relations among their constituent elements (their parts) properties that cannot be reduced to physical and chemical terms. One may reach a physical and chemical understanding of a kidney, a brain, and a liver. However, properties will be seen in the organism when considered as a whole that derive not from the separate organ systems per se, but from their relations with each other. When parts combine they produce a property that did not exist in the parts in isolation. The parts do not merely add up (e.g., $2 + 3 = 5$), but multiplicatively interact (e.g., $2 \times 3 = 6$; hence an extra unit than that present with additive combination is present), and this interaction brings about the emergence of a new property.

In essence, the organismic viewpoint asserts that the basis of the epigenetic (qualitatively discontinuous) emergences that characterize development lies in the multiplicative interactions of the constituent parts of the organism. When the parts combine they produce a new complexity, a characteristic existing only as a product of these parts in their interaction. This new property does not exist in any of the constituent parts—or in any of the lower organizational levels—even in precursory form.

Ludwig von Bertalanffy (1933), a leading formulator of the organismic viewpoint, suggests that nothing can be learned about the organism as such from a study of its parts in isolation. This inability occurs because an organism in its natural state, viewed as a whole being (and not just a bunch of constituent parts), shows phenomena that are so different from physical, mechanistic ones that entirely new concepts are needed to understand them. That is, if one accepts the epigenetic, organismic point of view, a mechanistic, reductionistic view of organisms is entirely inappropriate. The characteristics of a whole living organism have nothing in common with the characteristics or structures of a machine. This is true because the characteristics—or parts—comprising a machine can be separated without a change in their basic properties. For instance, a car's carburetor will still be a carburetor, still have the same properties, whether or not it is attached to a car. But according to the organismic position, this is not the case with living organisms. With living organisms, at each new level of analysis an emergence takes place; with every step building up to the whole living organism, from an atom, to a molecule, to a cell, to a tissue, to an organ, new phenomena occur that cannot be derived from the lower, subordinate levels.

Thus, knowledge of the functioning of various subsystems comprising an organism does not lead to an understanding of the whole organism. For example, water ($H_2O$) has an emergent quality (its liquidness) that cannot be understood by reducing water to its constituent (and gaseous) elements ($H_2$ and $O_2$). Similarly, human beings have unique characteristics (or qualities), such as being able to love, to be governed by abstract principles of moral and ethical conduct, to show high levels of need achievement, which emerge as phylogenetically distinct (qualitatively discontinuous) and cannot be understood by mere reduction to underlying neural, hormonal, and muscular processes. As a basis for this position organismic theorists suggest epigenesis, which is the belief that at each new level of behavioral organization there emerge qualitatively new (discontinous) phenomena that cannot be reduced to lower levels.

In summary, the basic characteristics of the organismic position are:
1. It is an *epigenetic* viewpoint.
2. It is an *antireductionist* viewpoint.
3. It is a *qualitative* viewpoint.
4. It is a *discontinuity* viewpoint.
5. It is a *multiplicative, interactionist* viewpoint.

## Sources of Development

The conceptual dividing lines between the unity-of-science position and the organismic position should now be evident: the former position is basically a reductionistic, quantitative continuity position, while the latter is an emergent, qualitative discontinuity position. The position of these philosophies on the continuity-discontinuity controversy is clear. However, how do these points of view bear on the nature-nurture controversy?

The unity-of-science philosophical position, when translated into a psychological theoretical position, will typically take the form of either a nature or nurture position. Resting on an additive and a mechanistic assumption, the unity-of-science position tries to explain behavioral development in terms of a single set of source determinants. Because they are committed to a continuity position, these thinkers would thus, by definition, be committed to the view that the same set of laws can always account for behavior. If continuity is asserted, it is then most difficult to draw one's explanations of behavior development from different sources of development. (Of course it is always possible to argue that nature and nurture laws may be reduced to the same laws and are thus not different sources after all; but this type of appeal really begs the question, since once again we are back to one common set of laws.)

As we have seen, the unity-of-science–learning theorists view the environment (nurture) as the source of the determinants of behavior. Human beings are seen as a machine; they are energized to respond by stimulation, that derives solely from the environment. Hence, they are seen as essentially passive. They must await energizing stimulation to evoke behavior. As discussed in Chapter 10, these theorists also view human behavior as being amorphous, as having no (initial) shape or form. Since the source of all of human behavior is derived from the stimulus environment—independent of human beings—then human behavior has no original form; it is shaped completely by the environment, and hence processes or variables not involved with such environmental stimulation really do not at all contribute to the shaping of behavior. Thus, heredity (nature) is really never systematically incorporated into these theorists' ideas, and the environment is considered the source of the shaping of human behavior.

It is possible, however, to have a unity-of-science–nature theory. Such approaches would also view behavior development as deriving from a single source, but in this case the source would be nature. Behavior development would thus be the continuous unfolding of preformed, genetic givens. The major thrust of William Sheldon's (1940, 1942) position can be viewed as consistent with a unity-of-science–nature formulation, as can some of the work of some of the European animal behaviorists (the ethologists such as Lorenz, 1965). Sheldon views body type as the essential determinant of personality or temperament. In turn, he maintains that body type—whether essentially fat, muscular, or thin—is primarily genetically determined. Hence he views one's personality as derived essentially from a single source: genetic inheritance. Lorenz (1965) may similarly be viewed as a unity-of-science–nature theorist. He believes that in some animals there exist behavior patterns called instincts, whose structures are formed totally at conception—when one inherits one's genes from one's parents. Hence such instincts are totally unavailable to any environmental influence. Whether ideas such as those of Sheldon and specifically of Lorenz have any validity will be evaluated in Chapters 3 and 4.

The present point is that unity-of-science theorists typically emphasize either a nature or a nurture viewpoint. Although some, if not most, unity-of-science–nurture theorists do explicitly admit, for example, that nature may provide an important contributory source of behavior (for instance, see Bijou and Baer, 1961), this admission never seems to lead to any systematic consideration of the role of this other source. Because changes in behavior are held to be continuous and additive, and not multiplicative, both nature and nurture are not systematically taken into account. Such interactionism occurs, however, as one of the predominant points of view within the organismic philosophy of science.

## Epigenetic Sources of Development

Although all organismic-epigenetic positions have the basic characteristics listed earlier, the precise basis of the determinants of epigenesis is itself a controversial issue among organismic thinkers. What determines when and how the constituent parts comprising the whole organism interact to produce qualitative discontinuity? As one may have already guessed, the basic issue involved in this question is the nature-nurture problem. The question becomes simply, "Does the source of epigenesis lie in nature, nurture, or a combination of the two?" On the one hand there are those thinkers who maintain that epigenesis is predetermined through genetic inheritance. Environment is held to play no role in the qualitative emergences that define epigenesis. Although development is seen as going through qualitative changes, some epigenetic thinkers argue that these changes are completely determined by genes; the environment that these genes exist in is seen to play no role in producing the qualitative changes that characterize development (in this regard such epigenetic thinkers are indistinct from the unity-of-science–nature theorists such as Lorenz). Thus these epigenetic changes are predetermined by invariantly ordered maturational factors such as growth and tissue differentiation, which are held to simply unfold in a fixed sequence—a sequence that arises independent of any experiential context. This *predetermined epigenetic* viewpoint is well illustrated by Victor Hamburger: " . . . the architecture of the nervous system and the concomitant behavior patterns result from self-generating growth and maturation processes that are determined entirely by inherited, intrinsic factors, to the exclusion of functional adjustment, exercise, or anything else akin to learning" (1957, p. 56).

As will become evident to the reader of Chapters 3 and 4, this nature epigenetic viewpoint has rather severe conceptual limitations (akin to those involved with the type of view represented by Lorenz). The alternative conception of the source of epigenesis, *probabilistic epigenesis,* appropriately deals with the conceptual issues inherent in a consideration of psychological development. Moreover, this view represents, in opposition to both the unity-of-science and the predetermined epigenetic view, the notion that developmental changes are determined by a multiplicative interaction of two sources of development, nature and nurture. Since the probabilistic epigenetic position views development as qualitatively discontinuous and further views this discontinuity as arising from an interaction, it is understandable that two different sources of development (hereditary and environmental sources) can be seen to provide the basis of the multiplicative interaction that defines and brings about the qualitative discontinuity.

Schneirla (1957) argues that no behavior is predetermined, or preformed. The role of the environment must always be taken into account in trying to understand the qualitative changes that characterize epigenesis—specifically, the experience of various stimulative events acting on the organism throughout the course of its life span. These stimulative events may occur in the environment outside the organism (exogenous stimulation) or in the environment within the organism's own body (endogenous stimulation). No matter where they occur, however, the influence of patterns of environmental stimulation upon the contribution that genes make towards behavior must always be considered.

Genes must exist in an environment. They do not just float in nothingness. Changes in the environment may help or hinder the unfolding (better, the contribution) of the genes. In other words, the experiences that take place in the environment will play a role in what contribution genes can make. If X-rays invade the environment of the genes, or if oxygen is lacking, or if poisonous chemicals enter this environment, then the role that the genes play in contributing to behavior may certainly be different from their role had such environmental stimulative events not occurred. Moreover, one cannot say with total certainty what type of environmental stimulative influences will always occur or whether the environment will interact with genes to help or hinder development. Rather, one may say only that certain types of environmental influences will *probably* occur (as they do with the average organism of a certain species) and/or that a given emergence will *probably* take place *if* the gene-experience interaction proceeds as it usually does.

Thus, in order for development to proceed normally (that is, in the appropriate sequence typical for the species), environmental stimulative events must operate on (interact with) the maturing organism at specific (or critical) times in the organism's development. That is, since epigenesis is determined by both genetic (maturational) and experiential sources, experience must interact with maturation at certain times in the organism's development in order for specific emergences to occur. If the emergence of a particular behavioral development is determined by a maturation— experience interaction, and if for a particular species this interaction usually occurs at a certain time in the life span (e.g., at about six months of age), then if the certain experience involved in this interaction occurs either too early or too late for a given member of this species, there will be a change in the emergent behavioral capacity. Thus the species-appropriate timing of maturational-experiential interactions is essential in order for the emergences that typically characterize development to occur.

However, the timing of these interactions is not invariant. One can never expect with any complete certainty that these interactions will occur at their appropriate times for all members of a species. As suggested above, some animals may undergo these interactions earlier than others, while others may undergo these interactions at a later than average time. These alterations may or may not lead to substantial alterations in the emergence of the resulting behavioral capacity. The point is that although emergent behavioral developments find their source in the interaction between maturation and experience, one cannot expect the time of these interactions to always be the same for all animals in a species. And alterations in the timing of these interactions, if extreme enough, could lead to changes in the characteristics of the behavior that developed as a consequence of this interaction. Thus, one can say that certain emergences will probably occur, given fairly typical timing of maturation-experience interactions.

Hence, the probabilistic epigenetic position recognizes the following:

1.    Both experience and maturation are invariably involved in determining the qualitative changes that characterize development.

2.   The timing of the interactions between maturation and experience is a factor of critical importance in the determination of behavioral development.

3.   Since these interactions cannot be expected to occur at exactly the same time for every organism within a given species, one can say with a given level of confidence only that certain emergences will probably occur.

The probabilistic formulation of epigenesis should appear more complicated than its predeterministic counterpart, because it is! Development is an exceedingly complex phenomenon and any accurate conceptualization of it would have to take this complexity into account. Thus, Schneirla, recognizing both the complexity of behavioral development and the failure of preformistic developmental notions to recognize that complexity, illustrates the probabilistic epigenetic viewpoint by stating:

> The critical problem of behavioral development should be stated as follows: (1) to study the organization of behavior in terms of its properties at each stage, from the time of egg formation and fertilization through individual life history; and (2) to work out the changing relationships of the organic mechanisms underlying behavior, (3) always in terms of the contributions of earlier stages in the developmental sequence, (4) and in consideration of the properties of the prevailing developmental context at each stage (1957, p. 80).

I believe that this organismic-epigenetic viewpoint offers the most appropriate conceptualization of development. Accordingly, this viewpoint will be stressed again, and explained more fully, at various points in this book.

## The Role of the Organism's Action

Organismic theorists disagree with unity-of-science theorists also about human passivity. Since the organismic position focuses on the wholeness and organization of the organism, it follows that it should be concerned with the role that this organized whole (the organism) plays in affecting its behavior. Thus, organismic thinkers look at organism-environment interactions. Not only are maturation and environment seen as sources of an organism's behavioral development, but so are the organism's *own* characteristics and capacities. The literature on effects of physical attractiveness on children's personality/social development offers many straightforward examples of how the organism's own characteristics play a role in shaping its own development. For example, Dion (1972) found that the exact same behaviors of children were evaluated differently by adults depending on whether the child being evaluated was physically attractive or unattractive; the behavior of the physically attractive child was seen as more favorable than the exact same behavior when emitted by a physically unattractive child. Thus, even this relatively static organismic characteristic—attractiveness—can be seen to affect the organism's own development. Dion's results suggest that an organism will evoke differential reactions in its socializing (adult) environment as a consequence of its own characteristics, and these different reactions may certainly be expected to have a differential impact on the organism's future development. In Chapter 9 we will see how this notion provides the conceptual basis for one of the major longitudinal studies of child personality development—the study of how a child's behavioral individuality may provide a source of his or her own behavioral development, conducted by Thomas, Chess, Birch, Hertzig, and Korn.

The present point is, however, that to organismic theorists behavioral development becomes, at least in part, a matter of self-activated generation. These theorists view development as arising essentially by the multiplicative interaction of two qualitatively different sources—heredity and environment. Hence, it is a logical next step to focus on the meeting place of those factors lying primarily within the organism (hereditary) and those lying primarily outside (environment). This meeting place is of course the organism itself. By focusing on the contributions that the organism's own characteristics (e.g., its type of behavioral style, its physical beauty) make towards its own further development, organismic theorists are essentially studying the continual accumulations of the interacting contributions of nature and nurture. This focus brings about a concern with what role various aspects of the organism itself play in shaping its own behavior. A fuller explication of this aspect of the organismic viewpoint is made in Chapter 4.

## Unity-of-Science—Organismic Compromises
Although the unity-of-science and the organismic viewpoints have been presented to this point as distinct, it is possible to conceive of conceptual compromises between them. Two such conceptual compromises exist (see Nagel, 1957).

### The Levels-of-Organization Hypothesis
The first of these has been implied in much of what we have discussed above. It is termed the *levels-of-organization hypothesis* and is illustrated by the work of Schneirla (1957). This compromise notes that there are different levels of organic and/or pheno-

Howard H. Kendler

Tracy S. Kendler

menal organization and that the laws of the lower levels (e.g., physics and chemistry) are implied in the laws of the higher (e.g., the psychological) level. Yet the laws of the higher level cannot be reduced to or predicted from the laws of the lower level. This is true because such reduction will not lead to an understanding of the emergent quality of the higher level. The reader should recognize that this assertion has been presented as a basic part of the organismic-epigenetic viewpoint. The water example on page 33 is an illustration of this compromise. Another illustration is that although certain neural, hormonal, and muscular processes certainly underlie (are implied in) a person's being in love, reduction of love to these lower levels—or to the still lower levels of chemistry and physics—is unlikely to result in an understanding of this phenomenon.

An example of the application of the levels-of-organization compromise may be seen by reference to some of the phenomena reported in the literature on children's problem-solving behavior. Kendler and Kendler (1962) devised a way to study problem-solving behavior in various species of organism (e.g., rats and humans), as well as in humans of various ages (e.g., nursery school children and college students).. In the procedure they devised, subjects are presented first with two large squares and two small squares. One of each type of square is painted black and one of each type is painted white. Thus, there is a large black and a large white square, and a small white and a small black square. The subject's task is to learn to respond either to the color dimension (and thus ignore the size) or to the size dimension (and thus ignore the color). For example, a subject may be presented with a large black and a small white square on one trial and then perhaps a large white square and a small black square on another trial. Now, if size is the aspect of the stimuli that should be responded to and, further, a response toward the bigger of the two squares will always lead to a reward, the subject should choose the large stimulus in each trial, no matter what the color. In other words,

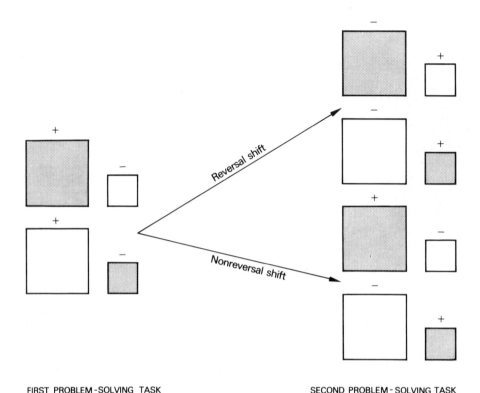

FIRST PROBLEM-SOLVING TASK                    SECOND PROBLEM-SOLVING TASK

**Fig. 2.3** Examples of a reversal shift and a nonreversal shift. *Source:* H. H. Kendler and T. S. Kendler, "Vertical and Horizontal Processes in Problem Solving," *Psychological Review* **69** (1962). Copyright 1962 by the American Psychological Association. Reprinted by permission.

the subject first learns that size is the relevant aspect of the stimuli; therefore, the subject learns to respond to the difference in size and to ignore (not respond to) differences in color of the squares.

Rats, nursery school children, and college students can all learn this first problem-solving task. The interesting thing about this type of problem solving is what happens when the rules about the relevant aspect of the stimuli are changed. In the first problem-solving task, size was the relevant dimension (the big squares were rewarded and the small squares were not). Now, without directly cueing the subject that this rule has changed, it is possible to still keep the size of the stimuli as the relevant dimension (and the color as the nonrelevant), but make choice of the small squares the response that will be rewarded. Thus, the same dimension of the stimuli (size) is still relevant, but there has been a reversal in which aspect of the size (from large to small) will lead to a reward. Kendler and Kendler call this type of alteration a *reversal shift;* the same stimulus dimension is still related to reward, but which of the two stimuli within this same dimension is positive and which is negative is merely reversed. A second type of shift may occur, however, in the second problem-solving task. Instead of size being the reward-relevant dimension, color can be. Now response to the black squares (regardless of their size) will lead to a reward, and response to the white squares (regardless of their size) will not. This type of change involves a shift to the other dimension of the stimuli and is not within the same dimension. Hence, the Kendlers term this second type of possible change a *nonreversal shift*. Figure 2.3 illustrates the reversal and the nonreversal shifts. In all cases the stimuli toward which a response will lead to a reward are marked +, while the stimuli toward which a response will not be rewarded are marked −.

Kendler and Kendler (1962) review the studies of reversal and nonreversal problem solving done with rats, nursery school children, and college students. After learning the first problem (for example, after making ten correct responses to the large sized stimuli), would it then be easier to learn a reversal shift or a nonreversal shift (again using the criterion of ten consecutive correct responses for learning)? The Kendlers' review indicates that rats learn a nonreversal shift easier than a reversal shift. Moreover, so do most nursery school children. Like rats, these human children reach the criterion for making a nonreversal shift faster than they reach the criterion for making a reversal shift. However, somewhat older children, as well as college students, find a reversal shift easier.

Now, the Kendlers interpret these age changes by suggesting that in development there emerges a new mental process in children such that they move from responding ratlike to college student–like; this new mental process, not present at earlier ages (e.g., efficient language processes), alters children's problem-solving behavior such that a reversal shift becomes easier than a nonreversal shift. Hence, while children's problem-solving behavior at the nursery school level can be accounted for by reference to processes apparently also identifiable in rats, their later behavior may be explained by the emergence of a new mental process. Certainly the processes present in the nursery school children provided a developmental basis for the processes seen among the older children. That is, it would be very unlikely to find children who now functioned like a college student but never functioned like a rat. Yet these former processes are not sufficient to account for the behavior of the older children. The problem-solving type of behavior reverses, and this alteration appears related to the emergence of a new mental function. Any attempt to reduce the laws of the later level to those of the earlier level will avoid dealing with the important emergent processes that apparently characterize the older age level. Thus, although other interpretations of these findings have been offered (see Esposito, 1975), the present point is that the work reported by Kendler and Kendler (1962) illustrates the level-of-organization compromise. The laws of the lower level may be involved in those of the higher one, but because of the emergent qualities involved in those of the higher one, the former laws will not suffice in accounting for the phenomena of the higher level if any attempt at reduction is made.

The levels-of-organization compromise is presented diagrammatically in Fig. 2.4. Here we see that at level 1 two gases, hydrogen and oxygen, are present; at level 2, however, the two gases combined produce a substance (water) that has a property (liquidness) that did not exist in either of the level 1 elements in isolation. Although the presence of the lower level's phenomena is certainly implied in the phenomena of the higher level, the latter level still has phenomena (e.g., liquidness) that cannot be understood through reduction to the lower level's phenomena.

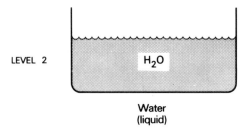

LEVEL 2

**Water
(liquid)**

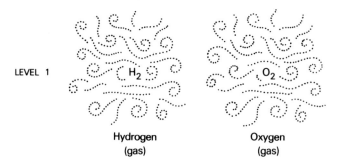

LEVEL 1

**Hydrogen
(gas)**          **Oxygen
(gas)**

**Fig. 2.4** Levels-of-organization compromise between the unity-of-science and the organismic positions.

## The General-and-Specific-Laws Compromise

The second compromise between the unity-of-science and the organismic positions maintains that there are general and specific laws that govern development: certain general laws apply to any and all levels of psychological functioning, yet each specific level of psychological development is also governed by specific laws. Such a compromise is often found in the work of organismic theorists, for example, Heinz Werner and Jean Piaget (see Chapters 5 and 7). Similar to other organismic developmental theorists who stress the concept of stage in their ideas, Piaget views development as involving two processes: first, a general, continuous process that is present at all levels, and in fact is used to account for the continual development of children through the various stages of cognitive development; and second, specific, qualitatively distinct phenomena, which actually serve as the definitional basis of the various stages of development they occur at.

Sigmund Freud, also an organismic developmental theorist, similarly makes use of a compromise between general and specific laws of development. Freud viewed sexual functioning as passing through various "psychosexual stages of development" (1949). However, he saw this development as being energized by a finite amount of mental

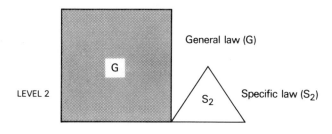

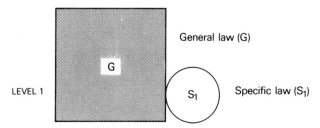

**Fig. 2.5** General-and-specific-laws compromise between the unity-of-science and the organismic positions.

energy present in every individual at birth. This mental energy passed through the body of a person in a prescribed sequence, concentrated at certain locations of the body at certain periods of the person's life. Now, although this same mental energy was seen as always being involved in sexual functioning at all times in a person's life—and as such represents a general law of development—the manner in which sexual functioning was expressed was dependent on exactly where the mental energy was centered. Thus, to Freud sexual functioning involved the combined contribution of a continuously applicable mental energy and a specific area (or zone) of the body wherein this mental energy happened to be located at a certain time in development; this specific characteristic of sexual functioning determined the mode of expression of one's sexuality. Hence, Freud's view of psychosexual development, which we will deal with again in Chapter 7, is an example of how organismic developmentalists may utilize the general-and-specific-laws compromise in their theories.

The general-and-specific-laws compromise is represented in Fig. 2.5. At both level 1 and level 2 we see that a general law, G, exists. However, at level 1 there is also present a specific law, $S_1$, while at level 2 there is present a different specific law, $S_2$.

If at each new developmental level of organization there is an emergence of new phenomena that cannot be reduced to lower organizational levels, how then may the laws governing—or variables involved in—these new phenomena be understood? Typical of other organismic theorists, Schneirla (1957) maintains that to understand this emergence one must look at the specific contribution of that developmental level's genetic inheritance (nature) and its environment, or experience (nurture). Within these two domains the sources of behavior must lie, and one must look at how each level's nature and nurture interact to produce the qualitatively new phenomena that characterize it. This consideration thus brings us to the organismic view of the nature-nurture controversy.

## Summary
Developmental psychology studies similarities and differences in psychological functioning across the life span, and this branch of psychological science has as its goal the discovery of the truth, the facts, about psychological development. The goal of developmental psychology is, then, to discern what actually stays the same and what changes over the course of development. However, whether or not behavior changes across life, developmental psychology is most basically concerned with why behavior takes whatever form it does. Respectively, then, the continuity-discontinuity and nature-nurture issues are raised, and they represent the basic, core issues of development.

The major thrust of this chapter has been a presentation of the unity-of-science and the organismic philosophies of science. The chapter has discussed how these two philosophical bases represent the philosophical forces underlying these core conceptual issues, as well as the conceptual dividing lines for the major theoretical positions and controversies within developmental psychology.

The unity-of-science position suggests that the subject matter of all sciences can be unified within a natural-science framework and that, therefore, the laws governing the most basic natural sciences—physics and chemistry—will apply at all levels of scientific analysis. Thus, there is continuity among all levels of scientific analysis; the laws of physics and chemistry can be used to understand the phenomena of any level of analysis. All that needs to be done in order to understand a higher level of analysis, like psychology, is to reduce the phenomena of the higher level to the terms of the lower, fundamental level. All that a scientist must do to discover the laws of all phenomena is to reduce these phenomena to the constituent elements of physics and chemistry and then discern the mechanisms by which these lower, but fundamental, components quantitatively add to comprise the higher level of analysis.

We introduced the translation of the unity-of-science philosophy into a psychological-theoretical view of development—the learning approach toward development—and discussed some of the philosophical problems with this translation, as well as with the unity-of-science position in general. These problems were seen to lead to the formulation of an alternative philosophical viewpoint.

The organismic position was presented as a view opposed to the unity-of-science viewpoint. This latter point of view suggests that one cannot simply reduce the phenomena of one level to the phenomena of another, lower level. The reason this antireductionist position is maintained is that it is believed that at each new level of analysis there emerge new characteristics that cannot be understood through looking at the laws of the lower level. This then is a belief in epigenesis: the emergence of new properties at each higher level of analysis. Such a position suggests that since one cannot understand the functioning of a higher level simply by reducing it to the phenomena of the lower level, there is then a discontinuity in the laws governing different levels of analysis. The same laws cannot be applied to all levels of analysis because you cannot use a common set of laws to explain the emergence of new properties at each higher level of analysis. Newness implies a change in quality, and the organismic position suggests that qualitative changes occur because when the parts comprising a lower level of organization combine to form the higher level they possess properties that in their combination did not exist in any of these parts in isolation. Thus, the parts comprising the whole organism (i.e., the parts contributing to the higher level) do not merely additively interrelate, but multiplicatively interact, and this type of relation accounts for the qualitative emergences that characterize higher levels of organization.

Thus, we have seen that the unity-of-science viewpoint is basically a continuity position—the same laws can be used to explain phenomena at any level of analysis—while the organismic viewpoint is essentially a discontinuity position—there are new laws at each higher level of organization.

We have also seen how these two views differ in regard to the nature-nurture controversy. While unity-of-science theorists focus on either nature or nurture as the source of behavioral development, many organismic thinkers believe that an interaction between these two sources is what accounts for development across the life span. Accordingly, although we have seen that some organismic theorists view maturation (nature) as the sole source of epigenesis (those adhering to a predetermined epigenetic point of view), we have also suggested that the interactionist, probabilistic epigenetic point of view appears most tenable. The latter stresses the timing of the maturation-experience interactions, which leads to a focus on the organism and the contributions that the organism itself makes to its own development.

Finally, the unity-of-science and the organismic philosophies of science are not mutually exclusive. Compromises can be made. Two such conceptual compromises were presented. The levels-of-organization compromise states that although the laws of the lower level are implied in those of the higher level, one cannot understand the functioning of the higher level simply by reducing to the lower level. The general-and-specific laws compromise states that although there are general laws that apply to all levels of functioning, each level has laws that apply only to that specific level. Examples of the application of each of these compromises, taken from the developmental research and theoretical literature, were given.

# 3

## The Nature-Nurture Controversy: Implications of the Question, How?

A child is born, and perhaps from its parents' initial point of view has few distinguishable capabilities. Soon, however, rather well-coordinated sensory-motor behaviors begin to be elaborated; later, other, more complicated motor patterns emerge and then, still later, the child's vocalizations turn to words!

A baby goose (a gosling), moments after it breaks through its shell, begins to walk after its mother. From then on in its life the goose will attach itself to other geese in all its social behaviors.

Rats, deprived throughout their early development of stimulus cues for depth, are separately placed on a platform that lies between an apparently deep drop-off and a shallow one. Almost all of the rats descend off the platform to the shallow side.

Newborn human babies, just a few days after their birth, consistently turn their heads toward a patterned visual stimulus rather than toward a plain gray stimulus.

What is the source of these diverse behaviors? In fact, what is the source of any behavioral development? Some psychologists have interpreted the emergence of behaviors such as those described above in a way that suggests that experience seems to play a minimal role, if any, and that innate, maturational, or hereditary factors seem to account for their appearance. Yet other psychologists claim just the opposite. Observing the same behaviors, they offer interpretations emphasizing environmental factors. Still other psychologists (myself included) attempt to interpret such behaviors in a way that takes into account the contributions of both intrinsic and experiential factors.

Where does truth lie? Perhaps all positions have elements of truth in them, but the arguments about where the sources of behavior lie are by no means resolved. The nature-nurture controversy is still very much an issue today.

From our discussion in Chapter 2 it should be easily surmised that the basic issue in developmental psychology is this nature-nurture controversy. This issue inquires into the sources of behavior determinancy and development. Stated in an extreme form, the issue asks whether the source of an organism's behavior lies solely in the genetic inheritance (heredity) or in environmental factors. The nature-nurture issue rears its head under many names, depending on the area of psychological inquiry—for example, perception, learning, or intelligence. Thus, we may sometimes hear the controversy termed *nativism versus empiricism, innate versus acquired, preformed versus epigenetic, maturation versus learning,* or *heredity versus environment.* Yet, no matter what terms are used, the basic thrust of the issue remains the same.

## Some Philosophical Roots of the Nature-Nurture Issue

The centrality of this issue is not unique to current developmental psychology but has been a perennial issue for philosophers as well as psychologists. When man, as philosopher, turned his attention from the nature of the universe to the nature of himself, different thinkers began to take different sides on the issue of the source of human behavior.

Illustrations of some of the positions taken are numerous and can start, for example, with the classical Greek era of philosophy. Plato, the teacher of Aristotle, believed that before birth the soul resides in something he termed the "realm of ideas." Plato viewed the body as the mere entrapment of the soul during the person's life. Thus, at birth the soul enters, or is trapped, by the body; because of the soul's existence in the realm of ideas before birth, a person is born with already existing ideas. Hence, in believing in preformed, or innate, ideas, Plato was maintaining a nature position.

A similar nativistic position was put forth by the medieval Christian religious philosophy. A forerunner of Calvinism and Puritanism, this influencial theological position had two basic tenets. First was the belief in original sin: all human beings are born with sin in them. The second element derived from the first. This is the notion of man's basic depravity; that is, human beings are basically depraved, evil creatures.

These two beliefs would be enough for one to argue that the medieval Christian position is appropriately classified as a nature point of view. Both tenets specify basic, inborn characteristics. Yet, another belief of those adhering to this viewpoint best illustrates how this position is a nature one. This is the *homunculus* theory, which maintains that at birth, preformed in the newborn's head, is a little man! The little man, termed the homunculus, is an exact model of a full-grown adult, only of course of smaller size. Instantly created with the child, the homunculus contains the sin, the basic depravity. So when parents having these beliefs applied stern physical punishment to their children, it was not to punish the children per se, but literally to "beat the devil out of them."

Other philosophical proponents of nature viewpoints can be mentioned. René Descartes, similar to Plato, proposed that human beings are born with innate ideas, which are present without any environmental contribution. Jean Jacques Rousseau, another French philosopher, also claimed that humans are born with certain intrinsic characteristics. As opposed to the medieval Christian nativistic position, however, Rousseau's position asserted that humans were born basically good.

The nature philosophical positions did not go uncountered, however. Other philosophies minimized the impact of nature and stressed the importance of nurture. Most notably, nativistic propositions such as that offered by Descartes were countered by a group of eighteenth century British philosophers who comprised the British school of empiricism. Members of this group included such men as Thomas Hobbes, David Hume, David Hartley, James Mill, John Stuart Mill, Alexander Bain, and John Locke.

Locke, for example, in part argued that when the child is born it has no innate ideas. Rather, its mind is like a blank slate, or what Locke termed a *tabula rasa*. Therefore, any knowledge that the child gains comes from its nurture, from experience. Thus, environmental stimulation, delivered to the child's mind through the avenues of its senses, is the source of the child's knowledge. Whatever the child becomes is due to environmental stimulation. This viewpoint is the essence of modern psychology's behaviorist position. Locke's philosophy can be seen as a forerunner of modern behaviorism and, if one may speculate, if John Locke were alive today he would probably be a learning-theory, behavioristic thinker. In Chapter 10 we will assess in greater depth the unity-of-science–learning-theory approach, of which Locke's position was a forerunner.

In sum, we can see that the relative contribution of nature and of nurture in determining human behavior was a well-debated topic throughout the history of philosophy. While one nativistic philosophy—the medieval Christian—specified that human beings are basically bad, another nature position—that of Rousseau—argued that human beings are intrinsically good. However, the nurture philosophy of Locke would probably not agree with either of the above. To Locke, humans are born neither good nor bad. They just are.

## The Nature-Nurture Controversy in Psychology

The philosophical roots of scientific psychology are numerous (Misiak, 1961), and they played an important role in shaping the nature of psychology when it became a science.

(The historical date of the advent of the science of psychology is 1879, the year that Wilhelm Wundt, the "father of psychology," opened his laboratory in Leipzig, Germany.) Accordingly, the nature-nurture debate in philosophy was readily translated into debates among scientific psychologists.

For example, as indicated in Chapter 2, some psychologists interested in the study of perceptual processes (the Gestalt school) claimed that nativistic factors are most important in determining a person's perception, while others (e.g., Hebb, 1949) took an empiricist point of view. In the area of personality, some (e.g., Sheldon, 1940, 1942) stressed what they claimed to be innate sources of a person's temperamental-behavioral functioning, while others (e.g., McCandless, 1967, 1970) maintained that acquired, socially learned responses are the source of such functions. In looking at certain types of animal behavior, some writers (e.g., Lorenz, 1965) postulated preformed, innate mechanisms to account for observed patterns, while others (e.g., Kuo, 1967; Lehrman, 1953; Schneirla, 1957) took an epigenetic approach. Researchers interested in verbal development stressed the primacy of maturation (Gesell and Thompson, 1941), while others viewing the same sort of behaviors offered interpretations that stressed learning (Gagné, 1968). Finally, some psychologists interested in intelligence suggested hypotheses that stressed the primacy of heredity factors (e.g., Jensen, 1969), while others apparently opted to emphasize the role of the environment (Kagan, 1969).

The details of each of the above controversies need not be specified here in order to make the point that psychology in no way takes a place behind philosophy in the intensity of its debate about the nature-nurture issue, and that in all cases the essence of each debate is always the same—the relative contribution of nature and nurture variables in providing a source of behavior.

## Toward a Resolution of the Nature-Nurture Controversy

By this time you are probably wondering how a controversy that has engaged so many bright men and women for over two thousand years can still remain unresolved. Can't the issues be detailed in such a way as to somehow diminish the seemingly endless confusion? I think they can. Rather than discuss all the details of the above controversies—which often led to what I feel were conceptual dead ends—let us turn to a review of various psychologists' formulations that were offered in an attempt to resolve the nature-nurture controversy; we will begin our analysis by a review of the seminal ideas of a famous psychologist, a former president of the American Psychological Association, Anne Anastasi. We will then use Anastasi's formulations as a general framework within which to begin to consider the issues necessary for our reconceptualization of the nature-nurture controversy.

## The Position of Anne Anastasi

The classic paper of Dr. Anne Anastasi, which first appeared in the *Psychological Review* in 1958, represents a most lucid and well-considered treatment of the nature-nurture controversy. The essential problem in appropriately conceptualizing the nature-nurture controversy, as Anastasi saw it, is that psychologists have been asking the wrong questions; therefore, they obviously could not get the right answers. Anastasi attempted to show why previous inquiries have led to dead ends, and what the appropriate question is.

Anne Anastasi

As we have seen, the first way that philosophers as well as psychologists inquired into this problem was to ask, "Which one?" Does heredity or environment, nature or nurture, provide the determinant source of behavior? Those who posed the issue in this way were assuming the independent, isolated action of one or the other in providing a source of a behavior. However, we should reject this way of posing the problem, because it is basically illogical. As Anastasi pointed out, there would be no place to see the effects of heredity without an environment and, alternatively, there would be no one in an environment without heredity. Thus we see that the two, nature and nurture, are inextricably bound. They are inseparable, although conceptually distinct. Nature and nurture are always present in everything, and it is simply not appropriate to ask "which one?" because they are both completely necessary for any organism's existence or for the existence of any behavior.

Some psychologists (e.g., Hebb, 1949; Lehrman, 1953; Schneirla, 1956, 1957), however, had recognized the inappropriateness of the "which one" question even before Anastasi's (1958) paper was published. Yet, others had asked another question that Anastasi maintained was also inappropriate, because it too led to a conceptual dead end. They put the issue this way: Granted that nature and nurture are always involved in any behavior, that both of them are always needed, *how much* of each is needed for a given behavior? For intelligence do you need 90 percent heredity and 10 percent environment, or perhaps is intelligence only 2 parts heredity and 8 parts environment? Or, some might ask: For personality may it be 50 percent of each, for perception is it 7 parts of one, 3 parts of the other? In essence, then, psychologists asking this question would attempt to ascertain how much of each source was needed for a given type of behavior.

But this question also leads to a fruitless end, because it, like the "which one" question, is based on an inappropriate underlying assumption. In the case of the "how much" question the assumption may be termed the independent, additive-action assumption. It suggests that the way in which nature and nurture are related to each other is that the contribution of one source is added to the contribution of the other to provide the behavior. We can see that this solution puts the controversy into the terms of a recipe. *Add* one part of X to some part of Y: add some unknown part of nature to an unknown part of nurture to get behavior.

However, such a question raises many others. For example, does not nature play a role with the nurture part? If not, then what can that one part of nurture possibly contribute to? And what of the (unknown) contributory part of nature? Can it contribute to behavior without any environmental support? Where does it contribute if not in an environment? Thus, the "how much" question soon leads to separating out the independent, isolated effects of nature and nurture, a conceptual route we have just taken by means of the "which one" question. We rejected this route, with its notions of either heredity or environment, because we saw that nature and nurture are always inextricably bound. Thus we must also reject the "how much" route because it really does not take us well beyond the "which one" path. In fact, the "which one" question can be seen to be just a special case of the "how much" question. That is, the former question implies a 100 percent–0 percent split between nature and nurture, while the latter implies some percentage split less than that.

Thus we see that a conceptualization of the independent action of either source (in either an isolated or an additive manner) will lead us to a conceptually vacuous dead end. We should conclude, then, two assertions that follow directly from our above argument. First, nature and nurture are always completely involved in all behavior. Put another way, 100 percent of nature and 100 percent of nurture always make their contribution to all behavior. Any method of inquiry into the source of behavioral development which does not take cognizance of this statement and seeks to make artificial distinctions between nature and nurture can lead only to conceptual confusion and an empirical blind alley. Second, since independent-action conceptualizations of the contributions of nature and nurture similarly lead to conceptual dead ends, an alternative conceptualization of their contributions, that of *interactive action,* seems more appropriate.

This alternative, which seems logically appropriate from all our considerations, is one that implies that both nature and nurture interact to provide a source of behavioral development. Since both sources have been seen to be necessarily completely present, and since we have seen that it is inappropriate to speak of their contributions as adding to each other, then it seems that we should ask, *How* do nature and nurture interact to produce behavioral development? *How* do the effects of each multiply to provide a source of development? Thus the organismic notion of a multiplicative interaction between nature and nurture as providing the basis of development is necessarily derived.

This third question, the question of "how," would seem to lead to the appropriate route of investigation of the contributions of nature and nurture. This, Anastasi argued, is the appropriate way to formulate the issue, because it takes cognizance of the logical necessities. It is based on what we may term the interactive, multiplicative-action assumption, which implies that: (1) nature and nurture are both fully involved in providing a source of any behavioral development; (2) they therefore cannot function in isolation from one another but must always interact in their contribution; and (3) interaction (which, as we have seen, cannot be appropriately construed to mean addition) can be conceptualized as a multiplicative type of interrelation—that is, a type of relation in which the full presence of each source is completely intertwined with the other.

The question "how," then, leads the psychologist to a consideration of the interactive effects of nature and nurture in providing a source of development. It seems that only this question casts aside fruitless polemics and allows the psychologist to begin to unravel the assuredly complex interrelations of nature and nurture.

**Heredity-Environment Interactions.** Assuredly, if after making the above point Anastasi had ended her paper, her contribution to the conceptual clarification of the nature-nurture controversy would have been considered substantial. Anastasi's paper provided additional information, however. After indicating that the appropriate way to conceptualize the nature-nurture controversy is in terms of how these two sets of sources interact, Anastasi proceeded to attempt to specify how each source—heredity and environment—may provide a basis of behavioral development.

**Nature: The Continuum of Indirectness.** Let us focus first on hereditary factors. Anastasi argues that the effects of heredity on behavior are diverse and are always indirect. That is, no psychological function is ever inherited as such; heredity always relates to behavior in an indirect way. At the very least, any hereditary influence on behavior must be mediated by, must occur in the context of, a supportive, facilitative environment. This assertion, we can see, is derived from the rationale that was used to object to the "which one" question: you need the environment to see the effects of heredity; there would be no place to see the contribution of nature if there were no environmental context. Accordingly, the specific contribution of heredity to behavior will depend on the specific environment that that contribution is occurring in. Consistent with our specification of the probabilistic epigenetic-organismic position in Chapter 2, we may assert that any hereditary contribution must occur in an environmental context, and the particular expression of the hereditary contribution that will eventually be seen will depend on the specific characteristics of the environment it is occurring in.

This is why hereditary effects are indirect. Indirectness means that a priori we cannot specify what behavioral effect a particular hereditary contribution will have. Hereditary contributions can express themselves only within the context of their interaction with a mediating environment, and without knowing how this environment will mediate the hereditary effects, we can make no before-the-fact statement about what specific behaviors will result from a particular hereditary contribution. (This is a particularly essential point; and in Chapter 4 it will be seen as an important foundation stone of others' interactionist organismic views about the nature-nurture controversy.)

Thus, there can be no preformed, direct, or invariant hereditary contribution to behavior. As we indicated in Chapter 2 in our discussion of the probabilistic epigenetic viewpoint, the most accurate way of conceptualizing the contribution of nature factors to behavior development is: (1) to recognize the necessary and crucial role that nurture factors play in providing an interactive context for nature factors; and (2) to recognize that the time at which these factors interact will play an important role in shaping development; that is, the interactive contribution of one factor to the other will not be the same at different points in development. Since the characteristics of nature and nurture factors as well as their time of interaction cannot be expected to occur at a time or in a manner in exactly the same way for every organism, before the fact one can say only that certain things will probably occur. Because of our recognition of points 1 and 2, the best we can do is take a guess, with some given degree of confidence in our chances of being correct (i.e., make a probabilistic statement), about what sort of specific be-

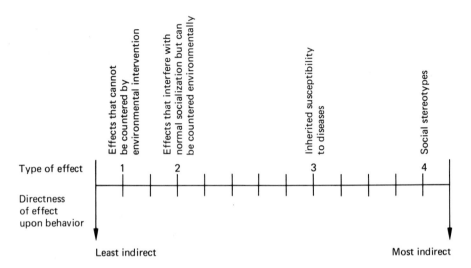

**Fig. 3.1** Contributions of heredity to behavioral development vary along a continuum of indirectness. Numbers 1 through 4 refer to some points along this continuum. *Source:* Adapted from comments by A. Anastasi.

havioral development will eventually result from a particular hereditary contribution.

Thus, any statement that in effect says that a given hereditary contribution will invariably (in all environmental contexts) result in a certain specific behavior is simply incorrect. Therefore, because it is necessary to adopt an interactionist position, we can make several statements about the indirect effects of heredity on behavior. First, the following points should be clear:

1.    The same hereditary influence can be expected to have a different behavioral effect in different environmental conditions; and

2.    Alternatively, the reverse may also be true—different hereditary influences can lead to the same behavioral development in varying environmental situations.

To be complete, we should also point out that

3.    The same environmental effect may be expected to lead to different behavioral outcomes under differing hereditary contributions; and

4.    Different environments can lead to the same outcome in the context of varying hereditary contributions.

The point of all this is that the sources of behavior interact with each other in complex ways. And any analysis of behavioral development that attempts to be appropriate in its recognition of this complexity must always attempt to understand the varying status of the interactions of both nature and nurture factors.

Thus, heredity always contributes to behavior in an indirect manner. Accordingly, Anastasi conceptualizes the contributions of heredity to behavior as varying along a continuum of indirectness, a hypothetical line whose end points are "least indirect" and "most indirect." Such a hypothetical continuum is represented in Fig. 3.1. The left end represents those hereditary contributions to a person that are *least indirect* (or, most direct) in their influence. One may speculate that such effects may be represented by such physical characteristics as eye color or eventual shape of the nose. But, be careful to remember that even these least indirect hereditary effects need, at the very least, the supportive, facilitative influence of the environment. The right end of the continuum represents those hereditary contributions to a person that are *most indirect.* Here the possible number of types of interrelations with the environment increases, and accordingly, resulting behavioral outcomes are much more numerous. Thus, as hereditary influences become more indirect, the range of possible behavioral outcomes of the interaction between heredity and environment similarly increases.

What are some possible illustrations of the range of indirect hereditary contributions to behavior? Anastasi suggests four points along the continuum of indirectness to illustrate this range of effects. These four hypothetical points are ordinal in nature; that is, they are ordered consecutively from "least indirect" effect through "most indirect" effect, although no exact specification of the exact location of these points can be made. Thus, although we may be sure that these effects are ordered appropriately, we are sure neither of their exact locations along the continuum nor of the relative distances between the four points. Despite these limitations, Anastasi's specification of these four points serves well to illustrate the range of heredity's indirect effects on behavior. Let us now consider these four points.

1. *Hereditary effects that in no way can be countered through environmental intervention.* Hereditary contributions to behavior that cannot be ameliorated through the intervention of environmental manipulations are considered to comprise the class of hereditary effects that are least indirect in relation to behavior. Although these effects need a supportive, facilitative environment in which to exert their contribution, once they make their contribution to behavior there is nothing that one can do, through changing the environment, to change that contribution. For example, let us say that because of an unfortunate genetic inheritance a child comes to possess a chromosome trisomy; instead of having the normal inheritance of a pair of a specific chromosome, the child has a third chromosome added to the pair. In normal cases the human complement of chromosomes is 46, divided into 23 pairs. Now, if the child is born with an extra chromosome, occurring with chromosome pair 21, then certain inevitable developments will occur. The child will develop a disorder termed Down's syndrome. As depicted in Fig. 3.2, such a child has rather distinctive physical (particularly facial) characteristics. However, such a child is also invariably mentally retarded; typically the child's intellectual capacities fall into the moderate to severely retarded range. Thus, after the inheritance of such a chromosomal anomaly, there is nothing we can do through environmental intervention, with our current state of knowledge, to avert the inevitability of the child's being mentally retarded. Although we can certainly attempt to train the child to maximize his or her potential, there is nothing we can do to raise the potential to the level that it might have been at had the child not inherited a trisomy of chromosome pair 21. In short, there is nothing we can do to bring the child's intelligence into the nonretarded range. This inheritance represents the least indirect contribution of heredity to behavior, a contribution that cannot be countered through environmental manipulation.

2. *Hereditary deficits that interfere with normal socialization but can be countered*

**Fig. 3.2** Photograph of a child with Down's syndrome. Courtesy of The National Foundation — March of Dimes.

*through environmental intervention.* Moving a little further along on the continuum of indirectness brings us to a second class of indirect hereditary effects. These are more indirect in their contribution to behavior because their contribution can be somewhat ameliorated by changes in the environment. Thus, although effects of this second class may interfere with the process by which a child acquires the behaviors that society may define as being necessary and appropriate, such interference may be somewhat counteracted with appropriate environmental modifications.

For example, let us say that because of a genetic anomaly a child is born blind or deaf. Certainly such handicaps would retard the development of the child's communication skills, and in this way interfere with normal socialization. Because the child cannot see or hear, the process by which the child develops the behaviors that society designates as necessary or appropriate will not be as efficient as it will be for a nonhandicapped child. However, having such an unfortunate inheritance interfere with the development of your communications skills and your socialization in general does not mean that these developments are lost to you forever. As dramatically illustrated in *The Miracle Worker,* the story of Helen Keller and her teacher, the handicaps of blindness and deafness can be counteracted. Thus, although a hereditary effect can interfere with socialization, certain environmental modifications can be instituted to modify or possibly even eliminate the effects of that hereditary contribution to behavior.

3. *Inherited susceptibility to diseases.* A third, still more indirect hereditary contribution to behavior is that type of inheritance that may predispose you to contracting certain diseases. Let us say that as part of your inherited physical/physiological characteristics you develop relatively weak musculature in one chamber of your heart. This hereditary contribution may or may not exert any influence on your behavior. But certain environmentally based characteristics you may possess (e.g., you are overweight, lack regular exercise, eat a poor diet, and are middle-aged) may interact with your constitution and make you very likely to have a heart attack. Yet, in another person not similarly predisposed but having the same characteristics, heart disease may never develop.

Similarly, consider the malady of hay fever. If we may argue that this disease is hereditarily based, then we can see that our inherited susceptibility may or may not lead to a behavioral effect, depending on the specific environment we live in. If we live in an area where the pollen count is extremely low, our susceptibility to this disease may never affect our behavior. In fact, because there would be little if any pollen to precipitate an attack of hay fever, we might never know that we have the disease. But if we live in an area in which the pollen count varies seasonally, then at certain times of the year our behavior will certainly be affected. We will sneeze, our eyes will water, and we will try to seek the comfort and release provided by air-conditioned rooms. Our behavior might be affected even at times of the year when no pollen is present in the air. We might, for example, find ourselves going to a physician all winter in order to get a weekly injection that will diminish the effects of the pollen during the late summer. This third point along the continuum of indirectness well illustrates a point made earlier: the same hereditary contribution will have a different effect on behavior under different environmental conditions.

4. *Social stereotypes.* A final point along the hereditary continuum of indirectness, certainly representing the *most* indirect effect, may be termed social stereotypes. This may seem somewhat paradoxical; how can social stereotypes be a hereditary effect, albeit the most indirect one, on behavior? Let us follow the reasoning underlining this classification carefully, not only to demonstrate its tenability, but also to illustrate the complex interactions between heredity and environment which provide the source of behavioral development.

As we have noted above, the least indirect hereditary contribution to a person may be physical characteristics. Thus, certain physical characteristics such as sex, eye color, or skin pigment are to a great extent very directly hereditarily determined. The range of variation in these characteristics, despite environmental differences, is not as great as it is with other types of characteristics.

How may such physical characteristics lead to social stereotypes? In attempting to function efficiently in the real world, people find ways to reduce the complexity of the situations around them. When we are out in the real world we are literally bombarded with stimulation coming from numerous, diverse sources. Obviously we cannot respond to all these stimuli simultaneously or even successively. If we did so we would never get anything done, and this certainly would not make us very adaptive organisms. So we attend to some stimuli in our environment and disregard others, depending in part on what information we need or want at that time and in that situation. In this way we can be economical in our social interactions.

A person is one type of stimulus object we encounter in our environment. But a person, too, is a complex stimulus, having many dimensions (sex, age, race, style of dress, apparent status, etc.), and we cannot respond to all characteristics of a person at once if we are to be efficient and economical. So in order to be economical, we tend to attend to as few dimensions of a person as possible. Depending in part, for example, on the type of information we need in order to function efficiently at that moment, we attend only to certain stimulus attributes, or cues. On the basis of these cues we place people into certain categories; that is, we associate specific stimulus attributes of the person with specific categories of information, behavioral characteristics, or social attributes. By doing this we need only respond to certain few person dimensions, and still we are able to function efficiently and economically in the real world.

This process of categorization is a very basic one, permeating all our interactions in the real world. For example, if we were lost in a big city late at night it might be successful, but relatively inefficient, to stop and ask various people how to find the way to a certain location. But if we perceive a person wearing a uniform and a badge standing by an intersection, we might respond by placing that person in the category of police officer. We would then attribute to that person the possession of certain attributes (e.g., knowledge of directions), we would ask for this information, and we would then be on our way. Thus, we see that whenever we perceive other people, (1) we respond to certain stimulus attributes, or cues, they possess (in order to maintain economical interpersonal perceptions); (2) on the basis of these cues we place these people into certain categories; and (3) on the basis of this categorization we attribute to these persons the possession of certain information or characteristics of behavior.

Now, Anastasi suggests, and from much accumulated evidence (for example, see Lerner and Korn, 1972; Secord and Backman, 1964) it seems clear, that one major type of cue that people readily use in organizing their interpersonal perceptions and interactions is physical characteristics such as sex and skin color. These are the very same characteristics that are least indirectly hereditarily determined. Thus, it is probable that in some societies, (and here I am intentionally understating my argument) people are categorized on the basis of certain inherited physical characteristics. If this occurs, we will probably make certain invariant personality attributions and maintain certain invariant behavioral expectancies about all people placed in that category. We will do this because, after all, the reason that we categorize in the first place is to efficiently tell us what to expect about that class of people stimuli. It would defeat the purpose of economical categorization processes to admit exceptions to our attributions.

What may be the effects of categorizing people on the basis of inherited physical characteristics? In answering this question we will see how such inherited characteristics provide the most indirect hereditary source of behavior: social stereotypes. To address this question though, let us offer a not-too-imaginary example.

Suppose that there is a society that has as a most salient cue for the categorization of people a certain inherited physical characteristic: skin color. Now, for argument's sake, let us further imagine that one of the two skin color groups in this society is

categorized in an unfavorable way. That is, people in that group, when put into this physically cued category, are afforded negative behavioral expectations and personality attributions—for example, they are thought of as lazy and shiftless and unable to profit very much from educational experiences. Now certainly, at least some people in this imaginary category probably could profit from education and are not lazy, but it is likely that such categorizations would be maintained despite experience of such exceptions. If this is the case—that our categorization involves an overgeneralized belief or attitude—then we may term such a categorization a *stereotype*. Thus, it is possible that in response to a physical attribute we place a person in a category and in so doing maintain stereotyped expectations about that person.

Now, if the skin color group were stereotyped as uneducable and lazy, it would not make sense to put much effort into attempting to educate people of that group. Because we would not expect them to learn too much we would not spend much money on their schooling. In fact, such a group might have a history of going to inferior schools where there were inadequate facilities and poorly qualified teachers. Thus, because of the stereotype, this skin color group would experience inadequate, inferior, or substandard educational opportunities.

Finally, years later, someone might come along and decide to see if the categorization of these people involves an overgeneralization. This person finds that this group does not seem to be doing very well educationally; many people in this group do not score high scholastically, do not seem to have as high intellectual aptitudes as members of the other skin color group, often do not go on to higher education, and accordingly do not often enter into the higher prestige, higher salary, higher socioeconomic-status professions. Thus, the person doing this study might conclude that the facts show that this skin color group cannot profit from educational experiences to any great degree. And many of those in this imaginary society, who may have often made such an attribution about those in this category, might say that they knew it all along.

But our analysis of the situation is certainly different. What occurred with this stereotyped skin color group was as follows:
1.   On the basis of their relatively direct inheritance of a physical characteristic—their skin color—people in this group were placed into a certain unfavorable category.
2.   In turn, on the basis of this categorization, certain negative behavioral expectations were invariably afforded members of this category (we might suggest here that a basis of both the initial categorization and the concomitant attributions and expectations might lie in the social and economic history of this group).
3.   These attributions were associated with differential experiences (different as opposed to the society's other skin color group) and opportunities.
4.   These differential situations delimited the range of possible behaviors that this group could develop. In other words, the group was channelled into a selected, limited number of behavioral alternatives, the very same behaviors that they were stereotypically held to have.
5.   Finally, many members of the group developed these behaviors because of the above channelling. That is, the end result of the physically cued social stereotype was a *self-fulfilling prophecy*.

In sum, we see that on the basis of a physically cued categorization we may make a stereotypic attribution and, accordingly, channel the people of that category into certain behavioral patterns by creating social situations within which the people in this category cannot do other than develop along the lines of the social stereotype. Our social stereotypes about relatively directly inherited physical cues may have a very indirect effect on behavior. It may result in a self-fulfilling prophecy.

Of course, the example that we have just considered is not, unfortunately, imaginary at all. Although this social stereotypical effect on behavior can obviously function either favorably or unfavorably for the categorized people, the illustration above is probably the most pernicious example of social stereotypes. From our analysis we can see that a strong argument can be made that the black people of our country have perhaps experienced the most unfortunate effects of this most indirect type of hereditary contribution to behavior—social stereotypes. Thus it seems that black Americans may have been involved in an educational and intellectual self-fulfilling prophecy in our country for many years. This possibility will be important to remember below when we consider in detail recent controversy (e.g., Hebb, 1970; Herrnstein, 1971; Jensen, 1969, 1973; Layzer, 1974) about the nature and nurture of black-white differences in intelligence and educability.

At this point, however, suffice it to say that social stereotypes certainly seem to represent a potent source of behavioral development. Although this is the most indirect hereditary contribution to behavior, it does nonetheless appear to play a ubiquitous role in our behavioral development. We have used the example of skin color to illustrate the effects of physically cued social stereotypes, but others, more subtle or more obvious, could be mentioned—for example, hair texture, shape of nose, breast size in women, or body build. In fact, the effects of social stereotypes about body build is a topic I have devoted much time to (Lerner, 1969, 1972, 1973; Lerner and Gellert, 1969; Lerner, Karabenick, and Meisels, 1975a, 1975b; Lerner, Knapp, and Pool, 1974; Lerner and Korn, 1972; Lerner and Schroeder, 1971a, 1971b), and the interested reader may consult these references to see that the processes involved in the social stereotyping of body build appear to be the same as those involved in the social stereotyping of skin color. With both types of cues, people seem to be channelled into a self-fulfilling prophecy by their society.

To this point we have considered implications of Anastasi's suggested four points along her theoretical continuum of indirectness, the continuum along which heredity contributes to behavior. But the major implication of the question "how?" is that nature interacts with nurture to affect all behavior. We must then consider the ways in which the environment contributes to behavioral development. In so doing we can continue to use Anastasi's (1958) paper as a model. Thus we will now look at another continuum, the environmental continuum, or as Anastasi conceptualizes it, the "continuum of breadth."

**Nurture: The Continuum of Breadth.**  Let us now turn our attention to environmental factors. Anastasi conceives of the environment as making its contribution to behavioral development along a continuum of breadth. In other words, environmental factors vary in terms of their pervasiveness of effect on behavior. Some environmental factors, then, may be seen to have very broad, pervasive effects on a person, relating to many dimensions of functioning and enduring in their contribution for a relatively long period of time. Alternatively, other environmental factors may have narrow, minimal effects, making

ENVIRONMENTAL - EFFECTS CONTINUUM

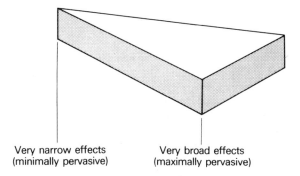

Very narrow effects          Very broad effects
(minimally pervasive)        (maximally pervasive)

**Fig. 3.3** The contributions of environment to behavioral development vary along a continuum of breadth. *Source:* Adapted from comments by A. Anastasi.

their contribution to only a small or limited segment of the person's behavior and exerting their influence for a relatively short, transitory period. Such a continuum of breadth is illustrated in Fig. 3.3. Those environmental effects that are derived from the left end of the continuum exert narrow, minimally pervasive effects on behavior, while those at the right end are broad and maximally pervasive in nature.

But what are examples of environmental effects? Just what sort of variables are there in the environment that can contribute to behavioral development along such a continuum of breadth? Anastasi suggests two general categories of environmental effects, and within these lie the nurture variables that affect behavior.

1. *Organic effects.* The first category of environmental effects may be labeled organic. There are some environmental occurrences that lead to changes in the makeup of the organism; they affect what the organism has and how what it has functions. In short, these factors change the constitution of one's physical and/or physiological processes.

Typically, one may adventitiously encounter environmental variables that affect the organic makeup of one's body through either contracting a disease or having an accident. However, the eventual behavioral outcomes of such organic changes may, in turn, be either broad or narrow in nature. For example, losing half one's cerebral cortex in an auto crash, or an arm or a leg, or having permanent facial scars following a burning may all be considered environmentally mediated changes in a person's organic makeup which will have obviously pervasive, enduring effects on behavior. Alternatively, loss of a single finger or of a toe, while being organic changes, would probably not have as great an effect. Moreover, accidents such as stubbing one's toe certainly affect behavior, but in an obviously trivial, narrow, and transitory way.

Disease contraction may also be broad or narrow in its behavioral contributions. Contracting a disease such as polio, sickle-cell anemia, or muscular dystrophy would certainly have a very pervasive effect on a child's behavioral development and functioning. The range of behaviors that children with such disorders could engage in would differ greatly from those that children not similarly affected could engage in. On the other hand, some diseases, although affecting the makeup of the organism, do so in only limited or short-term ways. Thus catching a common cold or contracting one of the childhood diseases such as chicken pox would affect behavior, but only for a minimal amount of time and probably in not too pervasive ways.

Of course, the environment can contribute to behavioral development through organic changes in ways that do not have to be construed as negative. Environmentally based organic changes that facilitate or improve behavioral functioning, rather than deteriorating it, can be induced. Thus, such things as changes in diet, climate, physical regimen, or medical treatments can result in changes in organic makeup which may have facilitative effects on behavioral functioning and development.

2. *Stimulative effects.* The second category of environmental effects on behavior may be termed stimulative. These are environmental events that act as direct stimulative influences on behavioral responses. Here, too, such variables may be broad or narrow in their contribution to behavior. Perhaps the broadest stimulative environmental variable is social class. Differences among social classes in modes of living, values, presence of material goods, and availability of cultural and educational opportunities represent variations in the types of stimuli that children of different social classes are exposed to. For example, a black child growing up in an urban ghetto is exposed to vastly different stimuli than is a white, middle-class child living in a suburban area. These differential stimulus sources, permeating all aspects of the developing child's world, serve to shape varying response repertoires.

A somewhat narrower, less pervasive stimulative influence may be, for example, the college experience. Events in this specific environment certainly evoke intellectual, attitudinal, and behavioral responses among students, and such responses are, in turn, probably different in nature from responses among youth not exposed to the college experience. For example, many people today believe that a generation gap exists between today's adolescent and adult generations. Yet, researchers like Adelson (1970) have argued that the generation gap may be more apparent than real. Adelson suggests that people may believe that such a gap generally exists because most research studies and media portrayals of the generation gap focus on college students. Most American youth do not go to college, however, and one may argue that the attitudinal and behavioral responses they exhibit are not representative of the attitudes and behaviors of all similarly aged youth. Youth exposed to different stimulative environmental effects, he suggests, may be expected to respond differently. These assertions were borne out in a series of studies (cf. Lerner, 1975; Lerner, Karson, Meisels, and Knapp, 1975; Lerner and Knapp, 1975; Lerner, Pendorf, and Emery, 1971; Weinstock and Lerner, 1972) on the generation gap. Thus, the college experience may be seen as one type of differential stimulative influence on behavior along the continuum of breadth.

Finally, some stimulative influences are exceedingly narrow, trivial, and of short duration in their contribution to behavior. Such minimally pervasive effects are numerous, occurring daily in our interactions in the real world. Thus, having a particularly rude, discourteous cab driver or sales person may affect us momentarily, but not to any great extent.

In sum, then, Anastasi has suggested that the effects of the environment on our behavioral development vary in their pervasiveness. Whether these effects are organic or stimulative in type, they present a range of environmental influences that will interact with indirect hereditary contributions to provide the source of our development. Heredity and environment, nature and nurture, are always present, always involved in providing a source of our development. The specific indirect contribution of nature can be understood only in the context of the particular broad-to-narrow contribution of nurture that it is interacting with, and in turn, an exact understanding of how a certain environmental contribution affects behavior can be reached only with an understanding of how it interrelates with the organism's nature.

Thus, in trying to conceptualize how nature and nurture interact, Anastasi drew on a concept used by a leading geneticist, Dobzhansky, who suggests that the *norm of reaction* might be a useful concept in conceptualizing the interacting influences of nature and nurture.

## The Norm of Reaction

The concept of norm of reaction has been a popular and useful one for geneticists since it was introduced in the early part of the twentieth century by Woltereck (Dunn, 1965). To understand the concept we must first recognize that what we inherit from our parents, what they transmit to us when fertilization occurs, is a particular set of genes. This genetic endowment, or *genotype* (Hirsch, 1963), represents our hereditary developmental potential for all our eventual physical, physiological, and behavioral characteristics. However, there is not a one-to-one relation, an isomorphism, between our genotype and the eventual characteristics that we do develop. That is, our genotype does not represent a genetic blueprint; we cannot simply specify how a particular genetic contribution will manifest itself behaviorally merely by knowledge of the genotype. As we have pointed out at length above, no psychological trait is ever directly inherited. So the eventual manifestation of our genotype, how the genotype will express itself when behavior develops, depends on the interaction of that genotype with the environment. And of course, this expression will vary under different environmental conditions.

Thus, what we see in the developed or developing person is the product of the interaction of the environment with the person's genotype. What we see is termed the *phenotype*. Therefore, because phenotypes can be expected to be different in varying environmental conditions, despite genotypic invariancy, what our genetic inheritance actually represents is not a predetermined, inevitable blueprint of our eventual characteristics; our phenotype is neither a mere replica of our genotype, nor is it isomorphic with it. Rather, our genetic inheritance represents a *range of potential outcomes,* and the developmental outcome that eventually manifests itself will occur due to the interaction of the environment within this range of genetic potential.

This, then, is the norm-of-reaction concept: "The same genotype can give rise to a wide array of phenotypes depending upon the environment in which it develops" (Hirsch, 1970, p. 73). In other words, our genotype—our heredity—gives us a range, or sets the limits, for the development of our characteristics; but the environment, interacting within these limits, plays an essential role in determining what will eventually be developed, what our phenotype will be. In sum, the norm-of-reaction concept asserts that our genetic inheritance sets the broad limits, the upper and lower boundaries, for our behavioral development; but the eventual behavioral outcome that we do develop (our phenotype) will depend on the specificities of the environment interacting within our hereditary limits.

Before assessing some of the implications of this concept, let us use an example to illustrate its meaning. We have suggested that the genotype may be conceived of as a range of potential behavioral outcomes, as the hereditary upper and lower limits for the development of a particular psychological characteristic. Now let us suppose that a given child's genotype for intelligence represents a range of from a low of 40 to a high of 160 IQ points. What will the child's measured IQ be? In other words, what will the phenotypic IQ be? This will depend, of course, on the specificities of the environment that the child is reared in.

If we reared the child for the first twelve years of his or her life in a clothes closet and then measured the child's IQ, we might suppose that the phenotypic IQ would fall near the lower limit set by the child's genotype, most likely near 40. However, we would expect a different phenotypic IQ if we took another child with the same exact genotype and reared him or her in a perhaps more stimulating environment, let us say in the home of a professional couple who provided facilitative general learning tools and excellent language models and who fostered high achievement motivation (see Bloom, 1964). A child reared in such an environment would be likely to have a measured IQ near the upper limit of his or her norm of reaction. Thus, although both children in our example had the same exact genotypic intelligence, their phenotypic intelligence would be quite different because of their markedly varied rearing environments.

In sum, then, we see that the phenotype for any observed psychological characteristic does not depend solely on the person's genotype, or genetic endowment; rather, the phenotype is the end result of a complex interaction of the environment within the genotypic range of potentials represented by that person's norm of reaction.

Psychologists other than Anastasi (e.g., Hirsch, 1963, 1970; Schneirla, 1957) recognized the utility of the norm-of-reaction concept in conceptualizing the nature of heredity-environment interactions. Hebb (1949), for instance, offered a conceptualization of intelligence consistent with the notions implicit in the norm-of-reaction concept. He suggested that humans are endowed with a range of intellectual potential, a genotypic intelligence. This inherited range of intellectual potential Hebb termed "intelligence A." However, psychology has not devised a means of assessing intelligence A; that is, there is no existing technique to appraise a person's genotypic intelligence. Rather, what can be measured is what Hebb termed "intelligence B"—the outcome of an individual's history of environmental interactions within the context of the person's norm of reaction. Thus, this phenotypic intelligence, intelligence B, is a measurement of the result of an interaction between environment and hereditary endowment.

To the extent then that Hebb's (1949) notions are tenable, the norm-of-reaction concept as it applies to this conceptualization of intelligence suggests the following:
1.   We are all born with a genotypic intelligence (intelligence A), which represents a range of potential intellectual developments.
2.   However, psychologists do not measure intelligence A when administering an IQ test; no means exists to measure this hypothetical construct (see Layzer, 1974).
3.   Another type of intelligence exists, which is the product of an interaction between the person's environmental history and genotypic intelligence. This second type of intelligence (intelligence B) represents the phenotypic intelligence of the person.
4.   This phenotypic intelligence is what is measured by current IQ tests.
5.   However, the genotype-phenotype intelligence correlation remains unknown; that

is, if the genotype represents a range of possible intellectual outcomes, then whether the phenotype represents a low, middle, or high point within this range remains unknown. The person has been endowed with a specific genotype, and through environmental interaction this genotype has provided a basis of the person's phenotype; however, whether this environmental interaction led to a phenotype that is expressive of the high part or the low part of the person's genotype cannot be assessed (again, see Layzer, 1974, for detailed mathematical reasons).

6. Finally, all this suggests that given another environmental history, the same genotype can be expected to have led to a different phenotype. Still, however, the portion of the norm of reaction that this new phenotype related to would remain unknown.

These points illustrate how one psychologist has used the norm-of-reaction concept in relation to a specific psychological construct: intelligence. Shortly, we will review in greater detail the implications of this concept for the topic of intelligence, but for the moment let us continue our analysis of the norm-of-reaction concept.

The last implication of Hebb's ideas about intelligences A and B (point 6 above) suggests that although we may expect the same genotype to lead to different phenotypes in different environments, what portion of the genotype is reflected by a specific phenotype remains unknown. This suggests that there are limitations of this concept, and it is important that these limitations be made clear.

**Limitations of the Norm-of-Reaction Concept.** The relation between genetic endowment and behavior has been a continuing research and theoretical concern of Dr. Jerry Hirsch. In recent statements (1970), Hirsch argues that although there is a norm of reaction associated with the observable outcomes of an individual's ontogenetic development (i.e., a person's phenotype), this range is not predictable in advance. In other words, before the person has developed, it is impossible to say that because of his or her genotype, given certain environmental manipulations one type of phenotype will develop, while given other environmental circumstances another phenotype will result. In essence, at the human level there is really no way to directly assess the expected range of phenotypes to be associated with a given genotype. We can only, at best, make statements about particular genotype-environment interactions *after* they have occurred.

In fact, at any level of life organization, the norm of reaction remains largely unknown in most cases (Hirsch, 1970). This is the case because in order to be able to specify with exactness the norm of reaction for any living animal (or plant for that matter), one must be able to reproduce an individual, specific genotype exactly, many times. In effect, one must be able to reproduce several genetically identical organisms. These replicated genotypes must then be exposed to as diverse an array of environments as possible. The range of phenotypes that develop from these exposures would give an estimate of the norm of reaction for that specific genotype. Ideally this exposure should be totally inclusive of all possible environmental conditions that the genotype might be exposed to. Of course, such an infinite exposure could only, in reality, at best be approximated, so the most that can be done is to offer an approximation of the norm of reaction for any one genotype.

We can agree, then, with Hirsch's conclusion:

Even in the most favorable materials only an approximate estimate can be obtained for the norm of reaction, when, as in plants and some animals, an individual genotype can be replicated many times and its development studied over a range of environmental conditions. The more varied the conditions, the more diverse might be the phenotypes developed from any one genotype. (From "Behavior-Genetic Analysis and Its Biosocial Consequences," *Seminars in Psychiatry* **2** (1970), pp. 69–70. Quoted by permission.)

Further clarifications of the norm-of-reaction concept need to be made. Hirsch points out that different genotypes should not be expected to have the same norm of reaction. The norm of reaction associated with each individual genotype can be expected to be differentially unique, that is, differentially broad or narrow. Therefore, the range of phenotypes that would develop from a specific genotype, under varying environmental conditions, can be expected to be different from individual to individual. The point here is that each and every person who walks this earth (possibly, but not assuredly, with the exception of identical—monozygotic—twins) has his or her own individual norm of reaction. As Hirsch (1970, p. 70) has simply put it, "We must expect norms of reaction to show genotypic uniqueness." Even if one simplifies the situation enormously in order to make an estimate, there are over *70 trillion* potential human genotypes; we can assume then that no two living people share the same genotype (Hirsch, 1970, p. 73; Jensen, 1973, p. 8).

Because of this uniqueness, all individuals will interact with their environments in unique, specific ways. This assertion points to the necessity of trying to determine individual laws of human behavior—laws that account for the individual's unique pattern of development within his or her environment. Alternatively, Hirsch's argument suggests the futility of attempting to specify general "laws of environmental influence" or of attempting to account for all the variation in human behavior merely through recourse to invariant, overt environmental stimuli and responses.

These implications—first, that each individual is genotypically unique and will interact differently in a given environment than other, genotypically unique people, and therefore, second, that a complete focus on the environment in an attempt to account for all behavioral variation is both misguided and incorrect—are important. They will apply to our discussions of the organismic and the unity-of-science–learning theories in the following chapters, as well as to our analysis of the ipsative theoretical approach to developmental psychology. Thus, our considerations lead us to stress the inescapable fact of human uniqueness; this fact is derived from an appropriate understanding of the genetic basis (or contribution) of individuality, and is well documented in a review by Jensen (1973).

At this point though, we can summarize our discussion of the norm-of-reaction concept by stating what it does and does not tell us about how nature and nurture interact to produce behavioral development.

1.  Heredity alone does not determine behavior. An isomorphism does not exist between a genotype and a phenotype.

2.  Rather, what our genotype represents is a range of possible outcomes of development. These outcomes will result from the varying specificities of the interactions of the environment with the genotype, and different phenotypes can be expected to result from different interactions.

3.  However, the norm of reaction can neither be predicted in advance nor, on the human level, even be well estimated or approximated.

4.   Therefore (and this is a crucial point) in actuality, those limits set by our hereditary endowment, by our genotype, can never be specified (Hirsch, 1970, p. 70). We cannot reproduce individual human genotypes and expose them to all possible environmental situations. Because of this fact, we cannot know any given individual's range of genetic potential.

5.   But what we can do is recognize that the norm of reaction is unique with each individual, and therefore, since it can be expected to vary from one individual to another, people will interact individually differently with their environments. This process will result in basic phenotypic uniqueness among people.

Thus, the norm-of-reaction concept highlights the necessity of focusing on the interaction of nature and nurture in order to understand behavior development. This concept's implications illustrate that "extreme environmentalists were wrong to hope that one law or set of laws described universal features of modificability. Extreme hereditarians were wrong to ignore the norm of reaction" (Hirsch, 1970, p. 70).

To this point in this chapter we have considered general concepts in the nature-nurture controversy and dealt with some of their rather broad implications. At the beginning of this chapter, however, I indicated that the nature-nurture issue is very much alive today and still rears its head in many currently researched and debated content areas of psychology. In order to illustrate how these general concepts may be appropriately applied to a specific topic, we will turn to a discussion of the nature-nurture controversy as it bears on a topic of recent scientific and public concern: intelligence. More specifically, we will consider immediately below the nature and nurture of the intellectual differences between black and white Americans.

## The Nature and Nurture of Intelligence

In the late 1960s the different average group scores of black and white American children on IQ (intelligence) tests became a point of major public concern. The mean (i.e., the arithmetic average) difference between these two groups is often reported to be as high as 15 IQ points (e.g., Scarr-Salapatek, 1971a) in favor of the white children. That is, white children, as a group, typically score higher than do black children, as a group, on standardized intelligence tests. However, this does not mean that blacks always do worse on IQ tests than do whites. In fact, as Jensen quite precisely points out:

Although the average IQ of the Negro population of the United States, for example, is about one standard deviation (i.e. 15 IQ points) below that of the white population, because of the disproportionate sizes of the Negro and white populations there are more whites with IQs below the Negro average than there are Negroes (1973, p. 16).

Now, psychologists (as a group) seem to orient themselves toward the left end of the political-social spectrum on matters of social concern, and accordingly, the favored interpretation of these racial differences in IQ is that they are environmentally based. Taking a position consistent with what may be termed a liberal political viewpoint, psychologists stress the cultural disadvantages of black Americans—the hypothesis that a complex of environmental factors associated with poverty, a complex as yet largely undefined, prevents a child from achieving optimum development (Scarr-Salapatek, 1971b). Such environmental disadvantage, they argue, accounts for the in-

Arthur R. Jensen

ferior performance of black children on standardized IQ tests. In essence it is hypothesized that it is not black children but their environments that are deficient.

Assuredly, no one could argue against the point that black Americans as a group have experienced a history of inferior and possibly even pernicious environmental circumstances. In fact, in our previous discussion of social stereotypes we saw how environmentally based social attitudes may have a pernicious effect on blacks' intellectual development. Accordingly, psychologists working with the above hypothesis have attempted to determine the nature of the environmental variables that led black children to their inferior performance on IQ tests. They also have contributed to social projects designed to ameliorate blacks' environmental disadvantages (e.g., Project Head Start).

What brought the IQ difference between blacks and whites to the general public's attention was that an alternative hypothesis suggested by Dr. Arthur R. Jensen (1969) was offered for investigation. Simply, Jensen proposed a genetic-differences hypothesis as an alternative to the above environmental-differences explanation of the black-white IQ differences. Jensen suggested that if behavior, and characteristics of behavioral functioning (such as intellectual behavior, as indexed by IQ), can be measured and found to have a genetic component, then such behavior can be regarded as no different from other human characteristics, at least insofar as a genetic viewpoint is concerned. Moreover, he asserted that "there seems to be little question that racial differences in genetically conditioned behavioral characteristics, such as mental abilities, should exist, just as physical differences" (Jensen, 1969, p. 80). Accordingly, after carefully reviewing several lines of evidence bearing on the general idea of race differences in intelligence and their possible sources, Jensen advanced:

a not unreasonable hypothesis that genetic factors are strongly implicated in the average Negro-white intelligence difference. The preponderance of the evidence is, in my opinion, less consistent with a strictly environmental hypothesis than with a genetic hypothesis, which, of course, does not exclude the influence of environment or its interaction with genetic factors (1969, p. 82).

Thus, Jensen proposed that the black-white differences in mean IQ are not due largely to differences in environmental opportunity, but to differences in the gene distributions for these groups (Scarr-Salapatek, 1971a). In his attempt to support this hypothesis, Jensen presented empirical data bearing on the racial difference in IQ scores and interrelated these findings with data bearing on another concept in this area of research: the concept of heritability.

*Heritability* refers to the proportion of a group's individual differences in a trait (e.g., a psychological characteristic such as intelligence) that is due to the genetic individual differences in that group. If a group of people is given a test, not everyone in the group will get the same score; there will be differences between people. Heritability is a concept that indicates the percentage (or proportion) of these differences which can be attributed to ("accounted for by") genetic differences between these people.

Jensen argued that IQ is a very highly heritable trait—that is, that individual differences (variation *between* people) in IQ scores within a group are mostly due (e.g., 80 percent) to the genetic variation in that group. He pointed out that about 80 percent of the differences between the people in certain groups are attributable to genetic differences between these people. Therefore, because of these relations it might seem tenable to argue that since heritability appears to be genetically based, the IQ differences between blacks and whites are in turn genetically based. Of course, Jensen recognized that most of the studies done to assess the heritability of intelligence have been done on white subjects; such estimates—of how much of the differences in IQ scores between members of specific populations can be attributed to genetic differences between these people—are not appropriately applied to other populations. Thus, he pointed out:

Although one cannot formally generalize from *within*-group heritability to *between*-groups heritability, the evidence from studies of within-group heritability does, in fact, impose severe constraints on some of the most popular environmental theories of the existing racial and social class differences in educational performance (Jensen, 1973, p. 1).

Thus, although Jensen recognized that it is not perfectly legitimate to attempt to apply heritability findings derived within groups of whites to an analysis between these white groups and black groups, he still felt that the findings with whites were impressive enough to cast doubt on the environmental-differences hypothesis.

Thus, Jensen offered for consideration the genetic-differences hypothesis. He proposed this hypothesis in an attempt to explain why major educational intervention programs such as Head Start were apparently failing in the attempt to raise the IQs of both black and white lower-class children. On the basis of this hypothesis, he suggested that this failure was due to the high heritability of IQ (Scarr-Salapatek, 1971a). Since to some reviewers of Jensen's ideas (cf. Jensen, 1973), high heritability of a trait indicates that the trait is minimally available to environmental influence, then it follows that: (1) since IQ is a highly heritable trait, there is little influence that the environment can have in affecting the expression of that trait, and (2) therefore, programs such as Head Start that attempt to present alternative environmental influences to some children have little effect because the target of influence is IQ.

This hypothesis is both complex and important; its evaluation will be the major burden of the rest of this chapter. Yet, we should first consider another aspect of the hypothesis—the social reaction to the offering of the hypothesis per se and, in turn, the social reaction to Jensen in offering it. I think in such discussion there is an important lesson to be learned about the nature of scientific inquiry in today's world.

## Social Reactions to Jensen's Hypothesis

First, and without question, Jensen offered his formulations in the spirit of science's quest for truth. After reviewing past studies of black-white IQ differences, he offered a hypothesis that he believed could better account for these differences than could previously offered hypotheses. As must be all scientists, Jensen was committed to producing the best explanation of the phenomena under scrutiny. Scientists may not limit themselves to generating hypotheses and offering interpretations that are consistent with prevailing social and political views of reality if they are to remain committed to the discovery of empirical reality. If separation between scientific work and prevailing political views is not maintained, then it is the current political climate rather than scientific, empirical investigation that determines "truth."

Hence, if Jensen thought that the genetic-differences hypothesis had any validity whatsoever—and he apparently did—he was scientifically obligated to advance it and thus to subject it to the evaluation of the scientific community. Yet, numerous members of the scientific community—as well as members of the media—do not think that Jensen did the correct thing in advancing the genetic-differences hypothesis. Although many scientists have genuine differences of opinion on the validity of Jensen's interpretations, there is also a seemingly large group of psychologists, as well as scientists in general, who think Jensen does not have the right to advance the hypothesis, despite its correctness or incorrectness. Basically it is argued that even an unastute observer of contemporary America can recognize that the hypothesis advanced by Jensen may have pernicious social implications. Although Jensen was writing to a scientific audience, it is probable that his ideas will filter down to the lay public and thus serve to reinforce racist prejudices and even serve as a basis for the formulation of social governmental policy before the ideas are appropriately scientifically tested or countered. Since, as indicated above, the genetic-differences hypothesis as applied to the heritability of IQ is interpreted by some to mean that individuals' IQ scores cannot be very influenced by environmental manipulations, then several apparently appropriate statements might follow. For example, it might then be said that the genetic-differences hypothesis really means that blacks are genetically inferior intellectually to whites, that there is a good reason to exclude blacks from jobs requiring high intellectual ability (and having high status) because they are less likely than whites are to have the requisite abilities, and that governmental funds devoted to environmental enrichment programs are thus being wasted. Moreover, such pejorative and faulty statements might increase in frequency when, after the appropriate scientific evaluation begins and some publications present views consistent with the genetic-differences hypothesis (e.g., Eysenck, 1971; Herrnstein, 1971, 1973), there is the perception by the public of more scientific unanimity than actually exists. Thus, despite whether or not Jensen has advanced an hypothesis that is veridical with reality, the inevitable result of the mere offering of the hypothesis is an increment in both racist attitudes and policies. If the hypothesis is incorrect, its advancement can only do social mischief. However, if the hypothesis is correct, it is still better not to advance it; since we do not want more racism, it is better to pretend that the environmental-differences hypothesis is correct because we can do something about the environment (Jensen, 1973, pp. 17–21).

Such an argument is scientifically unacceptable. We cannot allow the prevailing social climate to dictate what sort of hypotheses may be offered for investigation. For example, what if we reverse the case. Would we have shouted down a scientist working in Nazi Germany who had the "audacity" to suggest that the accepted genetic differences hypothesis was incorrect, i.e., that Jews were not genetic mongrels possessing inferior genes, that Aryans were not the superior race? No, we would have applauded the bravery of the scientist and have hoped that there would be someone to carry on his work (for in societies that make a rule of dictating what is permissible to believe as true, there is little room for dissenters). We would have wanted these ideas subjected to scientific, empirical test.

Jensen is not a naive abettor of racism. All one has to do is read what Jensen actually says (Jensen, 1969, 1973) and not what people say he says to see that he is not a racist. What Jensen was, and is, is a scientist, functioning in accordance with science's search for empirical truth. In our country, those who support his ideas have a right to be heard; and in regard to science, there is a need for these ideas to be heard if we continue to seek every avenue for the establishment of empirical fact. "Preordained notions and inhibitions concerning what is and what is not respectable grist for research are intrinsically antithetical to scientific investigation" (Jensen, 1973, pp. 4-5). But what of the socially pernicious implications of the genetic differences hypothesis? By referring to a statement by Hebb we may see that those who would suppress Jensen's thoughts may be creating a basis for the very racist reactions they wish to avoid, as well as functioning against the necessary orientation of scientific psychology:

> May I add that Jensen is not immoral, or unethical, or antisocial to make his argument, even if he has made errors of interpretation, and even if—as I think—he is wrong in supposing that compensatory education has been given a real try? I am appalled at the quality of the criticism from social scientists. Their reaction is dogmatic and emotional, and the hell with logic. If Jensen's argument is "socially dangerous," it must be more dangerous in the long run to suppress it. The idea is that we would be suppressing falsehood; but the result is to prevent criticism of the argument and, worse still, convincing the racist that it is the *truth* that is being suppressed. Though I think Jensen is wrong, I do not know that he is entirely wrong—or I think he is not nearly as right as he thinks he is—and I consider that he has done psychology a service in making his argument available for inspection and criticism (1970, p. 568).

I too feel that the genetic-differences hypothesis must be evaluated only on its scientific merits. Further, like Hebb, I believe that the genetic-differences hypothesis is not tenable; I believe that it has serious, if not fatal, shortcomings. But, to use a cliché, I disagree with Jensen but believe he did a service by saying what he said.

Accordingly, we must scientifically evaluate the genetic-differences hypothesis, and to do this we must concentrate our attention on evaluating the essential concept of heritability. We will do this by using the ideas of Dr. Jerry Hirsch as a framework for discussion.

## Uses and Misuses of the Concept of Heritability

If psychologists are interested in measuring a certain psychological construct or characteristic of people, such as intelligence, they will often formulate a test to measure this characteristic, or trait. Now, if a group of people is given such an intelligence test it is very unlikely that the people taking it will all get the exact same score. Rather, some will score low, some high, and some intermediate. The scores of the group will form a distribution, ranging from high to low. This is similar to when we, as students, take several tests in a course over a semester and our test scores distribute themselves from high to low.

Now, if we are interested in representing the way the group functioned on the test in general (or if we want to know how we are doing overall in the course), the first thing we might opt to do is find the mean (the average) score of the distribution. To do this we would simply add up all the individual scores in the distribution and divide this total by the number of people in the distribution.

Secondly, we might want to know about the distribution of scores per se. In other words, not everyone in our group got the same score. Rather, within the group there was *variation*. Many people scored near the group mean, a few scored way above it, and a few scored way below it. Statistical analysis would allow us to represent the amount of variation in a distribution through the use of the term *variance* ($\sigma^2$). The magnitude of the variance would indicate how much or how little variation in test scores occurred in the distribution.

For our purposes, the important question is not how much variation was present but rather what the source of the variation was. For our consideration of the concept of heritability, we would want to know how much of the variation in the test scores comprising the distribution was due to variation in the gene distribution of the people tested and how much was due to variation in the environments of the people tested.

Since we have a distribution of scores, this means that there are differences between the people in our population in their test scores. Now, we may ask several questions—all similar in purpose—about these differences. Why do these people differ? Why do they vary? What is the source of the variation between them? How much of this variation may be attributed to genetic differences between them? How much to environmental differences between them? What percentage of these differences between these people—what proportion of this variance—involves genetic differences between them? What percentage of these differences between people may be attributed to the corresponding gene differences—the corresponding gene distribution? Note that we are here asking what proportion of the test differences between people corresponds to the *gene differences* between people; we are *not* asking about how much of a given person's test score is determined by his or her genes. It should be clear that these are two different questions. We should keep this distinction in mind and see that since these are two different questions, we can in no way answer the second question by coming to an answer for the first.

However, when we answer questions such as the first one—when we are trying to find out how much of the variation between people is due to gene differences between them—we are addressing questions that will lead us toward the calculation of heritability. Such questions inquire about what proportion of variation in a group of people (a population) who have been measured for a particular psychological characteristic is related to the gene variation between these people.

Therefore, consistent with our brief definition of *heritability* above, we may now define this concept as the proportion of trait variation in a population that is attributable to genetic variation in that population. After McGill (1965), we offer the following simplified formula for the definition of heritability:

$$h^2 = \frac{g^2}{g^2 + e^2}$$

where $h^2$ = heritability, $g^2$ = the genetic variation in the population, and $e^2$ = the environmental variation in the population.

Now, if all the variation in a trait (such as intelligence) could be attributed to the concomitant variation within the gene distribution of the population under study, then no variation in the trait whatsoever would be due to environmental variation. Thus, in such a case, the value for $e^2$ would be zero, and accordingly, $h^2$ would equal plus one. Alternatively, if no trait variation could be attributed to genetic variation, all the trait variation in the population would have to be a function of $e^2$. Therefore, in this case, $h^2$ would equal zero. Thus, we see that $h^2$ values can range anywhere from zero to plus one, increasing in proportion to the extent that the population's genetic variation accounts for the trait variation.

Typically, the heritability of a trait falls somewhere within this zero to plus-one range, and a heritability score can be calculated in several ways. Basically, however, the main thrust of all calculation methods is to determine the degree to which a specific population of organisms has responded to being bred for the expression, the degree of presence, of some trait (Hirsch, 1970). For example, let us say that a particular population of organisms (a specific population of fruit flys, *Drosophila,* for instance) can be distributed in terms of a particular trait (e.g., the tendency to fly toward light). Now, if the distribution of this trait in this population remains the same despite any changes in the genetic similarity of the parents of these flys, then heritability would equal zero. That is, if the genes transmitted to the offspring comprising our fly population could be varied and this transmission does not differentially affect the population's trait distribution, then heritability would equal zero. This would be the case because if changes in the genetic similarities or differences among the parents do not lead to any variation in the population's trait distribution, then genetic variation within the population does not contribute to the variation in this population's trait distribution. Thus, in terms of our above formula, $g^2$ would equal zero, and accordingly so would $h^2$.

However, if in another population of *Drosophila* similarly distributed in terms of a particular trait the genes transmitted by the parents do lead to a change in the population's trait distribution, then, obviously, genetic variation within the population does account for some of this variation; therefore, in this case, the heritability value would be greater than zero. The exact numerical value of heritability would be thus determined by calculating the magnitude of the relationship (the correlation) between the parents and their offspring comprising the population under study.

From these illustrations we should recognize an essential point. Heritability values for the same trait vary in relation to the particular populations under study. That is, the heritability for the same exact trait may be plus one in one population, zero in another, and somewhere in between these two scores in still another population. Therefore, it should be clear *that heritability is a property of populations and never of traits* (Hirsch, 1963). Therefore, a trait in an individual cannot be appropriately spoken of as heritable; one cannot correctly speak of the trait intelligence as being heritable. Rather, all that heritability refers to is the extent to which genetic variation among the members of a specific population of organisms accounts for the trait *distribution* in that population. Jensen makes the same point. In discussing the appropriateness of applying the concept of heritability to a population of people and the inappropriateness of such application to any individual within that population, Jensen states:

> Heritability is a population statistic, describing the relative magnitude of the genetic component (or set of genetic components) in the population variance of the characteristic in question. It has no sensible meaning with reference to a measurement or characteristic in an individual. A single measurement, by definition, has no variance (1969, p. 42).

Hence, heritability describes something about a group and not anything about an individual. Heritability relates to the source of differences between people in a population; it says nothing about a given psychological trait within any person in that population.

Therefore, we can see that heritability is a far less meaningful, more limited piece of information than most people seem to realize (Hirsch, 1970, p. 72). As we will discuss in greater detail below, *heritability does not mean genetically determined.* Nor, as the genetic-differences hypothesis implies,does heritability mean unaffectable by the environment. Implicit in all we have said about heritability up to this point has been the assumption that the environments of the populations under study have been constant and unvarying. Of course, except under specifically designed conditions, possible to achieve with *Drosophila* but not with humans, environmental conditions can be expected to vary. Thus, it is possible that $h^2$ for a population under one set of environmental conditions might be plus one, while $h^2$ might equal zero for that same population reared under a different set of environmental circumstances. If this is the case, then $h^2$ values are obviously affected by environment, and one can in no way speak of $h^2$ as telling anything about genetic determination. Thus, as Hirsch (1970) has cautioned, heritability is only an estimate of the proportion of phenotypic variation of a trait that can be attributed to genetic variation in some *particular generation of a specific population under one set of environmental conditions.* Similarly, Jensen (1969, p. 43) states that heritability estimates " . . . are specific to the population sampled, the point in time, how the measurements were made, and the particular test used to obtain the measurements."

The above, then, is the only bit of information that a heritability estimate conveys. Thus we should now recognize that this limited information has little potential generalizability due to the facts that (1) a particular heritability estimate can be used only in reference to one particular generation of (2) a particular population (3) that is reared in a specific, invariant environment. In addition, Hirsch (1970) reports that when a heritability estimate is made on a population more than once, that is, when repeated measurements of $h^2$ are taken, some studies report that $h^2$ increases, others report that it decreases, and yet others report that $h^2$ varies randomly. Thus, in addition to its other limitations, $h^2$ values seem to fluctuate in a largely unpredictable manner from one time of measurement to the next. In psychological parlance, this is termed *unreliability*. This is a devastating, seemingly fatal, flaw. If a measurement does not come out to be the same value from one time of testing to the next (which means that the measurement is not reliable), what confidence can we place in that measurement? If we cannot even measure a concept reliably, of what use is the concept? And if a concept cannot be measured reliably, can we make any safe statements about the populations that are measured? Can we recommend any social or educational policies on the basis of such unreliable measurement? I think the answers to these questions are obvious. Thus, a heritability estimate is not what it may seem to be; in addition, it may not even be a good measurement of what it is supposed to be! In sum then, we must agree with Hirsch: "The plain facts are that in the study of man a heritability estimate turns out to be a piece of 'knowledge' that is both deceptive and trivial" (1970, p. 74).

## Heritability Versus Development: A Necessary Distinction

With our understanding of the meaning (or lack of meaning, as the case may be) of the concept of heritability, we can now turn to a consideration of the past use of the concept of heritability in the case of the alleged genetic intellectual inferiority of black Americans. As the reader may already be able to surmise, the use of heritability notions in this case is fraught with fallacious reasoning and conceptual misunderstanding. By carefully summarizing the arguments involved in this controversy, I hope to clarify exactly what psychology can and cannot correctly say about the nature and nurture of intelligence and in so doing perhaps put the genetic-differences hypothesis in proper perspective.

Let us follow Hirsch's (1970) analysis of the steps that lead to the faulty reasoning involved in the assertion that black Americans are genetically inferior to white Americans in intellectual capacity.

1.    First, as noted above, a trait (such as intelligence) is defined.

2.    A means of measuring this trait is devised; a psychological test, designed to measure the trait (intelligence) is constructed. Needless to say, if another definition of the trait were offered, and if other tests of the trait were constructed and used, the empirical expression of the trait could be expected to be different. The possibility that the use of different intelligence tests could lead to different findings in terms of black-white differences in intelligence is important. Intelligence tests do not correlate with each other perfectly; that is, the scores for the same individual on two different intelligence tests are often not exactly equivalent. Therefore, if other tests are given to black and white populations—tests not standardized exclusively on white, middle-class populations, for example, but that take into account the specificities of the black cultural milieu—then the status of racial differences in IQ might be different. Holding the tenability of this point in abeyance, however, let us assume for argument's sake that the same test is used to measure the trait expression in people.

3.    Through a series of studies of test scores for this trait done on populations comprised of people of various degrees of kinship (relationship), the heritability of this trait is estimated.

4.    Black and white racial populations are then tested, and their performances on this test of the trait are compared.

5.   If the racial populations differ on the test, then because the heritability of the trait measured by the test is now known (and in the case of intelligence has been found to be high), the racial population with the lower mean score is considered to be genetically inferior (Hirsch, 1970, p. 69).

In essence, it is known that data indicate that intelligence has been estimated to be highly heritable—$h^2$ for intelligence is often estimated to be $+.80$ (e.g., see Scarr-Salapatek, 1971a, 1971b). Therefore, the argument goes, most of the variation in intelligence is genetically determined and there is little that environmental intervention can be expected to do to boost IQ. But by this point in our discussion we should immediately recognize the limitations of the concept of heritability and the incorrectness of using it as in the above reasoning process—that is, as equal in meaning to genetically determined. At this point we should also be prepared to see the other major fallacies involved in this whole controversy. As delineated by Hirsch (1970) there are two such major fallacies.

**The First Fallacy: Between Is Not Within.**   People who attempt to use $h^2$ as an indication of genetic determinancy appear to be involved in asking and attempting to answer the question "how much?" This is one of the two questions that we have seen Anastasi (1958) reject as being illogical. In essence, they ask, "How much heredity and how much environment go into the determination of intelligence?" Or, "Which of the two is more important in determining intelligence?" However, as we know, answering this question is both logically impossible and inappropriate.

As detailed by Hirsch (1970), people working from this orientation typically test a population on the intelligence trait at a single time in their development. In then making a heritability estimate, all that is being done is a determination of the relative proportions of the variation between the individuals in the population which can be assigned to genetic and environmental variation. That is, the reason that a distribution exists is, by definition, that individuals differ from each other in their scores on the test for that trait. All that $h^2$ does, then, is provide an estimate of how much of these *between-individuals differences* are due to genetic variation and how much are due to environmental variation between the population members.

But people mistakenly use these values to estimate how much of the expression of the tested trait *within a single individual* of that population is determined by heredity and environment. Between-individual data are applied to alleged within-individual phenomena. Thus, not only is an attempt to ask, "How much of each?" illogical, but the collected data can in no way be appropriately used to begin to address the question. As Hirsch emphasized, people taking this approach "want to know how instinctive is intelligence (*with*) *in* the development of a certain individual, but instead they measure differences *between* large numbers of fully, or partially, developed individuals" (1970, p. 77; italics added).

The apparent confusion of those people taking this approach is further confounded. We have seen that the norm-of-reaction concept leads us to recognize that all individuals in the world, no matter to what race they belong, can be expected to have a unique, individual genotype. In addition, we recognize the impossibility of ever determining with any degree of exactness a human's norm of reaction (or, as Hebb would term it, intelligence A). Moreover, because of genotypic uniqueness, members of the same racial group cannot be appropriately equated in order to attempt to assess a racial group's norm of reaction. In fact, such a concept makes no sense. Even if it did, however, an exposure of each population genotype to the range of possible environments that it could interact with in order to assess phenotypic variability would remain a theoretical and practical impossibility. In sum, then, there is absolutely no empirical or theoretical basis for any general statement assigning fixed proportions to the contributions of nature and nurture to the intellectual development of a single individual (Hirsch, 1970), *much less within every individual in an entire group of people*! Accordingly, Jensen stresses, "There is no way of partitioning a given individual's IQ into hereditary and environmental components, as if a person inherited, say, 80 points of IQ and acquired 20 additional points from his environment. This is, of course, nonsense" (1969, p. 42).

**The Second Fallacy: Heritability Is Not Developmental Fixity.** The second fallacy in the racial-differences controversy which Hirsch (1970) points out is derived from the first. People who equate heritability with genetic determination assume that as the magnitude of $h^2$ increases from zero to plus one, less and less can be done through environmental modifications to alter the expression of the trait. Of course, they alternatively assume that if the value of $h^2$ is low, this leaves more room for altering the trait through environmental manipulation.

This argument is fallacious. As carefully summarized in a critique by Jensen of such reasoning, those espousing this position believe:

that there is an inverse relationship between heritability magnitude and the individual's improvability by training and teaching; that is to say, if heritability is high, little room is left for improvement by environmental modification, and conversely, if heritability is low, much more improvement is possible. Hirsch is quite correct in noting a possible fallacy that may be implicit in this interpretation of heritability. . . (1973, pp. 55-56).

But if this argument is fallacious, what is the actual relationship between $h^2$ and influence by experience? We are saying that a trait for a population can have high $h^2$ *and* be available to alteration by experiential influence. We are saying that $h^2$ does not mean developmental fixity. Yet, how can a population characteristic have high heritability and still be influenced by the environment? An example by Hebb clarifies this situation:

The conception of "heritability" is a misleading one in this context, and some of the geneticists who use it are as confused as the social scientists, so its origin in genetics does not guarantee logical use by psychologists. In a 1953 paper, I showed that the amount of variance attributable to heredity (or to environment) cannot show how important heredity (or environment) is in determining an aspect of behavior. . . . I give here a new example. . . .
Mark Twain once proposed that boys should be raised in barrels to the age of 12 and fed through the bung-hole. Suppose we have 100 boys reared this way, with a practically identical environment. Jensen agrees that environment has *some* importance (20% worth?), so we must expect that the boys on emerging from the barrels will have a mean IQ well below 100. However, the variance attributable to the environment is practically zero, so on the "analysis of variance" argument, the environment is not a factor in the low level of IQ, which is nonsense (1970, p. 568).

Hence, in Hebb's example, environment had no differential effect on the boys' IQs; presumably, in all boys it had the same (severely limiting) effect. In having this same effect, environment could contribute nothing to differences between the boys. There was no difference —or variation —in the environment, and so it could not be said to contribute anything to differences between the people. Yet it is also obvious that the environment had a major influence on the boys' IQ scores. It is clear that even with IQ heritability equal to plus one, the intelligence of each of the boys would have been different had he developed in an environment other than a pickle barrel. Even if the heritability of IQ for American blacks were plus one, then, alterations in their environmental experiences could favorably alter the distribution of their IQ scores. Hence, high $h^2$ does not mean developmental fixity. A high $h^2$ estimate means that environment does not contribute very much to differences between people in their expression of a trait; yet, environment may still provide an important (although invariant) source of the expression of that trait.

Thus, consistent with Hebb's (1970) example, Jensen asserts:

First of all, the fact that learning ability has high heritability surely does *not* mean that individuals cannot learn much. Even if learning ability had 100 percent heritability it would not mean that individuals cannot learn, and therefore the demonstration of learning or the improvement of performance, with or without specific instruction or intervention by a teacher, says absolutely nothing about heritability. But knowing that learning ability has high heritability does tell us this: if a number of individuals are all given equal opportunity—the same background, the same conditions, and the same amount of time—for learning something, they will still differ from one another in their rates of learning and consequently in the amount they learn per unit of time spent in learning. That is the meaning of heritability. It does not say the individuals cannot learn or improve with instruction and practice. It says that given equal conditions, individuals will differ from one another, not because of differences in the external conditions but because of differences in the internal environment which is conditioned by genetic factors (1973, pp. 56-57).

Hence, in both Hebb's and Jensen's statements we see the view that although heritability may be high, the characteristics in question may still be influenced by environment. In turn, we also see that even when conditions are "equal" (and in actuality this probably could never occur) and the differences that people will still assuredly manifest are attributable to genetic factors, this genetic influence is still not absolute, not environment independent. Even when differences are due to internal differences, such sources are only conditioned by genetic factors, that is, such genetic factors only contribute to this internal environmental source. Clearly, then, when environment contributes nothing to the differences between people in population, their gene distribution accounts for these differences; but this, again, does not mean that the population characteristic is fixed by heredity or that it is unavailable to environmental influence. As both Hebb and Jensen well point out, while contributing nothing to differences between people, environment can still be a uniformly potent source of behavior development and functioning within each of the people in a group.

A point consistent with the ones above has been made by Lehrman (1970), a former student of Schneirla. Lehrman points out that when a geneticist speaks of a trait as being heritable, all he means is that he is able to predict the trait distribution in the offspring population on the basis of knowing the trait distribution in the parent population. We can predict the distribution of eye color in the offspring generation merely by knowing the distribution of eye color among the parents. Thus, while the geneticist may use the terms *hereditary* or *inherited* as interchangable with the term *heritable,* he is not, by such interchangable usage, making any statements about the process involved in the development of this trait. In other words, the geneticist is not saying anything at all about the way that nature and nurture provide a source of a heritable trait. Thus, the geneticist is not saying anything about the extent to which the expression of the trait may change in response to environmental modification. In short, a geneticist would not say that a highly heritable trait cannot be influenced by the environment. Rather, the geneticist would probably recognize, as we now must, that even if the heritability of a trait is plus one, an almost infinite number of phenotypic expressions of that trait may be expected to develop as a result of an interaction with the almost infinite number of environments that any one genotype may be exposed to. The norm of reaction is a biological reality that cannot be ignored!

In sum, heritability research, particularly as it has been done in relation to IQ, has involved advancement of fallacious arguments and misapplication of data (see Layzer, 1974). At best, heritability is a concept of extremely limited utility. If misunderstood and misapplied it leads to the assumption that high heritability means developmental fixity—that a highly heritable trait cannot be altered in its expression through environmental changes, that the trait is simply innate and unavailable to environmental influence (Lehrman, 1970). However, in this chapter, we have indicated that no psychological trait is preorganized in the genes and unavailable to environmental influence. Our assessment of the implications of the question "how?" makes such an assertion simply not plausible!

Thus, any alleged genetic difference (or "inferiority") of black Americans based on the high heritability of intelligence would seem to be an attribution built on a misunderstanding of concepts basic to an appropriate conceptualization of the nature-nurture controversy. An appreciation of the interactive interrelation of heredity and environment, of the parameters of how they in fact interact, of the norm-of-reaction concept, and of the meaning, implications, and limitations of the concept of heritability should lead us to an important conclusion. *All our considerations strongly suggest that the hypothesis of genetic differences makes little compelling scientific sense.* The heritability (in the sense of developmental fixity) of intelligence, or of any other psychological trait for that matter, must be recognized as psychological unreality. Such terms have, at best, so little scientific utility as to make them functionally worthless (see Layzer, 1974).

Hence, in a thorough review of the scientific and mathematical status and bases of the calculation of heritability analyses of IQ, Layzer (1974) argues that there are significant cultural differences between blacks and whites in today's society which militate against any attempt to evaluate race differences in IQ scores (even with so-called culture-free tests). He states:

> Among the relevant systematic differences between blacks and whites are cultural differences and differences in psychological environment. Both influence the development of cognitive skills in complex ways, and no one has succeeded in either estimating or eliminating their effects. "Culture-free" tests deal with this problem only on the most superficial level, for culture-free and "culture-bound" aspects of cognitive development are inseparable. The difficulties cannot be overcome by refined statistical analyses. As long as systematic differences remain and their effects cannot be reliably estimated, no valid inference can be drawn concerning genetic differences among races.
> Precisely the same arguments and conclusions apply to the interpretation of IQ differences between socioeconomic groups (Layzer, 1974, p. 1265).

In addition to these general problems involved in making any valid statements about the genetic basis of IQ differences between the races, Layzer also sees specific problems inherent in the calculation of heritability estimates.

Estimates of IQ heritability are subject to a variety of systematic errors.

The IQ scores themselves contain uncontrollable, systematic errors of unknown magnitude. These arise because IQ scores, unlike conventional physical and biological measurements, have a purely instrumental definition. The effects of these errors are apparent in the very large discrepancies among IQ correlations measured by different investigators.

The only data that might yield meaningful estimates of narrow heritability are phenotypic correlations between half sibs reared in statistically independent environments. No useful data of this kind are available (1974, p. 1265).

Thus, Layzer reaches a conclusion similar to our own about the scientific utility of heritability analyses and programs of social change based on such research. He writes:

Under prevailing social conditions, no valid inferences can be drawn from IQ data concerning systematic genetic differences among races or socioeconomic groups. Research along present lines directed toward this end—whatever its ethical status—is scientifically worthless.

Since there are no suitable data for estimating the narrow heritability of IQ, it seems pointless to speculate about the prospects for a hereditary meritocracy based on IQ (1974, p. 1266).

It is perhaps appropriate to end our presentation of the controversy over the nature and nurture of intelligence with the summary statement about this topic offered by Hirsch, since his ideas have been seminal in the clarification of the issues:

. . . the relationship between heredity and behavior has turned out to be one of neither isomorphism nor independence. Isomorphism might justify an approach like naive reductionism, independence a naive behaviorism. Neither one turns out to be adequate. I believe that in order to study behavior, we must understand genetics quite thoroughly. Then, and only then, can we as psychologists forget about it intelligently (1970, p. 81).

We have defined our terms in this chapter and in so doing have been introduced to the problems involved in appropriately conceptualizing the nature-nurture issue. In the next chapter we will see how the general consideration dealt with in this chapter will allow us to deal with a specific theoretical formulation of psychological development. This formulation takes an interactionist, organismic, and probabilistic epigenetic view of psychological development. As we will see, the person providing the seminal impetus to the ideas to be expressed in the following chapter is T. C. Schneirla. Thus, we will interrelate the general issues involved in the nature-nurture controversy discussed in this chapter with the specific issues raised in the interactionist theory of Schneirla.

## Summary

The nature-nurture issue is the core conceptual issue of psychological development. Basically, the issue revolves around the ways in which nature variables (such as heredity) and nurture variables (such as environment) provide sources of behavior development.

Concern with this issue has not been unique to psychology. The respective philosophies espoused by Plato, Descartes, and the medieval Christians are examples of nativistic (nature) positions, which maintain that there are preformed, innate aspects of human behavior. On the other hand, philosophers of the British school of empiricism—for example, John Locke—took empirical (nurture) positions, which maintain that the source of human behavior is the environment.

In psychology the nature-nurture controversy involves various areas of concern—for example, perception, personality, and learning. This issue persists in psychology because psychologists have been asking the wrong questions about the relative contributions of heredity and environment. Thus, we saw that Anastasi indicated that questions like "which one?" (heredity *or* environment) or "how much?" (of each) are based on faulty logic. Because there would be no one in an environment without heredity, but no place to see the effects of heredity without environment, one must recognize that both sources are always fully present in any behavioral development. Thus, hereditary and environmental effects cannot be separated out; they are inextricably bound, each contributing 100 percent to all behavior. Thus, the correct question to ask is, "How?".

Anastasi conceptualizes the interactive contributions of nature and nurture in a manner consistent with the ideas of organismic, probabilistic epigenetic developmental theories. Accordingly, her ideas about how nature and nurture interact were used as a framework for discussing: (1) how heredity, interacting with environment, contributes to development; (2) how environment, in interaction with heredity, contributes to development; and (3) how the effects of heredity will be different under different environmental conditions and how, in turn, the effects of environment will be different under different hereditary conditions.

Heredity was seen to contribute to behavioral development along a continuum of indirectness; that is, heredity always contributes to behavior within the context of particular environmental circumstances. The more indirect the contribution, the more numerous the behavioral developments that can result. Four points along this continuum of indirectness were discussed. Ranging from least indirect to most indirect these points are: (1) hereditary effects that in no way can be countered through environmental intervention, (2) hereditary deficits that interfere with normal socialization but can be countered through environmental intervention, (3) inherited susceptibility to diseases, and (4) social stereotypes. We saw how this last type of contribution can affect behavior development through the establishment of self-fulfilling prophecies. These prophecy effects are based on an initial categorization of a person based on the person's physical characteristics. Once such categorization is made—and such categorizations were seen to be inevitable in order for people to be economical and adaptive in their perceptions of the world—invariant attributions are maintained about people put into the category. On the basis of these invariant expectations—these stereotypes—the possibility of behavioral delimitation was seen, and accordingly, the basis of the self-fulfilling prophecy was depicted.

Nurture, or environment, was seen to contribute to behavioral development along a continuum of breadth. Environmental effects can be broad, affecting a wide array of behavior for a long time, or they can be narrow, affecting only a small portion of behavior and only for a short duration. Thus, there are two types of effects of environment. Environment can affect the very physical makeup of the organism; such organic effects can result from accidents, disease, or the alterations produced by diet or exercise. Second, there are effects in the environment that serve as stimuli for the person, evoking responses as a consequence of particular stimulation. Such stimulative effects on behavioral development can be broad or narrow.

The interactive contribution of nature and nurture continua to behavioral development was conceptualized through reference to the concept of norm of reaction. We inherit from our parents a genotype, a complement of genes, which represents a range of potential behavioral outcomes. What we see eventually resulting from our genotype, however, is the end result of a complex interaction of the environment and this range of potentials represented by our genotype. What we see, then, is the phenotype, the product of this genotype-experience interaction; yet we must recognize that we see only the phenotype and never the genotype. We do not know what portion of the genotype is reflected by a particular phenotype. And since the only way to know the actual range of possible outcomes represented in our genotype is through reproducing a given genotype an infinite number of times in order to expose it to an infinite number of environments, the norm of reaction for any genotype will remain unknown. Moreover, because it is likely that, except for monozygotic twins, no two people have the same genotype, every person will have his or her own, unique norm of reaction; yet the limits for our phenotypic development represented by this norm of reaction can never be specified.

A major portion of the chapter was devoted to an application of these ideas about nature-nurture interaction to an understanding of the issues involved in investigating the sources of black-white differences in IQ scores.

The leading interpretation of such racial differences has been an environmental-deficit hypothesis, which basically says that the reason that blacks as a group tend to score about 15 IQ points lower on intelligence tests than do whites as a group is that blacks suffer environmental and cultural disadvantages. However, another hypothesis, the genetic-differences hypothesis, has been advanced in an attempt to account for these racial differences. Offered by Jensen, this hypothesis asserts that these average IQ differences between black and white populations may best be understood in reference to the gene distributions among the populations.

We evaluated the social reactions to the offering of this hypothesis and concluded that it is scientifically necessary and proper for such a hypothesis to be advanced and that Jensen performed both a useful scientific as well as social purpose in advancing the genetic differences hypothesis. We argued that this hypothesis should be evaluated only on its scientific merits. In the rest of the chapter we attempted to do this and found that there is no compelling evidence to support the hypothesis.

Our interpretation rested on our criticism of the core notion in this controversy: the concept of heritability. This concept relates to the extent to which differences in the scores for a trait within a population of people may be accounted for by differences between these people in their genes. Heritability was defined as the proportion of trait variation in a population that is attributable to genetic variation in that population. We saw that this concept thus refers to a characteristic of a population and does not apply to any individual within that population. Moreover, we saw that the concept refers to the source of differences between people and does not in any way refer to the extent to which heredity (or environment) contributes to the characteristic in question for any individual. In addition, a given estimate of heritability may not be generalized to other populations of people, or to the same people measured at another point in time, or to populations measured in ways different from that used with the original population.

Thus, although some people have estimated that 80 percent of the differences in IQ scores of people in some specific populations may be accounted for by reference to the population gene distribution, we saw that this estimate does not have much utility or meaning. This is because of the above limitations of a heritability estimate and because of some other conceptual limitations. Even if heritability is very high (e.g., .8), this does not mean that 80 percent of any individual's intelligence is determined by heredity; such differences between people may not be generalized to what exists within any one of these people. As indicated by Anastasi's arguments and as supported by Jensen, there is no way of partitioning a given person's IQ into separate hereditary and environmental components. In addition, high heritability does not mean that development is fixed by heredity. That is, even if a trait is highly heritable that trait is still available to influence and alteration by the environment. All that a high heritability estimate indicates in this regard is that the environment does not account for much variation in the population. However, although environment may contribute nothing to differences (variation) in a population, it may still have the same, although invariant, effect on each member of that population.

Thus, because of the limitations in the meaning and use of the concept of heritability we rejected it as having any psychological utility. In turn, we similarly reject the genetic differences hypothesis—as it is based on this concept—as having any utility.

# 4 The Nature-Nurture Controversy: An Interactionist Position

The work of T. C. Schneirla and his colleagues and students (e.g., Ethel Tobach, Daniel Lehrman, Herbert G. Birch, and Howard Moltz) represents an attempt to systematically deal with the problems of behavioral development. Schneirla clearly recognized that unraveling the unknowns of behavioral development is a necessarily complex task, for development itself is very complex. Accordingly, Schneirla spurned facile solutions; he rejected as naive and overly simplistic theoretical conceptions that stressed the exclusive role of either nature (hereditarily preformed mechanisms) or nurture (shaping of behavior solely by environmental stimulation). Thus, consistent with the arguments presented in Chapter 3, Schneirla focused on an interaction between nature and nurture factors in attempting to find the sources of behavioral development. Because he rejected the notion that development is a simple process, he also rejected the idea that methods used to study this process can be simple. Hence, in commenting on the relation between a nature-based variable, maturation, and a nurture-based variable, experience, he said:

> It would seem to be the prevalence of an intimate, dynamic relationship between the factors of maturation and experience that renders analytical study of behavioral ontogeny so difficult. Methods must be devised appropriate to the complexity and subtlety of these processes. . . . In such work, little may be expected from attempts to estimate the specific or the proportionate contributions of the innate vs. the acquired in ontogeny. (Schneirla 1956, p. 407).

Thus, Schneirla presented a theoretical position consistent with what we have said above about interactionist, organismic conceptions of development. Let us turn, then, to a more detailed analysis of the ideas of Schneirla and his students so that we may evaluate the extent to which such conceptions provide a fruitful, integrative framework with which to consider concepts of development. We may begin by focusing on an important issue raised in a classic paper of Schneirla's, published in 1957.

## The Notion of Homology Rejected

At times, a developmental theorist (e.g., Hamburger, 1957) finds it convenient to use the concept of *homology*. Although there are many definitions of this concept (see Atz, 1970), one of them asserts that homology describes a specific, invariant type of relation between the structure of an organism and that organism's functioning. The same structure leads to the same function and, conversely, identical functions are underlain by identical structures; that is, there is an isomorphic relation between structure and function. If two animals have the same neurophysiological structures in their brains, for example, these structures would have the same function. Similarly, if two animals of different phyletic levels have the same function—for instance, learning—then the underlying structure of this function is the same.

Schneirla begins his 1957 paper by asserting that this notion of homology is not valid. Rather he argues that the relationship between structure and function is not always the same for organisms of different phylogenetic levels. The same functions may not be homologous, in the above sense, but simply analogous; that is, a particular function (e.g., learning) may be present in both a rat and a human or in an infant human and an adult human, and this function may play an analogous role for each of these organisms: it may allow the organism to adapt to its environment, to survive. However, the

T. C. Schneirla

presence of this analogous function in no way in and of itself indicates that the underlying structure of learning is the same for an infant or an adult, for a rat or a man.

Schneirla suggests that, on the contrary, the relation between structure and function is exceedingly complex, but, more importantly here, will occur with varying degrees of directness at different phylogenetic and ontogenetic levels. Thus, the degree of directness of relation between the two would be different for the rat, ape, horse, and human being.

Schneirla noted (1956) that behavioral patterns often reach similar developments in different phylogenetic levels as a result of parallel adaptive (evolutionary) process. To some, such similarity indicates equivalent underlying organization, or structure. But this is neither empirically universal nor logically necessary, since the attainment of equivalently adaptive developments tells nothing whatsoever about the antecedent developmental processes that brought about these adaptive functions . All mammals learn; but to assert that because both a rat and a human being develop this adaptive function, then the laws, or structures, underlying their learning are the same is not necessarily correct. The developmental processes by which learning comes about may be totally different for these two organisms. That is, antecedent developmental processes may be completely disparate for two different types of organisms, despite the fact that both demonstrate a similarly adaptive function. Thus, as Schneirla points out, these processes "may involve complex anticipations, as in a socialized human being, or may be reflex-like and automatic, as in a lower invertebrate" (1956, p. 392).

In essence, Schneirla is suggesting that the underlying structure of even evolutionary similar behavioral developments is different for different phylogenetic levels. Although certainly not denying that structure underlies function, he emphasizes rather that one must expect the relationship between structure and function to be differentially direct at different phyletic levels. Each level must be understood in and of itself, because the structure-function relationships of other phylogenetic levels will not hold for another level in question. In other words, the laws of one phyletic level will not apply to another phyletic level, since the same structure-function relationships do not hold, and therefore one cannot completely understand one phyletic level by merely reducing it to another phyletic level. Similarly, as we will see, Schneirla views ontogenetic development in a manner analogous to phylogenetic development. That is, ontogeny progresses through levels just as phylogeny does. Accordingly, structure-function relations between different ontogenetic levels can also be expected to be different.

It should be clear to the reader that Schneirla is taking a now familiar viewpoint. He is advancing the organismic notion of qualitative discontinuity between levels: each different phylogenetic level has its own structure-function relationship, or said in other words, its own laws. Thus, because of its own laws, each different level is qualitatively different from the next. This is true, Schneirla asserts, if one is talking of different phylogenetic levels—what Schneirla calls *psychological levels*—and if one is talking of different ontogenetic levels—what Schneirla calls *functional orders*—because "on each further psychological level, the contribution of individual ontogeny is a characteristically different total behavior pattern arising in a different total context" (Schneirla, 1957, p. 82).

In addition to adopting the organismic viewpoint, Schneirla also adopts the levels-of-organization compromise discussed in Chapter 2. He is not, of course, denying that there is an important underlying structural basis for any functional (behavioral) development. But he is asserting that knowledge of the structural basis is not sufficient for understanding the behavioral development at any given psychological level or functional order. Structure does not simply give you function; and because something else is needed, each different level must be studied in its own terms. At best, structure is only half the story. There is that something else that must be understood in interrelation with structure in order to ascertain the relation between structure and function, in order to understand the laws of any given level. That something else is, of course, the environmental, or experiential, context within which the organism develops. Structure-function relationships can be understood only in interrelation with their environmental context. Thus Schneirla, too, asserts that a nature-nurture interactionist concept is necessary for understanding development.

Hence, we may state Chapter 2's levels-of-organization compromise in terms of Schneirla's position by stating that for any given psychological level or functional order, the laws (variables) of the structural (lower) level are involved with (implied in) the laws of the functional, behavioral (higher) level, but function cannot be understood merely through an understanding of structure. Knowledge of structure alone is insufficient for understanding function. This is the case because function develops out of a complex interaction between structure and environmental factors, an interaction that produces at each different level a qualitatively different developmental context.

In sum, Schneirla sees phyletic and ontogenetic development as qualitatively discontinuous. He sees different structure-function relationships at different levels. He maintains that the same psychological function may, therefore, be underlain by different processes at different points in development. Thus, Schneirla takes a position that is central in developmental theory and is shared by many other developmental theorists (e.g., Kohlberg, Piaget, Turiel, Werner): the same behavior is often determined by different variables at different points in ontogeny (or phylogeny).

## Behavioral Stereotypy versus Behavioral Plasticity

Schneirla has suggested that psychological levels differ qualitatively from one another, because different organisms have qualitatively different structure-function relationships, which are based on different organismic structural-experiential interactions.

But what is the nature of these different interrelationships? What is the basis of the differences between different psychological levels? As we might guess, Schneirla suggests an answer consistent with his organismic, levels-of-organization position. He suggests that one important dimension of difference between psychological levels is the degree to which their behavioral development shows *stereotypy* or *plasticity*.

If an organism's behavioral development is stereotyped, there is a relatively fixed relation between the stimulation the organism receives and the concomitant responses it emits; that is, an almost unchanging relation exists between what goes in (stimulation) and what goes out (response). What we see is little, if any, variability in response to stimulation. Thus, if we deprive a normal frog of food for some time and then present a fly to the frog in its immediate field of vision, we will inevitably see the frog flick out its tongue to catch the fly. Assuming that we take no steps to intervene in this interaction and that the frog continues to exist in its natural habitat, we will see little variation in the response to this stimulation.

Plasticity, on the other hand, refers to the ability to show varying responses to the same stimulus input; that is, a more variable relation exists between what goes in and what will come out.

Now, some of us may be in the habit of "flicking out" our tongues whenever our favorite food goes by—for example, dessert. However, at times a reprimand from our spouse (e.g., "If you get any fatter, you won't fit through the door") will result in our varying our response to the dessert stimulus; we may take a smaller helping than usual, or perhaps none at all. Similarly, although it would be relatively easy to train a rat to find its way in a maze, it would be extremely difficult to train it to develop a large repertoire of alternate routes that it could efficiently interchange when more habitual routes were blocked. Humans, however, develop this alternate-route repertoire quite readily. Thus, as illustrated in Fig. 4.1, if our most direct, and thus habitual, route for driving from home to the market is one day suddenly blocked, we can quite efficiently adopt an alternate route.

An organism that shows stereotypy in its ontogeny develops little behavioral variability in response to stimulation. Alternatively, an organism that shows plasticity develops a relatively considerable degree of variability in response to stimulation. Moreover, as we might expect, organisms with differing degrees of plasticity or stereotypy are on different psychological levels; the more plasticity shown in an organism's development, the higher the organism's psychological level. Thus, as Schneirla has stated: "The appearance of behavioral stereotypy through ontogeny, if found characteristic of a species, indicates a lower psychological level, whereas a systematic plasticity through experience indicates a high level" (1957, p. 83).

Of course, neither plasticity nor stereotypy is an all-or-none thing. One cannot say that the behavior of a particular species is either all stereotyped or all plastic. Rather, we may think of stereotypy and plasticity as forming a continuum, with stereotyped and plastic behavior at either end. Different psychological levels will fall at different points along this continuum, and the closer any species is to the plasticity end, the higher its psychological level. A hypothetical example of the ordering of species of different

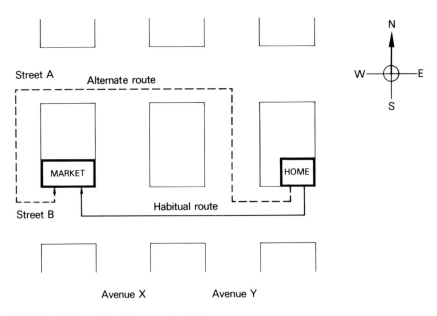

**Fig. 4.1** An illustration of human plasticity.

psychological levels along this continuum is presented in Fig. 4.2. Ants are at the lower end, because their behavior is less plastic than that of any other represented species. Human beings are closest to the plasticity end, because human behavior is more plastic than that of the other represented species, and, accordingly, the human psychological level is higher than that of any of the other species.

Donald O. Hebb

PLASTICITY

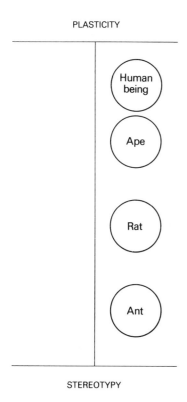

STEREOTYPY

**Fig. 4.2** An illustration of a hypothetical stereotypy-plasticity continuum.

## Hebb's A/S Ratio

What is the structural contribution to these contrasting functional capabilities? What nervous-system structures, for example, may contribute to plasticity or stereotypy of different psychological levels? One answer to this question might lie in a concept found in Hebb's (1949) writings.

The cerebral cortex of the brain of mammals (e.g., rats, monkeys, dogs, or human beings) has various sections. One section is comprised of nerve cells (neurons) that constitute the cerebral centers for sensory information—information that comes from the outside world through our receptors (e.g., the rods and cones of the retina of the eye) and into our bodies. Another area of the cerebrum is comprised of neurons that constitute our motor cortex—that part of our cerebral cortex that sends messages to our muscles and thus allows us to behave. Still another section of our cortex is comprised of association neurons, cells that integrate and associate information from various parts of the brain. For example, one role of the association cortex is to integrate information from the sensory cortex, pertaining to what is stimulating us, with information to the motor cortex, relating to our (motor, or muscular) actions, our behavior.

Now, it seems clear that the more association cortex we have, the more associations we can have between a given stimulus input and behavioral output. That is, the more association fibers that exist, the more variable should associations be to any stimulus, and, accordingly, behavior should be more variable in relation to stimulus input. In 1949 Hebb proposed to express the relation between the amount of sensory cortex and the amount of association cortex in a species in terms of a ratio . This ratio was termed the *association cortex/sensory cortex ratio,* or simply the A/S ratio.

Some organisms have a low A/S ratio, expressed as A/S ratio = < 1.0; simply, they have more sensory cortex than association cortex. For such organisms, sensory input will be more directly related to response than will be the case for organisms with higher A/S ratios. With organisms that have relatively little association cortex in comparison with their sensory cortex, sensory input (stimulation) will more directly determine behavior. Such organisms can be called sense dominated. Because such organisms have little association fibers with which to integrate their sensory input, their behavior in response to sensory input will be less variable. It will be relatively directly controlled by environmental stimulation. It will be stereotyped.

Animals with higher A/S ratios will, however, show relatively less sense domination. Animals with more association fibers relative to sensory fibers (whose A/S ratio =>1.0), will integrate their sensory input with the information provided by their association fibers and thus demonstrate more variable behavior in response to stimulation. The behavior of such organisms will be more a product of an interrelation between their association cortex and their sensory cortex than would be the case with organisms having a low A/S ratio. Accordingly, their behavior will be more variable in response to stimulus (sensory) input. It will be more plastic.

Thus, differences in A/S ratios may account for different degrees of plasticity and stereotypy among different psychological levels. Consistent with Schneirla, Hebb (1949, p. 125) suggested that for widely differing phylogenetic levels a hierarchy of psychological complexity can be assumed which corresponds to gross differences in the proportion of sensory to association neurons. Similarly, Schneirla (1956, p. 411) pointed out that a deficiency in the brain's association capacity seems to be a prime condition for certain fixed responses to specific stimuli, since stereotyped response tendencies are strongest in animals with the lowest supply of association neurons.

In sum, we see that Hebb's notions allow us to speculate about a structural basis for the functional differences in stereotypy-plasticity seen on different psychological levels. Animals with more sensory cortex than association cortex are more stereotyped in their behavioral development than are animals with more association cortex relative to their sensory cortex. These latter animals are more plastic in their behavioral development than are the former. Thus, the higher an animal's A/S ratio, the more functionally plastic its behavioral development. Conversely, the lower an animal's A/S ratio, the more functionally stereotyped its behavior development. To make an analogy, then, low A/S ratios are to stereotypy (and low psychological levels) as high A/S ratios are to plasticity (and high psychological levels).

## Ontogenetic Implications of Stereotypy-Plasticity and of the A/S Ratio

As might be surmised, Hebb, as well as Schneirla, maintains an active interest in the developmental implications of his ideas. Accordingly, Hebb qualified his notions about the A/S ratio by pointing out differences in the ontogeny of animals with different A/S ratios. We will see that Schneirla, in talking of stereotype-plasticity, reaches conclusions similar to those of Hebb.

Animals with low A/S ratios are more stereotyped in their eventual behavioral development and, accordingly, are on low psychological levels. Yet, such animals reach their final level of functional organization—behavioral functioning—much sooner in their development than do animals with high A/S ratios. Animals with few association fibers compared to sensory fibers progress through their ontogeny relatively rapidly; they reach their final, albeit stereotyped, level in a relatively short time in their development.

One way of understanding this is to realize that such animals have comparatively little association-area cortex fibers that have to be organized through their development; they have relatively few associations that can be developed. Thus they organize their association cortex comparatively rapidly. But at the same time, because of their comparatively limited association capacity, their behavior can never develop much variability, and hence it will be relatively stereotyped.

On the other hand, animals with high A/S ratios are comparatively more plastic in their eventual behavioral development and therefore are on higher psychological levels. However, such animals develop toward their final level of development relatively slowly. These high A/S ratio animals reach their final level of functional capacity—of behavioral organization—much later in their development than do low A/S ratio animals. High A/S ratio animals have more association cortex compared to their sensory cortex, and they progress through their ontogeny relatively slowly. These animals reach a higher, more plastic psychological level, but it takes them a longer time to do this.

In sum, lower A/S ratio animals develop more rapidly, but their behavior remains relatively stereotyped; it is sense dominated and shows little variability. On the other hand, higher A/S ratio animals develop more slowly, but their eventual behavioral development will be relatively plastic; it shows considerable variability. For example, a rat is on a lower psychological level than is a human being. Similarly, the rat has a lower A/S ratio than does a human being. But in the time span of just a few weeks a rat may be considered to be fully developed, while a human infant, of course, after only a few weeks of life is not at all like an adult human in terms of behavioral functioning. The human infant will take years to reach the analogous level that the rat pup reaches in just a few short weeks. Yet the human, when an adult, will be capable of considerably more complex, plastic behavior than any adult rat will ever be able to produce. In fact, this will be true of the not yet fully developed human; the human will surpass the adult rat when still a child.

An empirical instance of the point can be found in the results of a classic study by Kellogg and Kellogg (1933). The Kelloggs reared a newborn ape in their home and attempted to treat it like their own newborn child, who, by the way, also happened to be living there at the time. They diapered both infants and prompted their behavioral development, including language, in the ways that parents typically do. At first the ape was ahead of their child in terms of behavioral development. Soon, however, the child overtook the ape and was never bested again.

In summary, animals on low psychological levels will develop much more rapidly than will animals of high psychological levels. However, the gains that these two levels of animals will make through their ontogeny will be quite different. Animals on a low psychological level will be able to gain little behavioral variability through their ontogeny, because the nature of their development is restricted by their structural limitations, by their low A/S ratio. Animals on a high psychological level will be able to gain considerable behavioral variability through their ontogeny, however, because of the nature of their development occurs within the context of broader structural capabilities, their high A/S ratio.

## Concepts Representing Development

From the above consideration of stereotypy-plasticity, it is clear that Schneirla was just as concerned with the problems of ontogeny as he was with those of phylogeny. Although he viewed both as progressing through a series of qualitatively different levels, it will be remembered that he sought to draw a distinction between the progression from one phylogenetic level to another and the progression from one ontogenetic level to another; thus, he used the term *psychological levels* to refer to different levels along the phylogenetic scale (ants are on one psychological level, rats on another, and humans on yet another). He used the term *functional orders* to refer to different levels in the ontogeny of organisms of a particular psychological level. For example, the first two years of life may correspond to the first part of the functional order of a human, the next five years to another, separate portion of the functional order, and the following five years to still another part of this functional order.

We have seen how the concepts of stereotypy and plasticity serve to differentiate between different psychological levels, and how the relative degree of stereotypy-plasticity may serve to characterize the psychological level of a particular animal species. Let us now turn to a consideration of Schneirla's concepts characterizing the functional order of a species.

### A Definition of Development

To Schneirla (1957), *development* refers to progressive changes in the organization of an organism, an organism that is viewed as a functional and an adaptive system throughout all its life. Thus, development connotes progressive change within a living, functioning, adaptive, individual system. By continually functioning in an adaptive manner, this system—this individual organism—develops through progressive changes throughout its life, from womb to tomb.

But what are the characteristics of this system? What are the processes comprising the determinants of the organism's development? Schneirla (1957, p. 86) suggests two broad concepts that represent the complex factors comprising the progressive changes of development.

**Maturation.** The first of these two concepts is maturation. To Schneirla, *maturation* means growth and differentiation of the physical and physiological systems of an organism. *Growth* refers to changes in these systems by way of tissue accretion, that is, tissue enlargement. *Differentiation* refers to changes in the structural aspects of tissues with age, that is, alterations in the interrelationship among tissues, organs, or parts of either of these. For example, at certain stages in the development of the embryo a certain layer of cells exists. These cells mature not only via accretion (growth) but also through differentiation. Thus, when the embryo is in its blastula stage of development, it is divided into three layers of cells. One of these layers, for instance, is termed the *mesoderm*. Eventually, as the embryo goes through changes and the cells of the mesoderm grow larger and differentiate, these cells will come to form the muscles and bones of the body. Hence, maturation refers to changes in the organism which result from the growth and differentiation of its tissues and organs.

Schneirla cautions, however, against thinking that maturation can in any way occur independent of environmental contribution. Consistent with what we have said in Chapter 3 about the interactionist position on the nature-nurture issue, Schneirla emphasizes that maturational processes must *always* occur within the context of a supportive, facilitative environment; because of this interdependence, the exact path that maturation will take will be affected by what is happening in the environmental context of the organisms. Just as maturation is not independent of environment, structure, then, is not independent of function. Hence, as Schneirla stated:

> Maturation is neither the direct, specific representative of genic determination in development, nor is it synonymous with structural growth. Much as an environmental context is now recognized as indispensable to any development . . . , students of behavioral development . . . emphasize the roles of structure and function as inseparable in development (1957, p. 86).

**Experience.**  The second concept needed to represent the complexity of the factors comprising developmental changes is *experience.* To Schneirla, experience refers to all stimulus influences that act on the organism throughout the course of its life. Experience is a very broad, all-encompassing concept. Any stimulative influence, any stimulus that acts on the organism in any way, is part of experience; and this stimulative influence can occur at any time in the organism's travels from womb to tomb. Experience may affect the organism at any time in its ontogeny.

It is clear, then, that experience can affect the organism before it is born. For example, stimulative influences may act in the form of chemicals, drugs, or disease entities affecting the fetus. Thus, a baby whose mother contracts German measles (rubella) during the early part of her pregnancy may be acted on by this experience in an adverse way. Effects of such experience may be a deformed heart or blindness. Similarly, experience will obviously affect the organism after it is born. This also may take the form of diseases or accidents, but includes experiences such as the type of care the infant receives.

In sum, experience is a term representing any and all stimulative influences acting on the organism as it develops. These stimulus influences may result from events taking place within the organism's body (endogenous stimulative influences) or outside the organism's body (exogenous stimulative influences). In either case, experience acting on the organism provides one of the two interacting factors determining development. Let us look, then, at how experience interacts with maturation to affect development.

## The Role of Maturation-Experience Interaction in Developmental Progress
Experience is necessary for any and all developments throughout ontogeny. Experience always has an effect on the organism, and it does this in a specific way.

Experience results in *trace effects.* To Schneirla (1957), trace effects are organismic changes that result from experience and that in turn affect future experience. Experience effects changes in the organism, and these changes—these trace effects—affect how future experience will act on the organism.

When experience acts on the organism it will leave a trace of its action. This trace effect now becomes part of the organism and thus changes the organism's nature. Hence, any later experience that acts on the organism will now act on a different organism, an organism that now has a residual effect, a trace effect, of its previous experience. The second experience will now result in an effect different from what it would have been had this previous experience not acted. For example, a young child may have an experience that results in a physical disability. Because of this handicap, which has changed the nature of the organism, future experiences—for instance, exposure to a physical education program—will affect the child differently from the way they would have had the child not had this previous experience.

However, the effects that experience can have are limited by the maturational status of the organism. The effect of the same experience will be different at different points in the organism's development, because the organism will be at different levels of growth and differentiation at these two times. Thus, because the organism's sensory, association, and motor portions of the nervous system are maturing with time, the effects of experience are limited. For example, an infant is capable of perception and can form trace effects resulting from some types of perceptual experience (Bower, 1966). At later developmental stages this same child will be capable of developing trace effects as a result of the perceptual experiences involved in reading. However, these later experiences would not have resulted in the same trace effects had they been presented to the relatively physiologically immature infant. Alternatively, the trace effects that do obtain as a result of the perceptual experiences involved in reading could never have occurred when they did had the child not had a particular series of perceptual experiences, resulting in trace effects, since the time of infancy. In sum, the nature of the behavioral gains that can result from experience are limited by the relative physiological maturation of the organism (Schneirla, 1957, p. 90).

By this time, however, the reader should recognize that, in turn, maturation also has limits. These limits are imposed by experience. Consistent with the interactionist position he espouses, Schneirla (1957, p. 90) points out that the limitation of experience imposed by maturation is in turn limited by the developmental stage of the organism, by the attained functional order the organism has reached in its ontogeny. The growth and differentiation of maturation do not occur without the supportive, facilitative effects of experience. This experience, leaving its effects on the organism in the form of trace effects, provides the milieu within which maturation occurs. Inappropriate experiences— such as loss of oxygen supply—will not allow maturation to proceed as it would have had the inappropriate experience not occurred. Thus, maturation must interact with experience in order for development to proceed, and in turn, the effects of experience are channeled by their interaction within the limits imposed by the maturational status of the organism.

Hence, a complex interaction between experience and maturation provides the basis of behavioral development. This complex interaction is represented schematically in Fig. 4.3. Experience results in trace effects, but the nature of the trace effects is limited by the maturational status of the organism. In addition, this interaction determines what behavior the organism can develop at any particular time in its ontogeny. The experience-maturation interaction provides the basis for the developmental stage reached at a particular time in an organism's ontogeny. In turn, this developmental

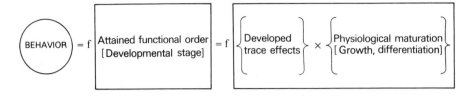

f = a function of
× = in interaction with

**Fig. 4.3** A complex interaction between experience and maturation provides the basis of behavioral development.

stage, comprised of the result of the interaction between experience and maturation, provides (1) the milieu within which further maturation proceeds, does not proceed, or proceeds at a different rate, and (2) the milieu that determines what trace effects will result from further experiences.

In sum, Schneirla said: "The nature of the gains made through experience is both canalized and limited by the relative maturity of species-typical afferent, neural, and efferent mechanisms, in dependence upon the developmental stage attained" (1957, p. 90).

What we have seen to this point, then, is that behavior emerges through the course of development as a function of an interaction between experience and maturation. If appropriate experiences do not occur, or conversely, if inappropriate experiences occur, then maturation will not proceed as it otherwise would have; accordingly, the behavior that would have developed will not therefore develop at that time. In other words, if inappropriate experiences occur (such as disease, loss of oxygen supply, loss of a mother's nurturance), or if appropriate experiences occur but do so at a time too late for appropriate development to proceed, then maturation will not develop appropriately, and it follows that the behavior that typically would have developed will be altered.

Conversely, if maturation does not proceed as it should (because of a lack of supportive, facilitative experiences), then the effects of experience—the trace effects—will be altered; in turn, the behavior that emerges at a particular point in time will be different. What we see, then, is that the ordered emergence of behavior in development depends critically on the nature and time of experience-maturation interactions. The attainment of developmental stages is critically dependent on the quality and timing of the variables involved in this interaction.

As we have seen in Chapter 2, this viewpoint is termed the *probabilistic epigenetic position*. It emphasizes that the nature and timing of interactions between maturation and experience are critical in determining behavioral development. Moreover, the nature and timing of this interaction cannot necessarily be predicted in advance for every organism within a species. At best, we can say only that if the nature and timing of the maturation-experience interaction occur in certain ways, then behavior will probably develop along certain lines.

Thus, norms for development, which are statements about when in people's lives a particular behavior is typically seen, can be used only as general guidelines for considering development. Statements such as "babies should sit up at six months," "babies should say their first word at eleven months," or "should walk at eighteen months" can be considered only as statements that apply in general. They may apply to a given group as a whole, but they may not necessarily apply to any individual in that group. That is, such norms do not mean that babies must do these things at these times in order to be considered normal. Rather, they mean only that for a given large group of babies, an average time exists for the emergence of a particular behavior. At the same time that this norm exists, however, differences in individuals also *necessarily* exist. Different people show a behavior either before or after the norm for their group. In fact, we would expect people *not* to all reach the same level of development at the same time.

We see that Schneirla's ideas culminate in a specification of the probabilistic epigenetic position: any behavioral development that occurs is obtained through an interaction between maturational and experiential factors. Thus, the emergence of any behavior at any time in an organism's development is critically dependent on the nature and timing of this interaction. In other words, behavioral development is not critically dependent on maturation or experience alone. This is because "factors of maturation may differ significantly in their influence upon ontogeny, both in the nature and in the timing of their effects, according to what relations to the effects of experience are possible under existing conditions" (Schneirla and Rosenblatt, 1963, p. 288). Hence, from Schneirla's theoretical point of view, any notion of behavioral development that stresses the exclusive contribution of either maturational or experiential factors is incorrect.

Despite the persuasiveness of Schneirla's argument, not all theorists agree with him. We will now consider two concepts that provide exclusively nature explanations of behavioral development: the *critical-periods* hypothesis and the notion of *instinct* (or innate behavior). These concepts have come under attack by Schneirla and his colleagues when they have been used to suggest that nature variables alone can account for behavioral development. Let us first turn to the critical-periods hypothesis.

## The Critical-Periods Hypothesis

The notion of critical periods in development was formulated in embryology. Within that science the idea was advanced that the various parts of the whole organism (e.g., various organs or organ systems) emerge in a fixed sequence; but more important, it was held that these parts develop in a fixed sequence with just a certain amount of time allowed for each; there is an overall timetable of development, and each part of the whole organism has its own fixed time of emergence, set by maturation. Each part has a critical period in which to develop.

This perspective holds that a part of the organism that is in its critical period can be easily stimulated. Such a part is highly responsive to both facilitating and disruptive influences. Thus, if the part does not develop normally or appropriately during its critical period, it will never again have a second chance. Because the time limits of development are invariably fixed by maturation, even if the part does not develop, the focus of development will switch. It will shift to another organ system, in accordance with the predetermined timetable of development, and that different organ system will be in *its* critical period of development. Hence, the part that does not develop during its own critical period will not have another chance.

Similarly, in psychology such a critical period refers to a time in the ontogeny of a species during which it is crucial for a particular psychological development to take place; the period is crucial because certain maturational processes then occurring would allegedly place time limits on the development (Schneirla and Rosenblatt, 1961). For example, as we will see in Chapter 8, Erik Erikson divides the human life span into eight critical periods. Each emerges in accordance with a maturational "ground plan" for development, which is built into the person (Erikson, 1959). So, Erikson maintains that in the first year of life the infant must develop a certain degree of a "sense of trust." If the infant does not develop this feeling at the time when the feeling is supposed to develop, not only will there never be another chance, but the rest of that person's development will be unfavorably altered.

Clearly, the critical-periods hypothesis places complete dependence on an intrinsic, maturationally determined timetable. What this formulation clearly implies, then, is that maturation in and of itself sets critical time limits for development; there are maturationally circumscribed periods in an organism's development and the time limits of these periods are somehow not related to experiential factors. However, from Schneirla's probabilistic epigenetic position we can see that such a conception of critical periods is not tenable. Rather than emphasizing the independent contribution of maturation, Schneirla would opt to investigate the process by which maturation and experience interact to enable a specific development to take place at a given time in ontogeny.

Schneirla is not saying that certain developments are not critical for some later developments. He would agree to some extent with other researchers concerned with the critical-periods notion—for example, Scott (1962)—that there *are* critical stages, for instance for the development of learning. He would agree that what is learned at a certain time in an organism's ontogeny may be critical for whatever follows (Schneirla and Rosenblatt, 1963; Scott, 1963). But all this really says is that what happens at time 1 in a person's life may be very important—in fact may be critical—for what can or will happen at time 2. Such an assertion just *describes* a relation between events that occur at two different times in ontogeny; it makes no statement about whether the first event was determined by maturation alone or by an interaction between maturation and experience.

It is the source of the "criticalness" in development about which Schneirla argues. Simply, maturationally fixed time limits for development, arising without the contribution of experience, are inconsistent with his probabilistic epigenetic position. Rather, Schneirla proposes a theory that places "emphasis upon the fusion of maturation (growth-contributed) and experience (stimulation-contributed) processes at different stages in behavior ontogeny, together with the . . . contributions both of maturation and experience . . . , as well as the interrelations of these contributions. . . . " (Schneirla and Rosenblatt, 1963, p. 288). Moltz, a leading student of Schneirla, experimentally found that the time limits of certain critical periods *could* be altered through specific environmental manipulations. Moltz and Stettner (1961) found that the alleged critical time limits for the development of certain following behaviors in ducklings could be altered by depriving these organisms of the opportunity to experience a structured perceptual environment. Hence, Schneirla's notion that one must always focus on the complex interaction between maturation and experience in order to account for behavioral development finds empirical support. Thus, as Sluckin (1965, p. 71) has emphasized, studies indicate that critical periods are not solely circumscribed by maturation but are determined by the interactive impact of experience on the developing organism.

Konrad Lorenz

Let us now turn to a second concept—that of instinct, or innate behavior—which also relates to the sole action of nature in behavioral development.

## Instinct: Innate Behavior

The notion of instinct, or instinctive behavior, is today perhaps most associated with the work of Konrad Lorenz. Beginning in the 1930s Lorenz, a European zoologist and physician, studied certain types of behavior termed *instinctive behavior.* By this term, Lorenz appears to mean behavior that is preformed in the genotype. He contends that we inherit a genotype, and built into this genotype is a "limited range of possible forms in which an identical genetic blueprint can find its expression in phenogeny" (Lorenz, 1965, p. 1). In essence, then, Lorenz contends that there is an isomorphism between certain genetic inheritances and certain behaviors, and this is what he means by instinctive behavior. Certain behaviors are preformed, they are innate; they are built into the organism through genetic inheritance and are thus simply unavailable to any environmental influence.

More specifically, Lorenz sees as innate certain inherited properties of nervous-system structures. Certain groups of neurons, he claims, have built into them specific, distinctive properties (Lehrman, 1970). They obtain these properties directly from the genotype, with experience having no influence. For example, as Lehrman (1970, p. 24) has pointed out, one such innate property of a given neural structure is "its ability to select, from the range of available possible stimuli, the one which specifically elicits its activity, and thus the response seen by the observer." All this, Lorenz claims, comes built into the organism. That is, certain nervous-system structures just come with the innate ability to select out certain stimuli from the environment; these are the stimuli that "just" elicit (bring forth) the built-in (preformed) functional component of the structure, that is, the response.

Since, Lorenz contends, experience plays no role in the presence of this instinctive behavior, one does not have to bother with the issue of how the relation between the stimuli and the responses comes to be established. All one has to say is that the behavior is there because it is innate, and innate behavior comes this way. Thus, to Lorenz no further analysis is needed. By advancing this argument Lorenz "solves" the problems of behavioral development—by avoiding them.

By this point the reader should be well aware of problems inherent in Lorenz's assertions By making a distinction between what is innate and what comes about through the environment, Lorenz is opting for the "which one" (nature or nurture?) question, which we rejected in Chapter 3 as inadequate. We also saw as inadequate notions such as genetic blueprint and genetically fixed. Thus, from our knowledge of Schneirla's interactionist position and from our discussion of the norm-of-reaction concept, we know that the notion of innate, or instinctive, behavior as formulated by Lorenz (1965) is not tenable, for the following reasons:

1. Nature and nurture are inextricably bound; it is inappropriate to assert that genes can directly give you behavior. Nature variables need the supportive, facilitative influence of experiential factors in order to contribute to behavior. (In turn, of course, experience needs nature variables with which to interact.)

2. Because of this interdependency, it is inappropriate to speak of innate as meaning developmentally fixed, that is, to speak of certain behavior as being unavailable to environmental influence or to say that an organism *must* develop certain behaviors because it inherited a certain genotype (Lehrman, 1970, p. 23). The interdependency of the nature-nurture interaction is more complex. Because genes exert their influence through experiential interactions, and because the outcome of their influence will be different under different environmental (experiential) conditions (remember the norm of reaction), it is therefore incorrect to speak of a genetic blueprint. Simply, there is no isomorphism between genotype and eventual behavior.

In sum, Lorenz uses the term innate, or instinctive, to refer to behavior that is genetically fixed and therefore unavailable to environmental influence. However, from our knowledge of the interactionist position we can reject such notions as being overly simplistic, as being based on faulty logic, and most important, as ignoring the problems and issues of behavioral development. To study the problems of behavioral development we must avoid terms such as innate. Such terms end scientific investigation by simply saying that a behavior develops in a certain way because the organism is built that way. Thus, use of the terms innate or instinctive avoids assessing the processes by which behavior develops and hence is of little, if any, scientific use.

Perhaps the most succinct summary of the criticisms that can be leveled against Lorenz's use of these terms was made by an adherent of Schneirla's interactionist position, Daniel Lehrman, in a classic paper published in 1953:

The "instinct" is obviously not present in the zygote. Just as obviously it is present in the behavior of the animal after the appropriate age. The problem for the investigator who wishes to make a closer analysis of behavior is: how did the behavior come about? The use of "explanatory" categories such as "innate" and "genetically fixed" obscures the necessity of investigating developmental *processes* in order to gain insight into the actual mechanisms of behavior and their interrelations. The problem of development is the problem of the development of new *structures* and activity *patterns* from the resolution of the interaction of existing ones, within the organism and its internal environment, and between the organism and its outer environment. At any stage of development, the new features emerge from the interactions within the *current* stage and between the *current* stage and the environment. The interaction out of which the organism develops is *not* one, as is often said, between heredity and environment. It is between *organism* and environment! And the organism is different at each stage of its development (Lehrman, 1953).

## Circular Functions and Self-Stimulation in Development

From our above discussion we have seen how Schneirla's theoretical position provides a way to conceptualize the interactive influences of nature and nurture in behavioral development. Moreover, we have seen how his probabilistic epigenetic formulations can be used to criticize and then appropriately conceptualize presumed nature concepts such as the critical-periods hypothesis and the innate, or instinct, concept. It is appropriate, then, to end our discussion of Schneirla's interactionist position by illustrating how it may be applied to the understanding of the phylogenetic and the ontogenetic development of a specific psychological process: perception.

However, let us first consider a related and extremely important concept that Schneirla offered in his 1957 paper—the role the organism's behavior plays in its *own* behavioral development.

### A "Third Source" of Development

Schneirla suggests that there is a "third source" of development. In addition to the interaction of nature and nurture, Schneirla says, there is another source of an organism's development: the organism itself!

As the organism develops, it attains certain behavioral characteristics through the effects of the maturation-experience interaction. These individual behavioral characteristics of the organism stimulate aspects of its environment—for example, the organism's parents. This stimulated aspect then responds to the organism and thus in turn again stimulates the organism. This is a *circular function*: the organism acts on its environment, and because of this action the environment acts on the organism.

In other words, the organism develops certain individual behavioral characteristics. These behaviors come about as a result of the specific maturational-experiential interaction influencing the organism. As a function of its individual behavioral capabilities which result from this interaction, the organism behaves in its environment. This action *on* the organism's environment provides a stimulus for reactions *from* the environment. The organism's behavior may stimulate other similarly aged organisms, or the organism's parents, or even itself. The stimulation will evoke responses, which in turn will serve to stimulate the organism and will become part of the experience that shapes its development. The circular stimulative process, initiated by the organism's own actions, creates a source of the organism's own development.

Hence, the organism provides an important, ever-present source of its own development. This source must be considered as important as the other sources of the organism's behavior—those that influenced the behavior that originally initiated these circular functions. In commenting on the importance of this third source of development, Schneirla said: "An indispensable feature of development is that of circular relationships of self-stimulation in the organism. The individual seems to be interactive with itself throughout development, as the processes of each stage open the way for further stimulus-reaction relationships depending on the scope of the intrinsic and extrinsic conditions then prevalent" (1957, p. 86).

An illustration of the important role of circular functions and self-stimulation in the development of the organism may be offered. Because of the specifics of his maturation-experience interaction, one child develops a certain style of behavior as an infant, consisting of the following:

1.   His behavior lacks regularity. For example, the child might sleep for two hours, wake for five, sleep for three hours, and then wake for seven. Sometimes he might eliminate almost immediately after feeding, while at others there might be a considerable length of time between feeding and elimination.

2.   The child, when awake, might show a considerably high activity level.

3.   This might be combined with a relatively negative mood; when awake, the child cries or screams quite often.

4.   And when he does cry and scream, he does so with a high intensity.

5.   Finally, all of this high activity, loud crying, and screaming seem to be set off by seemingly very minimal stimulation. That is, the child has a low threshold for responding.

Now, a second child may develop a quite different style of behavior as a result of the specifics of his maturation-experience interaction.

1.   For example, this second child, in contrast with the first, might be regular; he wakes, sleeps, and eliminates in predictable cycles.

2.   When he is awake, his activity level is of moderate magnitude.

3.   He has a positive mood; he smiles and laughs a lot.

4.   In addition, such behavior is of a moderate intensity.

5.   And finally, he maintains a moderate threshold for responding.

What we have, then, are two markedly different sets of individual behavioral characteristics. Both sets resulted from the specifics of each child's maturation-experience interaction, yet the implications of each set of characteristics for the development of the respective children are quite disparate. One might easily agree that the former child would present obvious difficulties for his parents. He would stimulate reactions that would be quite different from those stimulated in the parents of the latter child. Compared with the former child, the latter would be easy to interact with and would not create any serious problems for his parents.

If parents could choose, before the fact, either of the above two sets of characteristics for an expected child, I believe they would, almost without exception, choose the second set. They would rather have a predictable, smiling, moderately active baby than an unpredictable, loudly crying, highly active one. But parents cannot choose their baby's behavioral style characteristics. The former baby's behavioral characteristics would create reactions in his parents, and these reactions would in turn stimulate the baby and become part of his experience. For instance, the parents of such a child might find it difficult to handle the baby for long lengths of time, and so they might make their interactions with him relatively short and abrupt. Alternatively, however, if the baby's behavioral characteristics had been like those of the second child, he would have evoked different reactions in his parents, and in turn would have had different stimulation become part of his experience. Thus, if he had been easier to handle his parents might have sought to extend their interactions with him. Moreover, the interactions might have been of a different quality (e.g., warmer).

From this example we can see that an organism's own behavioral characteristics do provide an important source of its own development, through the process of circular functions and self-stimulation in development. In fact, the above illustration of this circular process is not quite imaginary. It is based on the research findings of Thomas, Chess, Birch, Hertzig, and Korn (1963), who, basing their work on Schneirla's conceptions about circular functions in development, studied the implications of behavioral individuality for the development of over one hundred children over the course of several years. Their work will be the focus of our discussion in Chapter 9.

In sum, then, Schneirla highlights the necessity of focusing on the organism and its own actions in trying to understand the sources of behavior development. His notions of circular functions and self-stimulation illustrate and emphasize a central idea in all organismic conceptions of development: the organism is central in its own development. An organism does not just sit passively; it does not just wait for maturation and experience to interact in order for its behavior to develop; and it certainly does not just passively wait for the environment to stimulate it to respond. Rather, the organism is always active, and its own activity provides an important source of its own development. Thus, development is in part a *self-generated* phenomenon.

This concept plays a central role in Schneirla's own ideas about the processes involved in specific psychological developments. As promised, then, let us now turn to an illustration of how all of Schneirla's ideas may be applied to an understanding of the development of a particular process in development, that of perception.

## Some Issues in the Development of Perception

All species of animals have processes available that are adaptive; that is, every living species, by virtue of its existence, has processes that allow it to adapt to its environment. All species have ways of taking in food and of eliminating waste products. But this does not mean that all species have available to them the same processes. That is, we may not assume a homology. Although all species take in food and eliminate wastes, they may do these things in different ways. Thus, organisms at different psychological levels may use different processes to serve the same function. Both the one-celled amoeba and human beings take in food and eliminate wastes, but they certainly perform these adaptive functions in different ways. This is because there are new processes available at different psychological levels; there is qualitative discontinuity among psychological levels.

Accordingly, although all psychological levels have the capacity to react to stimulation, it is not appropriate to attribute the capacity of perception to all psychological levels. All psychological levels must have the ability to react to stimulation in order to survive, what Schneirla (1957) terms the capacity for *sensation.* Even one-celled protozoa have this capacity. Yet it is not until we look at a much higher psychological level that we see the capacity for *perception,* that is, the ability to sense with meaning. Thus, at higher psychological levels a qualitatively discontinuous capacity emerges—

perception—which allows the organisms of that level to adapt to their environment. These organisms have the ability, for example, to make associations with their sensations, to integrate their purely sensory information with other information available to them. Such organisms can show different responses to the same stimulus; they can associate a different output with the same input. Thus, they sense with meaning.

If the capacity of higher psychological levels is qualitatively different from that of lower psychological levels, it follows that these differences should be reflected not in the degree to which different psychological levels can organize sensory information but in the kind of organization they achieve (Schneirla, 1957, p. 96). That is, these differences should be represented not only in how much sensory information can be handled but also in what is done with that information. Higher psychological levels should show greater associative variability—greater plasticity—than should lower levels.

Accordingly, Schneirla suggests that as one moves to higher psychological levels, one will see that sensory experiences result not merely in the *fixation* of trace effects, in the organism being able to develop a trace effect of a particular sensory input-reaction experience, but also in the *correlation* of these trace effects. In other words, organisms at higher psychological levels have the capacity for a kind of organization of sensory information that is different from the capacity of phylogenetically lower organisms. They have the ability to relate information coming from one sense modality (e.g., vision) with information coming from another sense modality (e.g., touch).

Thus, at higher psychological levels organisms have the capacity of *intersensory integration,* the ability to transduce (i.e., transfer, or transform) information from one sense modality to another. With this capacity, sensory input from vision, for example, may be "equated" with sensory input from touch; thus, the sensory input from the two different modalities (modes of sensing) can come to mean the same thing to the organism. For example, we can recognize a quarter coin by feeling it or seeing it. We can recognize an ice cube by touching it or by seeing it. The sensations from either of these objects can mean the same thing to us even though delivered through different modalities.

Hence, as we move up the phylogenetic scale, from lower psychological levels to higher psychological levels, we see perceptual ability emerging not because of new senses being present—not because higher psychological levels have more senses than do lower levels with which to fixate the trace effects of sensory experience—but because as we move to higher psychological levels better liaison among existing senses emerges. We see advances in the capacity to correlate information among the senses. We see increased intersensory integrative ability. Thus, as Birch and Lefford have pointed out: "In the emergence of the mammalian nervous system from lower forms, the essential evolutionary strategy has been the development of mechanisms for improved interaction among the separate sensory modalities" (1963, p. 3). Similarly, Sherrington stated: "Not new senses, but better liaison between old senses is what the developing nervous system has in this respect stood for" (1951, p. 289).

From the above we can see that an organism of a high psychological level—for instance, a human—has the capacity to develop considerable intersensory integrative ability, to make considerable gains through sensory experiences. However, we have also seen that humans, with their high psychological level, correspondingly have a high A/S ratio. This means that although human beings are capable of high levels of be-

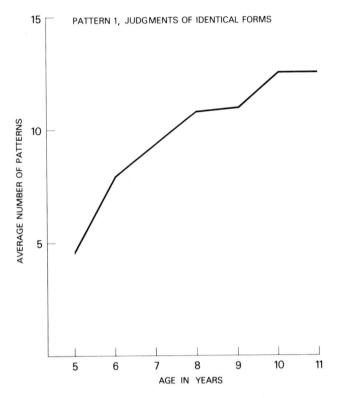

**Fig. 4.4** Some of the results of the Birch and Lefford study: Correct judgments for all intersensory pairings made when judging identical forms at different ages. *Source:* H. G. Birch and A. Lefford, *Intersensory Development in Children,* Monographs of the Society for Research in Child Development 28 (1963), p. 35. Copyright 1963 by The Society for Research in Child Development. Reprinted by permission.

havioral development, it takes them a relatively long period of time, as opposed to animals, to reach this developmental level, the highest point of their functional order. In essence, we can expect human beings, although capable of considerable intersensory integrative ability, to develop this ability over several years in the course of their ontogeny. Simply, we may hypothesize that human intersensory integrative ability is a developmental phenomenon!

This hypothesis was tested in an important study by Birch and Lefford (1963) of the ability of children of different ages (ranging from five to eleven years) to integrate information from three different sense modalities—vision, active touch (or the haptic sense), and passive touch (or the kinesthetic sense). The authors used geometric forms, such as blocks in the shape of a circle, square, triangle, star, and cross, as stimuli for the children. Two blocks at a time were presented. Sometimes the same object was presented for the child to see and touch; and at other times different objects were presented. In either case the child was asked to judge whether the two blocks were the same or different.

In support of the hypothesis that intersensory integrative ability increases with age (that it is a developmental phenomenon), Birch and Lefford found that "the ability to make the various intersensory judgments clearly improved with age" (p. 45). Figure 4.4 depicts some of the results of this study. The authors conclude that "the findings strongly indicate that information received by young children through one avenue of sense is not directly transduced to another sensory modality. . . . In fact, it may perhaps be argued that the emergence of such equivalence is developmental."

In essence, Birch and Lefford (1963) provided strong evidence in support of the notion that the intersensory integrative ability of human beings reaches its eventually high level only after years of development. However, they also found that even their youngest subjects—the five-year-olds—had relatively well-developed intersensory integrative ability. They suggested, however, that at younger ages, at about three years of age, this ability would be markedly inefficient but would rapidly improve.

Accordingly, in a similar experiment, Abravanel (1968) studied intersensory integrative development in children ranging in age from three to fourteen years. He found that at about three years of age the base level (the lowest level) for performing the various intersensory equivalences occurred. After this time, however, integrative ability improved greatly up through seven years of age, when it reached a high level of efficiency. Thus, consistent with the notions we have derived from Schneirla's ideas (1957) about perceptual development, we see that both the Birch and Lefford (1963) and the Abravanel (1968) studies provide findings that support the hypothesis that human ability to transduce information from one modality to another increases with age, that it is a developmental phenomenon.

Abravanel (1968) provides us with other findings that support Schneirla's concepts about development. He found that increases in intersensory integrative ability are associated with changes in the type of exploration activity the children showed when actively touching the stimulus. Specifically, younger, less accurate children explored the stimuli by either gross or passive movements. Alternatively, older, more accurate children used finer and more articulated movements, explorings with the fingertips, for instance, rather than with the palms.

Thus, as Schneirla would assert, children's own activity appears to be highly related to their perceptual development. Other studies, by Birch and Lefford (1967) and by Held and Hein (1963), also support this notion. Thus it appears that among the processes involved in perceptual development are some provided by the organism's own activity.

In summary, we see that we can use the ideas of Schneirla for understanding the development of a particular psychological process, that of perception. We have seen that the ideas and work of T. C. Schneirla and his students and colleagues provide us with the tools for appropriately conceptualizing many of the complexities of psychological development. His organismic and probabilistic epigenetic theory provides us not only with the knowledge for understanding specific issues in the nature-nurture controversy, but with a framework with which to look at many other concepts and issues in development. Accordingly, we will have reason to consider many of Schneirla's ideas again throughout the course of the following chapters.

We have come to the end of our discussion of the general (Chapter 3) and specific (Chapter 4) issues and implications involved in appropriately conceptualizing the nature-nurture issue. After summarizing this discussion we will turn then to a consideration of the second major conceptual issue in psychological development: the continuity-discontinuity issue.

## Summary

T. C. Schneirla presents an organismic, probabilistic epigenetic view of psychological development. According to this view, behavior at any level is the product of an interaction between the organism's nature and nurture. Schneirla rejects the notion of homology—the idea that identical functions are invariantly underlain by identical structures. Rather, he asserts that the relation between structure and function will be different at different phylogenetic or ontogenetic levels in dependence on the specifics of the nature-nurture interaction. Thus, the same behavior (function) may be underlain by different structures—that is, may have a different meaning—at different points in a person's life span.

Because different nature-nurture interactions may be expected to characterize different points along the phylogenetic span, Schneirla views different species as being qualitatively different. To characterize the differences among these various species—these different psychological levels—the concepts of stereotypy and plasticity were introduced. Organisms on lower psychological levels tend to be characterized by behavioral stereotypy as they progress toward their final level of development, or functional order. This is so because there is little response variability to stimulation; there is sense domination. Animals at higher psychological levels tend to reach a functional order characterized by behavioral plasticity, that is, varying responses to the same stimulus input.

A hypothetical interrelation was drawn between this stereotypy-plasticity dimension and Hebb's (1949) notions about the ratio between an organism's association and sensory neurons (an A/S ratio) being a basis for characterizing differences among species. The higher the A/S ratio, the greater the number of associations that can be made toward the same stimulus; hence, organisms with higher A/S ratios should show greater plasticity than organisms with lower A/S ratios. Thus, organisms with lower A/S ratios are more stereotyped in their final level of development than are the former type of organism, but because the lower organisms have less association area to organize, they reach their final level of development earlier in their ontogeny than do their more plastic counterparts.

To represent development Schneirla uses the concepts of maturation (growth and differentiation) and experience (all stimulative influences acting on the organism). The effects of one factor are canalized and limited by the status of the other. Thus, the type of trace effects that can result from experience is dependent on the maturational status of the organism, but factors of maturation will exert different influences depending on the experiential context. Since the status of each factor may not be the same for all organisms and may not be perfectly predictable for any one organism, the qualities emerging in development are dependent on the nature and timing of the interactions between these two factors.

Because development is characterized by probabilistic epigenetic emergences, emergences that arise as a function of the timing of specific maturation-experience interactions, a critical, negative evaluation is often made of the use of two concepts. The notion of critical periods, when used to mean that there exist time limits for the development of certain behaviors and that these time limits are set solely by maturation, and the notion of instinct, or innate behavior, when used to mean that certain behaviors are preformed in the genotype and hence unavailable to any environmental influence whatsoever, are inconsistent with Schneirla's organismic, interactionist views. Both concepts—as used above—are rejected because they ignore specific interactive interdependencies of maturation and experience as being involved in any developmental process.

Not only are such interactions always involved in any behavioral development, but because the timing and quality of such interactions will be different for different organisms, organismic individuality develops. Schneirla conceptualizes such characteristics of individuality as representing a "third source" of development. Through the establishment of circular functions and self-stimulation in ontogeny, the organism itself provides a stimulus source of its own future development. Its specific characteristics of individuality will evoke differential reactions in others in the organism's environment, and this will result in feedback stimulation for the organism.

Schneirla's interactionist ideas of development were applied to the understanding of one particular psychological process: the development of perception. We saw that across the phylogenetic span, increases in perceptual ability are characterized by increasingly better interrelation among existing sense modalities. Perhaps because of higher A/S ratios, and thus greater plasticity, organisms at higher psychological levels show the ability to efficiently translate (integrate) information from one sense modality to another. Yet, such plastic perceptual ability is attained through development. A study by Birch and Lefford demonstrated that there is an increasing ability among children of progressively older ages to make correct intersensory integrations. A related study by Abravanel also supported the view that intersensory integrative ability is a developmental phenomenon and provided evidence that increases in such ability are related to concomitant alterations in the child's mode of exploring and manipulating objects in the stimulus world. This finding, along with information derived from other studies, was interpreted to suggest that in perceptual development the role of the organism's own activity appears intimately involved in the developmental process.

# 5 The Continuity-Discontinuity Issue

The second central conceptual issue that pervades developmental psychology is the continuity-discontinuity issue. This issue can be derived from the former nature-nurture issue. Granted that there are laws governing behavioral development and that these laws lie within the province of nature and nurture, how do they function across the life span of a species? Do the variables involved in determining behavioral development remain the same or do they ontogenetically change in their functioning? If the same laws, or variables, account for behavioral development at different times in the ontogeny of a species, this is *continuity*. Alternatively, if different laws account for behavioral development at different times in the ontogeny of a species, this is *discontinuity*.

Of course, the continuity-discontinuity issue may be considered from either a phylogenetic or an ontogenetic perspective. Thus, if the same laws account for the behavior of animals of different phylogenetic levels, this would be termed phylogenetic continuity; if different laws account for the behavior of animals of different phylogenetic levels, this would be termed phylogenetic discontinuity. On the other hand, from an ontogenetic perspective, if the same laws account for the behavior of a person at time 1 and time 2 in life, this would be termed ontogenetic continuity; if different laws account for the behavior of a person at time 1 and time 2, this would be termed ontogenetic discontinuity. Simply, then, if the laws governing behavior remain the same with time, continuity exists; if the laws governing behavior change with time, discontinuity exists. These relations are illustrated in Fig. 5.1.

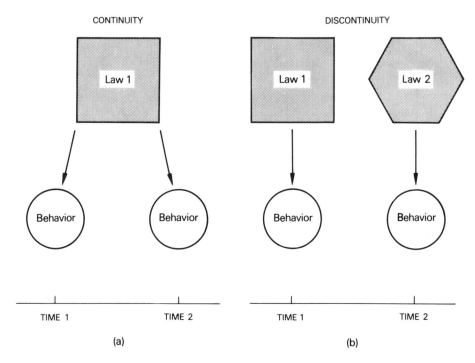

**Fig. 5.1** An illustration of (a) continuity and (b) discontinuity in development.

Heinz Werner

For a long time many psychologists considered the continuity-discontinuity issue an empirical issue. They contended that the existence of continuity or discontinuity for the development of a given psychological process could be determined only by the results of one's research. Of course, to some extent this position has a degree of validity. Whether one sees continuity or discontinuity in behavioral development *is* partially dependent on one's data. The point is, however, that the result of one's research is not the only factor that determines the existence of continuity or discontinuity. There are other, more important factors, and to understand them we must consider the work of Heinz Werner.

## The Contributions of Heinz Werner
Due primarily to the great contributions of Heinz Werner to the literature of developmental psychology, the other factors that determine the existence of continuity or discontinuity have been specified. Werner, like Schneirla (and like other great contributors to developmental psychology, such as Piaget) conceptualized development from an organismic point of view. Werner's writings, and those of his colleagues and students (for example, Seymour Wapner and Jonas Langer), have contributed immeasurably to the advancement of organismic theory as well as to the appropriate conceptualization of the continuity-discontinuity issue.

## Two Different Aspects of Change
Werner (1957) saw that considerable confusion existed among psychologists over the continuity-discontinuity issue and that at the crux of this confusion was a lack of understanding about two different aspects of change. He saw that psychological processes could change in one of two ways.

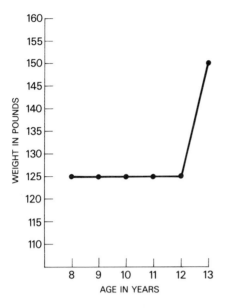

Fig. 5.2 An example of an abrupt change (quantitative discontinuity).

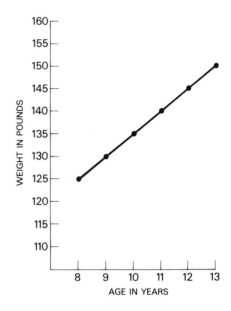

Fig. 5.3 An example of a gradual quantitative change.

**Quantitative Change.** First there is the quantitative aspect of change. Here things change in terms of how much of something exists; quantitative change is in amount, frequency, magnitude, or amplitude of a psychological variable or process. For example, a person's weight has been measured at the same time during each of his eighth through thirteenth years. He weighed 125 pounds when he was measured at years eight, nine, ten, eleven, and twelve; but he weighed 150 pounds when he was measured at year thirteen. Thus, between the times of measurement occurring at years twelve and thirteen a quantitative change occurred in how much weight existed. This example is illustrated in Fig. 5.2. This quantitative change is abrupt; there were no intermediate steps with which the person's weight gradually moved from one level (amount) to the next. In measuring this change there is a gap between one point in the measurement curve and another; that is, the curve representing the different measurements is not smooth (as in Fig. 5.3) but has an abrupt change in its direction (as in Fig. 5.2). There is a *gappiness* in the curve, a lack of an intermediate stage between the earlier and later levels of a variable (Werner, 1957, p. 133). When an abrupt change occurs, this is quantitative discontinuity.

Alternatively, the child's change in weight could have been gradual, as illustrated in Fig. 5.3. By gaining five pounds per year the child gradually changes from 125 pounds to 150 pounds between his eighth and thirteenth years. With gradual quantitative changes the rate of change stays the same—is continuous—from one measurement time to the next. This is *quantitative continuity*.

**Qualitative Change.** The second aspect of change that Werner specifies is the qualitative aspect. Here we are primarily concerned not with how much of something exists but with *what* exists—what kind or type of thing exists. Thus, we are concerned with whether or not a new quality has come to characterize an organism, whether something new has emerged in its development. When we are considering qualitative change we are dealing with *epigenesis,* with emergence.

In Chapter 2 we considered the central role of epigenesis in organismic conceptions of development. In distinguishing between quantitative and qualitative aspects of change, Werner highlights a core conception of the organismic position. Some of the types of changes that comprise development are emergent changes. These are changes in what exists rather than in how much of something exists. Something new comes about in development, and because it is new—because it is qualitatively different from what went before—it cannot be reduced to what went before. Hence, consistent with the analogy we presented in Chapter 2, if at time 1 we can be represented by ten oranges and at time 2 we can be represented by a motorcycle, we cannot reduce our motorcycle status of time 2 to our orange status of time 1.

To take another example: Before puberty a person may be characterized as being (in part) comprised of several drives: for example, a hunger drive, a thirst drive, a drive to avoid pain, and perhaps a curiosity drive. With puberty, however, a new drive emerges, the sex drive. With this emergence the adolescent begins to have new feelings, new thoughts, and even new behaviors, which may be interpreted as being a consequence of this new drive (A. Freud, 1969). The emergence of this new drive is an instance of qualitative discontinuity. The sex drive cannot be reduced to hunger and thirst drives, for instance.

Hence, qualitative changes by their very nature are discontinuous. A qualitative, emergent, epigenetic change is always an instance of discontinuity. Moreover, not only is an emergent change an irreducible change, but it is a change characterized by gappiness. As indicated above, gappiness in development occurs when there is a lack of an intermediate level between earlier and later levels of development. It should be clear that gappiness must also be a part of an emergent change. If there was an intermediate step between what existed at time 1 and the new quality that emerges at time 2, this would suggest that the new quality at time 2 *could be* reduced through reference to the intermediate step. Since we have just seen that an emergent change is defined in terms of its irreducibility to what went before it in development, we should also see that gappiness must also then be a characteristic of any emergence. In sum then, the characteristics of emergence and gappiness are needed to describe qualitatively discontinuous changes in development; on the other hand, the characteristic of gappiness (abruptness) alone seems to suffice for characterizing quantitatively discontinuous changes. Thus, as Werner stated:

It seems that discontinuity in terms of qualitative changes can be best defined by two characteristics: "emergence," i.e., the irreducibility of a later stage to an earlier; and "gappiness," i.e., the lack of intermediate stages between earlier and later forms. Quantitative discontinuity on the other hand, appears to be sufficiently defined by the second characteristic. . . . To facilitate distinction and alleviate confusion, I would suggest substituting "abruptness" for quantitative discontinuity, reserving the term "discontinuity" only for the qualitative aspect of change (1957, p. 133).

What Werner has provided us with, then, is a clarification of the concepts involved in appropriately considering the continuity-discontinuity issue. He has given us the conceptual means with which to discriminate between quantitative continuity-discontinuity and qualitative continuity-discontinuity. But which of these two concepts (continuity or discontinuity) best characterizes the changes that comprise develop-ment? In a sense, Werner's answer to this question is that both concepts characterize developmental changes! That is, Werner provides us with a concept that allows us to see the interrelation of continuity *and* discontinuity in development, and to see that the continuity-discontinuity issue is primarily a theoretical issue. Whether one posits continuity or discontinuity as characterizing development rests primarily on the theoretical assumptions and positions one maintains. The concept that allows us to see this state of affairs quite clearly is the principle of orthogenesis.

## The Orthogenetic Principle

Werner postulates that developmental psychology has one general regulative principle of development. This principle, which he terms the *orthogenetic principle,* states that "whenever development occurs it proceeds from a state of relative globality and lack of differentiation to a state of increasing differentiation, articulation, and hierarchic integration" (Werner, 1957, p. 126).

Thus, whenever development occurs, the changes that characterize it follow a specified sequence. At time 1 in development a particular psychological process, or variable, would be relatively global, that is, general, or undifferentiated. At time 2 in development, however, this same psychological process would have become relatively differentiated, that is, more specific. In addition, the differentiated status of the process would exist in the form of a hierarchy.

An illustration of the orthogenetic principle will help us understand its meaning. Consider a relatively young child, for example a child of about twenty months of age. We are spending a day with the child and decide to take a short walk. While walking we notice a dog come by. The child points and says, "doggie." We perhaps smile and say, "Yes, that's a doggie." But soon a cat is seen, and the child here also points and says, "doggie." Similarly, when later a picture of a raccoon is seen in a magazine the child also says, "doggie."

We might conclude then that this young child has a relatively global (undifferen-tiated) concept of animals. Any small, furry creature with four legs and a tail is called a doggie. In other words, the conceptual development of this child, at least insofar as animals are concerned, is in a state of globality, or lack of differentiation. Now, suppose that we visited this same child about a year or so later. On the basis of Werner's orthogenetic principle we would expect that if the child's animal concepts had developed, they would be relatively less global—they would be more differentiated. Thus, the child might now say "dog" only when a dog was in fact in view, and "cat," "raccoon," "horse," etc., when appropriate.

On another, still later visit with the child we might see some other things. The child might now show evidence of knowing that all dogs, cats, horses, etc., are animals, and in turn, animals are different from trees. Thus, we would see that the child's animal concepts not only had become more differentiated but also had formed into a hierarchy; that is, cats, dogs, and horses are all instances of the class "animals." Still later, perhaps, we would see that increasing differentiation and hierarchical organization had occurred. The child would have a concept not only of dog but also of different breeds of dogs, and in addition might be able to show evidence of knowing that within each breed there are puppies and adults, males and females of that breed. Moreover, the child might now be able to differentiate among types of plants (e.g., trees from flowers from vegetables) and might know that both plants and animals are in a similar, higher-order class (living things) and are different from nonliving things.

Thus, what we would see with the development of the child's animal concepts is a change from having relatively global, undifferentiated concepts to having concepts organized into a hierarchical structure. This development is illustrated in Fig. 5.4, which shows that the orthogenetic principle can be used to describe the nature of developmental change. This principle holds that all developmental changes should proceed from globality to differentiation and hierarchical organization. Thus, Werner asserts that the orthogenetic principle is a general, regulative law of all development. The principle describes the nature of developmental change, and in so doing gives one a framework within which to consider the continuities and discontinuities that may comprise a particular psychological development. Let us see how.

## The Orthogenetic Principle and the Continuity-Discontinuity Issue

Jonas Langer (1970), an eminent student of Werner, has contributed to clarifying how the orthogenetic principle helps us to understand the continuity-discontinuity issue. He points out that *both* continuity and discontinuity may be considered to characterize development. Discontinuity occurs as the relatively global organization of earlier times in development becomes differentiated. On the other hand, continuity occurs as the differentiated organism is hierarchically integrated. One stresses continuity in development by pointing out that earlier developments will become subsumed under later ones, that what went before will be subordinate to later superordinate developments.

Hence, development is characterized by a *synthesis,* an interweaving of two opposing tendencies. First is the tendency to become more differentiated. This involves the tendency for new characteristics to emerge from previous, global characteristics, the tendency for global characteristics to become different, specific characteristics. This differentiation is thus discontinuity. Second is the tendency to become hierarchically organized, the tendency for earlier developments to be continuously subsumed under later developments. This hierarchical organization is thus continuity. In sum, what Langer (1969, 1970) and Werner (1957) are suggesting is that there are *both* continuous and discontinuous aspects of development. To maintain an appropriate perspective of development, therefore, one must recognize that the organism develops in accord with both of these perhaps seemingly opposed processes. If one exclusively focuses, however, on one or the other of these two different processes, then one will miss the nature of the synthesis that characterizes psychological development and accordingly have an incomplete view. Thus, if one exclusively focuses on discontinuity, one might incorrectly view development as quite a disorderly process. Alternatively, if one exclusively focuses on continuity, one will not understand the qualitative changes of the interacting, developing organism (Langer, 1970, p. 733). What Langer and Werner

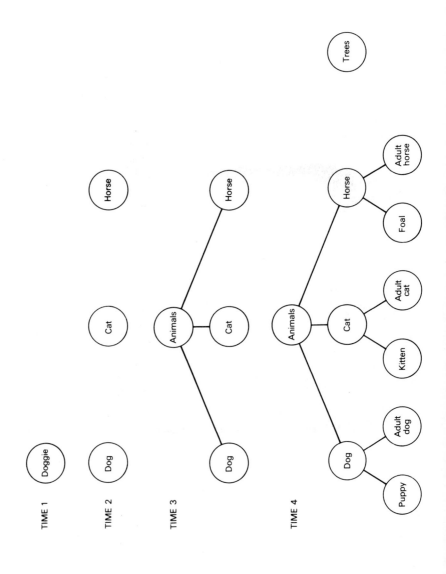

TIME 5

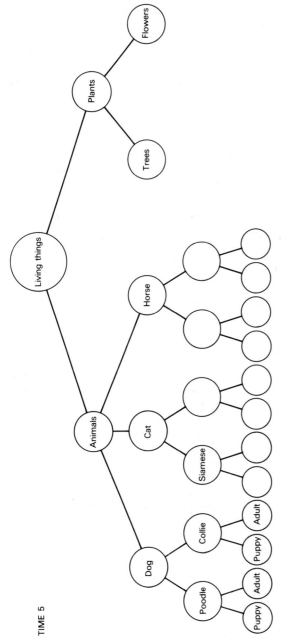

**Fig. 5.4** An illustration of the orthogenetic principle: The child's concepts of animals develop from a state of globality and lack of differentiation (Time 1) to a state of differentiation and hierarchical organization (Time 5).

are opting for, then, is a view of development that recognizes the existence of both general (continuous) and specific (discontinuous) laws of development. This general-and-specific-laws position has been outlined in Chapter 2, and we will see in Chapter 7 that Piaget too opts for this position and thus takes a theoretical stance quite similar to the organismic position of Werner.

In sum, the orthogenetic principle highlights the fact that one must consider both the continuous and the discontinuous aspects of development, because both can be seen to characterize developmental changes. Development proceeds from a state of globality and lack of differentiation to a state of differentiation (hence discontinuity) and integrated, hierarchical organization (hence continuity). In other words, development is actually a *dialectical* process, a synthesis between thesis and antithesis. Throughout the life span there is dialectical integration—a synthesis—between discontinuous differentiation (thesis) and continuous hierarchicalization (antithesis).

### Factors Influencing Decisions about the Continuity-Discontinuity Issue

A major implication of Werner's position, then, is that the continuity-discontinuity issue is *not* primarily an empirical question, but is dependent on one's theoretical views. If one adopts a theoretical position stressing the progressive, hierarchical integration of the organism (e.g., Gagné, 1968), one will necessarily view development as essentially continuous. On the other hand, if one stresses the progressive differentiation of the organism, one will view development as essentially discontinuous. For example, one's theoretical position might lead one to interpret a given piece of empirical evidence in one way (e.g., as consistent with a continuity position), while someone with a different theoretical position might interpret that same empirical fact in another way (e.g., as consistent with a discontinuity position). For instance, whether or not one views babbling as continuous or discontinuous with speech depends on one's particular theoretical perspective. Similarly, many researchers claim that an empirical fact of many adolescents' lives is "storm and stress" during these years. Some theorists interpret this in terms of the continuous functioning of an invariant process (e.g., A. Davis' "socialized anxiety"), while others (e.g., A. Freud) view it as evidence that a qualitatively discontinuous phenomenon has emerged.

A second factor, however, related to the first, is also responsible for decisions about whether one views development as continuous or discontinuous, and that is how one handle's one's data. To be fair, the influence of this factor on the issue is more subtle than the former factor and may not be as ubiquitous. However, a researcher may in fact analyze results in ways that subtlely reflect his or her theoretical beliefs.

For example, suppose that a researcher wants to study the level of aggression in play situations of girls from the ages of six through eleven years. The researcher develops a measure of aggression that is applicable to girls throughout this age range, studies a number of girls at each age level, and obtains scores for each girl. Now, let us imagine that the researcher has a theory about the development of aggression that predicts that aggression in girls of this age range should be discontinuous. Thus the researcher might specifically expect to see abrupt changes in the levels of aggression and accordingly graph the results of the study so that any year-by-year fluctuations in levels of aggression would be evident, as seen in Fig. 5.5(a). The graphed results would reveal abrupt fluctuations in measured aggression levels in play situations within

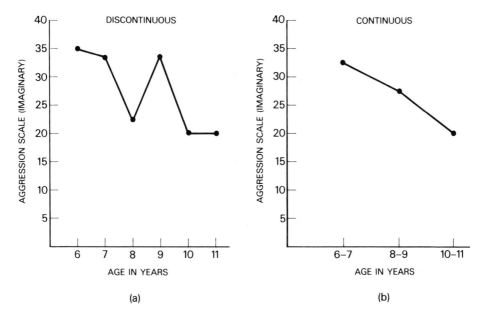

**Fig. 5.5** How one handles data may contribute to whether one views development as being discontinuous (a) or continuous (b).

the age range studied, and the researcher could use these results to support the notion that aggression in play situations is a discontinuous phenomenon in girls.

On the other hand, the researcher's theory might hold that aggression is a continuous phenomenon in girls of this age range. Accordingly, the researcher might not expect any abrupt changes in levels of aggression with age, but expect such development to be a gradual process. Thus, to make for ease and clarity in the analysis and presentation of the results of the study (and/or because it might be believed that it is a more reliable procedure), the researcher might use the average scores for a combination of both the six- and seven-year-olds as one data point on the graph, for the eight- and nine-year-olds as another data point, and so on, as seen in Fig. 5.5(b). The researcher could now use these results to support the contention that aggression in play situations decreases rather gradually over time with girls and therefore such aggression is a continuous phenomenon. Of course, this example has been made extreme in order to illustrate a point, which is that one's theoretical perspective can have a subtle effect on the way one handles research results.

Despite the apparent tenability of the above assertions, arguments about whether continuity or discontinuity characterizes phylogenetic and/or ontogenetic development still occur. One such debate has centered around whether the laws governing the phylogenetic development of learning are continuous or discontinuous. It will be useful to now consider this controversy because, first, the specifics of this debate will serve to well illustrate a particular and important instance of the continuity-discontinuity issue and, second, the information will be essential for our consideration of the continuity-discontinuity issue as it is applied to ontogenetic development.

## The Phylogeny of Learning: Continuity or Discontinuity?

Learning is a complex phenomenon. Although psychologists have spent a considerable amount of time and energy studying the learning process (e.g., see Kimble, 1961), there is no consensus about the nature of learning. Different theorists define learning in different ways and advance different notions about what processes comprise learning. For the purposes of our present discussion, though, we may consider learning as the acquisition of environmental-stimulation–behavioral-response relations, or simply, the acquisition of certain types of stimulus-response relations. If an animal acquires a bar-pressing response in the presence of a red light or a response of turning to the right at various points in a maze in order to obtain food, we may say that learning has occurred. Although this definition certainly does not allow us to point to all the complexities involved in a consideration of learning, it is not our goal to deal with all these issues; rather, we will focus on a particular aspect of the controversies involved in the study of learning, the issue of whether learning is a continuous or a discontinuous phenomenon. Are the laws governing learning the same for all species? Or must we posit new laws, to account for the learning of animals of different phylogenetic levels?

In the history of this controversy, M. E. Bitterman has come to play a central, clarifying role. In three important papers (1960, 1965, 1975), Bitterman presented arguments and empirical evidence that served to clarify the continuity-discontinuity issue in learning.

Bitterman (1960) noted that many psychologists interested in studying learning in different animals adopted, as a working assumption, the notion that learning processes are essentially the same in all animals. This assumption, he pointed out, found its basis in the ideas of no less an eminent figure than Charles Darwin. Darwin believed that differences among species in capacities such as learning are differences in amount (degree) and not in type (kind). Thus, beginning with Darwin many psychologists just assumed that the laws governing the learning of one phyletic level are qualitatively identical to the laws governing the learning of other phylogenetic levels.

This working hypothesis was extremely useful. Its adoption facilitated the experimental analysis of the learning process, because once continuity was assumed, psychologists could study one species and then apply the resulting data to other species. Hence, because it was easier to manipulate the stimulus-response relationships of laboratory rats, as compared with children for example, rats soon became almost the exclusive organism studied. Any laws found with rats could be *assumed* to apply to humans, because the only difference between these species was in quantity, not quality, of learning. The laws of rat learning could be used to understand how humans learned. Thus, by focusing on how the rat learned one could readily discover the universal laws of learning, the laws that applied to all organisms.

As Bitterman (1960, p. 485) points out, however, many "learning psychologists" (those psychologists interested in the study of learning) soon lost sight of the fact that their working assumption was only just that, an assumption, and that it needed to be put to empirical tests. One needed to see if, in fact, the laws of learning for one species were

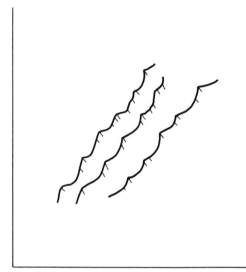

**Fig. 5.6** Learning curves for a pigeon, a rat, and a monkey. *Source:* B. F. Skinner, "A Case History in Scientific Method," *American Psychologist* **11** (1956). Copyright 1956 by the American Psychological Association. Reprinted by permission.

applicable to all species. This, of course, could not be done if learning psychologists continued to focus almost exclusive research interest on the laboratory rat.

Thus, unfortunately, many learning psychologists never put this assumption to the test, and soon many transformed this working assumption into an article of faith, an untested belief (Bitterman, 1960). Accordingly, we find such an early, famous learning psychologist as J. B. Watson saying, " . . . in passing from the unicellular organisms to man no new principle is needed" (1914, p. 318). Similarly, the more modern learning psychologists Dollard and Miller maintained that "any general phenomena of learning found in rats will also be found in people" (1950, p. 63). Indeed, the most prominent psychologist today identified with the psychology of learning, B. F. Skinner, espouses an identical position. He too has turned the working assumption that began with Darwin into an article of faith.

For example, in 1956 Skinner published an article that contained the graph seen in Fig. 5.6, which shows what we may term *learning curves* obtained by Skinner from the responses of a rat, a pigeon, and a monkey. But which curve belongs to which one of these three quite different animals? Skinner's answer to this question was, "It doesn't matter" (1956, p. 230). As Bitterman (1960) points out, Skinner did not present these curves to show that the learning processes of these animals are identical; rather, he assumed this. Although we can see that the behavioral products of these animals—their learning curves—are markedly similar, this does not necessarily mean that it doesn't matter which curve belongs to which animal. By asserting this position on the basis of functional (response) similarity, one is therefore assuming that the processes, or structures, underlying these functions are identical. Thus, one is asserting the notion of homology, and we have seen in some detail in Chapter 4 that this notion is not necessarily tenable.

Skinner is asserting that it does not really matter what processes underlie an animal's behavioral capability so long as one can demonstrate that one can shape the animal's behaviors in certain ways in specific situations. If one can make an animal emit a certain response, and make another species of animal make an identical response, then it is irrelevant if the processes by which these animals came to develop their response capabilities are different. As long as one can control the stimulus-response relations of animals and thereby demonstrate that different organisms can be made to respond in identical ways in these situations, then other differences among the animals are therefore irrelevant. They are irrelevant because in demonstrating that one can make different animals do the same thing (e.g., learn to press a bar in a given pattern) one has demonstrated that these animals are essentially the same.

In Chapter 4 we saw that such homologous-type thinking is inconsistent with Schneirla's views of behavioral development. In that discussion we saw some of the pitfalls of the position we now see Skinner espousing. Simply, just having techniques with which to manipulate the behavior of two different animals so as to make them emit markedly similar responses in similar situations does not necessarily mean either that the developmental laws governing the acquisition of their response capabilities are therefore the same, or that the different animals will typically show identical responses in all other situations. Thus, to summarize the essential difference between the continuity position of Skinner and the organismic position of Schneirla, we may offer an anecdote told about a famous student of Schneirla. Once, it is said, this student was called on to summarize the essential differences between the positions of Skinner and Schneirla. He did so in one sentence: "Professor Skinner is interested in finding out how animals come to do what *he* wants them to do, while Professor Schneirla is interested in finding out how animals come to do what *they* want to do!"

To Bitterman (1960) also, Skinner's reasoning is unwarranted. First, demonstrating that different animals can be made to do the same thing does not necessarily prove that they learn in the same way. Again, we have seen that the assumption that even identical behaviors are underlain by identical laws is not warranted. Second, demonstrating that animals can be made to acquire certain stimulus-response relations in specific situations does not therefore prove that they acquire all their stimulus-response relations in all of their life situations in that same way. Third, demonstrating that *some* animals can be made to perform the same way in a certain situation does not therefore prove that *all* animals can be made to perform identically. For example, we know that rats, pigeons, and some apes can be made to perform identically in some situations, but what about fish, elephants, pigs, three-year-old humans, and twenty-year-old humans? In fact, when some researchers *have* compared such other animals (e.g., pigs, raccoons, and chickens) on similar learning tasks, they have found that similar behaviors cannot necessarily be made to take place (Breland and Breland, 1961). In sum, a simple demonstration of similar learning curves among different species does not thereby demonstrate any universal laws of learning. The applicability of any law of learning to all species needs empirical verification, and Bitterman (1960) emphasized that such testing had by no means been provided by Skinner or any other learning psychologist. Thus, the assumption of phylogenetic continuity remains just an assumption.

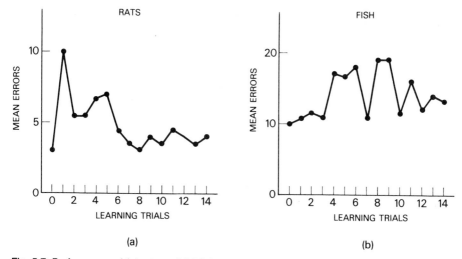

**Fig. 5.7** Performance of (a) rats and (b) fish on a specific type of learning task. *Source:* Adapted from M. E. Bitterman, "Phyletic Differences in Learning," *American Psychologist* **20** (1965). Copyright 1965 by the American Psychological Association. Reprinted by permission.

Bitterman did not just point to the need for testing this assumption, however. He began a series of important experiments designed to determine if the laws of learning are continuous across the phylogenetic scale. Accordingly, he chose for subjects species of animals other than laboratory rats. In a paper published in 1965 Bitterman reported on some of the results of his studies as well as studies by other researchers.

In some of the studies the learning capabilities of a particular species of fish were compared with rat learning. Bitterman found, when he compared the learning of these two types of animals in four different learning situations, that the laws governing the learning of this type of fish appear to be different from the laws governing rat learning. For example, Fig. 5.7, adapted from Bitterman (1965), shows that the performance of rats on one of these four learning tasks clearly improved with time. As the rats were trained, they made fewer and fewer errors. On the other hand, the performance of the fish clearly did not improve. In fact, from the curve we can see that their performance seemed to get worse. The more practice they had on the task, the more errors they seemed to make. Thus, for a given type of learning task, one species improved with practice, while the other species seemed to get worse. Clearly the laws governing this learning for these two species are not the same.

In addition, Bitterman compared the performance of the rats and the fish on the four types of learning tasks with the performances of other species on these four types of tasks. Not only did he find again evidence for discontinuity in the laws of learning, but he also found that on some tasks some species learned like rats, while on other tasks these same species learned in a manner similar to fish. Thus, while some species (e.g., monkeys) always learned in the way the rat learned and others seemed to learn in the way fish learned, some animals learned some problems the way rats did and other problems the way fish did. These findings by Bitterman are summarized in Table 5.1, adapted from his 1965 article.

**Table 5.1** Behavior of a variety of animals in four types of learning problems expressed in terms of whether their learning was similar to that of the rat or of the fish.

| Animal | Learning problem | | | |
|---|---|---|---|---|
| | 1 | 2 | 3 | 4 |
| Monkey | Rat | Rat | Rat | Rat |
| **Rat** | Rat | Rat | Rat | Rat |
| Pigeon | Rat | Rat | Rat | Fish |
| Turtle | Rat | Rat | Fish | Fish |
| **Fish** | Fish | Fish | Fish | Fish |
| Cockroach | Fish | Fish | — | — |
| Earthworm | Fish | — | — | — |

*Source*: Adapted from Bitterman, 1965.

In summary, Bitterman has argued against the seemingly well-ingrained assumption that there are universal laws of learning and only these universal laws, and that the laws of learning are necessarily continuous along the phylogenetic scale. He believes that the laws of learning of one species cannot be assumed to necessarily apply to all species. To test his argument he assessed different species of animal on different types of learning tasks and found that, simply, the same laws of learning do not seem to apply to all species. Thus, the import of Bitterman's work is to demonstrate the necessity of testing crucial developmental issues and not simply assuming that one's position on the issue is correct. Moreover, Bitterman has also provided developmental psychology with evidence against the notion that all psychological levels are the same. He has indicated that one common set of laws may not suffice in accounting for all the behavior of all species, but that there are qualitative differences among species. These differences are in kind as well as in degree. One implication of Bitterman's work is that discontinuity as well as continuity may characterize the phylogeny of learning. Another is that if there are differences among animals in the laws governing learning, it is also possible that there are differences *within* a given species. That is, ontogenetic development may also be characterized by discontinuity in the laws governing learning.

## Some Ontogenetic Implications

Support for this implication may be found in the writings of Kendler and Kendler (1962), which we reviewed in Chapter 2. However, we may now view their writings as relevant to the continuity-discontinuity issue in human development. In discussing research findings relating to the study of reversal-and nonreversal-shift problem-solving tasks, the Kendlers noted that discontinuity appears to exist in the laws governing the performance of two different species, rats and adult humans (college students), on these tasks. These two species were different in that the rats' problem-solving behavior was accounted for in terms of a relatively simple stimulus-response law, while for college students, more complex formulations involving different processes appeared necessary in order to account for behavior on this task. Kendler and Kendler viewed the differences as an instance of discontinuity (1962, p. 149).

More important here, however, the Kendlers also discussed evidence relevant to the continuity-discontinuity issue in ontogeny. They reported that comparisons of children of different ages on these same types of problem-solving tasks indicated that a marked transition appears to occur in ontogeny such that the changes could be termed discontinuous. Specifically, when very young (i.e., preschool) children were studied on these "shifting" tasks, their performance could be accounted for in terms of the same, relatively simple stimulus-response laws that appeared to govern the rats' behavior. However, when some older children ("bright" kindergarteners) were studied on these tasks, their behavior seemed best accounted for by those principles used to account for the behavior of the college students. In other words, some older children appeared to be governed in their problem-solving behavior by laws different from those that governed younger children but similar to those that governed quite older people (college students). Consistent with the organismic conceptions of development outlined in Chapter 4, the Kendlers' presentation may be interpreted to indicate that the ontogenetic development of human beings is characterized by transitions through qualitatively different functional levels; as humans progress through this functional order, the gains they eventually make are qualitatively different from the final gains achieved in the ontogeny of lower psychological levels.

Thus, the Kendlers (1962) suggest that insofar as some problem-solving tasks are concerned, the ontogeny of learning seems to be characterized by discontinuity as well as continuity. Discontinuity existed between the preschoolers and some of the kindergarteners, while continuity appeared to exist between this latter group and college students. Hence, the Kendlers provide contributions in regard to the continuity-discontinuity issue in the ontogeny of learning similar to those provided by Bitterman in regard to the continuity-discontinuity issue in the phylogeny of learning.

The contributions of both Bitterman and the Kendlers give us information essential for our consideration of the "learning position" in developmental psychology (see Chapter 10). As we will see in greater detail in that chapter, many of the notions and assumptions of learning psychologists in regard to phylogenetic development are also put forth when ontogenetic development is considered. Thus, many psychologists who opt for one universal set of laws to account for the behavior of different psychological levels also opt for one set of laws to account for ontogenetic behavioral development, and turn to "learning" to find this one set. Accordingly, many of our ideas about the continuity-discontinuity issue for phylogeny will also be relevant when we consider the learning view of ontogeny.

In fact, all of our discussions about the core conceptual issues involved in developmental psychology will be relevant to our discussions of the various theoretical views of ontogeny, which we will begin to present in the next chapter. However, let us first consider a final topic related to the continuity-discontinuity issue.

## The Stability-Instability Issue

In this chapter we have been considering the types of changes that the laws governing behavior may undergo. Thus, the assertion of continuity or discontinuity in an organism's development is really an assertion about how the laws governing an organism's behavior function and apply across its ontogeny. If the same laws apply across a person's development, this is continuity; if different laws apply, this is discontinuity.

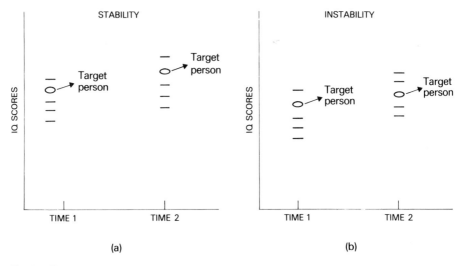

**Fig. 5.8** Examples of (a) stability and (b) instability in development.

These terms do not, however, necessarily specify what happens to a person as a function of the variables affecting his or her development. What happens to the person relative to other people as the relations among the variables that affect development change or remain the same? People may obviously be placed in groups, reference groups such as sex, age, race, ethnicity, or religion. What happens to the person's position in a reference group as the variables affecting the person function?

For example, let us consider the most common reference group in developmental psychology, an age group. Suppose that we have measured the IQ of every member of a five-year-old age group. We would expect that different people would get different IQ scores. In fact, we could rank every member of the age group from high to low, and any given person would therefore have a position in the age group. Now, what happens to this person when the variables that affect behavior function? The person's position could change, or it could remain the same relative to the other people in the age group.

Thus, whenever we consider the continuity-discontinuity issue, a second, subsidiary issue is also raised—that of *stability-instability*. If a person's position relative to his or her reference group changes with development, we term this instability. Alternatively, if a person's position relative to his or her reference group remains the same over development, we term this stability. Thus, these terms describe a person's ranking relative to some reference group. These relations are illustrated in Fig. 5.8.

Notice, however, in this figure, that in both the examples the IQ of the person in question (the target person) *increased* between time 1 and time 2 in development. This is an important point to see. Whether stability or instability occurs says nothing whatsoever about whether or not any *absolute* change took place. A person can change, and this change may still be labeled stability. This event could occur if others in the reference group also changed and thus the target person remained in the same relative position. On the other hand, a person could remain the same between time 1 and time 2 and yet his or her position relative to the reference group could be termed instable. This event could occur if others in the group changed while the target person did not. Hence, we should see that the terms stability and instability describe *relative,* not absolute, changes.

Let us illustrate this point. The concept of IQ, or intelligence quotient, is relative; it expresses a measure of a person's intelligence relative to his or her age group. For example, one way of expressing IQ is through use of the intelligence quotient formula of $IQ = MA/CA \times 100$, where $MA$ = mental age, $CA$ = chronological age, and the 100 is used to avoid fractions. Thus, if you are as bright as a five-year-old ($MA$ = 5 years) and you are five years of age ($CA$ = 5 years), then your IQ would equal 100. Similarly, if you are eight years old and you are as bright as an eight-year-old, your IQ would also equal 100. Used in this way then, we see that IQ is a relative concept. It expresses one's intelligence relative to one's age (reference) group.

Now, if a five-year-old child had an IQ of 120 and an eight-year-old child had an IQ of 100, it is clear that the five-year-old child is brighter than the eight-year-old child, because the five-year-old knows more relative to the five-year-old age group than the eight-year-old knows relative to the eight-year-old age group. Certainly if one could construct some imaginary scale of absolute knowledge, the eight-year-old would probably have more absolute knowledge than the five-year-old. Yet, we say that the five-year-old is brighter because IQ is a relative concept, and the younger child has a higher ranking in the five-year-old group reference group than the older child in his or her reference group.

Accordingly, a person's absolute knowledge may change, but if this person's age group keeps pace, then his or her IQ would be stable. Conversely, even if a person's absolute knowledge remains the same from time 1 to time 2, then his or her IQ could (1) remain the same, if the age group also did not change; (2) be unstable and even decrease, if the age group increased in its level of absolute knowledge; or (3) be unstable and even increase, if the age group decreased in its level of absolute knowledge.

We can see that stability and/or instability can be obtained in development in several ways. Stability between two times in a person's development can occur when (1) the person remains the same and so does the reference group; or (2) the person changes and so does the reference group to corresponding extents. On the other hand, instability between two times in a person's development can occur when (1) the person remains the same but the reference group changes; or (2) the person changes but so do members of the reference group to extents not corresponding with the person's degree of change. These instances of stability and instability are illustrated in Fig. 5.9, where we see, in reference to a given target person in each instance, the relative changes that comprise stability and instability.

## Relation of Continuity and Discontinuity to Stability and Instability

What we have seen is that the concepts of stability and instability describe the relative position of a developing person, while continuity and discontinuity pertain to the functioning of the laws affecting this development. In order to understand and describe the types of changes that characterize development, one can and must deal simultaneously with the two concepts (e.g., see Emmerich, 1968). That is, the processes

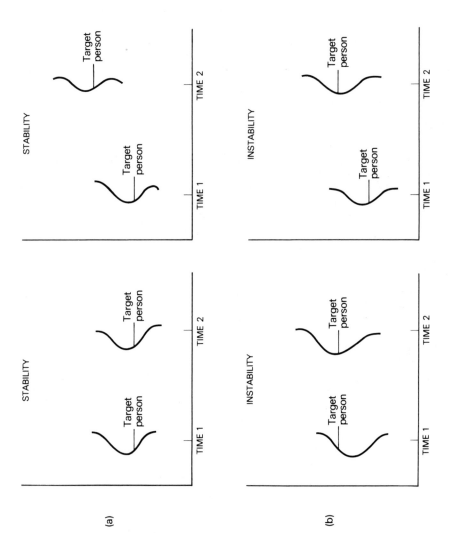

**Fig. 5.9** Two instances of the relative changes comprising (a) stability and (b) instability.

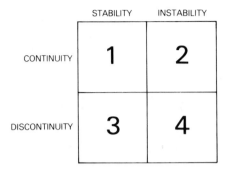

STABILITY     INSTABILITY

CONTINUITY     1     2

DISCONTINUITY     3     4

**Fig. 5.10** The interrelation of continuity-discontinuity and stability-instability.

that determine a person's development may be either continuous or discontinuous, and the functioning of these processes may result in a person's position relative to his or her reference group being stable or instable. Thus, a developmental change may be one of four types: (1) continuity and stability; (2) continuity and instability; (3) discontinuity and stability; or (4) discontinuity and instability.

These four types of changes are presented in Fig. 5.10. In box 1 we see continuity and stability. A change that is both continuous and stable is a change in which the laws governing behavior remain the same between two points in development *and* the rank ordering of people in a reference group affected by the continuous functioning of these laws remains the same. Thus, the variables involved in the determination of these people's behavior do not change, and the relative positions of the people in the group also remain the same.

In box 2 we see a second type of developmental change, continuity-instability. In this case, although the laws affecting development remain the same over time (continuity), people's relative position in their reference group changes with development. Changes of this sort would be comprised of no alterations in the variables affecting development but only changes in the ranking of people in a reference group.

In box 3 we see discontinuity and stability. Here, the laws affecting development are altered with time, but people's relative position in their reference group remains the same. Such changes are constituted by the nature of the variables involved in development changing over time (discontinuity), but people's rank ordering in their reference group remaining the same (stability).

Finally, in box 4 we see a fourth type of developmental change, discontinuity-instability. In this instance the laws governing behavioral development change, and so do the relative positions of people in a reference group affected by these changed laws. In this kind of change the variables involved in development are altered, and the rankings of people in a reference group affected by the discontinuous functioning of these variables are also changed.

In sum, we see that any developmental change may be characterized as being either continuous or discontinuous *and* either stable or instable. As we consider the theories and research in developmental psychology in succeeding chapters, we will find this cross-characterization of developmental changes quite useful because it gives us common and consistent labels to characterize any and all predicted or obtained developmental changes.

With this specification of the possible interrelations of continuity and discontinuity and stability and instability, we have concluded our presentation begun in Chapter 2 of the core conceptual issues in developmental psychology. After we summarize the points made in this chapter we will turn to a consideration of the various theoretical perspectives in developmental psychology. In making this transition we will find it useful to have an overview of the three major developmental theories, the topic of Chapter 6. As we consider each theoretical perspective, we will see the close and necessary interrelation of the concepts and the theories of psychological development.

## Summary

The continuity-discontinuity issue pertains to whether the laws involved in behavioral development remain the same (continuity) or change (discontinuity) across development. The work of Heinz Werner was drawn on in order to clarify the concepts involved in this issue.

Werner specified two different aspects of change. Quantitative change occurs when there is an abrupt change in how much of something exists. Such an abrupt change leads to gappiness in a developmental curve; this gappiness defines quantitative discontinuity. Qualitative change occurs when there is a change in what exists, when a new attribute of the organism emerges; because this emergence is something new, it cannot therefore be reduced to any earlier form. Such an epigenetic change also involves gappiness, and thus qualitative discontinuity involves both emergence and gappiness.

Werner indicates that both continuity and discontinuity should be expected to characterize development. This is the case because of the applicability of the orthogenetic principle, the general regulative principle of development. This principle asserts that whenever development occurs it proceeds from a state of relative globality and lack of differentiation to a state of increasing differentiation (i.e., discontinuity), articulation, and hierarchic integration (i.e., continuity). Hence, development is a synthesis between two opposing trends—discontinuous differentiation and continuous hierarchicalization. However, although Werner points out that both types of changes actually characterize development, whether one views development as essentially continuous or discontinuous is not primarily an empirical issue. Both Werner and Langer point out that one's theoretical view of what variables involved in development are and how they function, as well as how one in turn analyzes the data from research designed to test these theoretical ideas, influence decisions about the continuity-discontinuity issue.

We then evaluated the issues involved in deciding whether or not the phylogeny of learning is characterized by continuity or discontinuity. We saw that many "learning" psychologists assume that the laws of learning are continuously applicable to the behavioral development and functioning of all organisms. This assumption, however, is translated into a relatively untested belief. We saw that although there is evidence indicating that some animals can be made to perform in the same way in some situations, this does not mean that all animals can be made to perform in the same way in all situations. In fact, through reference to the work of Bitterman, we saw that there is considerable evidence that different laws of learning are involved in the performance of various species in the same learning situations. Hence, the same laws of learning do not necessarily apply to all species. Moreover, through reference to some of the work of Kendler and Kendler, we saw that the same laws of learning do not appear to characterize behavioral functioning at all points in the human life span. In investigating reversal- and nonreversal-shift problem-solving tasks, the Kendlers reported evidence for discontinuity in the laws involved in such task performance at various points in human ontogeny.

Finally, the subsidiary issue of stability-instability was interrelated with the continuity-discontinuity issue. This stability-instability issue pertains to the position of a person relative to a reference (e.g., age) group over the course of life. If the person's position relative to the reference group changes across development, this is instability; if the position remains the same, this is stability. Any combination between continuity-discontinuity and stability-instability may characterize the changes involved in development.

# 6

## Theories of Development: An Overview

In the previous chapters we saw the interrelation between the philosophical underpinnings and the core conceptual issues of developmental psychology. We also saw the interrelation among various conceptual issues. In turn, as we now turn to a consideration of the various general theoretical orientations in the discipline, we will see how these core conceptual issues are necessarily interrelated with the various theories of development. Just as certain philosophies of science provide an underpinning of the core conceptual issues of development, the core conceptual issues of development provide an underpinning of theories of development.

In developmental psychology several different types of theories—or approaches—to the conceptualization of psychological development have been advanced. As we will see, three of these are the *stage theory,* the *differential* approach, and the *ipsative* approach. A fourth major theoretical approach to development, the *learning-theory* approach, will be dealt with separately in Chapter 10. Here we will consider the similarities and differences among the stage, differential, and ipsative points of view, turning to the seminal work of Walter Emmerich (1968) for clarifications of the issues.

## The Stage-Theory View of Development

The *stage* approach to developmental theory may also be termed the *classical* approach, or simply, the *developmental* approach, perhaps because it was systematized first historically. Accordingly, we will use the terms stage theory, classical theory, and classical developmental theory interchangeably.

Although, as we will see in Chapter 7, various theorists have considered different aspects of development (e.g., the development of cognition, morality, and personality) using this approach, all classical developmental theories have specific, common characteristics. All of them hold that all people pass through a series of qualitatively different levels (stages) of organization and that the ordering of these stages is invariant.

To a stage theorist there are *universal* stages of development. If people develop, they will pass through all these stages, and they will do so in a fixed order. Moreover, the ordering of the stages is held to be *invariant;* this means that people cannot skip stages or reorder them. For example, let us say that a particular stage theorist postulates that there are five stages in development, such as the oral, anal, phallic, latency, and genital stages. This theorist (whom some of you may recognize as Sigmund Freud) would hold that if a person develops, he or she will pass through all these stages—that all of the stages apply to a given person's development and, in fact, all people's development— and that the order of these stages is the same for all people. Thus, it would be theoretically impossible for someone to skip a stage; one could not go right from the oral stage to the phallic stage but would have to develop through the intermediary stage, the anal stage. Similarly, one cannot reorder the sequence; thus, one could not go from the oral to the phallic and then to the anal stage. In essence, all people who develop must pass through each stage in the specified, invariant sequence.

Such theories also maintain that the stages are qualitatively different from each other. Thus, each stage has a qualitatively different organization from every other stage. In fact, the existence of qualitative differences among levels is the basis of the stage formulation. That is, the reason that one portion of time in development is labeled as one stage, while another portion of time is labeled as another stage, is because it is believed

Walter Emmerich

that within each of the two periods something qualitatively different exists. If different portions of development were not qualitatively different, there would seem to be no reason to maintain that they were in actuality different portions of development. Thus, it is necessary for the classical theorist to posit the existence of qualitatively distinct stages.

In sum, stage theorists are concerned with universal sequences in the development of all people. Thus, such theories describe the development of the *generic* human being, the general case of humanity. In addition, we can see that the laws which those advancing the stage approach theorize characterized development are laws which apply to groups of individuals (in fact, they apply to all individuals). Such laws are termed *nomothetic* laws. That is, the stage-theory approach is concerned with the postulation of general (group, nomothetic) laws of development, laws that apply to the generic human being.

## Individual Differences within Stage Theories

Despite their overriding attention to laws that characterize all people, stage theorists do recognize that people differ. But these individual differences are relatively minimal. That is, stage theorists maintain that there are only two ways in which people may differ (Emmerich, 1968). First, people may differ in their *rate of progression* through the stages, in how fast they develop. It may take one individual one year and another individual two years to pass through the same stage, but all people pass through the same stages in the same order.

The second way that people may differ, according to stage theories, is in their *final level of development reached*. Not all people will go through all the stages—for example, because of illness or death. The development of such people would stop. The point is, though, that as far as the development of such people does go, it will necessarily be in accord with the specified stage progression; and if these people had developed, they would have progressed through the stages in accordance with the specified sequence.

In sum, according to stage theory, people may differ in how *fast* they develop (rate of stage progression) and in how *far* they develop (final level of development reached).

## Developmental Transitions within Stage Theories

What happens to people as they progress through the various stages within a particular sequence? Specifically, what happens to the qualitatively distinct characteristics of a first stage when the person passes into a qualitatively different second stage?

As explained by Emmerich (1968), one of three things may happen to the characteristics of a previous stage when a person develops into the next stage. First, however, to understand any of these three possible events that may take place, we must understand that stage progression is never held to be an all-or-none event. That is, people do not progress from one stage to another overnight. It is not the case that one day a person goes to sleep in stage 1 and the next day awakes in qualitatively different stage 2. Development is *not* held to be a series of qualitative leaps, of saltatory, steplike functions. Rather, transitions from one stage to the next are gradual; they take place slowly over time.

For example, one way of determining if a person is at a particular stage in development is to see if the person shows behaviors consistent with what we would expect from knowledge of that particular stage. If the person does not show such behaviors, we could say that the person has not developed into that stage. On the other hand, however, just because a person does show responses representative of a particular stage of development does not mean that the person has fully developed into that stage. Because people progress from one stage to another gradually, they will therefore show behaviors that are representative of more than one stage at the same time. Thus, because stage progression is not an all-or-none process but rather takes place gradually over time, we would *expect* a person to show behavior representative of more than one stage of development at the same time.

How, then, may we determine what stage a person is in? Clearly, one or even a few behaviors would not be a sufficient sample to allow us to unequivocally determine a person's representative stage of development. Rather, it is necessary to get a large sample of the person's behaviors. Once we know which behaviors are representative of which stages of development, we have to observe many instances of the person's behavior. Only then can we make a stage determination. Then we may know within which stage the majority of the person's behavior falls. Thus, we are determining to which stage most of the person's behaviors relate. By determining the most frequently occurring (i.e., the modal) behavior, we are finding out what stage best represents the person's level of development.

Hence, whenever we say that a person is at a particular stage of development, we are saying this on the basis of the person's most frequently occurring (modal) behaviors. We are not saying that a person at a particular stage of development is functioning only at that one stage; in fact, as we have seen, we would expect quite the opposite to be the case. Yet, if we are judicious enough to obtain a large sample of a person's behaviors, we will also be able to ascertain which stage is most representative of his or her behaviors.

Thus, whenever we speak of a person as being at a particular stage of development, we are making a relative, not an absolute, statement, based on that person's modal response pattern. We are saying that relative to other stages of development, the modal behavior of the person is representative of a particular stage.

As we will see in Chapter 7 when we deal with specific stage theories of development, it is crucial to understand the meaning of saying that a person is at a particular developmental stage. Psychologists have not always understood that people function at more than one developmental level at a time and, that attributing the status of a particular stage to a person is based on a large sampling and determination of the person's modal behaviors. Hence, the discussion in Chapter 7 of the specific stage theories of Piaget and of Kohlberg will be particularly relevant. At present, however, we will consider each of the three different possible things that may occur to the characteristics of one stage when the person makes a transition to the next developmental stage.

As pointed out by Emmerich (1968, p. 674), the first thing that could happen when a person completes a transition from one stage of development into the next is that the characteristics of the first stage may be completely displaced. This is the most extreme view of what may happen when transition from one stage to the next is complete. In essence, this view holds that when transition is complete the person will be completely newly organized and the characteristics of the previous stage will be lost. Of course, even this radical transition takes place gradually, and accordingly, as we have explained above, even in this case the person will show evidence of behavioral characteristics of both developmental levels while the transition is still occurring.

In the second type of completed transition, the later stage becomes the dominant level of functioning, but the behavioral characteristics of the previous stage are still seen. This second possibility is similar to the general notions of gradual stage transition already discussed. It points out that stage development is a modal phenomenon. This alternative, then, stresses the notion that current stages are dominant in that behaviors representative of that stage are most frequent. However, the behavioral characteristics of earlier stages are not lost, although they do occur at a lower frequency than the modal behaviors. In fact, it is sometimes held that under some circumstances the lower frequency behaviors can for a time become dominant in frequency (Emmerich, 1968, p. 674).

The third possibility is similar to the second. Here, however, when the new stage has fully emerged, the behavioral characteristics of the earlier stage do not typically occur. That is, the characteristics of the new stage will be the only characteristics that are typically seen. The characteristics of the earlier stage lie dormant, or latent, and are not typically seen. In certain special circumstances, however, the earlier characteristics may emerge (Emmerich, 1968, p. 674).

In sum, several types of transitions between stages may occur within classical developmental theories. Different stage theories may opt for any one of these alternatives. Of course, the difficulty for the researcher who wants to test these different alternatives is in measuring differences that would be predicted by each alternative to occur. It would be difficult to discriminate among these three types of transitions because, in any event, all the transitions take place gradually. Hence, by the time a given stage has almost completely displaced a previous stage as a person's dominant level of functioning, another stage may be beginning to displace this now dominant stage. Hence, because of this *stage mixture* (Turiel, 1969), stage development is very complex, and it is most difficult to ascertain which of the three types of stage transitions best characterizes development. However, this very complexity is the major point of our present discussion. Because of the gradual nature of stage transition, a person functions at more than one qualitatively different stage at the same time. Thus, stage mixture is an essential component of any stage theory of development.

## Relation of Concepts of Development to Stage Theories

It should be clear where stage theorists stand in terms of at least some of the concepts we have considered in the earlier chapters—for example, the continuity-discontinuity issue. By definition, stage theorists consider development to include qualitatively discontinuous phenomena. In specifying that the sequential emergence of qualitatively different levels of functioning characterizes development, stage theorists are defining development as being qualitatively discontinuous.

On the other hand, however, most stage theorists also recognize that there are certain laws that function invariantly across a person's life span. Hence, the postulation of such functional invariants indicates that most stage theorists, for example, Jean Piaget, recognize that development is characterized by continuity as well as discontinuity. We will see in Chapter 7 that, consistent with the notions of Heinz Werner, Jean Piaget's organismic theory characterizes development as continuous (general laws) as well as discontinuous (specific laws). In sum, even though stage theorists define development as being qualitatively discontinuous, most theorists also recognize continuous laws that exist throughout development.

Second, as might be expected, stage theorists, in viewing development as an organismic phenomenon, typically take an interactionist viewpoint in respect to the nature-nurture controversy. Thus, to differing extents, all stage theorists look at an interaction between intrinsic (nature) and extrinsic (nurture) variables in accounting for behavioral development. However, different theorists put differing degrees of emphasis on nature and nurture factors. Thus, Piaget puts greater emphasis on an interaction between nature and nurture factors than do Freud and Erikson, who place greater emphasis on nature variables and view the nurture variables as either facilitators or inhibitors of primarily intrinsic emergences (Emmerich, 1968; Kohlberg, 1966). For example, we will see in Chapter 8 that Erikson places a good deal of emphasis on the "maturational ground plan" that he believes exists in all people. Thus, to Erikson, although a child must interact within society in order to develop normally, the stage emergences that characterize a child's development are primarily maturational in origin.

Moreover, just as stage theorists differ to some extent on the specifics of the nature-nurture interaction, they also differ about the subsidiary, critical-periods issue. It may be said that in one sense all stage theorists support a critical-periods notion, in that in each qualitatively different stage something unique is developing. This unique development, which gives the stage its qualitative distinctiveness, is by definition supposed to be developing at this particular point. Because stage theorists define development as being comprised of qualitatively distinct phenomena that arise in a universal, invariant sequence, they therefore maintain that not all periods in development have equal potentiality for any particular development. Thus, each specific stage has its own specific emergence, which by its very existence serves to define that period in ontogeny as a stage. In this sense, each stage has its own critical development.

Yet, different stage theorists have different ideas about "how critical is critical." They disagree about the implications for later development of inappropriate development within a given stage. For some stage theorists, if one does not develop what one should develop in a given stage, then one will never have another chance for such development. Thus, each given stage of development is truly critical, in that if one does not develop appropriately within a given period, irreversible, unfavorable implications will be inevitable. Such extreme views will be illustrated in Chapter 7 by the theory of Freud and in Chapter 8 by the theory of Erikson.

In addition, as might be surmised from the above, stage theorists similarly differ about the source of critical periods. Just as different stage theorists place contrasting emphases on nature and nurture factors in explaining the interactive basis of development, they correspondingly place different emphases on these factors in accounting for the critical nature of different stages. Those theorists who lay greater emphasis on nature (maturational) factors in accounting for stage development similarly place greater stress on maturation as being the source of the criticalness of critical periods.

In sum, we see that all stage theorists present theories that speak to the various core conceptual issues of development. In the next two chapters we will see how different stage theorists deal with these issues within the context of their specific theories. At present, however, let us turn though to the second type of approach that conceptualizes development.

## The Differential Approach to Development

Those concerned with a differential approach to development begin their inquiry by posing what is basically an empirical question: "How in the course of development do groups of people become assorted into subgroups, subgroups which are differentiated on the basis of status and behavior attributes?" (Emmerich, 1968, p. 671).

In its most basic form the differential approach to development is primarily an empirical, rather than a theoretical, system; it uses particular research methods to study differences among groups of people and individuals within these groups. Thus, as we will see, the differential approach does not necessarily connote any given theoretical point of view, but can be used by people having various theoretical perspectives.

The main focus of the differential approach is to discover how people become sorted into subgroups over the course of their development. Subgroups are formed, or differentiated, on the basis of one of two types of attributes. The first is status attributes. Status attributes are characteristics that place people in particular demographic categories or groups, such as those based on age, sex, race, religion, and socioeconomic status (SES). A differentiation of people into subgroups on the basis of age, sex, and race is illustrated in Fig. 6.1.

Obviously, however, there is nothing really psychological about differentiating a group of people on the basis of their status attributes. The psychological component of the differential approach arises when people are further differentiated on the basis of the second type of attributes, *behavioral attributes*. Behavioral attributes may be

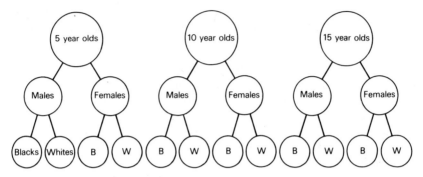

**Fig. 6.1** A group of people differentiated into subgroups on the basis of the status attributes of age, sex, and race.

considered bipolar behavioral or psychological dimensions. For example, a behavioral attribute would be any dimension such as:

extroversion_____introversion

dominance_____submission

aggression_____passivity

high activity level_____low activity level

independence_____dependence

trust_____mistrust

A behavioral attribute is really a continuum, which has opposite traits, or characteristics at either end. A differential psychologist using the term behavioral attribute, then, is referring to psychological traits considered as a bipolar continuum. Hence, behavioral attributes such as independence-dependence or high activity level-low activity level are really bipolar traits running along a continuum. People grouped toward one end of each of the continua might therefore be termed independent or high active, while people grouped toward the other end of each continua might be termed dependent or low active.

The goal of a psychologist using the differential approach for the study of psychological development would be, then, to discover the subgroups that people become assorted into on the basis of both their behavioral and status attributes. The differential psychologist would choose some behavioral attributes (e.g., aggression-passivity and independence-dependence) as well as some selected status attributes (e.g., age—five-year-olds and ten-year-olds—and sex) for study, and then try to discover how in the course of development people in these groups become differentiated.

For example, the psychologist would see if the five-year-old boys as a subgroup are located along the aggression-passivity and the independence-dependence continua at points different from the five-year-old girls. The psychologist would also ask these same questions of the ten-year-old male and female subgroups. Thus, in relation

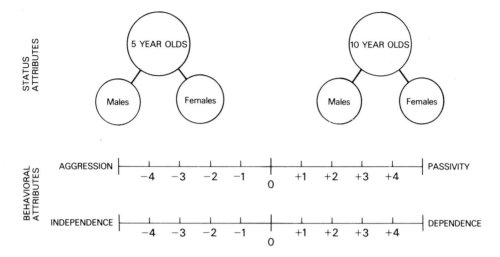

Fig. 6.2(a)  Design of a differential study of the relation of two status attributes to two behavioral attributes.

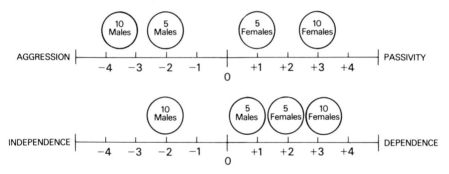

Fig. 6.2(b)  Some imaginary findings of such a study.

to the status attributes of age and sex, the psychologist would be able to discover if these people form subgroups located at different points along the behavioral dimensions. The psychologist would be able to see if five-year-old girls as a subgroup are more or less aggressive than five-year-old boys, for example; or for that matter, the psychologist would be able to see how each subgroup compares with every other subgroup in terms of relative location along each of the studied bipolar dimensions. The design of such an inquiry is illustrated in Fig. 6.2 (a), and in Fig. 6.2 (b) some imaginary results are depicted in order to illustrate the above points. In this figure we see that the four subgroups differentiated on the basis of status attributes are also differentiated on the basis of their location along the bipolar behavioral dimensions. That is, the spaces occupied on these dimensions by the subgroups are different.

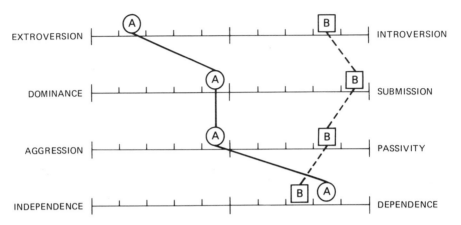

**Fig. 6.3** Individuality within the differential approach: Individual A and individual B have different locations on each of the four dimensions.

### Individual Differences within the Differential Approach

The differential approach is primarily concerned with groups, or better, subgroups, of people. Accordingly, in attempting to ascertain how such subgroups become differentiated with development, the differential approach is concerned with discovering nomothetic laws. Those taking the differential approach do not necessarily posit universal group laws of development and are thus different from the nomothetic stage theorists. Yet, differential psychologists *are* concerned with nomothetic laws, insofar as they are concerned with ascertaining the variables that predict how groups are differentiated into subgroups over the course of development.

However, more than is true with stage theorists, differential psychologists are interested in ascertaining the dimensions of individual differences in development. Consistent with the way that they conceptualize subgroup differences, they define individual differences in terms of different locations along various bipolar dimensions. Just as subgroups have different locations along each of these dimensions, so do individuals. Thus, each individual has his or her own location in multidimensional space. This is illustrated in Fig. 6.3 for two individuals, each of whom takes up a different space along each of the four shown dimensions. In sum, then, within the differential approach individuality is defined as one's location in multidimensional space (Emmerich, 1968, p. 678).

### The Study of Development within the Differential Approach

Although the differential approach can be used simply as an empirical approach within which to consider development, we will see that it also can be combined with specific theoretical formulations. For example, we will see in Chapter 8 that Erik Erikson, primarily a stage theorist, employs a differential formulation within each of his "eight stages of man." Similarly, just as stage theorists may use the differential approach within their qualitatively discontinuous theoretical point of view, other theorists may use differential ideas within theoretical approaches that stress continuity throughout development (e.g., Cattell, 1957). The point here is that the differential approach is not mutually exclusive of other approaches and, in fact, may be successfully interrelated with those such as the classical developmental point of view.

We have said, however, that the differential approach may be used in an initially empirical way. A researcher may have no previously formulated ideas about whether development is characterized by continuity or discontinuity and thus may adopt the differential approach in order to see which of these two concepts best describes the development of certain subgroups of people. Particular types of research methodology and statistical analyses of their results—for example, statistics that can readily show how many dimensions are needed to characterize subgroups of people—are typically employed by differential psychologists. Thus, such statistical procedures as correlational analysis, factor analysis, or cluster analysis are used. These procedures have common bases and, when used within the context of the differential approach, have a common goal—to see how variables comprised of status and behavioral attributes group together over the course of development.

For example, do the same groups of behavioral attributes characterize girls when they are five, ten, fifteen, and twenty years of age? Or do the dimensions that must be used to group these differently aged girls alter? Questions such as these are answered by the above statistical procedures. For instance, factor analysis, the most sophisticated of these procedures, would be used to discern whether the number of dimensions that differentiated the groups stayed the same or changed over time and whether the group of behavioral attributes that related to each other at time 1 in development remained in the same relation at time 2.

To specify the exact details of these statistical procedures is well beyond the purposes of the present discussion. Still, a simplified illustration of the use of these procedures within the differential approach will clarify and convey their utility. Suppose a researcher is studying boys and girls aged five, ten, and fifteen years of age. In relation to these status attributes the researcher wishes to learn how these people form into subgroups on the basis of fifty behavioral attributes, fifty bipolar dimensions. The researcher labels the fifty variables by their number and measures each of the subjects on each of the variables. He or she next performs a factor analysis on each of the age-sex subgroups, that is, statistically analyzes the scores on the variables (the behavioral attributes) to determine if some of the variables seem to relate to each other very much (and thus form a *factor*) while not similarly relating to the other variables. The researcher finds that for both the five-year-old males and the five-year-old females the same variables seem to group together, that is, the scores on each of the first twenty variables are consistent (correlated) with each other but are not so related to any of the remaining thirty variables.

Thus, the first twenty variables form a factor. Similarly, the next fifteen variables form a second factor, and the last fifteen variables form a third factor. Thus, the five-year-old males and females are found to be similarly differentiated on the basis of three similar groupings of variables. The structure of the relationship among the variables—*the factor structure*—is the same. With both subgroups of subjects the same variables cluster together.

This finding may not mean, however, that the males and females have identical sets of scores on each of the variables within a factor. Suppose that factor 1 is aggression-passivity and that some of the behavioral bipolar dimensions comprising this factor are:

looks for fights_____stays away from fights

teases others_____gets teased

yells when bothered_____quiet when bothered

Other variables within the factor are similar to these, and thus the researcher might reasonably opt to give this factor a name such as "aggression-passivity." In order for each of the variables in this factor to relate to each other, and thus form a factor, we would expect the scores on the variables within the factor to be consistent. For instance, we would expect a person scoring high (or low) on one variable in the factor to score similarly high (or low) on each of the other variables. Thus, despite whether a subgroup scores high and/or low on all of the variables, the variables would form a factor so long as all the people in the subgroup score similarly on each of the variables. Hence, the same factor could be obtained for both the five-year-old boys and girls even if each group's scores are not identical, even if they are in the opposite direction. For instance, the boys may have higher aggression scores than the girls on all the variables comprising the factor. Of course, this does not mean that boys and girls do not vary among themselves. The point here is that the boys may vary along the aggression-passivity continuum at points closer to the aggression end of the continuum than do girls.

Now, with the above findings about the factor structure of the five-year-old males and females, the differential psychologist may proceed to assess developmental changes or consistencies in the ten- and fifteen-year-old subgroups. In doing so, the psychologist will necessarily be addressing some of the core conceptual issues of psychological development—the continuity-discontinuity and the stability-instability issues.

**Continuity-Discontinuity.** When looking at results across age levels, the differential psychologist will be primarily concerned with whether the subgroup differentiations found at earlier age levels (e.g., with the five-year-olds) remain the same or change at older age levels. If the same variables seem to relate to each other in the same way at all age levels, this is continuity. If, however, differences from earlier patterns are found, this is discontinuity. Specifically, the differential psychologist may find continuity if, for example, the same number of factors, with the same variables comprising them, exist in the older subgroups. Alternatively, discontinuity may be discovered if, for example, a different number of factors exists within the older subgroups. Also, discontinuity may be found even if the same factors exist but different behavioral attributes comprise the factors. That is, bipolar dimensions not included in earlier age-level factors may be related to older age-level factors or vice versa.

In Fig. 6.4 we see an imaginary example of such differential research, illustrating the discovery of both continuity and discontinuity using the differential approach. Continuity exists between both the five-year-old male and female subgroups and both the ten-year-old male and female subgroups. The same number of factors exists in each subgroup and, in addition, the variables comprising each factor remain the same.

| | 5 YEAR OLDS | | 10 YEAR OLDS | | 15 YEAR OLDS | |
|---|---|---|---|---|---|---|
| | Males | Females | Males | Females | Males | Females |
| | Variables | | Variables | | Variables | |
| FACTOR A | 1−20 | 1−20 | 1−20 | 1−20 | 1−15 | 1−20 |
| FACTOR B | 21−35 | 21−35 | 21−35 | 21−35 | 16−30 | 16−25 |
| FACTOR C | 36−50 | 36−50 | 36−50 | 36−50 | 31−50 | 26−40 |
| FACTOR D | | | | | | 41−50 |

**Fig. 6.4** An imaginary example of hypothetical findings of differential research, illustrating both continuity (between five and ten years of age) and discontinuity (between ten and fifteen years of age).

However, discontinuity exists between the ten-year-old and fifteen-year-old subgroups. With the males, the same number of factors still exists at both age levels, but the meaning of the factors is different because different variables comprise the factors of the fifteen-year-old males as compared with the ten-year-old males. With the females discontinuity also exists. Here, however, the reason is primarily due to the emergence of a new factor (D) among the fifteen-year-old females.

**Stability-Instability.** In addition to being able to analyze whether or not the same variables account for differentiation throughout development (continuity-discontinuity), the differential psychologist is able to determine whether a person's rank on a variable and on a factor within his or her subgroup remains the same or changes with time. Each subgroup is, of course, composed of individuals who have scores on each of the measured variables. Although these scores may be similar, it will still be possible to rank order all of the individuals in a subgroup, from high to low. Thus, a person's rank for a variable may change with development; as we have seen, when such a change relative to one's reference group occurs, we term this instability. If a person's rank on a variable remains the same across time, we term this stability.

Consistent with what we have said in Chapter 5, Emmerich (1968, pp. 676–677) points out that any thorough analysis of development from the differential point of view must consider the issues of continuity-discontinuity and stability-instability at the same time. As illustrated in Chapter 5, any combination of continuity-discontinuity and stability-instability may occur. In reference specifically to the differential approach, Emmerich (1968, p. 677) points out the following:

1. *Continuity and stability* may occur when the factors (and the variables within them) remain the same for subgroups from time 1 to time 2, and accordingly, individuals' rankings with their respective subgroups remain unaltered.

2. *Continuity and instability* may occur when the factors (and the variables within them) remain the same for subgroups from time 1 to time 2, but despite this consistency, individuals' rankings within their respective subgroups change.

3. *Discontinuity and stability* may occur when factors (and/or the variables within them) are altered for subgroups from time 1 to time 2, but despite these changes individuals are ranked in similar ways within these new subgroupings.

4. *Discontinuity and instability* may occur when the factors (and/or the variables within them) change for subgroups from time 1 to time 2, and individuals' rankings are accordingly altered.

We will have reason to return in Chapter 8 to some of these possible interrelations, in order to understand the results of a specific instance of research done with a differential approach—the important work of Kagan and Moss (1962). At present, however, let us conclude our analysis of the differential approach by reviewing the relation of this approach to the conceptual issues of development we dealt with earlier.

### Relation of Concepts of Development to the Differential Approach

We have seen that those employing a differential approach deal primarily with the continuity-discontinuity and stability-instability issues and that the differential approach may be interrelated with other approaches to the understanding of development. When this approach is interrelated with stage theories of development, as in the case of Erikson's theory of psychosocial development (1959, 1964), the stage formulations in a sense take theoretical precedence. That is, when Erikson uses differential formulations within the context of his stage theory, the continuity-discontinuity of behavioral development does not remain an empirical question; rather, development is held to proceed through eight qualitatively different stages.

The above interrelation by Erikson really does not take anything away from the differential approach. As more of an approach to the study, rather than a theoretical view, of development, the differential approach does not *a priori* (before the fact) maintain a position relative to the continuity-discontinuity issue. Moreover, it in no way speaks to the nature-nurture or related issues. That is, the differential approach in no way offers formulations that specify the sources of differential developmental subgroupings, rather, it may be used within the context of contrasting theoretical perspectives. In sum, while we have seen that stage theory must necessarily take *a priori* theoretical stands relative to the continuity-discontinuity and nature-nurture issues, this is not necessarily the case with the differential approach. It is the case, however, with the ipsative approach, the last conceptual approach to the study of development we will consider in this chapter. Let us turn then to the ipsative approach to development.

### The Ipsative Approach to Development

As compared with the stage and the differential approaches to developmental psychology, the *ipsative* approach is primarily *idiographic* in orientation. That is, the goal of the ipsative approach is to discover individual (rather than group) laws of behavioral development. Those opting for an ipsative approach might argue that laws of behavioral development that apply only to groups, and not to the individuals within them, are meaningless, and would thus try to ascertain the variables involved in an individual's development. If these findings could then be applied to larger groups of people (e.g., to help better understand any qualifications in application of group laws to individuals), so much the better for the science of psychological development.

Accordingly, the ipsative approach considers intraindividual consistencies and changes in the development of the person (Emmerich, 1968). It asks whether or not the variables that comprise the individual remain the same or change throughout the individual's ontogeny.

Those taking the ipsative approach seek to understand the makeup of the individual in two ways. First, an attempt is made to ascertain the specific *attributes*, or psychological variables, that comprise the person (Emmerich, 1968). These attributes may be characteristics such as personality traits (e.g., dependency, aggression), temperamental styles (e.g., high activity level, low threshold for responsivity), or any such psychological/behavioral variables. Moreover, these attributes may be unique to the person or common among many people (like the personality traits illustrated above). In any event, the first task of the ipsative approach is to find out what attributes comprise the individual, to discover the individual's *attribute repertoire*. For example, a psychologist may be interested in discovering a person's values. Accordingly, the psychologist might discover that at age fifteen a given person was comprised of four values (e.g., values about one's body, about sex, education, and religion), while at age twenty-five an additional two values had come to comprise this person's value attribute repertoire (e.g., values about a career and about raising a family).

Second, attributes certainly have an organization. Some attributes may be central in that they serve to organize other attributes, while others may be subordinate. Alternatively, we may think of the organization of attributes in terms of attribute clusters. For instance, some attributes may be grouped together, while others may not. By analogy, one might view this attribute organization in terms of intraindividual attribute factors. Thus, a person may have several personality attributes clustered together, and these attributes may be independent of, for example, the person's cluster of value attributes and of temperamental attributes. Moreover, within a particular cluster, a specific attribute may be superordinate. Thus, the sex value may be superordinate to a person at a particular time in life, with all other values subordinate, viewed in terms of the overriding importance of the sexual value. In any event, the second task of the ipsative approach is to attempt to understand a person's *attribute interrelation,* how the attributes that comprise the person are related to each other.

For example, suppose an individual is comprised of three certain types of value attributes—religious, sexual, and economic. Although it is possible that these same three values may comprise the person's attribute repertoire at different times in life, the values may be interrelated differently over time. For instance, at age seventeen, the person's sexual value may be most important (superordinate), with the others subordinate. Now, this attribute interrelation may stay the same over time, but it might also change. For instance, at age thirty-seven, the economic value may be superordinate and the sexual value not as important—it has now fallen to second order importance perhaps, although the religious value maintains its previous intraindividual position. Still later, however, perhaps at age sixty-seven, these same three values may still comprise the person's repertoire, but once again they are interrelated differently. Thus, at this age the person's religious value may be most important, while the economic value has fallen to second and the sexual value to third.

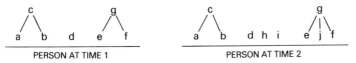

**Fig. 6.5** An example of ipsative change: The person's attribute repertoire changes from time 1 to time 2.

**Fig. 6.6** An example of ipsative change: The attributes in a person's repertoire are interrelated differently at time 1 and time 2.

In sum, those taking an ipsative approach to the study of development seek to discover the laws that account for an individual's development by attempting to find the person's attribute repertoire—those characteristics comprising the person—and attribute interrelation—the intraindividual organization of these attributes. Thus, the ipsative problem in development is to discern intraindividual consistencies and changes in the attributes and the organization of these attributes over the course of an individual's development. A person may change over the course of development as a function of new attributes existing in his or her repertoire. Such an intraindividual change in attribute repertoire is illustrated in Fig. 6.5, in which we see that at time 1 the person was comprised of seven attributes (a–g), while at time 2, three new variables (h–j) are in the repertoire.

But even if the attributes in a person's repertoire remain the same in development, the person may change ipsatively if the attributes are interrelated differently over time. This second type of change that can occur intraindividually in development is illustrated in Fig. 6.6, in which we see that although the same number of attributes exists in the person's repertoire at times 1 and 2 in development, the interrelation of the attributes is different at these two times. At time 1, attributes a, b (subordinate), and c (superordinate) cluster together, as do attributes e, f, g, and h. Attribute d does not cluster with either of these two groups. At time 2, however, the organization of the attributes is different. Here we see that attribute d now clusters along with attributes a, b, and c, while attribute g has now become independent of the attribute e, f, and h cluster.

Of course, *both* the number of attributes in the person's repertoire and the attribute interrelation may change over the course of development. If the attribute repertoire changes, then of course the person will have changed; but even if the attribute repertoire remains the same, the person can still change through a change in the attribute interrelation. Either or both of these changes may comprise an individual's development.

## Individual Differences within the Ipsative Approach

It should be clear that individual differences are the essence of the ipsative approach. The goal of this approach is to ascertain idiographic laws, that is, laws applying to an individual's development. Accordingly, the result is the formulation of highly specific generalizations about the course of an individual's development. Analysis begins at the level of the individual, because, it is held, general laws of development may not apply equally to all individuals. Hence, one should first understand how the individual develops before one tries to understand how large groups of individuals develop.

In stressing this view, however, those taking an ipsative approach are not denying either the necessity for studying, or the validity of, general laws of development. Rather, they are stressing a different aspect of the problem of developmental analysis. They are trying first to understand the role of the individual in his or her own development. Accordingly, they would suggest that particular attributes of a person may be unique; but they would not disregard the possibility that other attributes of the individual may be similar to those of other individuals. Thus, the stress of the ipsative approach is not that all people are *completely* different, but rather that in order to understand all of the phenomena of development one must deal with the particular intraindividual laws of development.

## Developmental Changes within the Ipsative Approach

In a general way, we have seen that within an ipsative perspective people may change through development on the basis of changes in their attribute repertoire and/or their attribute interrelation. But are such intraindividual changes systematic? Do they follow a predictable pattern, or are they unique to each and every individual? In other words, are there any principles that may be used to understand the nature of the intraindividual changes comprising development?

Due to the clarifications provided by Emmerich (1968, pp. 679–81), the answer to all these questions may be considered yes. Although Emmerich points out that traditionally there was little evidence of systematic ipsative developmental theorizing, he suggests that a principle exists allowing such conceptualization to proceed. This is a general, regulative principle of development, describing the course of developmental changes *whenever* development occurs. This principle is one we are familiar with — Werner's *orthogenetic principle.*

As discussed in Chapter 5, the orthogenetic principle holds that whenever development occurs, it proceeds from a state of globality and lack of differentiation to a state of differentiation, integration, and hierarchical organization. Individuals, of course, develop. Therefore, we would expect the orthogenetic principle to hold for the intraindividual development of a person. It would imply that no matter what the specific attribute repertoire of a person may be, the developmental changes in this attribute repertoire follow a specific, systematic course. All changes of the intraindividual attributes comprising any person would proceed in accordance with the orthogenetic principle.

Hence, even if all individuals were completely unique, their development would still be in accord with the descriptions provided by the orthogenetic principle. Therefore, we would expect that as an individual develops from time 1 to time 2, his or her attribute repertoire and attribute interrelation should develop along specific, systematic lines. Thus, we would expect that:

1. An individual's attribute repertoire should be relatively global and undifferentiated at time 1 in development but more differentiated at time 2. In other words, as an

individual develops, new and more differentiated attributes should emerge in his attribute repertoire. Thus, in terms of the ipsative attribute repertoire, the orthogenetic principle suggests that *discontinuity* should characterize development. Differentiated attributes should emerge from global attributes.

2. An individual's attribute interrelation should change, increasing in hierarchical organization with development. At time 1 a person's attribute interrelation would be less integrated, less hierarchically organized than at time 2. Thus, in terms of the ipsative attribute interrelation, the orthogenetic principle suggests that *continuity* should characterize development. The attribute interrelation should become increasingly more hierarchically organized over the course of an individual's development.

In sum, then, we see that when the orthogenetic principle is applied to intraindividual development, ipsative development may be held to follow certain systematic changes. There will be discontinuous changes when the person develops from time 1 to time 2 in his or her ontogeny, because the attribute repertoire will go from a state of globality to a state of differentiation. In addition, there will be continuous changes when the person develops from time 1 to time 2, because the attribute interrelation will become increasingly more hierarchically organized.

## Relation of Concepts of Development to the Ipsative Approach

We have seen that when the ipsative approach is interrelated with the orthogenetic principle, the ipsative approach takes a clear position on the continuity-discontinuity issue. As discussed in Chapter 5, the orthogenetic principle implies both continuity and discontinuity in development, and, accordingly, when this principle is applied to the ipsative approach, this approach also characterizes development as having both continuous and discontinuous components. Thus, when this interrelation is achieved, the continuity-discontinuity issue does not remain an empirical issue for those taking the ipsative approach but becomes a theoretical issue, because those taking this approach now maintain that development is both continuous and discontinuous in character.

The ipsative approach is also useful in its applicability to the nature-nurture issue. We have seen that an essential consideration of the ipsative approach is the role of the laws governing the individual. In other words, this approach is concerned with the contribution the individual makes to his or her own development. This is consistent with the orientation of Schneirla (1957) presented in Chapter 4. As Schneirla (1957) suggested, the experiential-maturational interaction that provides the source of all individuals' development functions to give each person an individual set of behavioral characteristics; this behavioral individuality provides, then, a "third source" of the individual's development through the establishment of circular functions and self-stimulation in ontogeny. Thus, ipsatively oriented psychologists, in focusing on the person's behavioral individuality, can ascertain how the individual—in interaction with his or her environment—provides a source of his or her own development. Thus, such psychologists would necessarily be taking an interactionist stance in respect to the nature-nurture controversy; and they would, by attempting to discover the contributions of the individual to his or her own development, be ascertaining important evidence bearing on this aspect of the nature-nurture interaction. In Chapter 9 we will see how a group of ipsatively oriented psychiatrists and psychologists (Thomas, Chess, Birch,

Hertzig, and Korn) has begun to study the contributions of a person's behavioral individuality to his or her own development and has thus begun to provide information about the organism-environmental interactions which comprise one essential dimension of nature-nurture interactions.

Moreover, another notion involved within the ipsative orientation is in accord with this person-environment interaction. We have noted that the ipsative approach recognizes that while it is possible for people to have completely unique attribute repertoires, it is also possible for people to have attribute repertoires that are very similar, if not identical. Accordingly, from an ipsative point of view we may identify people who have similar attribute repertoires at time 1 in their development and study them longitudinally, that is, across time. Some of these people will remain similar at time 2, while some will become different. Thus, by focusing on the different types of person-environment interactions these people experienced, we may discover how specific interactions provide a source of an individual's development. By discovering the laws that function to change people who were similar at time 1 into people who either remained similar or became different at time 2, we may learn about the specific characteristics of organism-environmental interactions as they provide a "third source" of behavioral development.

Alternatively, of course, we could also focus on people who had different attribute repertoires and/or interrelations at time 1 and study those people who remained different and who became similar at time 2. By assessing the organism-environmental interactions of these groups we might further discover how the characteristics of the individual in interaction with his or her environment provide a source of the individual's own development.

In sum, we see that the ipsative approach can be considered to take a stand on the continuity-discontinuity issue and to be potentially extremely useful in providing information about nature-nurture interactions as a source of development. The ipsative, the differential, and the stage approaches represent contrasting orientations toward the study of development. Yet, all elaborate concepts that bear on the core conceptual issues of development. These approaches—along with the fourth major theoretical view of psychological development, the learning-theory approach (which will be detailed in Chapter 10)—provide different theoretical ideas about development; and accordingly, the empirical questions and concomitant research studies done by those concerned with each respective approach are quite different. Still, all of the approaches to the theoretical conceptualization of development do provide us with ideas, and eventually with facts, which at our current state of knowledge are essential in attempting to understand the complexities of psychological development.

Accordingly, in the following chapters we will deal with specific examples of the three above approaches. Thus, in Chapter 7 we will discuss some major stage theories (those of Piaget, Kohlberg, and S. Freud); in Chapter 8 we will consider two examples of differential approaches (Erikson—who combines differential ideas within a stage-theory framework—and Kagan and Moss); and in Chapter 9 we will look at an example of the ipsative approach (the work of Thomas *et al.*). Finally, in Chapter 10 we will consider a last major approach that may be used to conceptualize development, the learning-theory approach (the ideas of such people as Skinner, Bijou and Baer, Gewirtz, and White).

## Summary

The stage, differential, and ipsative approaches to the conceptualization of development were presented. Within stage theories of development it is held that all people pass through a series of qualitatively different levels (stages) of organization and that the ordering of these stages is invariant. According to such theories, people differ in only two ways: in their rate of development and in the final level of development attained.

Stage transition is not viewed as an all-or-none process. That is, people pass from one stage to the next with gradualness. Accordingly, people may exhibit behaviors representative of more than one stage of development at a given point in their lives. Hence, stage determination becomes a matter of modal attribution. Although any of three types of stage transitions are possible in development, discrimination among these types of transitions is difficult because of the above described stage mixture.

While all stage theorists believe that qualitative discontinuity characterizes development, many such theorists also see development as a synthesis between such discontinuity and continuous laws of development. Stage theorists like Piaget view development organismically, that is, as representing a dialectical synthesis between continuity and discontinuity. Hence, because such an organismic position is taken, stage theorists typically maintain an interactionist conception of nature-nurture interrelations. This is the case despite a tendency on the part of some stage theorists (e.g., Erikson) to put primary emphasis on essentially maturational trends.

Within the differential approach to development a concern is taken about how, in the course of development, groups of people become differentiated into subgroups. These subgroups are differentiated on the basis of (1) status attributes—characteristics that place a person in a particular demographic category; and (2) behavioral attributes—bipolar behavioral or psychological dimensions. The differential approach may be used as an empirical approach to the study of development and may be incorporated into a theoretical system.

Differential psychologists attempt to specify the location of various status subgroups of people along each of the multiple number of bipolar dimensions usually assessed in such research. Similarly, the individual is also viewed as existing within such a multidimensional space. Through the use of such techniques as factor or cluster analysis, differential psychologists are able to discern whether the variable interrelation that characterizes a subgroup at a particular time in development continues (continuity) to similarly represent the subgroup across the life span, or whether the structure of such interrelation is altered (discontinuity) as a function of development. The differential psychologist's utilization of such techniques also allows a determination of the relative position of individuals within subgroups across the life span. Hence, the stability-instability issue is also addressed through application of this approach.

As compared with the stage and the differential approaches to development, which are relatively nomothetic in orientation, the ipsative approach is idiographic in orientation. The goal of this latter approach, then, is to discover laws of development that apply (primarily) to the individual. Thus, this approach seeks to specify intraindividual consistencies and changes in the development of a person across life. Such similarities or changes are considered in the context of the attributes that comprise the individual—the attribute repertoire—and how these attributes relate to each other—the attribute interrelation. People may change because the attributes in their repertoire increase (or decrease) across development and/or because the interrelation of one attribute to another is altered across life.

Ipsative psychologists do not deny the presence or applicability of general, group laws of development. However, such psychologists assert that general laws of development may not apply equally to all individuals and that therefore one should first understand how the individual develops before trying to understand how large groups of people develop. Hence, while placing primary focus on the individual course of development, such psychologists may also attempt to interrelate individual development with principles of development that appear to generally characterize changes across the life span. Thus, an interrelation of the ipsative view of development with principles such as orthogenesis may be made. The application of the orthogenetic principle to ipsative development would lead to the prediction that both differentiation of the individual's attribute repertoire and hierarchical integration of the person's attribute interrelation should characterize all individual development. Finally, in stressing the contribution of laws involved in individual development, those taking this viewpoint also express a concern with the contribution that the organism itself makes as a source of its own development; hence, the ipsative approach leads to an interactionist view of development.

# 7

## Stage Theories of Development

In this chapter we will consider three of the most prominent stage theories of psychological development: those of Piaget, Kohlberg, and Freud. Although all deal with different aspects of the developing person, they have certain similarities. Whether talking about the development of cognition (Piaget), of moral reasoning (Kohlberg), or about psychosexual development (Freud), these theorists all hold that all people who develop pass through the stages they specify in an invariant sequence. These stages represent universal sequences of development, qualitatively different developmental levels through which all people must pass in the same order if they develop. As we pointed out in Chapter 6, the essential ways in which people are thought to differ, from a stage point of view, are in how far they eventually develop (the final level of development they reach) and in how much time it takes them to move from one stage to the next (how fast they develop).

The stage theories we will consider in this chapter are also similar in that they take definite stands on the major conceptual issues we have considered in earlier chapters. Thus, these stage theories take a more or less interactionist viewpoint about the nature-nurture controversy. Similarly, they make specific statements about the continuity and the discontinuity of behavioral development. Because of their essential commitment to an interactionist, organismic point of view in regard to the nature-nurture controversy, stage theorists specify that development is in part characterized by qualitatively different phenomena across ontogeny. One portion of development is distinct from another, because of the emergence of qualitatively different attributes arising out of the interaction between the organism's characteristics and the characteristics of its experience. Hence, the term *stage* is used to denote this ontogenetic qualitative distinctiveness.

However, we will see that stage theorists also maintain that there are continuous elements in development. Thus, consistent with the organismic notions advanced by Heinz Werner (1957), the stage theorists considered in this chapter more or less explicitly view development as a dialectical process, an organismic synthesis of the discontinuous *and* the continuous variables affecting development.

In sum, then, while we will see that Piaget, Kohlberg, and Freud are often talking about different aspects of the developing person, they are also doing so within the context of some markedly similar views about the nature of psychological development. Let us turn, then, to a consideration of each of the above theorist's ideas; we will begin with the developmental theory of cognition of Jean Piaget.

## Piaget's Organismic Developmental Theory of Cognition

Jean Piaget was born in Switzerland in 1896. Young Piaget was quite an intellectually precocious boy. For example, he published his first scientific paper at the age of ten, and while still a teenager he had published so many high quality research papers on mollusks (sea creatures such as oysters and clams) that he was offered the position of curator of the mollusk collection in the Geneva museum (Flavell, 1963). As a culmination of these early research interests, Piaget received his doctorate in the natural sciences at the advanced age of twenty-two years!

Although receiving his doctorate in the natural sciences, Piaget maintained a broad intellectual interest. Thus, soon after receiving his degree in 1918, he found himself involved with work in psychology. In addition, he maintained an active interest in

Jean Piaget

epistemology, an area of philosophical inquiry concerned with the philosophy of knowledge. Perhaps it seemed to Piaget that the best way to understand knowledge was to study how it develops. In any event, he began to study the development of cognition in his own children. From these initial studies Piaget's first books resulted. What he began to discern, then, in his first endeavors, was a developmental theory of cognition rather than a cognitive theory of development! He viewed cognition as a developmental phenomenon rather than viewing all development as a cognitive phenomenon.

In terms of Piaget's theory the study of cognitive development can be defined as the study of knowledge and of the mental processes involved in its acquisition and utilization (Elkind, 1967). Moreover, as we have said, Piaget came to his interest in cognitive development from his training in natural science and his interest in epistemology; thus, not only is his theory colored by these intellectual roots, but as he himself pointed out (Flavell, 1963), he has never taken a course in psychology or even passed a test in the subject! Most of us forgive Piaget this limitation. He is one of the two (with Freud) unquestioned geniuses to have ever contributed to the field. However, like Freud, and due most probably to his doctoral training, Piaget's theory has a strong biological basis. To begin our assessment of Piaget's theory, then, let us first focus on his views concerning the biological basis of intelligence.

## Stage-Independent Conceptions
Although Piaget's theory is a stage theory, he advances several important conceptions relevant to all stages of cognitive development. That is, Piaget proposes certain stage-independent conceptions, principles of cognitive development that apply to all stages of development. There are general laws of development that continually function to provide a source of cognitive development throughout ontogeny. To understand them we must first focus on the biological basis of Piaget's theory.

To Piaget, cognition, or intelligence—terms we treat as synonymous for our purposes here—is just an instance of a biological system. Digestion, respiration, and circulation are examples of biological systems. Intelligence is, to Piaget, a biological system just like any of the above, governed by the laws that govern any other biological system; the functions and characteristics of the biological system "cognition" are identical to those involved in the organism's digestive, respiratory, and circulatory systems.

Like all biological systems, then, cognition has two basic aspects that are always, invariantly, present and functioning: *organization* and *adaptation*. Cognition always functions with an organization and it is always an adaptive system—that is, its functioning allows the organism to adapt to its environment; it has survival value.

The functional invariants of organization and adaptation are present throughout the organism's development; they are general characteristics of cognitive functioning applicable to any and all points in the organism's ontogeny. Although recognizing the fundamental importance of both of these general laws of cognitive functioning, Piaget chooses to devote the major portion of his theorizing to the second functional invariant, adaptation. By focusing on how cognitive development allows the organism to adapt to its environment, to survive, we can understand the dynamic interrelation between the organism and its environment which provides a source of intellectual development.

To Piaget, the process of adaptation is divided into two complementary component processes: *assimilation* and *accommodation*. They are always involved in the functioning of cognition to allow the organism to adapt to its environment.

**Assimilation.**  Let us first consider assimilation. This concept is used in a manner identical to the way it is used in any biological discussion; that is, when a cell assimilates food, what does it do? It takes the food in through its membrane and breaks it down to fit the needs of the cell. In other words, when the food is taken into the cell it does not retain its original form or structure but is altered; it is converted into energy and water, for example, in order to fit the already existing cellular structure. Thus, when a cell assimilates food it alters it in order to integrate it into its already existing characteristics. Hence, as Piaget has said: "From a biological point of view, assimilation is the integration of external elements into evolving or completed structures of an organism" (1970, pp. 706-7).

Cognitive assimilation functions in a similar manner. Let us imagine that a child has knowledge of a particular stimulus object—say an isosceles triangle like the one presented here:

Now the child is presented with another triangle, a right triangle like this one:

How may the child know what this second stimulus object is? If the child assimilates, the external object (the right triangle) will be integrated into the child's already existing cognitive structure; knowledge of that object will be distorted, or altered, so that the object will take the form of an isosceles triangle. When assimilation occurs the person "distorts reality" by changing the object to fit the subject (the person). Hence, assimilation involves changing the object, external to the subject, to fit the already existing internal structure of the subject.

Thus, an infant may have knowledge of its mother's breast. It has gained this knowledge through its *actions* on this external stimulus object. The infant has sucked on its mother's nipple and has developed an internal cognitive structure pertaining to this action-based knowledge. The infant "knows" the mother's breast through the actions it performs in relation to it. Hence the subject has an internal structure, derived from its actions on an external stimulus, which allows it to know that stimulus. Thus, objects are known through the actions performed on them. In other words, to Piaget the basis of knowledge lies in action.

When, however, the infant discovers its thumb and begins to suck on it, knowledge of this other external stimulus may be gained by assimilating it to the already existing action-based cognitive structure. That is, instead of changing its cognitive structure in order to know this new object, the infant may act on the thumb as it did the nipple and thus integrate the thumb to the already existing cognitive structure pertaining to the mother's breast. We may say that the infant alters its actions on the thumb, or rather fits its actions on the thumb, so as to incorporate these actions into an already existing cognitive structure. Thus, the infant would be changing the object to fit, or match, the structure of the subject; the infant would be assimilating.

**Accommodation.** As we have already noted, however, there is a process that is the complement of assimilation. This process is termed accommodation. Rather than the subject's altering the external object to match the internal cognitive structure of the person (assimilation), accommodation involves the altering of the subject to fit the object. For example, think of two people seated very comfortably on a rather small sofa. A third person comes along and asks to sit down. Either or both of the already seated people will have to alter their position on the sofa to accommodate this third person. The people seated on the sofa will have to change their already existing structure to incorporate this intrusion from the external stimulus. They will have to accommodate, to change themselves to fit with the external object.

Thus, cognitive accommodation involves the altering of already existing cognitive structures in the subject to match new, external stimulus objects. Rather than changing the object to fit the subject, accommodation involves changing the subject to fit the object. In the triangle example we offered above, accommodation would involve an alteration of the child's cognitive structure pertaining to triangles. Instead of altering the right triangle to fit in with the existing isosceles-triangle cognitive structure, the child would change the existing structure; he or she would accommodate by changing the structure to now include knowledge of both an isosceles and a right triangle.

Similarly, the infant could accommodate to its thumb rather than assimilate it. Instead of acting on the thumb as it did its mother's nipple and hence assimilating the thumb through integrating it into an already existing cognitive structure, the infant could incorporate these different actions through an alteration of its already existing cognitive structure. The infant could alter this structure to include its differential actions on this new object and thus could gain a new knowledge. By the subject's altered actions on the different object, a corresponding alteration in the subject's cognitive structure would occur. Rather than matching the object to the subject, in this case the subject—through differential actions—would match the object. Hence, accommodation would have occurred.

**Equilibration.** Why are assimilation and accommodation complementary processes? Piaget answers this question by postulating what he believes to be a fundamental factor in development. This factor he terms equilibration. Piaget proposes that an organism's adaptation to its environment involves a balance, an equilibrium, between the activity of the organism on its environment and the activity of the environment on the organism.

When an organism acts on its environment it incorporates the external stimulus world into its already existing structure (assimilation); alternatively, when the environment acts on the organism, the organism is altered in order to adjust to the external stimulus world (accommodation).

Hence, Piaget proposes, a balance must be struck between these two tendencies. In essence he hypothesizes that there is an intrinsic orientation in the organism to balance its actions on the environment with the environment's actions on it. In order for the organism to be adaptive, it must be able to incorporate the environment into its already existing structure and to adjust itself to fit the exigencies imposed on it by the environment. Piaget proposes that neither of these two tendencies must always override the other if the organism is to be adaptive. Thus, an equilibration between these two tendencies is needed in order for the organism to be adaptive.

Hence, for every assimilation there must be a corresponding accommodation. One process must balance the other. Just as the subject changes the object to fit its internal structure, the internal structure of the subject must be changed to fit the object. Thus, equilibration is, to Piaget, the balance of interaction between subject and object (Piaget, 1952). There is an inherent tendency in the organism to equilibrate, to balance between assimilation and accommodation. This tendency exists because of its fundamental biological significance; that is, it is what comprises the basis of an organism's adaptation to its environment. Thus, as Piaget has stated:

. . . cognitive adaption, like its biological counterpart, consists of an equilibrium between assimilation and accommodation. As has been shown, there is no assimilation without accommodation. But we must strongly emphasize the fact that accommodation does not exist without simultaneous assimilation either (1970, p. 708).

In essence Piaget proposes that there is a general, biologically based adaptive tendency that applies to the organism throughout its development. This factor—equilibration—is the moving force behind all cognitive development. There must be a balance between subject and object, between assimilation and accommodation. Whenever the organism alters the environment to incorporate it into its already existing internal structure, there must also be a compensatory alteration of the organism's structure to match the objects in its external environment. There must be a balance in action—the basis of all knowledge—between the organism and its environment.

## Functional (Reproductive) Assimilation

If, as we have seen, cognitive development tends to move toward a balance—an equilibration—between assimilation and accommodation, then why, when such a balance is reached, does cognitive development not just stop? Why, after the infant assimilates its mother's nipple and then accommodates to its thumb, does cognitive development not just stop there? If equilibration is the end point, or goal, of cognitive development, why does such development obviously continue after a given equilibration is reached?

It is not enough to argue that there are many things that impinge on the infant's world that necessitate further assimilations (and ensuing accommodations). If the infant is in equilibrium there would seem to be no reason to bother with other impinging stimulation. Let us make an analogy. Most of us have a favorite food. For example, let us suppose that we cannot resist cheeseburgers. Whenever we have the opportunity to eat a cheeseburger we do so; we "assimilate" as many cheeseburgers as we can. However, let us imagine that we have just finished Thanksgiving dinner at Grandma's house. Now, if we are offered a cheeseburger we certainly would not assimilate it; more likely, we would turn away protesting the inappropriateness of offering more food at that time. We would be in gastronomical equilibrium and wouldn't bother with any food stimuli that we would otherwise assimilate.

Of course, we do not remain in gastronomical equilibrium forever. Rather, our digestive system continues to function, and as a result the food is assimilated and we are no longer in equilibrium. Similarly, we do not appear to remain in cognitive equilibrium. Thus, the problem for Piaget is to account for continuing cognitive development while maintaining that equilibrium is the point toward which all cognitive development tends.

To address this problem Piaget introduces the notion of *functional assimilation* (the term *reproductive assimilation* may be used synonymously). In essence, this concept refers to the fact that any cognitive structure brought about through assimilation will continue to assimilate. That is, it is the nature of assimilatory functioning to continue to assimilate. This is the case for any biological system; although a biological system may be in equilibrium, such balance is necessarily temporary because the system must continue to function if the adaptive role of the system is to be maintained. Although ingested food may place the digestive system in equilibrium, such balance is transitory since the food must necessarily be assimilated if digestion is to continue to subserve its adaptive function. The cognitive system works like any other biological system. When a simple cognitive structure is developed on the basis of assimilation—such as that involved in our example of the infant's sucking on its mother's nipple—it continues to assimilate; it functions to reproduce itself. That is, such structures "apply themselves again and again to assimilate aspects of the environment" (Flavell, 1963, p. 55). Thus, the concept of functional (or reproductive) assimilation indicates that it is a basic property of assimilatory functioning to continue to assimilate. (Similarly, it is a basic property of the digestive system to continue to digest.)

Hence, any equilibrium that the infant establishes will be only transitory. The child assimilates and then accommodates and reaches an equilibrium. But, cognitive development goes on to higher and higher developmental levels. This occurs because of the fact that even though an equilibrium is reached, reproductive assimilation occurs.

Thus, the child assimilates other components of the environment and this, in turn, requires a compensatory accommodation. Hence an equilibration is again reached, but this too is short lived, because a disequilibrium will inevitably result when the child continues to assimilate. Once again, this assimilation will be balanced by a corresponding accommodation, again establishing a transitory equilibrium. Thus, because of the disequilibrium resulting from the continued functional assimilation of the child, higher and higher levels of cognitive development are reached.

Schematically, the steps in this continuous process of cognitive development may be seen as:

1. *assimilation,*
2. *accommodation,* which results in
3. *equilibration;*
4. *reproductive assimilation* then occurs and results in
5. *disequilibrium,* which necessitates a return to step 2 and a repetition of the sequence.

Hence, the occurrence of disequilibrium (through the process of reproductive assimilation) provides the source of cognitive development throughout all stages of life. In other words, with the postulation of this model Piaget has offered a set of stage-independent concepts about cognitive development; that is, these concepts apply at all stages of cognitive development. They represent general laws of development applicable to the development of cognition throughout all stages. In fact, these stage-independent concepts account for the person's continual cognitive development. With this understanding, then, let us now turn to a consideration of Piaget's stage-dependent concepts.

## Stage-Dependent Concepts: The Stages of Cognitive Development

**The Sensorimotor Stage.** The first stage of cognitive development in Piaget's theory is termed the sensorimotor stage. Although the age limits of any stage may vary from individual to individual, we may suggest rough boundaries for each stage. Thus, the sensorimotor stage may be held to last from birth through two years.

When the child is born and thus begins its sensorimotor stage, it enters the world with what Piaget terms *innate schema.* We need not argue here about whether or not by the use of the term "innate" Piaget means that these "schema" are unavailable to experiential influences. In fact, we might even assume that he does not mean this; as we will see, and as we have seen in our discussion, Piaget is quite aware of the necessity of conceptualizing development within an interactionist model. Hence, let us just assume that by innate schema Piaget means "congenital schema," schema that are fully present at birth.

But what is a schema? A schema to Piaget is the essential component, the main building block, of cognitive development. Precisely defined, a *schema* is an organized sensorimotor action sequence. By this term, then, Piaget refers to a structure:

1.  that has an organization;
2.  that has a sensory, or input, component, i.e., a component comprised of stimulation derived from the external environment;
3.  that has a motor component, i.e., a component comprised in part by some output component like a muscular movement; these mean

4.  that some action on the environment follows the sensory portion of this structure; and finally

5.  that the components of this structure function in a sequential order, i.e., there is a sequence to the organized sensory and motor actions that occur.

It may seem to you that a schema seems very much like what we typically term a reflex. In fact, the schema that the child is born with, as well as the schema existing throughout this first stage, may conveniently be thought of as reflexive in nature. Similar to a reflex, a schema is a rigid cognitive structure. That is, although the development of schemas throughout the sensorimotor stage represents considerable development in the cognitive functioning of the child, at the same time, the existence of schema during this period tends to place limitations on the cognition of the child. As we will soon see, schema tend to be unidirectional; that is, the direction of the sequence involved in the schema is always the same. Thus, a schema is in many ways analogous to a reflex. For example, in an eye blink reflex a puff of air would always precede and lead to an eye blink. Similarly, schema are also unidirectional in that the motor component of the schematic sequence cannot be reversed.

In essence, when we say that the newborn enters the world with a complement of innate schema, we may think of this as the beginning of the sensorimotor stage, characterized by the presence at birth of an assortment of reflexes, or sensorimotor structures. Such innate schema may be illustrated by the grasping reflex; the infant will grasp tightly around an object placed in its palm. Another example would be the Babinski reflex. This is a backward curling and fanning of the toes in response to tactile stimulation of the sole of the foot. (This reflex, by the way, disappears early in ontogeny due to the development of portions of the brain; in fact, the presence of this reflex in an older child is an indication of brain damage.) Another example of an innate reflex, or schema, would be the rooting reflex. Here, if the infant's cheek is stimulated, say by lightly running a finger from the bottom of the ear to the corner of the mouth, the infant will turn its head in the direction of the stimulation and promptly begin to suck. This is obviously an adaptive reflex. Typically it is the mother's nipple that so stimulates the infant, and head turning and sucking actions will increase the infant's proximity to the mother's nipple and hence food. In sum, then, the infant enters the world with a complement of innate schema.

However, these schema do not remain innate for long. That is, they do not retain their original structure. Once they function for the very first time they change. They begin to assimilate from the environment and hence become *acquired schema*. In other words, once the schema functions it does so by assimilating. This of course changes its structure and requires a complementary accommodation. Then, because of functional or reproductive assimilation, the structure of the schema continues to change.

To understand the process by which schema develop throughout the sensorimotor stage and the concomitant cognitive developments attained through these alterations in schematic structure, we must point out some other facets of the sensorimotor stage. First, Piaget divides this stage into six sequential periods. Within each the concept of circular reaction is involved.

*Circular reaction* refers to one or a series of repetitions of a sensorimotor response. The first response in any of these series is always new to the infant. When a schema first functions, its specific results cannot be anticipated by the infant; the results were not intended before the response was made. The important aspect of a circular reaction comes about, however, after this first, new response is made. Because of reproductive assimilation the infant will tend to repeat this new, chance adaptation over and over (Flavell, 1963, p. 93). What we see, then, is that a circular reaction involves a repeating of a given schema's functioning.

Thus, the first period of the sensorimotor stage involves the alteration of the infant's innate schema to acquired schema. Again, this alteration, this bringing into existence of initial, acquired schema, comes about through the functioning of reproductive assimilation. In period two of this stage, circular reactions are involved with, and affect, the infant's body itself; these circular reactions are termed *primary*. In period three, the infant's circular reactions come to involve objects in the outside world, such as toys or mobiles hanging over the crib; these circular reactions are termed *secondary*.

To this point in the sensorimotor stage, one could describe the infant's cognitive development with the phrase "out of sight, out of mind." The infant interacts with objects in the external world as if their existence depended on the infant sensing them (Piaget, 1950). When objects are not in the infant's immediate sensory world, the infant acts as if they do not exist. In other words, the infant is *egocentric;* there is no differentiation between the existence of an object and the sensory stimulation provided by that object (Elkind, 1967).

Although all stages of cognitive development contain functioning that may be described as egocentric, overcoming this sensorimotor egocentrism will involve the most important cognitive attainment of the child during this stage. We may think of all of the remaining periods within the sensorimotor stage as involving the elaboration of schematic structures that subserve the crucial function of allowing the infant to know that there is object permanency in the world.

We may think of numerous instances of the infant's apparent lack of a schema of object permanency. Before a certain point in cognitive development, games such as peekaboo hold the child's attention. The child acts as if the person playing this game appears and disappears throughout the peekaboo game by virtue of going into and passing out of existence. Thus, the person jumps in and out of the child's immediate sensory purview, and when the person is in the reappearing phase, the child responds with "surprise" (a smile or a laugh). Similarly, if an attention-getting toy or object is brought in and out of the child's sensory purview, the child will not, at these initial points in cognitive development, follow the object (for example, visually) when it leaves his or her immediate sensory world. It is only after series of circular reactions, involving many different objects, that the child is finally able to represent an object not in the immediate sensory world. Only after repeatedly acting on objects does the child become able to internally represent these objects. Thus, as a consequence of these repeated sensorimotor actions, resulting in an internalized representation of an object, the child comes to know that an object exists even though the child is not perceiving it. Thus, the child has *conquered the object* (Elkind, 1967). The child's egocentrism has diminished enough—the child has decentered enough—to now know the difference between an object and the sensory impression it makes. This *representational ability,* this ability to internally represent an absent object and thus to act as if one knows it continues to exist, represents the major cognitive achievement of the sensorimotor stage enabling the infant to progress to the ensuing stage of cognitive development.

David Elkind

**The Preoperational Stage.**   The age range associated with this second stage is usually two through six years of age. The major cognitive achievements in this stage involve the elaboration of the representational ability that enabled the child to move from the sensorimotor stage to the present one. In the preoperational stage, true systems of representation, or symbolic functioning, emerge. In fact, Elkind (1967) has termed this stage the period of *the conquest of the symbol.*

The most obvious example of the development of representational systems in this stage is language. Here the child's use of language develops extensively, as words are used to symbolize objects, events, and feelings. There are other indications of this representational ability as well. During this stage of life we see the emergence of symbolic play; for example, the child uses two crossed sticks to make a jet plane or uses his or her finger to make a gun. In addition we see the emergence of delayed imitation; for example, the child sees someone perform an act—e.g., daddy smoking a pipe and pacing across the room—and then repeats the act hours later.

Although cognitive development in the preoperational stage does have positive characteristics—by virtue of the fact that such elaborate systems of representational ability do develop—it also has limitations. The child in this stage is also egocentric, but here the egocentrism takes a form different from that seen in the previous stage. The child now has the ability to symbolize objects with words, to use words to refer to objects. But at the same time, the child fails to differentiate between the words and the things the words refer to. For example, the child believes that the word representing an object is inherent in it, that an object cannot have more than one word to symbolize it (Elkind, 1967). The child does not know that an object and the word symbolizing the object are two independent things. The child does not differentiate between symbols and what the symbols refer to (Elkind, 1967).

There are several consequences of this type of egocentrism. One is that the child acts as if words carry much more meaning than they actually do (Elkind, 1967). For instance, it is not uncommon to see a child in this stage of development ask someone for the "thing" and act as if enough information has been conveyed to the other person to have the request fulfilled. Since the child does not differentiate between symbols and their referents, he or she thinks the word belongs to (inheres in) the object.

A broader consequence of this egocentrism is the child's inability to hold two aspects of a situation separately in mind at the same time. That is, the child does not differentiate between objects and the words that refer to them and thus joins, or merges, these two dimensions of a stimulus—the object and the symbol. This failure suggests a more general lack of ability to take into account two different aspects of a stimulus array at the same time. One indication of this general inability may be found in the preoperational child's failure to show conservation ability.

*Conservation* refers to the ability to know that one aspect of a stimulus array has remained unchanged although other aspects of the stimulus array have changed. To understand this concept, let us imagine that we present to a five-year-old child two dolls, a mommy doll and a daddy doll. We then take four marbles and place them in a row beside the mommy doll and take four more marbles and place them beside the daddy doll in positions directly corresponding to the mommy doll's marbles. Our materials would look like those in Fig. 7.1 (a). Now, if we show the five-year-old these materials arranged in this way and ask, "Which doll has more marbles to play with—the mommy doll or the daddy doll?" the child would most probably say that both dolls have the same amount of marbles to play with. However, if we spread out the mommy doll's marbles right in the full view of the child (but leave the daddy doll's marbles in the same position) so that we have an arrangement that looks like Fig. 7.1 (b), and ask which doll has more, the preoperational five-year-old child will answer that the mommy doll has more!

What we see from this example, then, is the inability to conserve number. The child does not know that one aspect of the stimulus array—the number of marbles—has remained unchanged, although another aspect of the array—the positioning of the marbles—has changed. It would seem that the child cannot appreciate these two dimensions of the stimulus array at the same time. A cognitive error is made because in not being able to put these two dimensions in their proper interrelation, the child fails to know that the movements of the mommy doll's marbles can be reversed and be back to the original stimulus array. As we will learn when we discuss the next stage of cognitive development—the concrete operational stage—the child cannot understand this *reversibility* yet. The child's thought is still dominated by schemas, and as we have seen such structures are rigidly unidirectional. Thus, even though we spread out the marbles right in front of the child, the child will still maintain that the altered array has more marbles. We might even return the array to its original form and again ask which doll has more. The child would now probably say once again that they both have the same, and even if we repeat these steps several times the child's answers might correspondingly alternate between "same" and "more."

The lack of conservation ability seen with the quantitative dimension of number applies, too, with other quantitative aspects of stimuli. Thus, if we present two equal lengths of rope—as in Fig. 7.1 (c)—and ask which rope is longer, the child will probably answer that the ropes are equal in length. If, however, we move the location of one of

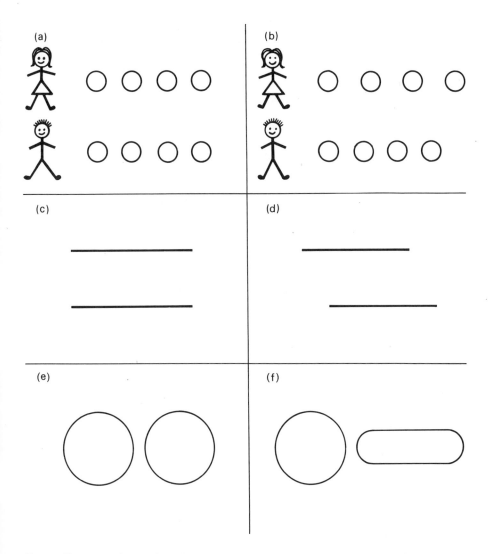

**Fig. 7.1** Examples of tests of number conservation (a and b), length conservation (c and d), and mass conservation (e and f).

these pieces of rope—as in Fig. 7.1 (d)—and repeat the question, the child will now claim that one piece of rope is longer than the other. Similarly, if we take two equally sized pieces of clay and roll them up into equally sized and shaped balls and present them to the child—as in Fig. 7.1 (e)—the child will say that each ball contains the same amount of clay. If, however, we reshape one of these clay balls into a sausage—as in Fig. 7.1 (f)—again doing this right in the full view of the child, and now ask which ball has more clay to play with, the child's answer will be different, now saying that the sausage-shaped piece contains more clay. In this example we see an instance of the inability to show conservation of mass. The child does not know that one aspect of the stimulus array—its mass—remains the same although another aspect of the array—its shape—is altered.

In sum, then, the preoperational child does not generally show conservation ability; this manifests itself in respect not only to quantitative aspects of stimuli such as mass, length, and number, but to other quantitative aspects of stimuli such as area and volume as well. Thus, although the preoperational child's thought has progressed well beyond that of the sensorimotor child's thought—due mostly to extensive representational abilities—the preoperational child's cognition still has the above limitations. However, as the cognitive conflicts produced by being unable to differentiate between symbols and the objects they refer to increase, and as the instances of inability to simultaneously appreciate two different aspects of a stimulus array similarly increase and cause conflict, the child must accommodate more and more. As the equilibrations and the disequilibrations comprising this process occur, the child's cognitive structure will be altered. When enough alteration has taken place, the child will enter into the next stage of cognitive development.

**The Concrete Operational Stage.** Up to the point when a child enters the concrete operational stage (which spans from about six years of age through eleven or twelve years), the child's cognitive structure is comprised predominantly of schemas. However, because a schema is a unidirectional structure, the child is generally unable to simultaneously appreciate contrasting aspects of a stimulus array. This limitation, as we have seen, is illustrated by the lack of conservation ability. The way in which preoperational thought thus limits a child is in not providing the ability to reverse various physical events. That is, if we as adults see two balls of clay and decide that each contains an equal amount of clay, we would continue to maintain this even if one of the balls were reshaped to look like a sausage. If this were done we would know—without having to see the action performed—that by reversing the action of reshaping the clay we would be back to the original two clay balls. Because nothing was added or subtracted to either ball, because reshaping does not alter the amount of mass present, we would assert that both pieces of clay are the same.

The emergence of *operational structures* gives the child this ability. An operation is an internalized action that is reversible. As opposed to schema, operations allow the person to know that actions can be counteracted by reversing them. Moreover, operations *are* internalized actions. That is, we do not have to see the action of rolling the sausage back into a ball to know that we can return the clay to its original shape. We can just think of this action. Our thought about concrete, physical actions does not depend on our actually seeing these actions. We can reverse the action in our heads and come to the same conclusion about the actions as if we actually, concretely viewed the reshaping actions.

Thus, the emergence of operational cognitive ability extends the child's capacity in dealing with the world. Because thought is now reversible, because the child can now appreciate the reciprocity in concrete actions on and with physical stimuli, the concrete operational stage is the period in which the child begins to show the conservation abilities lacking in the preoperational stage. Moreover, because operations are internalized actions, the child's cognitive abilities are also extended in that now the child need not actually see actions performed in order to know about them. Thus, the child now has cognitive structures that enable him or her to think about the actions of the world without having to actually experience these actions. Simply, operations extend the scope of action by internalizing it.

But, despite the great cognitive accomplishments inherent in the concrete operational stage, thought in this stage also has its limitations. Notice that the label for this stage is concrete operational. What this denotes is that although thought is operational, it is bound by concrete, physical reality. Although the child can deal with objects internally, that is, without having to actually experience them, these actions and objects must have a concrete, real existence. Things or events that are counterfactual—that are not actually represented in the real world—cannot be understood by the concrete operational child. An illustration of this point offered by Elkind (1967) is helpful. Suppose someone asks you to imagine that coal is white, and then further asks you to indicate what color coal would be when burning at its hottest. Most probably you would have an answer to this counterfactual question. You might think that since coal is actually black and when burning at its hottest is white, then if it were white, it would be black when burning at its hottest. The point here is not the particular solution, but the fact that you can deal with the counterfactual question. The concrete operational child, on the other hand, cannot do this. For example, the response might typically be, "But coal is black!" (Elkind, 1967). In essence, then, a major limitation of concrete operational thought is that it is limited to thinking about concrete, real things.

Other limitations of concrete thought also exist, however. As Elkind (1967) has pointed out, the concrete operational child is also egocentric. Here, however, the egocentrism takes the form of an inability to differentiate between actions and objects experienced directly and actions and objects the child thinks about. We have seen that the child's thought is now independent of experience, such that the child can now deal with an action whether it is experienced or just thought about. However, the child fails to distinguish between knowledge gained through experience and knowledge gained from thought alone. If given some information about a physical situation (say a scientific problem) and asked to give a solution to the problem, the child will not have to see the actual physical objects in order to reach a solution but will think about it and form an answer, a hypothesis. But the child will not recognize the answer as just a hypothesis, just one possible solution to the problem. Rather, the child will think that the answer is one and the same with the physical situation. The child will not see any difference between what he or she thinks and what is! Even if the child's ideas about experience are challenged and/or evidence is presented contradicting those ideas, the child will not alter the answer, but will just reinterpret the opposing evidence to fit into his or her ideas (Elkind, 1967).

Unable to think counterfactually and equating perceived and actual reality, the child cannot recognize that his or her thoughts about reality represent only hypotheses, that they are arbitrary; they are not necessarily imposed by or part of reality but are just one of many possible interpretations of reality. Thus, a child is egocentric in failing to view thoughts and experience as two independent phenomena. With further cognitive development, however, the child attains the ability to think counterfactually, to see that thoughts about reality and reality are different. Hence, the child's final stage of cognitive development begins.

**The Formal Operational Stage.** The last stage of cognitive development in Piaget's theory is termed the formal operational stage (which begins at about eleven or twelve years of age and continues thereafter). Here thought becomes hypothetical in nature. Now discriminating between thoughts about reality and actual reality, the child comes to recognize that his or her thoughts about reality have an element of arbitrariness about them, that they may not actually be real representations about the true nature of experience. Thus, the child's thoughts about reality take on a hypothetical "if . . . then" characteristic: "*if* such and such *were* the case, *then* that and that would follow." In forming such propositions, such hypotheses about the world, the child's thought can be seen to correspond to formal, scientific, logical thinking. This emergence accounts for the label applied to this stage—the formal operational stage.

For the first time the child's thought is completely free from any dependence on concrete reality. Now the child can and does think not only in the "if . . . then" or "as if" manner, but counterfactually and completely abstractly as well. Thus, anything and everything can become the object of the child's newly developed abstract and hypothetical cognitive ability. The child not only may recognize his or her own thoughts as only one possible interpretation of reality, but also may come to view reality as only one possible instance of a potentially unlimited number of possible realities. Hence, the concrete predomination of what *is* real is replaced by the abstract and hypothetical predomination of what *can be* real. Thus, all things in experience are thought about hypothetically, and even the child's own thoughts can become objects of the child's hypothesizing. In other words, the child can now think about his or her own thinking.

Understandably, the young person spends a good deal of time employing these new thought capabilities. The person's own thought processes thereby become a major object of cognitive concern. This preoccupation, or *centration,* leads, however, to a limitation of the newly developed formal operational thought. It leads to egocentrism within the formal operational stage.

The formal operational stage of cognitive development corresponds chronologically to the period in people's lives usually labeled adolescence. Hence, Elkind (1967) has labeled the egocentrism of this stage *adolescent egocentrism.* This adolescent egocentrism has two components. First, we have seen how the adolescent's own thoughts come to predominate his or her thinking. Because of this preoccupation, the adolescent fails to distinguish, or discriminate, between his or her own thinking and what others are thinking about. Being preoccupied with self, and not making the above discrimination, the adolescent comes to believe that others are as preoccupied with his or her appearance and behavior as he or she is (Elkind, 1967). Thus, the adolescent constructs an *imaginary audience.*

An illustration of the functioning of the imaginary audience and of some emotional concomitants of this cognitive development may be seen if we think back to our days of early adolescence. Assuredly, some new fad, perhaps in regard to a particular style of clothing, sprung up among our peers. Some of us were perhaps stuck with wearing the old, out-dated style and we were literally afraid to be seen in public. We were sure that as soon as we walked about without the appropriate uniform, everyone would notice its absence. Because we were so aware of the absence of this evidence of fitting in with everyone else, we were equally sure that everyone would immediately be aware of our shortcoming. Because we had to perform for our imaginary audience, assuredly as critical of us as we were of ourselves, it caused us great stress. We see here an instance of the emotional concomitants of the functioning of the imaginary audience, as well as an explanation for the socializing power of the peer group among adolescents and for the ubiquity of fads among this age group.

A second component of adolescent egocentrism also exists: the adolescent's thoughts and feelings are experienced as new and as unique. Although to the adolescent they are in fact new and unique, the young person comes to believe that they are *historically* new and unique. That is, the adolescent constructs a *personal fable,* the belief that he or she is a unique, one-of-a-kind individual, a person having singular feelings and thoughts.

Here, too, it is easy to think of an illustration of the functioning and emotional concomitants of the personal fable. Again, think back to adolescent years and your first love affair. No one had ever loved as deeply, as totally . . . no one had ever felt the intense compassion, the devotion, the longing, the overwhelming fulfillment that we felt for this, our one true love. . . . Then remember three days later. When it was over! The pain, the depression, the agony . . . no one had ever suffered as deeply, no one had ever been so wrongfully abused, so thoroughly tortured, so spitefully crushed by unrequited love. . . .

We sat in our rooms, unmoving; and our mothers would say, "What's wrong with you? Come and eat." Our inevitable answer: "You don't understand. What do you know about love!"

This admittedly overdramatized depiction of the functioning of the egocentric adolescent's personal fable illustrates some emotional implications of this cognitive phenomenon.

Finally, although the formal operational stage is the last stage of cognitive development in Piaget's theory, the egocentrism of this stage obviously diminishes over the course of the person's subsequent cognitive functioning. As the person continues to assimilate input from the world around, and plays new and different roles, notions of imaginary audience and personal fable will inevitably diminish because of the necessary, concomitant accommodations that must be made. Thus, although the formal operational stage is the last stage of cognitive development, and no new cognitive structures are held to emerge over the course of life, the person still continues to change, to assimilate and hence accommodate, and one outcome of this continuous functioning is the diminution of the components of adolescent egocentrism.

## Some Concluding Comments

What we have seen is that Piaget offers a theory of cognitive development that includes the positing of both continuous, stage-independent phenomena and discontinuous, stage-dependent phenomena. Piaget's is an organismic account of development; he views development as the outcome of organism-environment interactions and hence as an active, self-generated process. Action—the action of the organism on the environment and the action of the environment on the organism—is the basis of cognitive development. The disequilibriums continually caused by these actions provide the moving force of cognitive development, and the changes due to this process are characterized by developmental stages.

Although a stage theorist, Piaget does not view the person as making abrupt modal transitions from one stage of the development to the next. Rather, as is true of other stage theorists, he recognizes in several ways that people function at more than one stage of development at the same time. For instance, children do not gain the ability to make conservations in all quantitative dimensions at one time. Rather, number and length conservations appear first, area conservation appears later, and volume conservation typically develops last. Thus, in some areas of cognitive functioning a child may show behaviors indicative of the preoperational stage, while in other areas may show evidence of concrete operational functioning. Thus, stage transition becomes a matter of shifts in modal type of functioning. Moreover, Piaget also recognizes the fact that people frequently show similar cognitive phenomena at different points in their ontogeny through his concept of *décalage*. A repetition of a cognitive phenomena which takes place within the same, single stage of development and involves a single, general level of functioning Piaget terms *horizontal décalage*. The circular reactions that occur throughout the sensorimotor stage are illustrations of horizontal décalage. In addition, repetitions of the same phenomena at different stages of development Piaget terms *vertical décalage* (Flavell, 1963, pp. 21-22). Showing conservation ability at two different stages of development is an instance of vertical décalage, as is the continuous functioning of reproductive assimilation across ontogeny.

Thus, although different stages of development have different stage-specific laws governing their functioning, vertical décalage suggests that there are laws general to all levels of functioning. This, then, is the second "compromise" between the organismic and unity-of-science philosophies of science discussed in Chapter 2. This is the general-and-specific-laws compromise. That is, there are phenomena at all ontogenetic levels that can be understood by one or a common set of laws or principles; however, this does not alter the fact that each level may also be governed by specific laws, the specificity of which, in fact, serves as the criterion for calling a stage a stage. Thus Piaget, in agreement with Werner, sees both continuity and discontinuity as characteristic of developmental processes. Piaget's recognition of stage mixture as characterizing cognitive development and functioning is an indication of his understanding of the modal nature of stage transition and his belief in the orthogenetic nature of cognitive development; it will also be important to our understanding of Kohlberg's related stage theory, discussed in the following section.

In sum, Table 7.1 presents an outline of Piaget's stage theory, with the four stages of development and each of their concomitant cognitive assets and limitations.

## Kohlberg's Stage Theory of the Development of Moral Reasoning

Moral development has been a topic of considerable theoretical and research interest among psychologists. Freud, in his psychoanalytic theory, displayed extensive concern with the development of morality; many learning-oriented theorists (such as Sears, 1957, and Bandura and Walters, 1963) have also demonstrated a strong interest in how people develop and follow rules—that is, how they develop morally.

Piaget, too, was concerned with this issue from a cognitive developmental point of view and accordingly was an early contributor to this topic (1965). He devised a theory of moral development that was generally consistent with his other theories. For instance, he saw the child's morality as developing along several dimensions and presented a

**Table 7.1** Piaget's stages of cognitive development.

| Stage | Approximate age range | Major cognitive achievements | Major cognitive limitations |
|---|---|---|---|
| Sensorimotor | Birth–two | Schema of object permanency | Egocentrism: lack of ability to differentiate between self and external stimulus world |
| Preoperational | Two–six | Systems of representation Symbolic functioning (e.g., language, symbolic play, delayed imitation) | Lack of conservation ability Egocentrism: lack of ability to differentiate between symbol and object |
| Concrete operational | Six–twelve | Ability to show experience-independent thought (reversible, internalized actions) Conservation ability | Egocentrism: lack of ability to differentiate between thoughts about reality and actual experience of reality |
| Formal operational | Twelve on | Ability to think hypothetically, counterfactually, and propositionally | Egocentrism: imaginary audience, personal fable |

Lawrence Kohlberg

two-stage process for each dimension. Thus, on one moral dimension, younger children were seen to be objective in their moral judgments; that is, they judge an act to be right or wrong solely in terms of the consequences of the act. If I break a vase, I would be judged by a young child morally culpable, whether or not the breaking was an accident. Older children, however, were seen to be subjective in their moral judgments; that is, they take the intentions of the person into account when judging the moral rightness or wrongness of an act. Hence, if I break a vase out of spite or anger I would be judged morally wrong; if, however, I break it because I am just clumsy, then no moral culpability would be seen. Piaget's overall orientation toward the topic of moral development was consistent with his general organismic position. Hence, he viewed the person as an active participant in the development of his or her morality. Moral rules are obtained not just through the environment's action on the person, but through the person's active role in the construction of moral judgments as well. Moreover, the constructions obtained as an outcome of this process changed qualitatively with development; they progressed through stages.

Lawrence Kohlberg developed a theory of moral reasoning development which derives from the Piagetian tradition. Although finding some fault with some of the specific aspects of Piaget's theory of moral development (Kohlberg, 1963b), Kohlberg subscribed to the general organismic orientation employed by Piaget. Thus, Kohlberg presents a theory of moral development (1958, 1963a, 1963b) which is in agreement with the general organismic orientation of Piaget and in opposition to other leading views of moral development.

## Learning and Psychoanalytic Views of Moral Development
Kohlberg's cognitive developmentalist theory of moral development stands in opposition to the views of moral development expressed by many learning-oriented and

psychoanalytically-oriented theorists. The points of division between the cognitive developmental viewpoint and the latter two positions have been well detailed by Turiel (1969).

Basically, although psychoanalytic and learning theories represent considerably divergent views about the nature of human development, they converge in their determination of whether or not a person is morally developed. Both positions tend to agree with the notion that a person is morally developed when his or her behavior conforms to the rules of society. In other words, moral development involves increasing conformity to the rules of society. Thus, a morally developed person is one who has internalized, or learned, the rules of society and whose behavior is consistent with these rules.

Now, learning theorists (e.g., Eysenck, 1960; Sears, 1957) would suggest that this development occurs through the acquisition of a series of learned stimulus-response relations, associations acquired on the basis of external rewards and punishments. Psychoanalytic theorists (e.g., Freud, 1923), on the other hand, while not subscribing to the mechanistic, stimulus-response learning notions, also view moral development merely as the internalization of societal standards. They, however, see these developments as largely outcomes of biologically imperative processes (i.e., essentially universally maturationally determined processes). We will see some of Freud's views on moral development later on in this chapter. In sum, then, although these two positions have different explanations of *how* a person morally develops, the point is that both use the same indication of moral development—a morally developed person is one whose responses are in accord with the standards and rules of society. From both of these theoretical positions one would focus on the overt response in a moral choice situation if one wanted to empirically verify these notions.

From the cognitive developmentalist point of view, however, there are several things wrong with these notions. First, focusing only on the response in a moral choice situation is seen as insufficient for an understanding of moral development. As we saw when we reviewed Schneirla's (1957) criticisms of the concept of homology (in Chapter 4), the same response at two different points in ontogeny does not necessarily indicate that identical processes exist at these two points in time. One may see identical moral responses at different points in development, and the relation of these same responses to moral development may be totally different. What is being asserted, then, is the notion that the same response may have totally different meanings if it occurs at two different times in development. Similar responses do not necessarily indicate similar underlying structures.

For example, if we ask a five-year-old whether it is right or wrong to steal, assuredly the child would say it is wrong. Similarly, a twenty-year-old would give the same response to the same question. Thus, from the perspective of the learning- and psychoanalytically-oriented positions noted above, both the five-year-old and the twenty-year-old would be equally morally developed. Both give identical responses to a moral choice question; since both responses are in accord with the standards of society and since both may be seen to reflect the same internalization of these standards, the five-year-old is seen to be equal in moral development to the twenty-year-old. This is not necessarily so.

If we go on to ask *why* stealing is wrong, we would probably see very strong evidence for the fact that the two people are quite disparate in their moral development. We would probably see that despite their similar responses about the rightness or wrongness of stealing, the reasons offered for their responses reflect markedly qualitatively different thoughts. For instance, the five-year-old would be likely to assert that the reason that stealing is wrong is that you get punished for it. The twenty-year-old, however, would look at this answer as naive (or "immature"). This person, on the other hand, might say something to the effect that stealing was wrong because it violates implicit principles of mutual trust, that as a member of society you have an implicit agreement to respect the personal and property rights of others in society and that they, in turn, must respect your rights.

Thus, we see that by focusing only on the response in a moral situation, we may be ignoring important distinctions in the moral reasoning of people at different points in their ontogeny, reasoning differences that in fact may give different meaning to the exact same response at various developmental levels. Hence, the response alone does not give us a clue as to the underlying reasoning. To a great extent the study of responses alone does not tell us very much about the why of moral behavior, the reasons underlying a moral response, or the structure of moral thinking. As Turiel (1969, p. 95) has argued, "An individual's response must be examined in light of how he perceives the moral situation, what the meaning of the situation is to the person responding, and the relation of his choice to that meaning: the cognitive and emotional processes in making moral judgments."

Because of these problems, Kohlberg rejected these response-oriented approaches to the understanding of moral development and chose to investigate the *reasons* underlying moral responses (e.g., Kohlberg, 1958, 1963a). That is, he chose to investigate the structure of the thought processes involved in moral reasoning. He sought to ascertain whether or not people's thinking about moral responses goes through developmental changes in its structure. Let us see how Kohlberg's study led to his discovery of stages in the development of moral reasoning.

## Kohlberg's Method of Assessing Moral Reasoning

Kohlberg saw that it was necessary to study moral reasoning, and to do this he devised a series of stories, each presenting imaginary moral dilemmas, to assess this reasoning. Let us see one such story and then evaluate the features it offers in providing a technique for assessing moral reasoning.

One day air raid sirens began to sound. Everyone realized that a hydrogen bomb was going to be dropped on the city by the enemy, and that the only way to survive was to be in a bomb shelter. Not everyone had bomb shelters, but those who did ran quickly to them. Since Mr. and Mrs. Jones had built a shelter, they immediately went to it where they had enough air space inside to last them for exactly five days. They knew that after five days the fallout would have diminished to the point where they could safely leave the shelter. If they left before that, they would die. There was enough air for the Joneses only. Their next door neighbors had not built a shelter and were trying to get in. The Joneses knew that they would not have enough air if they let the neighbors in, and that they would all die if they came inside. So they refused to let them in.

So now the neighbors were trying to break the door down in order to get in. Mr. Jones took his rifle and told them to go away or else he would shoot. They would not go away. So he either had to shoot them or let them come into the shelter.

What are the features of this story that make it a moral dilemma? First, as is true of all of Kohlberg's moral dilemma stories (Turiel, 1969), the story presents a conflict to the listener. In this particular story the conflict obviously involves the need for a choice between two culturally unacceptable alternatives: killing others so that you might survive or allowing others and yourself and family to die. Other dilemmas may involve a conflict between two culturally acceptable alternatives. The point is, however, that the story presents a dilemma; it puts the listener in a conflict situation such that any response is clearly not the only conceivable one that is acceptable to make. Thus, the particular response the listener makes is irrelevant to the investigator. What is of concern is the reasoning the listener uses to resolve the conflict. Thus, Kohlberg asks the listener not just to tell him what Mr. Jones should do, but why Mr. Jones should do whatever the listener decides.

Thus, Kohlberg would first ask the listener, "What should Mr. Jones do?" Next he would ask, "Does he have the right to shoot his neighbors if he feels that they would all die if he let them in since there would not be enough air to last them very long? Why?" Then, "Does he have the right to keep his neighbors out of his shelter even though he knows they will die if he keeps them out? Why?" And finally Kohlberg would ask, "Does he have the right to let them in if he knows they will all die? Why?"

Through the application of such analyses of reasoning processes Kohlberg was able to evaluate people's moral reasoning. Moreover, through the application of these techniques to people who were of different ages (Kohlberg, 1958, 1963a), Kohlberg was able to discover that moral reasoning passes through a series of qualitatively different stages of structural organization. Qualitatively different reasons for identical moral choice responses—and hence qualitatively different thought structures—characterize people at different points in their development.

What Kohlberg discovered, then, was that there are six stages in the development of moral reasoning. He found that these six stages form a universally invariant sequence in full accord with all the requirements of stage theories. Moreover, he discovered that one could divide these six stages into three different levels, each of which has two stages. Let us turn now to a presentation of the levels and stages of moral development discovered by Kohlberg.

**Level 1. Preconventional Moral Reasoning.**  Within the first level, the first two stages of moral reasoning emerge. Although these two stages involve qualitatively different thought processes about moral conflicts, they do have a general similarity and hence are grouped together to form the first, the preconventional level of moral reasoning. For both stages of this level a person's moral reasoning involves reference to *external* and *physical* events and objects, as opposed to such things as society's standards, as the source for decisions about moral rightness or wrongness.

**Stage 1. Obedience and punishment orientation.**  This reference to external, physical things is well illustrated by the first stage of moral development. Kohlberg sees this stage as being dominated by moral reasoning involving reference merely to obedience or punishment by powerful figures. Thus, an act is judged wrong or right if it is or is not associated with punishment. Reasoning here is similar to what we have seen Piaget label as objective reasoning. From this perspective, one must be obedient to powerful authority *because* that authority *is* powerful; it can punish you. Acts, then, are judged as not moral only because they are associated with these external, physical sanctions.

**Stage 2. Naively egotistic orientation.**  Reference to external, physical events is also made in this stage. Here, however, an act is judged right if it is involved with an external event that satisfies the needs of the person or sometimes the needs of someone very close to the person (e.g., a father or a wife). Thus, even though stealing is wrong—because it is associated with punishment—reasoning at this level might lead to the assertion that stealing is right *if* the act of stealing is instrumental in satisfying a need of the person. For example, if the person was very hungry, then stealing food would be seen as a moral act in this instance.

Thus, although this second stage also involves major reference to external, physical events as the source of rightness or wrongness, the perspective of self needs (or sometimes the needs of significant others) is also brought into consideration (albeit egocentrically). Thus, the development in this second stage gradually brings about a transition of perspective, a perspective involving people. This transition then leads to the next level of moral reasoning.

**Level 2. Conventional Moral Reasoning.**  In this second level of moral reasoning the person's thinking involves reference to acting as others expect. Acts are judged right if they conform to roles that others (i.e., society) think a person should play. Thus an act is seen as moral if it accords with the established order of society. Let us see how this type of reasoning characterizes the two stages of level 2.

**Stage 3. Good-boy orientation.**  Here the person is oriented toward being seen as a good boy or a good girl by others. The person sees society as providing certain general, or stereotyped, roles for people. If you act in accord with these role prescriptions you will win the approval of other people, and hence you will be labeled a good person. Thus, acts that help others, that lead to the approval of others, or that simply *should,* given certain role expectations by society, lead to the approval of others will be judged as moral.

**Stage 4. Authority and social-order-maintenance orientation.**  Here a more formal view of society's rules and institutions emerges. Rather than just acting in accord with the rules and institutions of society to earn approval, the person comes to see these rules and institutions of society as ends in themselves. That is, acts that are in accord with the maintenance of the rules of society and allow the institutions of social order (e.g., the government) to continue functioning are seen as moral. Here the social order and institutions of society must be maintained for their own sake; they are ends in themselves. A moral person is one who "does his duty" and maintains established authority, social order, and institutions of society. A person is simply not moral if his or her acts are counter to these goals.

Thus, we see that reasoning at this level involves a consideration of a person's role in reference to society. But at stage 4, as opposed to stage 3, moral thinking also involves viewing the social order as an end in itself and the self as having to maintain these institutions in order to do one's duty and be moral. However, this thinking may lead the person to consider the alternative, or reverse side of the issue. The person may begin to think about what society must do in order for it to be judged as moral. If and when such considerations begin to emerge, the person will gradually make a transition into the next level of moral reasoning.

**Level 3. Postconventional Moral Reasoning.**  This is the last level of the development of moral reasoning. Here moral judgments are made in reference to the view that there are arbitrary, subjective elements in social rules. The rules and institutions of society are not absolute, but relative. Other rules, equally as reasonable, may have been established. Thus, the rules and institutions of society are no longer viewed as ends in themselves, but as subjective. Such postconventional reasoning also develops through two stages.

**Stage 5. Contractual legalistic orientation.**  Here the person recognizes that a reciprocity, an implicit contract, exists between self and society. One must conform to society's rules and institutions, do one's duty, because in turn society will do its duty and provide one with certain protections. Thus, the institutions of society are seen not as ends in themselves but as part of a contract. From this view a person would not steal because this would violate the implicit social contract, which includes mutual respect for the rights of other members of the society.

Thus, the person sees that any specific set of rules in society is somewhat arbitrary. But one's duty is to fulfill one's part of the contract (e.g., not to steal from others), just as it is necessary for society to fulfill its part of the contract (e.g., it will provide institutions and laws protecting one's property from being stolen). Hence, the person sees an element of subjectivism in the rules of society, and this recognition may lead into the last stage of moral reasoning development.

**Stage 6. Conscience, or principle, orientation.**  Here there is more formal recognition of the subjectivism of societal rules. Thus, one sees not only that a given, implicit contract between a person and society is a somewhat arbitrary, subjective phenomenon, but too that one's interpretation of the meaning and boundaries of this contract is also subjective. One person may give one subjective interpretation to these rules, while another person may give a different interpretation. From this perspective the ultimate appeal in making moral judgments must be to one's own conscience.

The person would here come to believe that there may be rules that transcend those of specific, given social contracts. Since a person's own subjective view of this contract must be seen as legitimate, a person's own views must be the ultimate source of moral judgments. One's conscience, one's set of personal principles, must be appealed to as the ultimate source of moral decisions. Thus, to paraphrase ex-Chief Justice of the Supreme Court Earl Warren, someone with this perspective might state, "I know that it is the law, but is it justice?"

In sum, stage 6 reasoning involves an appeal to transcendent, universal principles of morality, rules that find their source in the person's own conscience. Despite the law—the parameters of the implicit contract—one must live with one's conscience. One's conscience must be the ultimate source of one's moral judgments.

We see that Kohlberg has discovered six stages of moral reasoning development that people may pass through. These stages are summarized in Table 7.2. Let us finally turn to a consideration of some important characteristics of development through the stages.

## Developmental Transitions through the Stages of Moral Reasoning

Consistent with Piaget's view of cognitive development, Kohlberg and other cognitive developmentalists studying moral reasoning development (most notably Elliot Turiel) clearly recognize that development through the stages of moral reasoning is a gradual process. Transitions from one stage to another are not abrupt; rather, movement is

**Table 7.2** Kohlberg's stages of moral reasoning development.

---

Level 1.  Preconventional moral reasoning

   Stage 1.  Obedience and punishment orientation

   Stage 2.  Naively egotistic orientation

Level 2.  Conventional moral reasoning

   Stage 3.  Good-boy orientation

   Stage 4.  Authority and social-order-maintenance orientation

Level 3.  Postconventional moral reasoning

   Stage 5.  Contractual legalistic orientation

   Stage 6.  Conscience, or principle, orientation

---

characterized by gradual shifts in the modal type of reasoning given by a person over the course of development. Thus, as explained in Chapter 6, and again illustrated in the present chapter in our discussion of Piaget's concept of décalage, such stage mixture means that at any given point a person will be functioning at more than one stage at the same time.

Accordingly, one must have a large sample of instances of a person's moral reasonings in order to accurately determine that person's stage of moral reasoning. Only such a large sample will allow one to discover the modal (i.e., the most frequently occurring) type of reasoning the person uses to make moral decisions. Although research and writing by some psychologists interested in moral development (e.g., Ban-

Elliot Turiel

dura and McDonald, 1963) has ignored the existence and implications of stage mixture, the present discussion indicates that stage mixture is an ever-present facet of the developmental processes involved in moral reasoning.

In addition, Turiel (1969) has indicated that stage mixture is a *necessary* component of the development of moral reasoning. From a cognitive developmental perspective, changes in moral reasoning level should come about as a result of disequilibrium, which of course would necessitate the reestablishment of an equilibration. Turiel (1969) has demonstrated that when children are exposed to reasoning at a level one stage higher than their own, disequilibrium is caused. That is, the child perceives a contradiction between his or her own level of moral reasoning and the next higher one, and the conflict produced by this recognition is the product of disequilibrium. In order to reestablish an equilibration the child must accommodate to this higher stage, and this results in the child's movement towards a higher stage of moral reasoning.

But how is the child able to perceive a discrepancy between his or her own reason and the one that is from one stage higher and thus not modally the child's? Turiel suggests that the answer lies in stage mixture. Since the person is functioning at more than one stage at the same time, there are reasoning structures available from this higher stage that enable the person to perceive this discrepancy. Stage mixture, then, is not only a ubiquitous, but a necessary, component of moral reasoning development. As Turiel has said, " . . . stage mixture serves to facilitate the perception of contradictions, making the individual more susceptible to disequilibrium and consequently more likely to progress developmentally" (1969, p. 130).

## Some Concluding Comments

It is important to reassert the point that although Kohlberg's theory of moral reasoning development specifies six stages of development, not all people necessarily modally reach the sixth stage of development. People differ in how far they develop. Thus, although six stages exist, and if people *do* develop they will pass through each stage in the same invariant sequence, not all people must necessarily pass through all the stages. Moreover, even for those who do develop through all the stages, their rates of progression may be different. Hence, people may experience differing degrees of cognitive conflict—and therefore disequilibrium—in their lives, and accordingly they may pass through these stages at different rates if, in fact, they pass through them at all.

Thus, we can expect that different people will have reached different modal levels of moral thinking at a particular time in their life. In fact, Turiel (1969) has said that his research indicates that most Americans are modally at stage 4 in their moral reasoning development. That is, for the majority of today's Americans moral correctness is evaluated in reference to the maintenance of established social order and the institutions of that order. It is important to recognize, however, that being at stage 4 does not make one any worse of a person, or any better for that matter, than someone at another stage. It only makes one different from someone else. Thus, although a scientist may appropriately address the issue of how to modally shift people from stage 4 to stage 5, for example, it is important to recognize that while such research may have important theoretical and social-change implications, it is unfair to assert that such research is arbitrarily aimed at taking people and making them better. It is my contention that while such value judgments are inappropriate for a scientist *qua* scientist, a scientific researcher must also be aware of being a citizen of society as well. Scientists must thus be aware of the social implications of their research and concomitantly of the necessity of resolving any conflicts between their scientific commitment to the search for truth and their role as citizens of society. Thus, while they may have personal beliefs about what makes for a better society, they must constantly be vigilant against letting these beliefs bias their scientific search for truth. We will have more to say about the interrelation between scientists (as theoreticians and researchers) and their society in Chapter 11.

In sum, we have seen that Kohlberg, like Piaget, offers a stage theory that deals essentially with the development of aspects of cognition. However, Kohlberg's theory has been subjected to theoretical criticism (Simpson, 1974), and research based on the theory has some important methodological problems (Kurtines and Greif, 1974). Such criticism is likely to result in both reactions by Kohlberg and some revisions of his ideas; yet, such appraisals of future activity indicate that Kohlberg's theory represents an example of a current, provocative stage theory of an aspect of moral development, a theory perhaps not in its own final stage of development.

Processes other than cognitive ones also develop, of course. Let us turn, then, to the last stage theory we will present in this chapter. Our analysis of Freud's theory of psychosexual development will provide us with an instance of how other facets of the development of people—in this instance, their affective, or emotional, development— may be also conceptualized within the framework of a stage theory.

## Freud's Stage Theory of Psychosexual Development

Sigmund Freud was born in Freiberg, Moravia, in 1856 and died in London, England, in 1939. He lived most of his life, however, in Vienna, where in 1881 he obtained his medical degree. Thus, although able to practice medicine, Freud became a research physician after graduation and undertook a series of studies of the nervous system. However, as pointed out by Hall (1954), Freud was forced to leave the university setting and his neurological research; although he had shown himself to be an excellent scientific researcher, he was unable to support his family on the basis of the limited income given to low-status faculty members, and in turn was unable to receive faculty advancement due to the anti-Semitism prevalent at that time. Freud thus left university life and entered medical practice.

Freud began this private practice as an associate of another physician, Joseph Breuer. Breuer had been working to a great extent in the treatment of hysteria, a disease believed to afflict only women because it was held that the source of the disease was damage to the uterus. Breuer had successfully treated this disorder through the application of what he termed the "talking cure" (Boring, 1950). Breuer hypnotized his patients and allowed them to talk about the emotional events associated with their difficulty. Thus, through use of this catharsis, or emotional release, Breuer was able to cure his hysterical patients. Freud readily adopted this method but soon modified its use. He found it equally, if not more, effective to allow his patients to talk completely freely about whatever was on their minds. Thus, by supporting such *free association* in his patients, Freud found that the same emotional releases could be produced without the use of hypnosis. Freud soon found that once such emotions were released, his patients would talk about things that they themselves thought they had forgotten.

With this use of the free association method, Freud was able to get his patients to

Sigmund Freud

reveal to him, and to themselves, what he termed *repressed* memories. These were memories of unpleasant feelings (affects, or emotions) or events that patients had experienced and because of their negative emotional valence had actively kept out of their awareness. Because of the negative affective connotation of these experiences, they had repressed the memory of them; they had actively kept these unpleasant memories in an area of their mind, the unconscious, that contained only material normally not present in awareness. Thus, through the use of such methods as free association, as well as a subsequent method he developed—dream interpretation—Freud was able to discover the repressed, emotion-laden memories stored in the unconscious of his patients. He was also giving himself the major tools for the method of therapy he was developing and discovering information for his theory of development and personality. Thus Freud's practice resulted in two things: a method of treatment of emotional, or neurotic, disorders, termed *psychoanalysis,* and a psychoanalytic theory of development.

Freud's methods allowed him to ascertain his patients' repressed memories. He saw that most of these memories were of events that had occurred very early in the lives of his now adult patients, in fact, in the first five years. On the basis of these retrospective accounts he was able to formulate a theory of affective, or emotional, development. Let us see the characteristics of this theory. To do this we must first deal with a core concept in this theory necessary for the understanding of all of the developments that concerned Freud. This is the concept of libido.

## The Concept of Libido

Freud was trained as a scientist and understandably was influenced by work in many areas of scientific inquiry, including the field of physics. In that field notions relating to the concept of physical energy were being investigated, and one such idea—the law of the conservation of energy—appears to have had a profound influence on Freud's thinking. This principle states that physical energy can be neither created nor destroyed, but only transformed. For example, in the human visual system, energy in the form of light rays is transformed into chemical energy (when light hits the retina of the eye), which in turn is transferred into electrical energy (when the chemicals decompose and cause a nerve cell firing to occur). When this electrical energy reaches the appropriate area of the brain the sensation of vision is experienced.

Freud saw a parallel between the transformation of energy in the physical world and events that occur in people's mental life. That is, Freud hypothesized that humans are really just complicated energy systems (Hall, 1954). By this he meant that human mental life is energized just as other physical systems are energized. Human mental life, he hypothesized, is governed by its own energy, and this human mental, or psychic, energy he termed *libido*. Thus, libido could not be created or destroyed. Humans are born with a finite amount of libido. Instead of this psychic energy being transformed into another type of energy, an alternative type of transformation was seen to take place: libido changes its area of localization within the body over the course of development. Thus, people are born with psychic energy—libido—which energizes their psychological functioning, enabling them to perform such functions as thinking, perceiving, and remembering. But, although a person is born with a finite amount of libido, this libido is transformed throughout the course of a person's development in that it changes its area of localization within the body. As we will soon see, this alteration in bodily location is the essential determinant of a person's developmental stages. The law governing the movement of the libido is the factor accounting for developmental stage progression. Analogous to Piaget's equilibration model, libido movement is the continual process underlying stage development. But before we turn to a consideration of how libidinal movement accounts for stage progression, let us first consider some implications of the fact that libido is centered in different bodily areas, or zones, at different times in development.

As we have seen, libido is energy. This energy is held not to be distributed evenly across all parts of the body but, rather, at different points in time, to be localized in specific bodily zones. When energy is present in a zone, all the person's libido is concentrated in one bodily area. Such an accumulation of energy would lead to an excessive amount of tension if there were not some way for this energy-produced tension to be released. Freud specified, however, that such excessive tension could be avoided, that it could be released, if stimulation were applied to the appropriate bodily area. For example, if one's libido were centered in the area of the mouth, then stimulation of this zone would release tension. An unpleasant feeling state (tension) would begotten rid of, and in turn, a pleasurable feeling (tension reduction) would occur. We may term this tension reduction resulting from appropriate stimulation *gratification*. Stimulation to the appropriate bodily zone would provide libidinal gratification.

Now, the area of the body wherein the libido is centered is termed an *erogenous zone*. This term implies sexual arousal, but we may also see that Freud had a broad view of what "sexual" meant. Sexual gratification was seen as involving not only the genital areas (although, as we will see, at specific stages it did mean this); rather, any bodily area wherein the libido was centered was an erogenous zone of the body and therefore capable of providing as much sexual gratification as that provided by any other such zone. Accordingly, such sexual gratification could be obtained through appropriate manipulation and stimulation of that area (Hall, 1954).

In sum, Freud said that a person's libido "travels" to different zones of the body over the course of development, and depending on where this libido is centered, the person may receive sexual gratification from stimulation to that area. That is, such stimulation would give pleasure to the person in that it would diminish the tensions that tend to accumulate in such an erogenous zone due to the focusing of libido there. Hence, we see that Freud conceptualized the way in which people's emotional tensions were gratified. By implication, we also see how a person's emotions cannot be gratified. If the appropriate stimulation to a bodily area does not occur, then an unpleasant feeling state will remain. Freud believed that such an event would have a profound negative effect on the emotional-sexual, or psychosexual, development of the person. To learn of these effects, let us now turn to our consideration of the sequences that Freud postulated as characterizing the changes in bodily localization of the libido.

## The Psychosexual Stages

Freud saw the libido as changing its site of bodily localization several times in the course of development. Hence, several psychosexual stages resulted from this libidinal movement.

**1. The Oral Stage.** Freud believed that the location of the libido at a particular point in a person's development follows the sequence of what Freud saw to be invariant, universal stages. To Freud, the emergence of these stages is primarily maturationally determined, but as we will see, the effects of these emerging stages on a person's psychosexual functioning are dependent on the specifics of that person's experience.

Accordingly, Freud postulated that the first erogenous zone in development is the oral zone. Here the libido is centered in the mouth region, where it remains for approximately the first year of the child's life. The infant of this stage obtains gratification through stimulation of this oral area, which can occur two ways. The infant can bring things into its mouth and suck on them, or later, when teeth develop, can bite on things. Accordingly, the first portion of the oral stage can be thought of as the oral incorporative (or oral sucking) period. Again, stimulation appropriate for the obtaining of gratification would involve sucking on things such as the mother's nipple or the thumb.

We have indicated, however, that it is possible for such sexual gratification not to occur. For example, an infant might be deprived of some needed oral stimulation because of frequent or prolonged mother absence. When the infant's attempts to obtain appropriate stimulation are blocked, or frustrated, serious problems in the infant's psychosexual development may ensue. If such frustration is extensive enough, *fixation* may occur. That is, there may be an arrest of libidinal development. Some of the infant's libido will remain fixed at the oral zone; when the infant develops to the next stage—in accordance with its maturational timetable—all the libido that could have moved on to the next erogenous zone will now not so move. Thus, some libido will always be tied into the person's oral zone, fixated there for the rest of life! Such an oral fixation during the oral stage will mean that the person for the rest of life will attempt to obtain the gratification missed earlier. Said another way, the emotional and/or psychosexual problems the person has as an adult will be based on these early, stage-specific fixations.

Accordingly, a fixation in the incorporative portion of the oral stage might result in an adult who is always attempting to take things in, to acquire things (Hall, 1954). This might manifest itself through attempts to acquire wealth or power or, more obviously, through the taking in of excessive amounts of food. Other examples might be an older child who relentlessly sucks on his or her thumb or an adult who chain smokes.

Alternatively, a fixation in the oral biting period of the oral stage might result in an adult who continually uses orality to be aggressive. Thus, someone who constantly makes "biting remarks" about others—for example, an extremely sarcastic or cynical person—might be seen to be fixated in the oral biting portion of the oral stage.

**2. The Anal Stage.** From about the end of the first year of life through the third year, the libido is centered in the anal region of the body. Here the child obtains gratification through exercise of the anal musculature, the muscles opening and closing the anal sphincters allowing the fecal waste products to be let out or kept in. In this stage we may also speak of two subperiods: an anal expulsive period, wherein the child obtains gratification from loosening his or her anal musculature and allowing the feces to leave; and the anal retentive period, wherein gratification is obtained through keeping the feces in.

Fixations may result from frustrating experiences in this stage also. For example, since this stage usually corresponds in our culture to the time in which people are toilet trained, anal expulsive fixations may result from too severe toilet training. This may result in an adult who "lets everything hang out"—a messy, disorderly, or wasteful person (Hall, 1954). Alternatively, an anal retentive fixation might result in an adult who is excessively neat and orderly. Such an adult might also be seen to be "up tight," keeping everything in, including his or her emotions.

**3. The Phallic Stage.** Here for the first time in our discussion of psychosexual development we must distinguish between the development of boys and of girls. Although for both sexes the phallic stage, which spans from about the third through the fifth years, involves the moving of the libido to the genital area, it is necessary to discuss the sexes separately because of the structural differences in their genitalia.

**The male phallic stage.** The libido has moved to the boy's genital area. Here sexual gratification is obtained through manipulation and stimulation of the genitals. Although masturbation would certainly provide a source of such gratification, Freud believed that the boy's mother is the person-object most likely to provide this stimulation. Because mother is providing this stimulation, the boy comes to desire his mother sexually. That is, the boy experiences incestuous love for his mother. However, at the same time, he recognizes that his father stands in the way of the fulfillment of his incestuous desires. This recognition arouses considerable negative feeling in the boy for the father.

This complex of emotional reactions Freud labels the *Oedipus complex*. Oedipus was a character in Greek mythology who (unknowingly) killed his father and then married his mother. Freud saw a parallel between this myth and events in the lives of all humans. Freud believed that the stages of his theory are universally applicable to all humans and, further, that phenomena occurring within each stage—such as the Oedipus complex—are biologically imperative. They are biologically-based emergences and hence cannot be avoided, although their effects on the person's psychosexuality are interdependent on experience. Thus, all males experience an Oedipal complex; all experience incestuous love for their mother and feelings of antagonism towards their father.

However, when the boy realizes that the father is his rival for the mother's love, a new problem is presented. The boy comes to fear that the father will punish him for his incestuous desires and that this punishment will take the form of castration. Thus, as a result of his Oedipal complex, the boy experiences castration anxiety. Because of the power of this castration anxiety, the boy gives up his incestuous desires for his mother and, in turn, identifies with his father.

This identification with the father is a most important development for the young boy. As a result of this identification, the boy comes to model himself after the father. That is, the boy forms a structure of his personality which Freud terms the *superego.* The superego has two components. The first, the *ego-ideal,* is the representation of the perfect, or ideal, man (the "father figure"), and the second is the *conscience,* the internalization of society's standards, ethics, and morals. Thus, as a result of castration anxiety, the boy models himself after his father and in so doing becomes a "man" in his society. That is, the modeling, or identification, process results in the formation of the superego, which represents, in the ego-ideal component, the internalization of the attributes that are required to become an ideal man in society. Moreover, as a result of this process, the boy develops a conscience, the second superego component, and this internalization brings about moral development in the boy (Bronfenbrenner, 1960).

At many points in this complex series of events experiences can unfavorably alter the outcome of this stage. For example, if for some reason the boy does not successfully resolve his Oedipal complex, he may not give up his love for his mother. Thus, as an adult he may be inordinately tied to her, or he may in fact identify with her instead of with his father. If this event occurs, the male might incorporate the mother's superego; this might express itself in the choice of a sexual partner when the boy reaches adulthood. Part of the mother's ego-ideal involves the type of person she wants or has as a mate. Whatever her preference, however, the point is that she chooses a male as a mate and as a sexual partner. The young boy in adopting his mother's ego-ideal might also choose a male sexual partner when an adult. Thus, one possible outcome of an unresolved Oedipal complex would be male homosexuality.

**The female phallic stage.** Freud himself was never fully satisfied with his own formulation of the female's phallic stage (see Bronfenbrenner, 1960). Here, too, the libido moves to the genital area and gratification is obtained through manipulation and stimulation of the genitals. Although presumably it is the mother who provides the major source of this stimulation for the girl, the girl (for reasons not perfectly clear even to Freud himself) falls in love with her father. Then, analogous to what occurs with boys, she desires to incestuously possess her father but realizes that her mother stands in her way. At this point, however, the similarity with male development is markedly altered.

The female is afraid that the mother will punish her for the incestuous desires she maintains towards the father. Although it is possible that the girl first fears that this punishment will take the form of castration, her awareness of her own genital structure causes her to realize that, in a sense, she has already been punished. That is, the girl perceives that she does not have a penis but only an inferior (to Freud at least) organ, a clitoris.

Hence, the girl is unable to resolve her Oedipal complex in the same way as the male does. The male experiences castration anxiety and this impels him to resolve his Oedipal complex. However, since the girl does not have a penis to fear castration for, she cannot very well experience this emotion. Thus, the girl experiences only a roughly similar emotion; she experiences *penis envy.* The girl envies the male for his possession of a genital structure that she has been deprived of.

The effect of penis envy is, however, to impel the girl to resolve her Oedipal conflict, relinquish her incestuous love for her father, and identify with her mother. Accordingly, she then forms the superego component of her personality, which, again, is comprised of the ego-ideal (here the ideal female, or "mother figure") and the conscience. However, Freud believed that only castration anxiety could eventually lead to complete superego development and thus, because females experience penis envy and not castration anxiety, females do not attain full superego development. This lack, Freud believed, takes the form of incomplete conscience development. In short, to Freud (1950), females are never as morally developed as males!

Finally, as with males, difficulties in the female's phallic stage could have profound effects on adult psychosexual functioning. Thus, in a manner analogous to males, female homosexuality could result from extreme difficulties occurring in the female's phallic stage.

**4. The Latency Stage.**  After the end of the phallic stage—at about five years of age—the libido acts in a manner analogous to an iceberg. The libido submerges and is not localized in any body zone for quite a long time. From the end of the phallic stage until puberty occurs—typically at about twelve years of age—the libido plays no further role in the person's psychosexual functioning. Freud said that the libido is latent. It does not disappear but just does not localize itself in any bodily zone. Hence, until puberty, no erogenous zones emerge.

**5. The Genital Stage.**  At puberty the libido again emerges. This time, emerging again in the genital area, it takes a mature, or adult, form. Now, if the person has not been too severely restricted in his or her psychosexual development in the first five years of life, full, adult sexuality may take place. The person's sexuality can now be directed to heterosexual union and reproduction. Thus, although as we have seen, remnants—or traces—of the effects of the earlier stages may significantly affect the person at this time in life, it is still only when the genital stage emerges that the person's libido can be gratified through directing it into reproductive functions.

## Some Concluding Comments

We have seen that Freud described five stages involved in the development of one's psychic energy. This libido, he believed, changes its site of bodily localization over the course of development and in so doing determines how the tensions built up through the presence of the libido in one concentrated area may be diminished. That is, where the libido is centered determines how the person may be gratified. Thus, psychosexual development and modes of psychosexual gratification involve the stage-dependent alteration of libido localization. Moreover, since anything that can adversely affect adult psychosexual functioning seems to have to occur in the first three stages, one major implication of Freud's theory is that the first five years of life are most crucial for adult psychosexual functioning.

Although Freud believed these stages to be biologically based and universal, there is some question as to the source of the evidence he used to form these ideas. Freud worked in Victorian Europe, a period in history noted for its repressive views about sexuality; moreover, as a practicing psychiatrist his main source of data was the memories of his adult neurotic patients, people who came to him for the treatment of emotional and behavioral problems that were interfering with their everyday functioning. Freud used his psychoanalytic psychotherapy methods to discover the source of his patients' emotional problems. Hence, he attempted to construct a theory of early development through the study of adults, adults from one particular historical period of time. Yet, adults are not children, and most of Freud's patients were *not* children; however, he constructed a theory about early development in children without actually observing them.

Thus, Freud's adult patients reconstructed their early, long-gone past through retrospection. With Freud's help they tried to remember what happened to them when they were one, two, or three years of age. This is how Freud obtained the information to build his theory. Obviously, though, one may strongly suggest that Freud's patients forgot, distorted, or misremembered these early memories and therefore biased his information. Furthermore, one may assert that Freud's patients could not necessarily be viewed as representative of other, nonneurotic Victorian adults or, for that matter, of all other humans in general.

Similarly, one may question whether Freud, if he were working today, would devise the same theory of psychosexual development. It is possible that, in addition to the limits imposed on Freud by his use of adults who were neurotic and who reconstructed their past through retrospection, other limitations may have been imposed on Freud due to the historical period in which he was working. Would, for example, Freud today find females viewing their genital structure as inferior and thus experiencing penis envy? Would he still maintain that females are not as morally developed as males, and would he find no evidence of psychosexual functioning during the years of latency?

Despite these problems and limitations of Freud's theory we do see that he provided developmental psychology with a provocative and influential—if not readily empirically testable—stage theory of aspects of emotional development. Thus, with our analysis of Freud's theory we have seen three instances of stage theories of psychological development. All positions are similar in that they all view development as proceeding through a series of qualitatively different levels of organization. Moreover, while all positions thus see development in part as being qualitatively discontinuous in nature, they also include notions of continuity. That is, they posit general, as well as specific, laws. Thus, to Piaget and Kohlberg it is disequilibrium that continuously accounts for stage progression, while to Freud it is the continual movement of libido. Finally, to differing extents all positions share the organismic, interactionist view of behavioral development; in differing ways these three theorists see the outcomes of behavioral development resulting from an interaction between the organism's characteristics and the characteristics of its experience.

We have thus completed our presentation of stage theories of development. Although we have treated these theories apart from our consideration of other approaches to the conceptualization of development, stage conceptualizations are not necessarily mutually exclusive with these other approaches. Accordingly, we will see, as we next consider the differential approach to the study of behavior development, that it is possible to combine both stage and differential concepts into one integrated theory of development. Thus, we will begin our next chapter with a consideration of the developmental theory of Erik Erikson, a follower of Freud, who, however, went beyond Freud in that he contributed to the refocusing of the major directions of psychoanalytic theory. Before we learn of this, however, let us summarize the major points made in this chapter.

## Summary

In this chapter the developmental stage theories of Piaget, Kohlberg, and Freud were described. All theories are similar in that they view development as proceeding through a series of qualitatively different levels of organization in an invariant sequence; in addition, all theorists take (albeit to differing extents) an organismic, interactionist view of development and posit both general (stage-independent) and specific (stage-dependent) laws of development.

Jean Piaget proposes a developmental stage theory of cognition. Piaget views cognition as an instance of a biological system, and as such cognition has two functional invariants: organization and adaptation. Piaget devotes most of his theoretical interest to the second concept and, accordingly, specifies that adaptation is divided into two complementary processes. First there is assimilation—the incorporation of external stimuli into the organism's already existing cognitive structure (the alteration of the object to fit the subject). Second there is accommodation—the revision of the organism's already existing structure to match the external object (the alteration of the subject to fit the object). There is a tendency for the organism to be in balance, in equilibrium, between assimilation and accommodation. Thus, equilibration denotes the view that in order for an organism to be adapted there must be a balance between the action (influence) of the environment on the organism and the action of the organism on the environment. Hence, although neither factor must outweigh the other if the organism is to be adaptive, any equilibration achieved by the organism will only be temporary. It is a basic functional component of any biological system to continue to function (adaptively), and therefore even though equilibration may be reached, such a balance will be counteracted by the continual functioning of assimilation. Such functional assimilation will necessitate a balancing accommodation in order to reestablish an (albeit temporary) equilibration. The continual functioning of this equilibration model is the mechanism by which an organism progresses through the stages of cognitive development.

Piaget specifies four stages of cognitive development. The major cognitive achievement in the sensorimotor stage (which lasts from birth to about two years) is the development of the schema of object permanency. Thus, the attainment of this knowledge is indicative of representational ability. Such ability is involved in the major cognitive achievements in the preoperational stage (which lasts from about two through six years). Here, true systems of representation develop (e.g., as indexed by language, symbolic play, and delayed imitation). Still, the child does not generally show operational ability in this stage; rather, thought is still dominated by rigid, unidirectional schematic structures. Hence, the preoperational child does not show conservation ability (the ability to know that one aspect of an array has remained unchanged although other aspects of the array have changed). With the emergence of the concrete operational stage, however (which lasts from about six through twelve years), conservations are typically seen; thus, operational structures—internalized actions that are reversible—are evidenced. Yet, the child's thought, although operational, is bound by concrete, physical reality. The child cannot think counterfactually or hypothetically. Such ability characterizes the last stage of cognitive development, the formal operational stage (which lasts from about year twelve onward). However, here, too, thought initially has limitations. Because new thought capacities come to predominate the adolescent's own thoughts, the person experiences egocentric, distorted beliefs about his or her role and importance in the world.

Lawrence Kohlberg proposes a theory of moral reasoning development which is in the cognitive developmental tradition represented by Piaget. Like Piaget, Kohlberg rejects views of moral development which exclusively focus on the response in moral choice situations. Such responses may be identical across wide ranges of the life span, and yet these responses may have distinctly different developmental meanings. Hence, one must focus on the underlying reasons for a moral response, that is, on the underlying moral reasoning structure, in order to ascertain the meaning of responses in a moral choice situation.

Accordingly, Kohlberg devised a series of moral dilemmas, stories that presented equally appropriate (or inappropriate) responses to a moral choice situation. The response a given subject offered was viewed as not as important as the reason any particular response was made. By analyzing subjects' reasons for response choices to such moral dilemma stories, Kohlberg devised a theory of moral reasoning development that divided such development into six stages (two stages each within three succeeding levels).

In level 1 (preconventional morality) reasons for moral correctness or incorrectness are related to the association between a given act and external and physical events and objects. Hence, stage 1 involves a punishment and obedience orientation, while stage 2 involves a naively egotistic orientation. In level 2 (conventional morality) the person's moral reasoning involves reference to acting as others think one should act. Hence, stage 3 is termed a good-boy morality, while stage 4 involves authority and social-order-maintenance reasoning. In level 3 (postconventional morality) moral judgments are made in reference to the view that there are arbitrary and subjective elements in social rules. Thus, stage 5 involves a contractual legalistic view of morality, while in stage 6 a conscience, or principle, orientation towards moral choices is maintained.

While Kohlberg maintains that these stages fulfill the criteria of stage conceptions of development and offers evidence in support of this, these views have been subjected to criticism. Yet, Kohlberg's formulations do represent a provocative example of how one component of cognitive functioning may be conceptualized within a stage framework, and this work does provide some important clarifications of relevant concepts involved in stage theories of development—for example, the concept of stage mixture.

As opposed to Piaget and Kohlberg, Sigmund Freud proposed a stage theory of development pertaining to the development of affect (or emotions). Freud's theory of psychosexual stage development must be understood in the context of Freud's major stage-independent conception, the concept of libido. This general law of development provides the basis for stage development within the theory. That is, libido—mental, or psychic, energy—is present in a finite amount at birth within each individual. Rather than being equally distributed throughout the body, the libido is centered in certain areas of the body at certain periods in life. The concentration of this energy in a particular part of the body makes this zone erogenous, that is, an area wherein tension is built up and appropriate stimulation will result in pleasurable feelings (or gratification). Thus, where the libido is centered will be the prime determinant of how the person may obtain gratification (or be frustrated in an attempt to obtain gratification). Stimulation to the erogenous zone will result in such pleasure, and what area is such a zone depends on where the libido is centered; this centration thus determines the psychosexual stage.

Libido is first centered in the oral zone. This oral stage of development lasts for about the first year of life. Here the child obtains gratification through appropriate stimulation of the mouth area. Since this stage is divided into two periods (the oral sucking, or incorporative, and the oral biting, or aggressive), just what type of stimulation may be considered appropriate is dependent on which of these two periods the person is in. Of course, at this stage, as well as at all others, the child's attempts to obtain gratification may be frustrated, and this may result in a fixation (an arrest of libido development). The emotional and/or psychosexual problems an adult has are based on these stage-specific fixations.

The anal stage is the second psychosexual stage (and lasts from about the end of the first year through the third year of life). Here gratification is obtained through appropriate stimulation of the anus, and again what is appropriate stimulation is determined by the particular period within the stage the person is in (i.e., the retentive or expulsive period). From about three through five years of age the person's libido is centered in the genital area, but not in a manner consistent with adult sexuality. Hence, Freud termed this stage the phallic stage and here differentiated between the psychosexual development of males and females. While children of both sex groups typically experience incestuous desires for the opposite-sexed parent, such feelings result in castration anxiety for the male and penis envy for the female. Both occurrences, however, lead each sex group to identify with the same-sexed parent *if* appropriate resolution of the Oedipal conflict is achieved. Identification results in superego development within each sex group. During latency, the fourth stage of development (which lasts from about the fifth through the twelfth year), the libido is not centered in any bodily zone. However, in the last stage of development—the genital stage—the libido reemerges.

Although problems exist in Freud's formulations pertaining to the universal nature of the psychosexual stages, the cultural bias of the theory, and the nature of the method Freud used to obtain information relevant to his formulations, he did posit an extremely influential view of emotional development. Moreover, his views have had considerable heuristic significance.

# 8
## The Differential Approach

As discussed in Chapter 6, the differential approach to the study of behavioral development considers how people become sorted into various subgroups over the course of their development. Psychologists taking such an approach are concerned with the developmental interrelations among selected status and behavioral attributes. For instance, status attributes such as age, sex, and race are considered in their developmental interrelation with behavioral attributes, conceptualized as bipolar dimensions, such as dominance-submission, extraversion-intraversion, or aggression-passivity. The discovery of the developmental location of various subgroups of people—defined in terms of their status attributes—along these dimensions is, then, a major goal of the differential developmental psychologist. Also, given individuals can be denoted in terms of their own locations in multidimensional space.

The concern with the developmental interrelation of status and behavioral attributes may be expressed in either primarily theoretical terms or as a primarily empirical interest. Psychologists employing differential concepts as components of their theoretical writings may specify how specific status attributes will be interrelated with specific behavioral attributes. Such theoretical attempts may first posit particular status attributes and then specify, along with each status attribute, events that are thought of in behavioral-attribute terms—for example, events thought of as bipolar trait dimensions.

On the other hand, differential psychologists who have primarily an empirical orientation do not a priori specify the exact interrelation of these attributes. They certainly may have theoretical orientations that affect their choices of particular status and behavioral attributes for study and they certainly may make predictions about how status and behavioral attributes will interrelate, but they are primarily concerned with empirically discovering or verifying these interrelations. Thus, this approach attempts to empirically ascertain how people become differentiated into subgroups over the course of their development.

In the present chapter we will consider examples of both the theoretical and the empirical uses of the differential approach to psychological development. First, as an instance of the use to which differential concepts may be put within a given theoretical context, we will consider the theory of Erik Erikson. Next we will consider some instances of the empirical use of the differential approach through our review of the classic work of Kagan and Moss (1962) and of differential psychologists concerned with studying the relative contributions of ontogenetic and historical changes to psychological development (e.g., Schaie and Baltes). Let us first consider the developmental theory of Erik Erikson.

Following Freud, Erikson proposes a stage theory of human emotional development. But in addition, within each of the eight stages of development that Erikson specifies, we will see the inclusion of an emotional crisis in development, which is conceptualized in differential terms. We will see, then, that Erikson combines both stage and differential concepts of development in order to provide a theoretical account of the development of human beings across their entire life span.

## Erikson's Stage and Differential Theory of Psychosocial Development

Erik H. Erikson was born in Frankfurt, Germany, in 1902, and moved to the United States in the early 1930s. While still a young man, Erikson served as a tutor to the children of some of the associates of Sigmund Freud. While working in this capacity, Erikson came

Erik H. Erikson

under the influence of both Sigmund Freud and his daughter Anna. Accordingly, Erikson received training in psychoanalysis, and after moving to the United States and settling in the Boston area he soon established his expertise in the area of childhood psychoanalytic practice.

Through his practice, as well as through the results of some empirical investigations (see Erikson, 1963), Erikson began to evolve a theory of affective—or emotional—development which complemented the theory of Sigmund Freud. Erikson's theory altered the essential focus of past psychoanalytic theorizing. To understand this alteration let us consider, first, some of Sigmund Freud's views about the mental structures that comprise the human personality.

## The Id and the Ego

As indicated in Chapter 7, Freud's theory emphasized the biologically based components of a person's psychosexual development. That is, he emphasized an interrelation between biologically imperative emergences and psychological functioning. Simply, Freud emphasized the effects of human biology on human psychology.

In the terminology of psychoanalysis, the above relation might be cast in terms of Freud's emphasis on the id in psychological functioning. In Chapter 7 we saw that Freud specified several different mental structures comprising the human personality. One of these structures, the superego, arises out of the resolution of the Oedipal conflict. Other personality structures were held to exist, however, and one of these Freud termed the *id*. To Freud, the id is an innate structure, a part of the personality present at birth "containing" all the person's psychic energy, the libido. As we have seen, the libido functions in accordance with biological imperatives. For all people it changes its site of bodily localization in accordance with an intrinsic timetable of development. Thus, the id, originally possessing all of a person's libido, is intrinsically involved in all the person's attempts to obtain pleasure, or gratification, through appropriate stimulation. In fact, because the id is the center for all the biologically based libido, and since the focusing of the libido creates tensions necessitating appropriate stimulation for their release, and since the release of such tensions results in pleasure, Freud said that the id functions in accordance with the *pleasure principle*. Thus, in emphasizing the implications of the gratification or frustration of libidinal energy, Freud was emphasizing the implications of the biologically based id on psychological functioning.

However, in addition to the superego and the id, Freud specified a third structure of the personality, the *ego*. The function of the id is solely the obtaining of pleasure, the gratification of libidinal tensions. Thus, the id impels a person into the oral stage to seek appropriate stimulation—for example, the mother's nipple. Sometimes, however, the nipple is not present. At such times the id has available a particular type of functioning, or process, which Freud termed the *primary process*. Thus, when the mother's nipple is not present the child can imagine that it is there. Simply, the primary process was held to be a fantasy, or imaginal, process. Clearly, however, such fantasies are not sufficient to allow the child to obtain the appropriate stimulation. To do this, one cannot just fantasize, one has to interact with reality. Because of this situation, Freud hypothesized that another structure of the personality is formed, a structure whose sole function is to adapt to reality, to allow the person to actually obtain needed stimulation and hence adapt and survive. This other structure of the personality is the *ego*.

Thus, we see that the ego develops in order to deal with reality; it comes about to allow the person to adjust to the demands of the real world and hence to survive. Accordingly, Freud said that the ego functions in accordance with the *reality principle*. Moreover, the ego must have processes available that enable it to adjust to and deal with reality. Thus, the *secondary process* available to the ego involves such things as cognition and perception. Through the functioning of the secondary process the ego is capable of perceiving and knowing the real world, and hence adapting to it.

Although Freud spoke about the implications of all three of the structures of the mind—the id, the ego, and the superego, the sum of which comprise a person's personality structures—we have seen that he emphasized the implications of the id on human psychological functioning. Hence, in describing human psychosexual development, Freud was viewing human beings as essentially biological and psychological in nature. On the other hand, Freud did not spend a good deal of time discussing the implications of the ego. This focus is what Erikson provides.

## Implications of the Ego
When one turns one's focus from the id to the ego, one immediately recognizes the necessity of dealing with the society that the person is developing in. The function of the ego is survival, adjustment to the demands of reality. That reality is shaped, formed, and provided by the society that the person is developing in. An appropriate adjustment to reality in one society, allowing the person to survive, might be inefficient or even totally inappropriate in another society. Hence, when we say that the child is adapting to reality we are saying, in effect, that the child is adapting to the demands of his or her own particular society. How the ego fulfills its function of reality adaptation will necessarily be different in different societies.

For instance, although it is held that all infants pass through the same oral stage and need to deal with reality in order to obtain the appropriate oral stimulation, the way they obtain it may be different in different societies. In one society, for example, there may be prolonged breast feeding by the mother. Here the infant need only seek the mother's breast, which in turn may never be very far away, in order to obtain the needed oral stimulation. In another society, however, infants may be weaned relatively early. A few days after birth the mother might return to work and leave the infant in the care of a grandparent or older sibling (see DuBois, 1944). Although the infant might also still need oral stimulation, adjustments to reality different from those involved with the former infant will have to be made. We see, then, that the specifics of a child's society must be understood when we consider the implications of the ego's functioning.

Such a conclusion was reached by Erikson. Along with other psychoanalysts practicing after Sigmund Freud (e.g., Hartmann, Kris, Anna Freud, and Rapaport), Erikson believed that the implications of the ego on human psychological functioning were not given sufficient attention by S. Freud. When such attention was given, however, it seemed clear that humans are not only biological and psychological creatures, but *social* creatures as well. To Erikson, a child's psychological development can be fully understood only when considered within the context of the society in which the child is growing up. Perhaps we can see why Erikson's most famous book is entitled *Childhood and Society* (1963).

In sum, Erikson changed the focus of Freud's psychoanalytic theory by giving primary consideration to the implications of the ego rather than the id. Although Erikson too is dealing with the development of affect—or feelings—his alteration in theoretical focus broadens the scope of Freud's concern with the psychosexual stages of development. Erikson's theory stresses the interrelation of the ego and the societal forces affecting it; thus, rather than being concerned with biologically based psychosexual development, Erikson is concerned with a person's *psychosocial* development throughout life. He is able to see that human emotional development involves far more than only psychosexual development.

As psychosocial development proceeds, the ego has to continually alter to meet changing demands of society. At each stage of psychosocial development, new adjustment demands are placed on the ego and, accordingly, new emotional crises emerge. Hence, the consideration by Erikson of the ego and society led him to the formulation of stages of development different from those of Freud and to the formulation of psychosocial emotional crises specific to each stage of development. It is these emotional crises that are conceptualized in differential terms and, accordingly, allow us to use Erikson's theory as an instance of the interrelation of stage and differential theories of development. In order to understand Erikson's use of these concepts, as well as the specifics of his theory of psychosocial development, let us consider the eight stages of ego development he specifies. As a necessary introduction to these stages, however, we must focus on Erikson's epigenetic principle and his concomitant concept of critical periods. The former notion provides us with Erikson's model for stage transition, while the latter indicates the central importance of each stage for effective, integrated psychosocial functioning.

## Erikson's Epigenetic Principle

As the ego develops, new adjustment demands are continually placed on it by society. The ego must adapt to these new demands if healthy, or optimal, development is to proceed. Yet, when new adjustment demands are placed on the developing ego, new ego capabilities must be gained in order for these demands to be met; each new societal demand requires a different adaptation by the ego, a different capability to be developed, if the ego is to continue to develop optimally. Simply, healthy ego development involves appropriate adjustments to the demands of society.

In other words, as each new demand is placed on the ego, a new crisis must be faced. Can the ego meet the demands of the society by developing this new capability? Can it thus continue to function adaptively? In essence, psychosocial development involves the development of the ego's emerging capabilities for meeting society's demands; it involves the person's attempts to resolve the emotional crises provoked by these changing demands. Hence, each new demand placed on the ego evokes an emotional crisis, a new adjustment challenge. If the ego develops the appropriate capabilities, then the crisis will be successfully resolved and healthy development will proceed.

How does the ego develop the appropriate capabilities to deal with the changing demands of reality and hence to effectively resolve the concomitant changing emotional crises? To use Erikson's (1959, p. 52) terms, "How does a healthy personality . . . accrue . . . increasing capacity to master life's outer and inner dangers . . . ?" To address this question Erikson offers an *epigenetic principle*. As defined by Erikson " . . . this principle states that anything that grows has a *ground plan,* and that out of this ground plan the *parts* arise, each having its *time* of special ascendancy, until all parts have arisen to form a *functioning whole*" (1959, p. 52).

Thus, to account for healthy ego—or personality—development, Erikson offers a principle that is basically maturational in its emphasis. This epigenetic principle asserts the existence of a maturational ground plan, a timetable, for ego development. There are various capabilities that comprise a fully developed ego. These capabilities are not, however, fully developed or present at birth. Rather, each part of the ego has a particular period of time, or stage, in the life span when it must develop *if it is ever to develop*. When one capability is developing, the focus of development is centered around this function. However, when the next stage of development comes about, again in accordance with a maturationally fixed timetable of development, the focus of development has switched to it. This maturationally fixed alteration in developmental focus is represented schematically in Fig. 8.1.

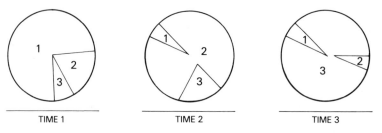

TIME 1                    TIME 2                    TIME 3

**Fig. 8.1** Schematic representation of maturationally fixed alterations in developmental focus. Here we see a developmental pattern involving three parts of a whole; each part has its own time period of ascendancy.

Clearly, we see that Erikson proposes a stage theory of psychosocial development. The emergence of each stage of development—of each ego part—is fixed in accord with a maturational timetable. Since each stage involves the development of a specific capability of the ego, a person has only a limited time to develop each stage-specific capability. Time is limited because the timetable of development will move on to the next stage of development, irrespective of whether or not the necessary capability was developed. Thus, to Erikson, each stage of psychosocial development is a *critical period*.

## Critical Periods of Psychosocial Development

Because stage development is governed by a maturational timetable, a person *must* develop what is supposed to be developed in each stage of development or else there will *never* be another chance. The timetable of development will move on, and another part of the whole—another capability—will be in *its* time of ascendancy. Thus, each stage of psychosocial development is critical in that if appropriate development does not occur when it is supposed to, two things will happen. First, that capability is doomed as an entity. The potential for the optimal development of that capability will be lost. Second, if what was necessary in order for healthy ego development to proceed was not developed, the rest of development will be unfavorably altered. When all parts of the whole should have arisen to form one synthesized, functioning whole, the person will be lacking the completed, or adequate, development of an ego part, an ego capability. Because to Erikson there are no second chances in development, once missing an appropriate development of part of one's ego, one will never be able to regain it, and the rest of development will be unfavorably altered. Hence, the person will, to this extent, be ineffective in dealing with reality. In this sense the second outcome of inappropriate development within each critical period of development is neurotic, as opposed to healthy, personality development.

In sum, Erikson proposes that ego development proceeds through eight stages of psychosocial development. In each stage a different ego capability must be developed in order for healthy ego development to proceed. Simply, developments within each psychosocial stage are critical for the final development of a fully integrated, whole ego. Such an ego will have all the necessary capabilities for meeting all the societal demands imposed on it. Thus, within each stage of development the component emotional crisis, which Erikson conceptualizes in differential terms, must be successfully resolved in order for healthy ego development to proceed.

## Stages of Psychosocial Development

As indicated above, Erikson was a follower of Freudian psychoanalysis. Thus Erikson saw the stages of psychosocial development as complementary to Freud's psychosexual stages. Accordingly, the id-based psychosexual stages exist, but along with the ego-based psychosocial stages. Hence, while these psychosocial stages have some similarity to the psychosexual stages, they go beyond them in that they comprise stages in the ego's continual functioning.

**Stage 1. The Oral-Sensory Stage.** Freud's first stage of psychosexual development is termed the oral stage. In that stage the infant is concerned with obtaining appropriate stimulation in the oral zone. Erikson believes, however, that when one changes one's focus to the ego, one sees that the newborn infant is concerned not merely with oral stimulation. Rather, the infant has newly entered the world, and therefore all its senses are being bombarded with stimulation—its eyes, ears, nose, and all other sense-receptor sites. Thus, in order to begin to deal effectively with the social world, the infant must be able to incorporate all this sensory information effectively. Hence, Erikson terms this psychosocial stage the oral-sensory stage, and in so doing indicates that the ego must develop the capability of dealing with the wealth of sensory stimulation constantly impinging on it.

However, the necessity of dealing with all this stimulation evokes a stage-specific emotional crisis for the infant. If the infant experiences the sensory world as relatively pleasant or benign, one sort of emotion will result. Alternatively, if the child's sensory stimulation experiences are negative or harsh, then another type of feeling will result. Thus, if the infant has relatively pleasant sensory experiences, he will come to *feel* that the world is a relatively benign, supportive place, that it will not hurt or shock him. To Erikson, then, the infant will develop a sense of basic trust. If, however, the infant experiences pain and discomfort, he will feel that the world is not supportive but that there is pain and danger in the world. Here the infant will develop a sense of mistrust.

The infant thus faces an emotional crisis, precipitated by the nature and quality of the sensory world he attempts to incorporate. He must develop a sense of trust or a sense of mistrust. It is this emotional crisis that Erikson conceptualizes in differential terms. The emotional crisis, then, is between *trust versus mistrust*. (We may delete the phrase "a sense of" for the sake of brevity of presentation, with the understanding that this phrase is always to be applied to all of the alternative stage-specific feeling sets.) Erikson thinks of these two alternative feelings as forming a behavioral attribute. That is, they represent bipolar, alternative end points along a single dimension. Erikson would represent the emotional crisis of trust versus mistrust as:

trust _____ mistrust

The ends of this bipolar continuum represent the alternative emotional outcomes of this stage of psychosocial development. In other words, Erikson stresses the point that people do not, and should not, develop *either* complete trust *or* complete mistrust. Rather, a given person will develop a feeling that falls somewhere along this dimension.

If a person develops complete trust, Erikson points out, this will be as unadaptive as developing complete mistrust—the person will not recognize the real dangers that exist in the world (e.g., he will never look when crossing the street because he will trust that no driver would ever hurt him, or he might never strive to provide for himself because he feels that the world will surely take care of him). On the other side, however, a person whose feeling falls on the far end of the mistrust side of the continuum will never attempt to venture interactions with the world because he feels that assuredly the world will hurt him. In a sense we might say that such a person would have absolutely no hope; he feels that there is no chance of anything but pain resulting from his interactions, his incorporations of the world. Thus we see that it is necessary to develop a feeling that lies somewhere between the two end points of the bipolar continuum. If one develops more trust than mistrust, then Erikson believes that healthy ego development will proceed. If, however, one develops greater mistrust than trust, then unhealthy, unoptimal ego development will proceed. Having a feeling located closer to the trust end of the continuum means that the ego has developed the appropriate incorporative capabilities allowing it to deal effectively with the sensory input from the world. Having a feeling located closer to the other side of the continuum, however, means that the appropriate ego capabilities have not developed.

In other words, for this first status attribute—the oral-sensory psychosocial stage of psychological development—a ratio of trust/mistrust greater than one will result in healthy ego development, while a ratio of trust/mistrust less than one will result in unoptimal ego development. For any status attribute (stage of development), a behavioral attribute location that results in a ratio (of positive-end to negative-end) greater than one means that the appropriate ego capabilities have developed, while a corresponding ratio less than one means that the appropriate ego capabilities have not developed.

We see that each stage of psychosocial development may be construed as a status attribute, and within each status attribute there exists an emotional crisis that is conceptualized as a bipolar dimension, as a behavioral attribute. One's location along this dimension defines the extent to which one has successfully resolved the emotional crisis precipitated by the reality demands put on the ego at this stage of development and thus the extent to which the appropriate ego capability has been developed. Further, this location will affect the ego's functioning as the child enters the next stage of psychosocial development.

**Stage 2. The Anal-Musculature Stage.**  Freud's second stage of psychosexual development is termed the anal stage. Here we may remember that the infant obtains gratification through the exercise of his anal musculature. To Erikson, however, psychosocial development involves the other muscles of the body as well. Here, then, psychosocial development involves developing the control over all of one's muscles, not just those involved in psychosexual development. Analogous to use of his anal muscles, the infant must learn when to hold on and when to let go (Erikson, 1963) of all his bodily muscles. He must develop the capability of being able to control his own overall bodily movements.

Accordingly, if the child feels that he is in control of his own body, that he *himself* can exert this control over himself, the child will develop a sense of autonomy. To the extent that the child can control his own movements, he will feel autonomous. On the other hand, if the child finds himself unable to exert this independent control over his own bodily musculature, if he finds that others have to do for him what he feels he is expected to do himself, then he will develop a sense of shame and doubt. He will feel shame because he is not showing the ability to control his own movements (e.g., bowel movements, movements involved in feeding himself), and this may evoke disapproval from significant other persons (e.g., parents). Moreover, because he is experiencing this inability to control himself he will feel doubt about his capabilities for so doing. He feels shame because he experiences others doing things for him that both he and these others feel he should be doing for himself; thus feeling shame for this lack of effectiveness, he further feels doubt about whether or not he has the capability to perform these expected functions. In sum, the second bipolar psychosocial crisis is one between *autonomy versus shame and doubt.*

**Stage 3. The Genital-Locomotor Stage.**  Here, if the child has appropriately developed within the anal-musculature stage and gained the ability to control his own movements, he will now have a chance to use these abilities. This third psychosocial stage corresponds to Freud's psychosexual phallic stage. Although Erikson does not dismiss the psychosexual implications of the Oedipal conflict, he specifies that such a development also has important psychosocial implications. That is, if the child is to successfully resolve the Oedipal conflict he must begin to independently move away from the parental figures. He must begin to employ his previously developed self-control over his muscles, take his own steps into the world, and thereby break his Oedipal ties. What Erikson says is that society expects the child not to remain "tied to his mother's apron strings," but rather to locomote (walk off) by himself and thereby eliminate such attachments. He must be able by himself to move freely in interaction with his environment.

Accordingly, if the child is able to step in the world without his parent being there to guide or prod him, he will develop a sense of initiative. He will feel that he himself can decide when to use his locomotor abilities to interact with his world. On the other hand, if the child does not move off on his own, if he remains tied to the parent for directives about the exercise of his locomotor functioning, he will not feel a sense of initiative. Rather, the child will feel a sense of guilt. That is, the child's Oedipal attachments remain relatively intact, and to the extent that they continue to exist while at the same time his society expects him to show evidence of their being eliminated, he will feel guilt. Thus, in this stage a child will develop towards either *initiative or guilt,* and again, of course, this emotional crisis is conceptualized as a bipolar dimension. People should develop towards the initiative side of this emotional attribute continuum such that the ratio of initiative to guilt is greater than one.

**Stage 4. Latency.**    Freud did not pay a good deal of attention to the psychosexual latency stage because of his belief that the libido is submerged and consequently the stage has little if any psychosexual importance to Freud. However, Erikson attaches a great deal of psychosocial importance to the latency years. Erikson believes that in all societies children begin at this stage to learn the requisite tasks necessary for being adult members of society. In our society this psychosocial directive takes the form of the child's being sent off to school. In other societies this same psychosocial orientation may take the form of teaching the child to farm, cook, hunt, or fish.

Accordingly, if the child learns these skills well, if he learns what to do and how to do it, he will develop a sense of industry. The child will feel that he knows what to do to be a capably functioning adult member of society. He will feel that he can be industrious, that he has the capability to do. On the other side of the continuum lies the feeling associated with failures in these psychosocial developments. If the child feels that he has not learned to capably perform the requisite tasks of his society (while others around him, he feels, have acquired this), he will feel a sense of inferiority. Thus, to the extent that children feel that they have or have not developed the requisite skills of their society, they will develop feelings toward either *industry or inferiority.*

**Stage 5. Puberty and Adolescence.**    This stage of development corresponds to the genital stage of psychosexual development in Freud's theory. Erikson too is concerned with the implications of the emergence of a genital sex drive occurring at puberty. But as with the previous stages of psychosocial development, Erikson here looks at the broader, psychosocial implications of all the physical, physiological, and psychological changes that emerge at puberty.

There are numerous changes that occur when a person enters puberty. In fact, one may even suggest that every dimension of the person undergoes quantitative and/or qualitative change. With puberty comes the emergence of the secondary sexual characteristics (e.g., pigmented pubic hair, changes in the voice, changes in the muscle and fat distributions of the body, menarche and breast development for females, the first ejaculation and pigmented facial hair for males). There are even changes in the primary sexual characteristics, the genitalia (for instance in males there is a thickening and an elongation of the penis). Moreover, the person experiences new bodily sensations: the person now has a sexual drive—a genital capacity—and this evokes new bodily sensations that have to be dealt with and understood. Yet the person's mental structures also undergo a qualitative change at about this time. As we have seen in our discussion of Piaget's theory in Chapter 7, the person at this time begins to think differently; formal operations emerge and this means that the person will become predominantly centered on himself (what we have seen termed adolescent egocentrism) and will think about himself abstractly and hypothetically.

Erikson sees all these changes occurring with puberty as presenting the adolescent—for this is the label that society now attaches to him—with serious psychosocial problems. The child has lived for about twelve years and has developed a sense of who he is and of what he is and is not capable of. If he has developed successfully, he will have developed more trust than mistrust, more autonomy than shame and doubt, more initiative than guilt, and more industry than inferiority. In any event, all the feelings he has developed have gone into giving him a feeling about who he is and what he can do. Now, however, this knowledge is challenged. The adolescent now finds himself in a body that looks and feels different, and further finds that he is thinking about these things in a new way. Thus, all the associations the adolescent has had about himself in earlier stages may not now be relevant to this new person he finds himself to be.

Accordingly, the adolescent asks himself a crucial psychosocial question: Who am I? Moreover, at precisely the time when the adolescent feels unsure about this, society begins to ask related questions of the adolescent. For instance, in our society the adolescent must now begin to make his first definite steps toward career objectives (e.g., he has to make a decision about whether or not he will enter into college preparatory courses). Thus, the adolescent must find out who he is both for himself and for his society. This question—Who am I?—is basically a question of self-definition, necessitated by the emergence of all these new puberty-related feelings and capabilties (e.g., the sex drive and formal thought), as well as by the new demands placed on the adolescent by society.

Accordingly, Erikson says that such self-definition is the most important psychosocial task of adolescence. The changes of puberty and the psychosocial demands placed on the adolescent bring about an *identity crisis*. To feel that he has answered the unavoidable question of self-definition, the adolescent must discover who he is; he must achieve an identity. However, because of its complexity, this attainment can represent an arduous task. It involves the development of several things, all of which the person must coordinate—or feel he has coordinated—in order to resolve the identity crisis.

For instance, the adolescent must find out what he believes in, what his attitudes and ideals are. These factors, which can be said to define one's *ideology,* provide an important component of one's *role*. That is, when we know who we are, we know what we do, and when we know what we do, we know our role in society.

Along with any role (e.g., wife, father, student, teacher) goes a set of orientations toward the world which serves to define that role. These attitudes, beliefs, and values give us some idea of what a person engaged in a particular role in society thinks of and does. Thus, there is an ideology that serves to define a societal role. We know fairly well what the ideology of a Catholic priest is and how it is similar to and different from the ideology associated with a military general, or a professional artist, or a professional politician. The point is that along with any role goes a role-defining ideology. To solve one's identity crisis one must be committed to a role, which in turn means showing commitment—or fidelity—toward an ideology.

If the adolescent finds his role in society, if he can show fidelity toward an ideology, he will have achieved a sense of identity. He will feel that he knows what his role is, and he will feel that he knows who he is and what he believes in (his ideology). Alternatively, if the adolescent does not find a role he can play in his society, he will remain in his identity crisis. He might typically complain that he "does not know where he is at" or that he cannot "get his head together." To resolve this crisis and redress these problems he might find himself trying one role one day and another the next. He might successfully, but only temporarily, invest himself in many different things. Accordingly, Erikson maintains that if the adolescent does not resolve his identity crisis, he will feel *a sense of role confusion* or *identity diffusion*. These two terms denote the adolescent's feelings associated with being unable to adopt a role and hence define himself.

Several possibilities exist for an adolescent who is in his identity crisis. One is to simply adopt a readily available role supplied by society. For instance, the adolescent could go into the father's business, enter the service, or get married and define him or herself as a husband or wife. Another possible route would be to adopt an identity also readily available but deemed socially unacceptable by society. For example, one could become a delinquent and thus achieve what Erikson terms *negative identity formation*. Finally, instead of first finding a role, one could adopt an ideology. That is, one could show intense commitment to some set of beliefs (e.g., those associated with some current social cause) and thus achieve a feeling of having a role. Since ideology and role go hand in hand, if one adopts an ideology, one must therefore have a role. One would be someone who stands for that cause. Such a solution would give a feeling of having found one's role. Thus, one would feel "older now"; one would feel that one has gotten past one's identity crisis. Perhaps, however, because such a solution does not really represent a true internalization of a role, this intense commitment toward an ideology and the concomitant feeling of being "older now" are not enduring. One might become disillusioned with this ideology, and then if one develops further and finally achieves an actual identity, one might look back at these previous commitments and feelings of being "older now" as being premature.

**Stage 6. Young Adulthood.**   In this and the last two psychosocial stages, Erikson departs from the psychosexual model and provides a description of the psychosocial stage changes involved with the rest of the human life span. Thus, after the adolescent years the person enters into young adulthood and accordingly is faced with a new set of psychosocial requirements.

In young adulthood the person is oriented toward entering into a marital union. Hopefully, the person has achieved an identity and now knows who he is. The society now requires the person to enter into an institution that will allow the society to continue to exist. Accordingly, the formation of a new family unit must be established—for example, through marriage. The young adult must form a relationship with another person which will allow such an institution to prosper. This psychosocial directive, however, leads the person into another emotional crisis.

Erikson argues that to enter into and successfully maintain such a relationship, a person must be able to give of himself totally. Such openness and complete give and take is not limited, argues Erikson, only to sexual relations. Rather, Erikson means that by giving of oneself totally, all the facets of one person (e.g., feelings, ideas, goals, attitudes, and values) must be unconditionally available to the other person; moreover, the person must be unconditionally receptive to these same things from the partner. Accordingly, to the extent that one can attain such interchange, one will feel *a sense of intimacy*. Again, this is not limited just to sexual intimacy but includes the mutual interchange of both partners' most intimate feelings, ideas, and goals. If, however, one has not achieved an identity in stage 5 and thus does not have a total sense of self (to give of completely), then of course one will not be able to achieve this sense of intimacy. One cannot give of one's self if one does not have a self to give. Thus, rather than being able to have a complete mutual interchange, one will be restricted in what one is capable of giving. Accordingly, there are limits to being intimate with another; if one cannot (for whatever reason) share and be shared, then one will feel *a sense of isolation*.

Erikson's theorizing provides a suggestion about why divorce is becoming so prevalent in today's society. Perhaps people enter into marriage unions with the expectation of finding their identities. They expect to define themselves through marriage and thus discover who they are. However, because, according to Erikson, less than two identities can never be made to equal two identities, such people would be disillusioned by marriage. Instead of finding out who they are, they experience feelings of isolation. Although they are now joined with another person, this union, this other person, is a disappointment. This other person has not provided them with what they expected—an identity—and thus this union has instead brought on feelings of being alone.

**Stage 7. Adulthood.** If a successful, intimate union has been consummated, however, the person can now attempt to meet the next set of psychosocial requirements, presented by adulthood. In this stage society requires the person to play the role of a productive, contributing member of society. Farmers must grow produce, artists must paint pictures, and professors must generate ideas (and publications).

Accordingly, if the person is successfully playing the role society expects of him, if he is contributing and producing what is expected, then the person will have *a sense of generativity*. He will feel he is performing his role appropriately. He will feel he is being generative. On the other hand, if the person finds that he is not fulfilling the requirements of his role, if he is not producing as he should, he will feel *a sense of stagnation*. The person will find that his output is below expectations.

Traditionally, American society has drawn important distinctions between men and women in what behaviors they may appropriately engage in. Thus, how men and women achieve feelings of generativity has been different. While men's generative feelings could be achieved through engaging in professional or business activities, women's generational feelings could traditionally be attained only through the generation (or production) of children! Women who chose not to have children or opted for entering the "men's world" (of business or professionalism) were negatively evaluated by society and viewed as inappropriately fulfilling the roles of women. Such pejorative orientations toward women obviated the possibility of women making their maximal contribution to our society. This situation is, of course, changing, and Erikson points out that well it should. If women are limited to the production of children as their only way of attaining this needed feeling of generativity, then, Erikson feels, eventually our society and the world will be faced with a severe problem: overpopulation. Thus, in addition to the moral and human rights reasons for widening women's roles in our society, Erikson provides us with a psychological and an ecological reason for this alteration. Women must, he argues, be allowed to channel their generational behavior along other lines if society is to survive. Society must then come to view as appropriate women's fulfilling their generational feelings in all possible ways. The choice for women should not remain children versus stagnation. If this choice is not altered, then we will enter into a most dangerous spiral. More and more people will be produced and they, in turn, will produce more and more people.

**Stage 8. Maturity.**   In this stage of psychosocial development the person recognizes that he is reaching the end of his life span. If he has successfully progressed through his previous stages of development—if he has experienced more trust than mistrust, more autonomy than shame and doubt, if he has had an identity, had an intimate relationship, and been a productive, generative person—then he will face the final years of life with enthusiasm and élan. He will be childlike, says Erikson, in his enthusiasm for life. Thus, Erikson argues that he will feel *a sense of ego integrity*. He will feel that he has led a full and complete life.

Alternatively, if the person has not experienced these events—if, for example, he has felt mistrustful, guilty, a sense of identity diffusion, isolation, and stagnation—then he will not be enthusiastic about these last years of his life. Rather, he will perhaps feel cheated or bitter. He might be "childish" in his behavior, as if trying to go back to earlier years and attain the feelings that he never experienced. In this case, Erikson says, the person would feel *a sense of despair*. He would feel that time was running out and that he had not gained everything out of life that he felt he needed.

### Some Concluding Comments

We have seen that Erikson describes eight stages in the psychosocial development of human beings. In addition, we have learned that within each of these eight stages Erikson conceives of an emotional crisis, conceptualized in differential terms. That is, while each of the stages may be thought of as a separate status attribute, each concomitant emotional crisis is conceptualized as a bipolar trait dimension. A person develops a feeling within each stage that lies somewhere between the end points of each feeling dimension. Thus, each of these bipolar dimensions may be thought of as representing a behavioral attribute. In turn, since a person may develop a feeling at any particular location along each of these continua, a person's individual psychosocial developmental pattern may be represented as his location in this multidimensional feeling space.

In sum, then, Erikson uses differential concepts to theoretically conceptualize people's psychosocial development. He uses his stages as analogous to status attributes and, in addition, theoretically specifies the existence of differentially conceptualized emotional crises within these stages. Thus, through our presentation of Erikson's theory we have seen how a differential approach to the understanding of

**Table 8.1**  Erikson's theory of psychosocial development.

| Psychosocial stage | Bipolar emotional crisis | | |
| --- | --- | --- | --- |
| | A sense of: | *versus* | A sense of: |
| 1. Oral-sensory | basic trust | | mistrust |
| 2. Anal-musculature | autonomy | | shame, doubt |
| 3. Genital-locomotor | initiative | | guilt |
| 4. Latency | industry | | inferiority |
| 5. Puberty and adolescence | identity | | role confusion |
| 6. Young adulthood | intimacy | | isolation |
| 7. Adulthood | generativity | | stagnation |
| 8. Maturity | ego integrity | | despair |

psychosocial development may be employed within what is primarily a theoretical framework. Erikson uses differential concepts to best depict what he considers to be, theoretically, the important components of psychosocial development. Although we would take issue with several of Erikson's specific formulations, on the basis of our discussions in Chapters 3 and 4 of organismic, interactionist positions on the nature-nurture controversy, his theory is still important. It represents a unique integration of stage and differential conceptualizations of human development within a theory that attempts to describe aspects of development across the entire life span.

We have said, however, that the differential approach may be utilized also as primarily an empirical mode of investigating the phenomena of psychological development. Thus, one may employ research methods that allow people who possess different status attributes to be differentiated into subgroups on the basis of studied behavior attributes. Hence, the use of such methods will allow one to make an empirical determination of the developmental interrelation of status and behavioral attributes. Although numerous examples exist of such an empirical use of the differential approach, we will now consider perhaps one of the most outstanding examples of such work, the longitudinal study by Kagan and Moss (1962). However, let us first offer, as a final summary of Erikson's theory, Table 8.1, which presents his eight psychosocial stages and their respective bipolar emotional crises.

## The Kagan and Moss Study of Birth to Maturity

In their 1962 book, *Birth to Maturity,* Jerome Kagan and Howard Moss report the results of a longitudinal study of psychological development. A *longitudinal study* involves the study of the same group of people over the course of their development. Through such repeated measurement the researcher obtains data allowing an assessment of the continuity-discontinuity and/or the stability-instability of the developing behaviors being studied. Accordingly studies that have a long duration (like those of Kagan and Moss) are suited for studying these issues.

However, longitudinal studies are difficult to do, and they usually have important limitations. It is difficult to obtain a large group of people who are willing to submit to repeated, and often intensive, psychological investigation. Accordingly, longitudinal samples are usually comprised of a small number of people, and these people can be presumed to be different from other people in important ways. After all, these people are willing to take part in a long-term psychological investigation of their own lives. Thus, longitudinal samples may not be representative of any larger population. This makes results from such a study difficult to generalize to other groups of people. In addition, longitudinal studies are expensive, in terms of both money needed to pay for ongoing research costs and the great deal of time it obviously takes to do such studies. As the years go by, some subjects may drop out (possibly making the sample even more un-representative), or in one way or another the researchers themselves may drop out of the study. In addition, repeated measurements with the same subjects may allow prac-tice to affect responses. Yet, despite these limitations, longitudinal studies seem suited for assessing the continuity-discontinuity and/or the stability-instability of selected be-haviors.

Alternatives to the longitudinal research strategy do exist. One such alternative is called the *cross-sectional* study. Here, rather than using the same subjects at different ages, different subjects at different ages are used. The researcher attempts to match subjects of different age groups on all variables (such as socioeconomic status, intelli-gence, and sex) except one: age. If such matching is successful, then when all these differently aged subjects are measured at one given point in time, the researcher can see how they differ in respect to the behavior being studied. Obviously, this approach is less expensive (in time and money) and is quicker to complete than is the longitudinal study. Yet, problems exist with this type of study also. When age-group differences are seen in the expression of some psychological phenomenon, the researcher cannot be sure whether these changes are actually developmental changes (i.e., ontogenetic changes due to developmental processes of people who are now of a given age) or *historical* changes. That is, such changes—or age-group differences—may be due to the fact that the people who are of different ages, but who have been studied at one point in time, have in fact lived and developed in historically different periods of time.

Because of these problems with the cross-sectional approach—in addition to the problems we have seen with the longitudinal type of study—some developmental psychologists (e.g., Schaie) have suggested compromise methods of research, methods that adopt the assets of each technique. We will consider such an alternative approach in the last main section of the present chapter, and we will again turn to more general issues in developmental research in Chapter 11. However, at this point we should see both the assets and limitations of longitudinal research, and in so doing we should recognize why major longitudinal studies of psychological development are few and far between. Thus, our consideration of the Kagan and Moss study allows us to focus not only on one of the best but on one of the relatively few major longitudinal studies of psychological development. Let us now turn to a consideration of the methods that Kagan and Moss used to assess the development of various psychologi-cal phenomena from birth to maturity.

## The Methods of the Kagan and Moss Study

Kagan and Moss present a summary of the results of a longitudinal study of personality development which began in 1929 and continued through the late 1950s. Because Kagan and Moss believed that "only systematic longitudinal observations can discover those behaviors that are marked for future use and those that will be lost along the way" (1962, p. 1), they employed longitudinal observations to assess personality development. Thus, children enrolled in the Fels Research Institute's longitudinal population during the years between 1929 and 1939 were selected for such repeated observations. In this way 89 children (44 boys and 45 girls) were selected for study. Subjects were mainly from the Midwest, Protestant in their religious affiliations, white, of middle-class socioeconomic backgrounds, and the children of relatively well-educated parents. In other words, some of the differential status variables that Kagan and Moss considered were, of course, age and sex; in addition, religion, socioeconomic status, and parents' educational backgrounds were also considered.

Obviously, not everyone who develops has the above status characteristics. Thus, we see that one limitation of the Kagan and Moss longitudinal study is that the sample is not representative of broader populations. Accordingly, while we may be unsure about the extent to which we may generalize the specific results of the Kagan and Moss study, we may at least expect the findings to provide us with some interesting (if tentative) suggestions about the course of personality/behavioral development.

**Sources of Data.** The major purpose of the Kagan and Moss study was to discover the interrelation of selected status variables (primarily age and sex) to various behavioral dimensions. Through such an interrelation an indication of the relation between psychological development in childhood and adult psychological functioning might be discovered. Accordingly, information about the subjects was gathered in a manner allowing the information to be divided into two broad age periods.

The initial information about the children pertained to their development from birth through early adolescence. The children were administered various tests of their intelligence and their personality, and these assessments were combined with live observations of them in their homes, their nurseries, and later, their schools and day camps. In addition, assessments of the mothers of the children were made, and teacher interviews were conducted. Through these procedures, data allowing for the measurement of many different variables across the first fourteen years of life were obtained. Each variable was conceptualized as representing a differential (behavioral) dimension, with end points lying at 1 and 7. For example, for the variable "dependency," a score of 7 might indicate high dependency and a score of 1 might indicate low dependency, and a person's score could fall anywhere along this dimension.

Before interrelation between these attributes began, the status variable of age was further reconceptualized. Instead of differentiating their subjects continuously—that is, into fourteen consecutive age groups, one year to the next—Kagan and Moss reduced the first fourteen years of data into four consecutive and overlapping age periods: birth to three years (infancy and early childhood); three to six years (preschool); six to ten years (early school years); and ten to fourteen years (preadolescent and early adolescent years). In sum, for the first fourteen years or their subjects' lives, status variables such as age period and sex were interrelated with several psychological variables, each conceptualized as seven-point behavioral attribute dimensions.

Of their 89 subjects studied in their first fourteen years of life, 71 participated in the second phase of data gathering. When they returned, in the time between mid-1957 through late 1959, they were between nineteen and twenty-nine years of age. Thus, a final age period—adulthood—was now introduced into the study. Again, these subjects had to be tested and measured to ascertain their location along the various psychological dimensions under study.

Kagan and Moss now had a considerable amount of data bearing on the psychological development and later adult functioning of a group of people, a group whose development from birth to maturity had been longitudinally studied. They now began the arduous process of interrelating these measurements in their attempt to discover how these people were differentiated into various subgroups over the course of their development. They began to analyze their information in order to discover how development in the first fourteen years of life (the first four age periods) related to the psychological functioning of the adult.

Did behaviors seen early in life remain present throughout the first fourteen years, and further, did early behavior relate in any way to the psychology of the developed adult? How did one's multidimensional location throughout childhood relate to one's multidimensional location as an adult? Let us now turn to the results of the Kagan and Moss study to see how the information they obtained answered such questions.

## The Status Variables of Age Period and Sex

Perhaps the most consistent finding obtained by Kagan and Moss was that many of the child's behaviors shown in the third age period (the early school years, from six to ten years of age) were fairly good predictors of similar early adulthood behaviors (Kagan and Moss, 1962, p. 266). Similarly, a few behaviors seen in the second age period (the preschool years, from three to six years of age) were also related to theoretically similar adult behaviors. Thus, such adult behaviors as dependency (on the family) or anxiety (in social interactions) seemed to be related to analogous behavior/personality characteristics in these early or middle childhood periods. In this way, Kagan and Moss found that knowledge of a child's position on a given variable at a particular age period in the child's life allowed one to make some predictions about that child's related adult functioning. In other words, the person's position along many dimensions seemed to remain stable; and in turn, because these same variables seemed to characterize the person at these different age periods in his life, continuity in the personality development of the person seemed to have occurred. Accordingly, Kagan and Moss conclude that such findings "offer strong support to the popular notion that aspects of adult personality begin to take form during early childhood" (1962, pp. 266-67).

Despite such overall continuity in personality development, however, an important qualification must be made. Despite the fact that changes in the status variable of age period were often associated with continuity in the expression of various behavior/personality attributes, another status variable—sex—affected this relation. Kagan and Moss found that age-period continuity in various behavioral characteristics was essentially dependent upon whether or not that behavior was consistent with traditional sex-role standards. For example, degrees of childhood passivity and childhood dependency remained continuous for adult women but were not similarly continuous for adult men. Kagan and Moss argue that traditional sex-role standards in our culture place negative sanctions on passive and dependent behaviors among males. Studies of stereotypes about the ideal masculine figure in our society find that the most positively evaluated male figure is one who is viewed as dominant, aggressive, and instrumentally effective (Lerner and Korn, 1972). Men who do not display such characteristics are negatively evaluated (Lerner and Korn, 1972). Kagan and Moss believe, however, that no corresponding negative sanctions about such behaviors exist for women in our society. Thus, the authors found continuity between childhood passivity and dependency and adult passivity and dependency for females. A similar relation for males was not found.

On the other hand, through an analogous argument we might expect aggressive, angry, and sexual behaviors to be continuous for males but not continuous for females. In fact, such a finding was obtained. For example, "Childhood rage reactions and frequent dating during preadolescence predicted adult aggressive and sexual predispositions, respectively, for men but not for women" (Kagan and Moss, 1962, p. 268).

Of course, certain behaviors could be expected to remain similarly continuous for both sexes. Intellectually oriented behaviors (e.g., attempting to master school work) and sex-appropriate interest behaviors (e.g., fishing for males, knitting for females) are consistent with traditional sex-role standards for either sex. Society approves such behaviors among members of both sexes. Accordingly, Kagan and Moss found that such behaviors showed a marked degree of continuity for both sexes from their early school years through their early adulthood.

In sum, Kagan and Moss found overall age continuity for many personality/behavior characteristics. For many behaviors one could predict the adult's type of functioning through knowledge of his or her functioning in respect to conceptually consistent childhood variables. Yet, whether or not such overall continuity was found depended on whether a particular behavior was consistent with traditional societal sex-role standards. Those behaviors that were consistent with sex-role standards remained stable; for those that were not, discontinuity was seen. Kagan and Moss summarize this portion of their results by stating:

It appears that when a childhood behavior is congruent with traditional sex-role characteristics, it is likely to be predictive of phenotypically similar behaviors in adulthood. When it conflicts with sex-role standards, the relevant motive is more likely to find expression in theoretically consistent substitute behaviors that are socially more acceptable than the original response. In sum, the individual's desire to mold his overt behavior in concordance with the culture's definition of sex-appropriate responses is a major determinant of the patterns of continuity and discontinuity in his development (1962, p. 269).

## The Sleeper Effect

The above results present an important illustration of the potential empirical outcomes derived from longitudinal application of the differential approach. However, this technique provides the opportunity for finding other types of results. For instance, it may be the case that an important event occurs early in a person's life. The event will provide a cause for some of the person's behaviors but this effect may not be seen right away. Simply, " . . . there may be a lag between a cause and open manifestation of the effect" (Kagan and Moss, 1962, p. 277). In other words, one may see a *sleeper effect* in development.

The Kagan and Moss method was well suited for the discovery of such sleeper effects. Through their repeated measurements of the same people over the course of their development, Kagan and Moss could ascertain if a behavior or event measured early in a person's life, while not showing effects at middle periods, was highly related to a similar behavior found in later adult life.

Two such instances of a sleeper effect in development occurred in the Kagan and Moss study. First, among males, passivity and fear of bodily harm measured in the first age period (zero to three years) were found to be better predictors of a conceptually similar adult behavior (e.g., love-object dependency) than were the other measurements of the childhood behaviors. Thus, males who were passive and feared bodily harm in their first three years of life (and thus may be surmised to have been dependent on their mothers for support and protection) were found to be similarly dependent on their love object (e.g., their wives) when they reached adulthood. Yet, measurements of passivity and fear of bodily harm in the other three childhood/adolescent age periods did not predict adult male dependency. Although one may attempt to account for this finding through reference to possible problems in the measurement of dependency (perhaps the measures during the intervening periods were not sensitive enough to adequately measure dependency), one may also speculate that this sleeper effect is an instance of qualitative continuity and quantitative discontinuity. For some males there was an abrupt change in their measured dependency-related behaviors, between the first age period and the next three ones, and in turn between these three periods and the adult period. These two abrupt changes represent quantitative discontinuity. Yet, because the first period behavior measurements *were* highly predictive of adult behavior measurements, and because these two sets of measurements seem to be reflective of analogous behavioral tendencies, one may say that the same, underlying personality characteristic was expressed in these two measurements. Thus, one may interpret the relation between the two widely separated age periods as being reflective of qualitative continuity and speculate that perhaps factors related to differential social situations can account for this complex finding. Perhaps quantitative discontinuity was seen because the dependency-related behaviors measured in the first period and in adulthood were measures of the male in relation to a female (mother and wife, respectively), while the measures of dependency-related behaviors in the intervening three age periods were measures of the male in relation to his peers (presumably mostly other males). Since we know that such dependency-related behaviors are negatively sanctioned for males, it may be the case that although the personality characteristic remained present, it was not manifested in the later-childhood/adolescent age periods because these periods presumably involved major interaction with males and not females. Admittedly this is speculation, but the point is that the discovery of sleeper effects in development, through the application of longitudinal diffe.ential methodology, provides rich grist for future research.

A similarly interesting sleeper effect was also found with females, when certain measures of the mother's behavior toward the child during the first three years of the child's life were related to various aspects of the child's own adolescent and adult functioning. If mothers had critical attitudes toward their daughters during the first age period (zero to three years), this was highly predictive of adult achievement behavior on the part of the daughter. However, a similar attitude in the middle three age periods was not so related to adult female behavior. Similarly, maternal protection of the female child during the child's first three years of life was related to a conceptually consistent adult female behavior on the part of the daughter (e.g., withdrawal from stress), while similar maternal behaviors during the child's later age periods were not so related to adult female behaviors. Thus, through these findings we see that Kagan and Moss were able to discover events and/or behaviors that occurred early in a child's life that, while not relating to similar behaviors in immediately succeeding age periods, did highly relate to later, adult functioning.

## Some Concluding Comments

We see, then, that the application of a longitudinal, differential approach allowed Kagan and Moss to discern some important ways in which people may become differentiated into subgroups over the course of their development. Although their specific results are certainly provocative, as noted above, they are difficult to generalize to broader populations of people. Yet, their method and findings do suggest the importance of employing such a longitudinal strategy if one wants to discover the continuities and the discontinuities in a child's development. A cross-sectional approach might not have been able to uncover the fact that sex-appropriate behaviors in a child seem to be destined for continuity, while sex-inappropriate behaviors seem to be discontinuous. Moreover, a cross-sectional approach certainly would not have been able to discover the sleeper effects involved in particular children's development. Since a cross-sectional study assesses different children at different ages, it would not have been possible, for example, to discover that if a female had a protective mother in her first three years of life, she would show withdrawal from stress as an adult. Still, despite the wealth of empirical findings that are possible from longitudinal differential studies, such studies do have their limitations. We have seen some of these in earlier discussions in this chapter, and we will have reason to refer to those points again in Chapter 11. However, before we conclude the present chapter, let us turn to a relatively recent methodological development in the empirical application of the differential approach, which attempts to address the problems not only of longitudinal investigations but of cross-sectional studies as well.

## Schaie's General Developmental Model

We have seen that there are two major research strategies typically employed to ascertain the developmental differentiation of people into subgroups: longitudinal and cross-sectional. Yet, while both can be used to assess the developmental differentiation of people into subgroups and might even involve the study of the same status and behavioral attributes, they often do not yield the same—or even similar—results. In our discussion of the sleeper effect found by Kagan and Moss in their longitudinal study, we suggested that a cross-sectional study involving the same variables (e.g., maternal protection in early childhood and adult female withdrawal from stress) probably would never have discovered a sleeper phenomenon.

Accordingly, Schaie and Strother (1968) point out that the age changes typically associated with the results of longitudinal studies are not consistent with the age changes typically found with cross-sectional research. For example, when studying intellectual or cognitive development with a cross-sectional design, most researchers report that highest performance occurs in the early twenties or thirties and considerable decreases in performance levels occur after this period (e.g., see Horn and Cattell,

1966). With longitudinal studies of these same variables, however, no decrease in performance is seen at all. In fact, some studies (e.g., Bayley and Oden, 1955) have found some increase in performance levels into the fifties.

Why do these contradictory age trends occur? Certainly if the goal of the differential developmental psychologist is to obtain a valid account of the developmental differentiation of people into subgroups along certain dimensions, we cannot be satisfied with one type of research design indicating one type of result and another type of design, used to study the very same thing, indicating an opposite result. These contradictions must be resolved.

Some people have attempted to resolve this contradiction by suggesting that the nature of the subjects typically used in the longitudinal design is considerably different from that of subjects used in the cross-sectional study. Longitudinal studies are comprised of a considerably select sample to begin with, and as the study proceeds some people will drop out of the research. Rather than being a random process, such attrition may be due to the fact that subjects of lower ability leave the study. Hence, at least in regard to studies of cognitive or intellectual development, this biasing would account for lack of decreases in level of performance (as is the case with the cross-sectional studies). In addition, as Schaie and Strother (1968) point out, these longitudinal studies of intellectual development have not reached the assessment of the sixties and seventies, the age periods during which the greatest performance decreases have been seen in the cross-sectional studies (e.g., Jones, 1959). Thus, comparisons of the age-associated changes found with the two methods are not appropriate. On the other hand, cross-sectional samples have not escaped criticism. Schaie (1959) has argued that such samples do not give the researcher a good indication of age-associated changes because of the fact that the samples of subjects used to represent people of widely different age ranges are difficult to adequately match.

Although these arguments may be appropriately used to reconcile the discrepancies (or perhaps to explain them away), Schaie (1965) suggests that these arguments miss an essential point: they do not show a recognition of an essential methodological problem involved in the consideration of longitudinal and cross-sectional designs. Schaie (1965) argues that these two designs are only special cases of a more general developmental research design, and in fact, the longitudinal and cross-sectional methods should not even be expected to result in similar age-associated changes.

Schaie (1965) points out that the cross-sectional method compares scores from subjects who are of different age groups. Thus, each different age group represents a different *generation* of people, or what Schaie terms *cohorts*. Yet, each different generation is measured at the same point in time, in order to allow the researcher to efficiently obtain the data. Thus, differences between age groups could occur because of (1) actual age differences in the expression of the psychological phenomenon under study; (2) differences between the generations per se—that is, historical differences; and (3) a combination of age and cohort difference. For example, in a cross-sectional study of the development of attitudes towards war, age-group differences in attitudes might be a function of age-associated changes in the ontogenetic, or developmental, processes involved in people's cognitions and affects about war; alternatively, such age-group differences may be related to the fact that one group grew up during a war, and thus historically experienced war, while the other grew up in a time of peace. Of course, such

K. Warner Schaie

cross-sectional age-group differences may result from a combination of these two fac-tors. Simply, as indicated by Nesselroade and Baltes (1974), the conventional cross-sectional design confounds age and cohort differences.

In longitudinal studies, on the other hand, the subjects belong to the same genera-tion, or cohort. This single generational group is then repeatedly measured at different points in time. Differences here in the expression of a psychological phenomenon can, of course, be due to ontogenetic age changes. But they may also be due to cohort-specific effects the environment has on the people over the course of time. Longitudinal subjects all come from the same cohort, and thus any findings may reflect only idiosyn-cratic events particular to that historical era. In addition, differences may be due to re-peated exposure to the same measures; for example, subjects may "learn to" respond to a test that has been repeatedly administered to them. Of course, longitudinal differ-ences may be due to a combination of all these sources.

Now, Schaie argues (Schaie, 1967; Schaie and Strother, 1968) that the typical cross-sectional study confuses age differences with cohort differences, while the usual longitudinal study will confuse age differences with time differences. Accordingly, it will be unusual indeed if both types of studies indicate similar age-associated changes (Schaie and Strother, 1968). Thus, Schaie has in a sense accounted for the contradic-tory results of longitudinal and cross-sectional studies. However, by doing so he seems to have seriously criticized the effectiveness or usefulness of either. This is not the case. Schaie offers a new design for developmental research which will employ features of both the cross-sectional and longitudinal approaches. This new method, representing a most significant advancement in the application of the differential approach to the study of development across the entire life span, allows the confusions and contradictions to be eliminated.

**Features of the General Developmental Model: Sequential Strategies of Design**

The respective confusions involved in the cross-sectional and longitudinal designs may be resolved, Schaie (1965) argues, through utilization of the *sequential methods of analysis* of developmental data. By combining features of the longitudinal and cross-sectional designs, this new strategy allows a researcher to assess the relative contributions of age, cohort, and time differences in one study, to know what differences (or portions of the differences) between groups are due to age differences, to cohort (historical generation) differences, or to time (of testing) differences. In addition, such a sequential design has the feature of allowing these sources of differences to be ascertained in a relatively short period of time. In commenting about the sequential features involved in Schaie's model, Nesselroade and Baltes similarly define the components of developmental functions which may be discerned through application of sequential designs:

> In the behavioral sciences it was Schaie (1965) who first presented a General Developmental Model describing the relationship between three components characteristic of descriptive developmental functions: age, cohort, and time of measurement. While age and time of measurement are self-explanatory, the term cohort requires definition. As used here, cohort refers to birth cohort—a group of people born at the same time or during an arbitrary period of time, say in 1950 or 1965. The term generation is sometimes used as an alternative to cohort, especially when larger time units are involved (1974, p. 3).

Thus, application of sequential strategies of data collection in developmental research will allow empirical statements to be made about the relative contributions of age, cohort, and time of assessment. Such statements may be made because the

> literature on sequential strategies is fairly consistent with regard to aspects of data collection; for example, all authors seem to agree that application of cross-sectional and longitudinal sequences (as proposed by Baltes, 1968) will result in all data points that one may need for examining the relationships between age, cohort, and time of measurement. The same is true for the three sequential startegies proposed by Schaie (1965), that is, cohort-sequential, time-sequential, and cross-sequential, if they are applied simultaneously for data collection. In fact, all sequential methods espoused in principle lead to the same data matrix (Nesselroade and Baltes, 1974, p. 6).

In other words, all sequential methods of analysis in principle provide data that allow empirical statements to be made about the relative contributions of age, cohort, and time, statements independent of the pitfalls involved with observations based solely on conventional cross-sectional or longitudinal designs. Thus, although there is some disagreement pertaining to mathematical bases of the design and interpretations of results derived from use of such designs (cf. Baltes, 1967, 1968; Buss, 1973; Schaie, 1965, 1970), all researchers using this approach agree about its advantages relative to conventional research designs.

Research based on sequential designs is complex, due in part to the necessary involvement of multivariate statistical analyses and to the numerous measurements that have to be taken of many different groups, but a simplified example of such a design may be offered. It will indicate how use of such a design allows the developmental researcher to discriminate among the relative contributions of age, cohort, and time and

Paul B. Baltes

thus avoid the potential confoundings involved with traditional cross-sectional and longitudinal approaches.

Basically, a sequential design involves the remeasurement of a cross-sectional sample of people after a given, but fixed, interval of time has passed. In other words, a researcher selects a given cross-sectional sample, comprised therefore of various cohort levels, and measures each cohort level longitudinally (with the provision that each set of measurements occurs at about the same point in time for each cohort level).

John R. Nesselroade

In addition, if, for example, two times of testing are included (as the longitudinal component of the design), then control cohort groups, assessed only at the second testing time, are used to control for (to assess) any retesting effects. Hence, this design calls for obtaining repeated measures from each of the different generational groups (cohorts) included in a given cross-sectional sample. Thus, the researcher now has a measure of age changes both *within* each generational (cohort) level and *between* cohort levels—for every time of measurement. In other words, the researcher now has repeated measures on different cohort groups, and since data from control groups are also present, information about any effects of retesting these groups per se is also available. The researcher is thus in a position to make empirical statements about the relative influences of age, cohort, and times of measurement upon any observed developmental functions in the results.

To see how this is the case, let us consider a possible design of such a sequential study. Such a design is presented in Table 8.2. Different cohort levels are comprised of different groups of people born at different historical periods (e.g., some were born in 1915 and some in 1970). Thus, at the time of the first testing (June 1975 for this design), the study has the attributes of a cross-sectional study. However, the sequential feature is introduced when these same subjects are again measured (again at the same point in time). Now the researcher can answer a number of questions, all of which involve the potentially interrelated influences of cohort, age, and time influences. That is, by repeatedly measuring a cross-sectional sample of different generational levels and, of course, comparing these measures to those obtained with respective retest control groups, the researcher can determine if the within-generation (cohort) changes, among the various cohort levels, are similar or different. If they are different, then such discrepancies could be attributed to the historical differences among the different generations. Referring to Table 8.2, if for example, the cohort comprised of people born in 1940 underwent age changes between the two times of measurement and were found to be different at age forty from the people in the 1935 cohort group when they were forty, then there must be some historical difference between these two cohort levels. In other words, if differences are due simply to age changes, then one should see across the same exact period of time similar performance for every generational level. A younger cohort group should show performance when its members get older similar to that of an older cohort group when its members were first measured at this age, *if* there are no historical differences between cohorts. Again from Table 8.2, the 1955 cohort should show a level of performance on its second measurement comparable to that of the first measurement for the 1950 cohort, *if* there are no historical differences between the generations. What we see, then, is that since all groups are measured at the same time periods, the effect of time is constant for all groups, and therefore the repeated measures for the different cohorts should all result in similar performance levels *if* age changes alone account for performance changes. If, however, similar performance changes do not occur during these same time intervals between the different cohorts, then these cross-sectional differences may be due to historical differences between generations, or to the effects of repeated measurement. An assessment of this second possibility may be made through comparing a cohort's performance at the time of the second measurement with that of its control group. If repeated exposure to the tests does not affect performance, then both groups should perform the same.

## Some Concluding Comments

Through the application of the above sequential design, Schaie and his colleagues (e.g., Baltes and Nesselroade, 1972; Nesselroade and Baltes, 1974; Schaie and Strother, 1968) have been able to empirically differentiate between historical and ontogenetic sources of change in differential research. By applying such a sequential design to differently aged cross-sectional subsamples, these researchers have given developmental psychology a sensitive method not only for better determining how people of different ages become assorted into subgroups over the course of their development, but for ascertaining some of the sources of this differentiation. This technique provides a convenient and necessary combination of both longitudinal and cross-sectional methods and allows the researcher to differentiate between historical and ontogenetic sources of change across the entire life span. It also allows an assessment of development across the life span to be made in a relatively short time. For example, we see in Table 8.2 that it is possible to sequentially study development from ages five to eighty within the context of a five-year study. If results from the different cohort levels suggest that age changes are the source of the differences between groups (rather than historical changes), then the portions of the life span represented by the performances of the different cohorts may be combined—or pieced together—to form an overall developmental curve for that portion of the life span assessed.

In sum, we have seen that the empirical utilization of the differential approach to developmental psychology provides a rich and a varied assortment of techniques to ascertain the course of the phenomena involved in the developmental differentiation of

**Table 8.2**  A possible design for a sequential study.

| Cohort (generational) level | Time of first measurement | Age at this time | Time of second measurement* | Age at this time |
|---|---|---|---|---|
| People born in 1970 | June, 1975 | 5 | June, 1980 | 10 |
| People born in 1965 | June, 1975 | 10 | June, 1980 | 15 |
| People born in 1960 | June, 1975 | 15 | June, 1980 | 20 |
| People born in 1955 | June, 1975 | 20 | June, 1980 | 25 |
| People born in 1950 | June, 1975 | 25 | June, 1980 | 30 |
| People born in 1945 | June, 1975 | 30 | June, 1980 | 35 |
| People born in 1940 | June, 1975 | 35 | June, 1980 | 40 |
| People born in 1935 | June, 1975 | 40 | June, 1980 | 45 |
| People born in 1930 | June, 1975 | 45 | June, 1980 | 50 |
| People born in 1925 | June, 1975 | 50 | June, 1980 | 55 |
| People born in 1920 | June, 1975 | 55 | June, 1980 | 60 |
| People born in 1915 | June, 1975 | 60 | June, 1980 | 65 |
| People born in 1910 | June, 1975 | 65 | June, 1980 | 70 |
| People born in 1905 | June, 1975 | 70 | June, 1980 | 75 |
| People born in 1900 | June, 1975 | 75 | June, 1980 | 80 |

*Both the original cohort groups and the retest controls will be assessed here.

people into subgroups. Both the empirical and the theoretical uses of the differential approach allow us to see the ways in which people may be conceptualized to differ over the course of their development. We may turn now to a third approach—the ipsative approach—for still another framework within which to understand a child's development. We will summarize the major points made in this chapter, however, before we turn to our discussion of the ipsative approach.

## Summary

The differential approach to the study of development considers how people over the course of development become sorted into various subgroups, differentiated on the basis of status and behavioral attributes. This concern with developmental differentiation into subgroups may be expressed in either primarily theoretical terms or as a primarily empirical interest.

Erikson uses differential constructs within the context of his stage theory of psychosocial development. While Freud focused primarily on the contributions of the id to development, Erikson focuses on the role of the ego. This perspective leads Erikson towards an emphasis on the role of society in determining what the ego must do to fulfill its function of reality adaptation.

The development of ego capabilities is seen as progressing through eight stages of psychosocial development; the emergence of these stages is governed by an epigenetic principle that, to Erikson, is primarily maturational in emphasis. Within each stage a particular capability of the ego must be developed if the ego is to meet the adjustment demands placed on it by society. Hence, each stage is viewed as a critical period, since stage development will proceed in spite of whether or not the capability is developed. Thus, within each stage there emerges a crisis between developing a feeling of the appropriate capability or developing the feeling that the appropriate capability is lacking. It is this crisis that is conceptualized in differential terms.

Hence, within the first stage of psychosocial development (termed by Erikson the *oral-sensory* stage) there emerges a crisis between developing a sense of trust or of mistrust toward one's world. If favorable sensory experiences are encountered, the child will develop toward the former feeling state, while if unfavorable experiences occur, a feeling closer to the latter state will obtain. Thus, in this stage, as well as all others, a child typically develops somewhere along a hypothetical differential dimension; in this first stage the crisis is one between trust versus mistrust. Healthy ego development will proceed if the ratio of the former to the latter is greater than one, while unhealthy ego development will proceed if this ratio is less than one.

The second stage is termed the *anal-musculature* stage, and here the crisis is between developing toward a sense of autonomy or a sense of shame and doubt. The third stage is termed the *genital-locomotor* stage, and the crisis involved is between initiative versus guilt. In *latency* (stage 4) the crisis is between developing toward a sense of industry or a sense of inferiority, while in *puberty* and *adolescence* (stage 5) the crisis involved identity versus role confusion. Erikson divides adult life into three succeeding stages. In stage 6 (*young adulthood*) there is an emotional crisis between developing toward a sense of intimacy versus a sense of isolation. In stage 7 (*adulthood*) the crisis is between generativity versus stagnation, while in the final stage (*maturity*) the emotional crisis is one between ego integrity versus despair.

An example of the empirical use of the differential approach was the study by Kagan and Moss. Kagan and Moss longitudinally studied a group of 89 children from their early years through their young adulthood. Through the use of interviews, test administrations, and live observations, data were collected on these people's psychological functioning throughout this period. From these data, measures for many different variables were obtained (e.g., dependency), and each variable was conceptualized as representing a differential behavioral dimension with end points lying at 1 and 7.

Kagan and Moss found that many of the child's behaviors shown in the early school years (from six through ten years) were fairly good predictors of similar early adult behaviors. Similar findings pertaining to other relations between childhood and adulthood periods were seen. Yet, despite such continuity, Kagan and Moss found that the extent to which age-period continuity was seen in various behavioral characteristics was essentially dependent on whether or not that behavior was consistent with traditional sex-role standards. Finally, evidence for what Kagan and Moss termed a *sleeper effect* was found. Sometimes a behavior or event measured early in a person's life was highly related to a similar behavior found in later adult years but not in the age periods between these two points. An example of such a lag between a cause and a measurable indication of the effect was found among males. Passivity and fear of bodily harm measured in the first few years of life (birth to three years) were found to be better predictors of a conceptually similar adult behavior in males (love-object dependency) than were other measurements of the childhood behaviors in the intervening age periods.

While the Kagan and Moss study illustrates the empirical use of the differential approach within the context of a longitudinal research design, recent methodological advancements in the empirical application of the differential approach avoid some of the problems encountered with both this type of differential research design and the cross-sectional research design. Both longitudinal and cross-sectional designs were seen to have some serious methodological problems, but these are overcome through use of the sequential data analysis strategies involved in developmental research designs derived from Schaie's general developmental model. Thus, it was seen that conventional cross-sectional designs confound age and cohort (or generational) effects, and conventional longitudinal designs confound age and time of measurement effects; such respective confounding may contribute to the basis of the differences in developmental functions discerned through application of the two techniques. Yet, since the sequential design strategies combine features of both of these techniques while avoiding their shortcomings, an unconfounded assessment may be made of the relationship between the three component characteristics of descriptive developmental functions: age effects, cohort effects, and time-of-measurement effects. While the mathematical and statistical bases of the sequential design are complex, the application of these ideas in actual empirical research has been demonstrated in several studies by Schaie, Baltes, and Nesselroade, the researchers largely responsible for the formulation of the model. While there is variation between studies, sequential designs typically involve the remeasurement of a cross-sectional sample after some fixed interval of time has passed. Thus, various cohort levels are assessed longitudinally, and control cohort groups are included in the repeated measures component of the design to provide a means to assess retesting effects. Through application of such a design the unconfounded contributions of age, cohort, and time of measurement may be assessed in life-span differential research.

# 9
## The Ipsative Approach

In this chapter we turn to a consideration of the last of the three approaches to the study of child development described in Chapter 6. We learned there that the ipsative approach to developmental psychology assesses intraindividual consistencies and changes in the attribute repertoire and the attribute interrelation of a person over the course of development. As opposed to the relatively more nomothetically oriented stage and differential approaches, the ipsative approach is essentially idiographic in orientation. That is, it seeks to understand the laws that govern an individual's behavior; it attempts to formulate highly specific generalizations, applicable to the development of a single individual.

In seeking to understand the variables involved in an individual's development, those taking an ipsative point of view are not necessarily formulating specific laws of development applicable only to that given person. Rather, they stress that an understanding of the individual is a necessary basis for any more general understanding. Although developmental psychology must be concerned with ascertaining nomothetic, or group, laws, as well as idiographic laws, those taking this point of view suggest that the science would suffer if the former were emphasized to the exclusion of the latter. As pointed out in Chapter 6, general laws of development may not apply equally (or at all) to all the individuals in a group. Hence, one must also understand intraindividual laws if one wants to get a full account of development. In other words, one must understand the contributions that an organism's own individuality makes towards its own development in order to fully comprehend development.

We see, then, that a basic, necessary orientation of the ipsative approach is an assessment of the role of the organism's own characteristics in its own development. An organism's lawful, systematic characteristics of individuality provide an important source of that organism's own development. Thus, those taking an ipsative point of view seek to assess an individual's attribute repertoire and the concomitant interrelation of this repertoire over the course of the individual's development. From this perspective, ipsatively oriented developmentalists follow an organismic, developmental point of view in focusing on how the organism itself contributes to its own development. While not necessarily denying the validity of other approaches to the study of psychological development (e.g., the stage approach), the ipsative approach suggests that these other formats are incomplete because they do not pay sufficient attention to the organism's lawful (and potentially unique) characteristics of individuality and the contributions of this individuality to the organism's own development.

We see, then, that the ipsative approach shares with other organismically oriented positions, such as those of Schneirla (1957) and Piaget (1966), the idea that the organism's own characteristics play an active role in its own development. Yet, despite the similarities between the ipsative approach and other organismically oriented positions, little systematic developmental research has been conducted from an essentially ipsative point of view. (Some of the reasons for this have been suggested in Chapter 6.) One major study of development from the ipsative point of view does exist, however. This study, the New York Longitudinal Study, has been conducted by Alexander Thomas, Stella Chess, Herbert Birch, Margaret Hertzig, and Sam Korn, a group of psychiatrists and psychologists. Because it is the best example of ipsative research about psychological development and has especially important theoretical and practical implications, the rest of this chapter will review its features and

Alexander Thomas

implications. Our intense review of this study will serve several purposes. First, it will give us some knowledge and appreciation of how a major study of psychological development is initially conceptualized. Second, it will illustrate how developmental psychologists move from conceiving of a study to implementing it. Third, it will illustrate the problems encountered very often in developmental research and some ways in which developmental psychologists seek to address these problems. Fourth, our analysis will allow us not only to appreciate a major ipsative study of development but,

Stella Chess

Herbert G. Birch

further, to make some more general, important statements about the viability of the organismic, interactionist theoretical point of view.

## The New York Longitudinal Study

The New York Longitudinal Study (NYLS) began in 1956 in New York City and continues through this writing. The study involves a longitudinal assessment of a relatively large (i.e., for a longitudinal study) group of children from their first days of life onward.

Margaret Hertzig

Sam J. Korn

Although, of course, it is essential for us to understand the methods, findings, and implications of this study, we must first focus on the theoretical issues that led to the study. Only by beginning here can we understand the rationale of the entire NYLS and thus see why the study took the form that it did.

## Why Are Children Different?

Any developmental psychologist would of course admit that children are different. We have seen, for example, that both stage and differential approaches to the study of child development incorporate concepts of individuality into their respective systems. Thus, any debate about developmental individuality does not focus on whether or not children are different. Rather, it concerns either the ways in which children differ (e.g., stage theorists say children may differ in their rate and final levels of development, while differential psychologists conceptualize individuality as one's location in multidimensional space) or the sources of differences. In other words, people may recognize all children as having individualistic characteristics, yet they may debate about where these differences come from.

If such a debate seems reminiscent of the controversy surrounding the nature-nurture issue dealt with in Chapters 3 and 4, this is because nature-nurture is precisely the issue involved in such debate. Arguments about the source of behavioral individuality have traditionally advanced either a *preformationist* viewpoint or an environmentalist viewpoint. Those taking a preformationist view have essentially stressed inborn sources of individuality, which are thought to be largely genetic in origin and apparently unavailable to environmental influence. Those taking an environmentalist position have stressed stimulus-response relationships, acquired through the empirical laws of learning. This position views people as malleable balls of clay. Where the genetically oriented preformationists stress that a person enters the world as an already formed ball, the environmentalists opposingly argue that the person enters the world with little but the potential to be completely shaped by stimulus-response relations. Thus, instead of different genetic inheritances being the source of individuality, the environmentalists suggest that different—although lawfully identical—stimulus-response relations provide the source of individuality.

Of course, although the environmentalist position has traditionally been predominant in American psychology, we have seen in Chapters 3 and 4 that both this and the preformationist position are inadequate in giving complete accounts of behavioral development. Rather, we have seen that it is necessary to focus on an *interaction* between both hereditary and environmental sources. Thus, as Schneirla (1957) and other organismic developmentalists (e.g., Piaget) have stressed, it is necessary to focus on factors both intrinsic and extrinsic to the organism in order to gain a full understanding of development. Not only will such organism-environment interactions provide the source of development, but too, from the probabilistic epigenetic point of view (discussed in Chapters 2 and 3), the timing of these intrinsic-extrinsic interactions will be different for different organisms, and such differences will provide a source of organismic individuality.

Furthermore, we have seen that such organismic individuality may have profound influences on the organism's own development. We have seen that Schneirla (1957), in describing a "third source" of development, has indicated that an organism's characteristics of individuality, arising out of its unique maturational-experiential interaction, accordingly stimulate differential reactions on the part of the other organisms in the organism's environment. These differential reactions then feed back on the organism, providing a further source of the organism's experience and thus contributing to the organism's development.

Because the Thomas researchers subscribed to this organismic, interactionist view, they rejected both the preformationist and the environmentalist views of behavioral individuality. Rather, they conceptualized the source of a child's characteristics of individuality as being the interaction between the organism's intrinsic and extrinsic factors; further, because of the theoretical implications of this interactionist point of view, they sought to ascertain the role that such behavioral individuality plays in contributing to a child's development. Thus, the Thomas group's (1963, p. 1) study was "concerned with identifying characteristics of individuality in behavior during the first months of life and with exploring the degree to which these characteristics are persistent and influence the development of later psychological organization" (quoted by permission of New York University Press from *Behavioral Individuality in Early Childhood* by Thomas, *et al.* Copyright © by New York University).

Because of their theoretical point of view, the Thomas researchers felt it necessary to focus on intraindividual consistencies and changes in the characteristics of a child over the course of development. Such an ipsative analysis would yield information regarding the contribution that such behavioral individuality makes to the child's own development. In other words, such an assessment of the contributions and implications of a child's individually different *style of behavioral reactivity*—the child's style of responding or reacting to the world—might supply important information bearing on unanswered but crucial problems of child development.

## Implications of the Thomas Group's Theoretical Position

We have developed the general theoretical stance of the Thomas group through addressing the question, Why are children different? An exploration and empirical assessment of this point of view would seem to have important theoretical implications. That is, if the Thomas group's view of the source and the implications of behavioral individuality is correct, some revisions in our thinking about both the preformationist and the environmentalist views would be warranted. In addition, the approach and findings of the Thomas group might have implications for other controversies in child development study. For instance, as Thomas and Chess have suggested, an approach such as theirs might provide answers about such important developmental questions as:

Why do youngsters exposed to the same kind of parental influences so often show markedly different directions of personality and development? . . . Why do some parents who show no evidence of any significant psychiatric disturbances and who provide a good home for their children sometimes have a child with serious psychological disturbances? Why do the rules for childcare in feeding, weaning, toilet training and so on never seem to work equally well for all children, even when applied by intelligent and conscientious mothers? (From *Development and Evolution of Behavior: Essays in Memory of T. C. Schneirla,* edited by Lester R. Aronson, Ethel Tobach, Daniel S. Lehrman, and Jay S. Rosenblatt. W. H. Freeman and Company. Copyright © 1970.)

Clearly, we see the theoretical suggestion that some portion of the answers to these questions must lie in the fact that children have important characteristics of individuality. These individual differences serve to promote two things. First, different reactions in different children to the same environmental stimulus situation will occur. The interactionist viewpoint suggests that as a result of an organism's unique maturation-experiential interaction, the organism will develop its own characteristics of individuality; this means that though an identical stimulus may impinge on two different children, the resulting reaction may not be the same. For example, one child might react intensely to a loud noise, while another may hardly react at all. Thus, because of such individual differences in a child's style of reactivity, what might be a part of the *effective stimulus environment* for one child—that is, a stimulus in the child's environment which evokes a reaction—may not be part of the effective environment for another child.

Second, because the same environmental event (e.g., a particular parental child-rearing practice) will have a different effectiveness for different children, such differential reactivity characteristics will differently influence others in the child's environment. Because different children can be expected to interact differently, each individual child will influence even similarly acting parents in different ways. The child who reacts intensely to even the slightest noise will certainly evoke parental responses different from those that would be evoked by a child who showed hardly any response at all to noise. Thus, one's characteristic style of reactivity to the world will differentially influence and stimulate other people in one's world. The reactions from these other people will, in turn, provide a further component of the child's stimulus world. Since such experiences play an integral role in affecting the child's further development, we see that here, too, the child's style of reactivity plays an active, contributory role in the child's own development.

## From Theory to Research

Thus we see the basic theoretical rationale of the Thomas, et al. project. Further, we see that the study holds the promise of providing data bearing not only on the accuracy of the interactionist position but on important empirical and practical concerns of child development as well. Moreover, on the basis of its theoretical rationale, the study will necessarily have to focus on a child's characteristics of individual reactivity, the child's style of behavior in interaction with the world. If the implications and contributions of such reactivity are consistent with the study's theoretical rationale, the authors will have to demonstrate not only that such behavioral style may play a role in a child's behavior at a given point in life but also that such individuality continues to contribute to the child's functioning over the entire course of development as the child continues to interact with the world.

Accordingly, in order to translate their theoretical ideas into empirical facts, Thomas et al. will have to do several things:

First, of course, they must have some idea how to measure individual characteristics of behavioral reactivity. They must know exactly what behaviors or aspects of behavior constitute such behavioral style and how to measure these behaviors in children as they develop.

Second, they must be able to find out the extent to which children's individualistic styles of behavior remain individually different or are similar at various points in their development. Third, they must continually assess the ways in which such individuality (to the extent that it is found to exist) continues to provide an important source of the child's development. Thus, they must ascertain how children with different styles of reactivity interact differently with the world over the course of their development and how such differential interactions continue to provide a source of the child's development. Accordingly, Thomas et al. must study their subjects longitudinally.

In sum, we see both the theoretical rationale of the Thomas et al. study and the manner in which this theoretical viewpoint must be translated into an empirical procedure in order for the ideas to be tested. Let us turn now to a consideration of the procedures of the Thomas group's study.

## The Method of the Thomas Group's NYLS

The first major publication of the Thomas, et al. NYLS came out in a 1963 book, in which the authors presented their findings about the development of 80 children (39 girls and 41 boys) throughout the first two years of their lives. Although other publications have dealt with these children, as well as additional children also longitudinally studied as part of this project, the method described in the 1963 book applies to the method essentially used throughout the study. Accordingly, we will use the descriptions supplied in this first major publication as the basis for our presentation of the NYLS method.

**The Subjects of the Study.** Longitudinal studies typically have problems relating to the representativeness of their sample of subject and hence the generalizability of their findings. We have seen these problems before, in our discussion in Chapter 8 of the Kagan and Moss (1962) study. Of the 80 children described in the 1963 book, all were from middle- to upper-middle-class backgrounds, most were white, most were Jewish in their religious affiliation, all were residents of the greater New York City area, and most had college-educated fathers. Clearly this sample is not broadly representative of large segments of American society, and accordingly we may generalize any specific findings from the NYLS to broader samples only with caution.

**Sources of Data.** Having delineated their sample, the Thomas group was next faced with the crucial problem of how to obtain data about the development of a child's characteristic style of reactivity. This problem involved two things.

1. *What is temperament?* First, at the time of the study's inception there existed no acceptable definition of the dimensions of a child's characteristics of reactivity, or what the Thomas group called *temperament.* Although other psychologists (e.g., Sheldon, 1940, 1942) had provided definitions of temperament (or behavioral style), these had been linked to preformationist theoretical conceptions and were thus unacceptable to the organismically oriented Thomas group. Accordingly, although the authors wanted to objectively study the aspects of a child's behavioral style, they had no preformed ideas about what constituted such aspects. They knew that they wanted to concern themselves with the *how* rather than the *what* of behavior. How does a child react to whatever he reacts to? What is the style of behavioral response, or reactivity, a child typically demonstrates in doing any and all of the things that a child does?

Thus, although the Thomas group knew that by *temperament* they meant only a general term representing the various aspects of how a child individually reacted to the world, they had no preconceived ideas about what sort of different reactive characteristics comprised a child's temperament. Simply, the crucial conceptual problem immediately facing the authors was that although they knew generally what aspect of a child's development they wanted to study (characteristics of temperament), they did not know what constituted the various aspects of temperament. In terms of the ipsative approach, they did not know what attributes comprise the child's intraindividual attribute repertoire.

2. *How to measure temperament?* More basic than this definitional problem was the immediate problem of temperament measurement. Assuming for the moment that the authors knew the particular attributes of temperament that they were to measure, how were they going to go about obtaining these measures? Where was the information about the development of the child's temperament going to come from?

This problem was complicated by the fact that the authors felt it crucial to obtain measures of the child's temperament in all situations the child engaged in. If the authors wanted to accurately ascertain how the child did whatever he did, and not just how he went about doing certain things (for instance, those things that might be involved in a once-a-month experimental assessment session), they would have to observe the child's temperamental style continuously. They would have to observe the child each and every day of the child's life. Thus, observations could not be limited to those at the authors' laboratory but would have to include observations of the child in the real, nonlaboratory world.

A possible way to obtain such observations would be to hire and train eighty different observers to live in each child's household around the clock and thus observe and rate the child in how he does everything. Such a procedure presents problems, however. The hiring and training of eighty observers would be economically prohibitive. Moreover, probably three times as many observers would have to be hired, since the observers would probably work no more than eight hours a day. Furthermore, few if any families would allow one (not to mention three) people to permanently enter their homes to observe each and every interaction made by their child. Thus, how were Thomas *et al.* to obtain the necessary, continuous, total observations of each of their subjects?

Fortunately, someone did exist who observed the child continuously, who at no cost to the researchers lived with the child daily, and who always worked a twenty-four-hour day. This, of course, was the child's parent. Hence, the Thomas group decided to use each child's parent as the observer of the child's temperament; thus through interviews with each parent, the researchers were able to obtain the needed information about the child's style of reactivity in all daily interactions with the world. Since the parent continually observed the child, an appropriately designed interview of the parent could turn these observations into data about the child's developing temperament.

**Problems of Data Accuracy.** However, such reliance on the parent presented other problems. Obviously, one would not be quick to nominate a child's parent if one wanted an objective description or appraisal of the child. Such parental observations held the danger of being subjectively biased. Yet, the Thomas group decided that there was a way to avoid the subjectivism typically involved in parental reports. The interview of each parent was structured so that *descriptions,* rather than *interpretations,* of behavior were elicited. Although the interviewer recorded both interpretations and descriptions, only descriptions were considered for use as data. At times when parents insisted on interpreting rather than describing, the interviewer carefully reworded, rephrased, or repeated the question so as to obtain in each case a step-by-step description of the behavior in question. This insistence on description rather than interpretation was illustrated by Thomas *et al.* (1963, p. 25) in the following example of a segment of a parental interview:

INTERVIEWER:   "What did the baby do the first time he was given cereal?"
PARENT:            "He couldn't stand it."
INTERVIEWER:   "What makes you think he disliked it? What did he do?"
PARENT:            "He spit it out and when another spoonful was offered he turned his head to the side."

Thus, when questions were asked about bathing or meeting new people, for example, and the parent responded with an interpretation (e.g., "He likes to be bathed," or "He is afraid of new people"), the interviewer always insisted on a description. The only answers used for data about temperament were those that responded to the question, "What did he *do*?"

In this way the Thomas group took a first step toward ensuring that the data derived from parental interviews were accurate. However, other steps were also followed. In Chapter 7 we saw that one of the major limitations of Sigmund Freud's method was that he obtained retrospective accounts of the early lives of his adult patients. He asked adults to reconstruct their long-gone past by remembering back to their early years of development. Such retrospections may be biased through such factors as selective remembering or forgetting, or distortion. Similar biases could enter into the parental responses. Such retrospective accounts are less accurate than *anterospective* descriptions, descriptions of a child's behavioral development given at about the very same time the behavior is occurring. Thus the Thomas group used anterospective interviews, conducted at three-month intervals during the child's first year of life. For example, the first interview occurred when the child was about three months old and was used to provide information about the child's temperamental development during these first three months; the second interview, conducted when the child was six months old, was used to obtain temperamental information about his fourth, fifth, and sixth months of life. After the first year, subsequent interviews were conducted at six-month intervals.

Further steps were taken to ensure data accuracy. It was possible that although a parent was providing descriptions rather than interpretations of the child's behavior, such descriptions were themselves inaccurate or distorted. To check this possibility, the accuracy of parental descriptions were ascertained by two independent observers entering the homes of several children. Not only did each observer tend to agree in his or her own descriptions with those provided by the parent, but the two observers also tended to agree between themselves. Finally, although such procedures indicated that parents were in fact providing accurate descriptions of their children's temperament a loss of accuracy could have resulted from the researchers' scoring of these parental interview responses. Because of the large number of response descriptions resulting from each of the several interviews of each of the many parents, different people would have to be used to score and interpret these answers. The researchers had to be sure that each different person would score the same responses in the same way and, moreover, that the same person would always score the same response in the same way, or else considerable inaccuracy would be introduced into the information. To check this possibility the researchers had different people score the same set of parental responses and had the same people score the same parental responses twice (after a three-month interval had gone by). In both cases, there was over 90 percent agreement between the two sets of responses.

In sum, we see that after taking several necessary steps to ensure the accuracy of their data, the Thomas researchers were able to conclude that they had consistent, accurate measures of the child's developing temperament. Yet, they still did not have an indication of what constituted the temperamental attribute repertoire of their subjects. Although they now considered that they had accurate, consistently scored information describing the "how" of children's reactivity to their world, they did not know the particular aspects of that reactivity. What were the variables, or attributes, comprising the child's temperamental repertoire? Although such knowledge obviously lay in their already obtained information, they now had to tease this knowledge out. Let us consider how they went about ascertaining this knowledge and what, in fact, they discovered.

## The Attributes of Temperament

The Thomas group did not have any predetermined theoretical notions concerning what the attributes of temperament are. Accordingly, the researchers could not deductively derive what the particular temperamental attributes should be—they could not say that since their theory about temperament said x, then y should be an attribute of temperament.

Moreover, the group wanted to avoid limiting the analyses of the interviews to a scoring of just one or two possible temperamental attributes; this methodological route would clearly introduce the possibility of ignoring large or important aspects of the data.

On the other hand, there was so much information contained in the interviews that some categorization of the descriptions was necessary. One had to score, or place, the various parental descriptions into categories in order to reduce the vast number of bits of data, while at the same time not thereby producing as many different categories as there were bits of information. The group wanted to move from data to more general organizational categorizations; they wanted to induce (discover) categories in the data that would organize it.

Accordingly, a sample of parental interviews was read, and by careful reasoning the Thomas group was able to discover nine categories of temperament. That is, by performing an *inductive content analysis* of their data, they were able to generate nine reliably scored attributes of temperament into which their various behavioral descriptions could be placed.

Although there seemed to be other than the nine categories in some of the parental descriptions, the group decided to focus on the nine attributes of temperament induced by the above method. The nine attributes included the following:

1. *Activity level.* This category refers to descriptions of the child's motor behavior (muscular functioning). Such descriptions answered several questions: Was the child very highly active all the time, or were very low levels of general activity seen? Did the child move around a lot, or a little, when eating, playing, sleeping, etc.?

2. *Rhythmicity.* This category refers to the cyclicality of behavior. Was the child's behavior very predictable? For example, did the child sleep for four hours, wake for four hours, sleep for four hours, etc? Did the child always eliminate one hour after eating, always get hungry at the same time? Or, was the child's behavior irregular? Did the child sleep for seven hours, wake for two, then perhaps sleep for three, but then wake for five, etc.? Did he sometimes eliminate right after eating and sometimes hours after? Was he sometimes hungry a short time after eating, while at other times go for hours without getting hungry?

3. *Approach or withdrawal.* Did the child tend to move toward—approach—new stimuli (for example, toys, people) or to move away—withdraw—from all such stimuli?

4. *Adaptability.* Did the child tend to adjust easily to new situations (after his initial approach or withdrawal response to it), or did the child tend to take a good deal of time to adjust to new situations and stimuli?

5. *Intensity of reaction.* This attribute refers to the strength of a response. Whenever the child responded to a situation or stimulus, was this response indicative of a high level of energy? Did the child respond with vigor or with little energy? For example, did the child tend to whimper rather than scream loudly when crying?

6. *Threshold of responsiveness.* A threshold refers to the smallest amount of energy necessary to evoke a response. If, for example, a noise has to be very loud for it to bother you, then you have a high threshold; if even a pin dropping causes you to react, you have a low noise threshold. This category, then, relates to the child's general threshold for responding.

7. *Quality of mood.* Was the child generally pleasant and friendly? Did he smile and laugh a lot and thus have a positive mood? Or was the child's behavior generally unpleasant? Did he cry and frown a lot and thus have a negative mood?

8. *Distractibility.* Once the child was engaged in a given behavior (e.g., watching television), was it very easy to alter this behavior (e.g., by calling him to dinner)? That is, was the child easily or highly distractible in that external stimulation would easily change

his ongoing behavior? Or was the child hard to distract? Was it difficult to change his ongoing behavior through introduction of another stimulus to the situation? Did the child thus show low distractibility?

9.  *Attention span and persistence.* How long did the child tend to stay at a given behavior he was engaged in? Did he tend to persist in doing a task for a long time, or did he stay with one task for a few minutes or so and then move to another task, and then another? If the child tended to stay with tasks for a long time, he would have a long (or high) attention span. He would be persistent. If the reverse were true, then he would have a short (or low) attention span. He would not show high persistence.

These categories comprise the nine attributes of temperament discovered by the Thomas group. Note that the nine categories refer to descriptions of the "how," the style, of behavior. They refer to how a child goes about doing whatever behaviors he engages in. Thus, they comprise a description, rather than an interpretation, of the dimensions of a child's style of behavioral reactivity to the world. Thus, the parental descriptions of how the child behaved in respect to such content topics as sleep, feeding, toilet training and toilet activities, bathing, grooming, meeting other people, playing, learning rules, talking, etc., were used by the Thomas group to obtain a broad sample of descriptions of the child's characteristics of reactivity. These descriptions were then used to discover the categories of temperament which inclusively described these behavioral style characteristics. In turn, the child's characteristics of reactivity were then placed into these various temperamental attribute categories. Each of these nine attributes was scored on a three-point scale. For example, for threshold of responsiveness, a child could be scored as having a low threshold, a high threshold, or a moderate threshold. The nine attributes of temperament and the three levels of scoring—or rating—for each attribute are presented in Fig. 9.1.

| ATTRIBUTE OF TEMPERAMENT | POSSIBLE "SCORES" FOR EACH ATTRIBUTE | | |
|---|---|---|---|
| Adaptability | adaptive | variable | nonadaptive |
| Rhythmicity | regular | variable | irregular |
| Activity level | high | moderate | low |
| Approach—Withdrawal | approach | variable | withdrawal |
| Threshold | high | moderate | low |
| Intensity | intense | variable | mild |
| Mood | positive | variable | negative |
| Distractibility | yes | variable | no |
| Attention span; persistence | high | variable | low |

**Fig. 9.1** The nine attributes of temperament found by Thomas, *et al.* (1963), and the possible "scores," or ratings, for each attribute.

In terms of the ipsative approach, the attribute repertoire of temperament for any given child would be comprised of the child's "score" on each of the nine attributes. Since a child's score on one dimension would not necessarily affect his score on any other attribute, the attribute interrelation of the repertoire could be different for different children. In other words, with the discovery and scoring of the nine attributes of temperament, the Thomas group defined a temperamental attribute repertoire that could exist differently in different children, that is, different children could have different scores on the various attributes; therefore, of course, the interrelation of the attributes would then be different for these different children. One child might combine a low threshold with high activity and a positive mood, while another child might combine a moderate threshold with low activity and a negative mood.

Was this in fact the case? Did different children show different attribute repertoires? Were different attribute interrelations seen? And did the children's repertoires remain the same as the children developed? To address these questions let us turn to the results of the NYLS.

## Results of the NYLS

The NYLS is an ongoing, longitudinal project. The data from the study are still being analyzed, and the children of the project are still being studied. Thus we may speak only of those results of the investigation that have already been published (e.g., in Chess, Thomas, and Birch, 1965; Thomas and Chess, 1970; Thomas, Chess, and Birch, 1968, 1970; Thomas, *et al.*, 1963). We will focus on data describing intraindividual consistencies and changes in the individual's temperamental attribute repertoire and repertoire interrelation over the course of the first ten years of development.

The first task of data analysis for the Thomas group was to discover if, in fact, children did possess individually different temperamental repertoires in early infancy. Second, the group had to determine the developmental course of such individuality. The first major finding, then, was that children *do* show individually different temperamental repertoires and interrelations; moreover, these individual differences in temperament do become distinct—they can be discerned—even in the first few weeks of the child's life. Although some children tend to be similar in their temperamental styles—a point whose implications we will consider below—different arrays of scores for each of the different attributes were found. Thus, in particular for the attributes of activity level, threshold, intensity, mood, and distractibility, marked individual differences in temperamental repertoires were evident (Thomas *et al.*, 1963, p. 57).

Moreover, these individually different temperamental styles were not systematically related either to the parents' method of child rearing or to the parents' own personality styles (Thomas *et al.*, 1970). This finding indicates not only that children are individually different but, too, that these characteristics of individuality are not simply related to what the parent does to the child or to the parents' own personality characteristics.

The second major finding of the NYLS is that these characteristics of individuality, first identified in the child's first three months of life, tend to continue to characterize the child over the course of later years. For example, one may look at the most frequent score given a child for each of his various nine temperamental attributes. That is, although a child in various instances may score high, moderate, or low in threshold, most of the ratings might be one of these scores, e.g., high. If one looks at these scores, one sees that the child's temperament tends to remain the same over his life; e.g., the preponderance of his threshold scores across his life tends to be high (Thomas *et al.*, 1963, p. 71). Moreover, the child's other scores, both within a particular attribute category and between the different attribute categories, tend also to remain similar over the course of the first ten years of life. This finding indicates not only that the attribute repertoire of the child tends to remain consistent but that the attribute interrelation also tends to remain consistent. The expression of such temperamental similarity over the course of the first ten years of life is illustrated in Table 9.1. This table displays two ratings for each of the nine categories of temperament, along with behaviors indicative of the consistency in temperament at each of the age periods ranging between two months through ten years of age.

We may conclude that to a great extent a child is born with an individually different temperament and that this individuality remains with the child over the course of his first ten years of life. The ipsative study of the Thomas group indicates that individually different attribute repertoires and attribute interrelations characterize the individual over the course of his development. These findings of course have important theoretical implications for organismic, interactionist theory, as well as important practical implications. Before turning to a consideration of these implications, however, let us turn to a final aspect of the results of the study. Although children were found to be characterized by individually different temperamental styles, we have also said that certain characteristics of temperament tended to be similar in some children. That is, for some children—not all, by any means—certain attribute scores on one dimension tended to occur at the same time with certain other attribute scores on other dimensions. Let us see the implications and meaning of such occurrences.

**Temperamental Types.** Among some children, scores on some temperamental attributes tended to consistently go along with scores on some of the other attributes. That is, a cluster, or grouping, of attribute scores was found for some children. For instance, for some children low thresholds tended to go along with high adaptability and high attention spans. In fact, the Thomas group was able to identify three such temperamental clusters. Some children had one type of temperamental-attribute grouping, while other children possessed another type. These three types were given different labels to describe the reactivity patterns of the children who possessed them.

1. *The easy child.* Some children were characterized by a temperament comprised of a positive mood, high rhythmicity, low or moderate intensity reactions, high adaptability, and an approach orientation to new situations and stimuli. About 40 percent of the children in the NYLS sample possessed this temperamental type (Thomas, *et al.,* 1970). Such children slept and ate regularly as infants, were generally happy, and readily adjusted to new people and events. As older children, they also adjusted easily to changing school requirements and adapted and participated easily in games and other activities. Hence, the Thomas group labeled such a child as easy because such a child obviously presents few difficulties to raise. Such a child is easy to interact with.

2. *The difficult child.* On the other hand, however, there is the child who possesses a temperamental style that makes for difficult interactions. These children are characterized by low rhythmicity, high intensity reactions, a withdrawal orientation to new situations and stimuli, slow adaptation, and a negative mood. About 10 percent of

**Table 9.1** Behavioral illustrations for ratings of the various temperamental attributes.

| Temperamental quality | Rating | Two months | Six months | One year |
|---|---|---|---|---|
| Activity level | High | Moves often in sleep. Wiggles when diaper is changed. | Tries to stand in tub and splashes. Bounces in crib. Crawls after dog. | Walks rapidly. Eats eagerly. Climbs into everything. |
| | Low | Does not move when being dressed or during sleep. | Passive in bath. Plays quietly in crib and falls asleep. | Finishes bottle slowly. Goes to sleep easily. Allows nail-cutting without fussing. |
| Rhythmicity | Regular | Has been on four-hour feeding schedule since birth. Regular bowel movement. | Is asleep at 6:30 every night. Awakes at 7:00 A.M. Food intake is constant. | Naps after lunch each day. Always drinks bottle before bed. |
| | Irregular | Awakes at a different time each morning. Size of feedings varies. | Length of nap varies; so does food intake. | Will not fall asleep for an hour or more. Moves bowels at a different time each day. |
| Distractibility | Distractible | Will stop crying for food if rocked. Stops fussing if given pacifier when diaper is being changed. | Stops crying when mother sings. Will remain still while clothing is changed if given a toy. | Cries when face is washed unless it is made into a game. |
| | Not distractible | Will not stop crying when diaper is changed. Fusses after eating even if rocked. | Stops crying only after dressing is finished. Cries until given bottle. | Cries when toy is taken away and rejects substitute. |
| Approach/Withdrawal | Positive | Smiles and licks washcloth. Has always liked bottle. | Likes new foods. Enjoyed first bath in a large tub. Smiles and gurgles. | Approaches strangers readily. Sleeps well in new surroundings. |
| | Negative | Rejected cereal the first time. Cries when strangers appear. | Smiles and babbles at strangers. Plays with new toys immediately. | Stiffened when placed on sled. Will not sleep in strange beds. |
| Adaptability | Adaptive | Was passive during first bath; now enjoys bathing. Smiles at nurse. | Used to dislike new foods; now accepts them well. | Was afraid of toy animals at first; now plays with them happily. |
| | Not adaptive | Still startled by sudden, sharp noise. Resists diapering. | Does not cooperate with dressing. Fusses and cries when left with sitter. | Continues to reject new foods each time they are offered. |

**Table 9.1** (Continued)

| | | | | |
|---|---|---|---|---|
| Attention span and persistence | Long | If soiled, continues to cry until changed. Repeatedly rejects water if he wants milk. | Watches toy mobile over crib intently. "Coos" frequently. | Plays by self in playpen for more than an hour. Listens to singing for long periods. |
| | Short | Cries when awakened but stops almost immediately. Objects only mildly if cereal precedes bottle. | Sucks pacifier for only a few minutes and spits it out. | Loses interest in a toy after a few minutes. Gives up easily if she falls while attempting to walk. |
| Intensity of reaction | Intense | Cries when diapers are wet. Rejects food vigorously when satisfied. | Cries loudly at the sound of thunder. Makes sucking movements when vitamins are administered. | Laughs hard when father plays roughly. Screamed and kicked when temperature was taken. |
| | Mild | Does not cry when diapers are wet. Whimpers instead of crying when hungry. | Does not kick often in tub. Does not smile. Screams and kicks when temperature is taken. | Does not fuss much when clothing is pulled on over head. |
| Threshold of responsiveness | Low | Stops sucking on bottle when approached. | Refuses fruit he likes when vitamins are added. Hides head from bright light. | Spits out food he does not like. Giggles when tickled. |
| | High | Is not startled by loud noises. Takes bottle and breast equally well. | Eats everything. Does not object to diapers being wet or soiled. | Eats food he likes even if mixed with disliked food. Can be left easily with strangers. |
| Quality of mood | Positive | Smacks lips when first tasting new food. Smiles at parents. | Plays and splashes in bath. Smiles at everyone. | Likes bottle; reaches for it and smiles. Laughs loudly when playing peekaboo. |
| | Negative | Fusses after nursing. Cries when carriage is rocked. | Cries when taken from tub. Cries when given food she does not like. | Cries when given injections. Cries when left alone. |

**Table 9.1** (Continued)

| Temperamental quality | Rating | Two years | Five years | Ten years |
|---|---|---|---|---|
| Activity level | High | Climbs furniture. Explores. Gets in and out of bed while being put to sleep. | Leaves table often during meals. Always runs. | Plays ball and engages in other sports. Cannot sit still long enough to do homework. |
| | Low | Enjoys quiet play with puzzles. Can listen to records for hours. | Takes a long time to dress. Sits quietly on long automobile rides. | Likes chess and reading. Eats very slowly. |
| Rhythmicity | Regular | Eats a big lunch each day. Always has a snack before bedtime. | Falls asleep when put to bed. Bowel movement regular. | Eats only at mealtimes. Sleeps the same amount of time each night. |
| | Irregular | Nap time changes from day to day. Toilet training is difficult because bowel movement is unpredictable. | Food intake varies; so does time of bowel movement. | Food intake varies. Falls asleep at a different time each night. |
| Distractibility | Distractible | Will stop tantrum if another activity is suggested. | Can be coaxed out of forbidden activity by being led into something else. | Needs absolute silence for homework. Has a hard time choosing a shirt in a store because they all appeal to him. |
| | Not distractible | Screams if refused some desired object. Ignores mother's calling. | Seems not to hear if involved in favorite activity. Cries for a long time when hurt. | Can read a book while television set is at high volume. Does chores on schedule. |
| Approach/Withdrawal | Positive | Slept well the first time he stayed overnight at grandparents' house. | Entered school building unhesitatingly. Tries new foods. | Went to camp happily. Loved to ski the first time. |
| | Negative | Avoids strange children in the playground. Whimpers first time at beach. Will not go into water. | Hid behind mother when entering school. | Severely homesick at camp during first days. Does not like new activities. |
| Adaptability | Adaptive | Obeys quickly. Stayed contentedly with grandparents for a week. | Hesitated to go to nursery school at first; now goes eagerly. Slept well on camping trip. | Likes camp, although homesick during first days. Learns enthusiastically. |
| | Not adaptive | Cries and screams each time hair is cut. Disobeys persistently. | Has to be hand led into classroom each day. Bounces on bed in spite of spankings. | Does not adjust well to new school or new teacher; comes home late for dinner even when punished. |

THE NEW YORK LONGITUDINAL STUDY 243

**Table 9.1** (Continued)

| | | | | |
|---|---|---|---|---|
| Attention span and persistence | Long | Works on a puzzle until it is completed. Watches when shown how to do something. | Practiced riding a two-wheeled bicycle for hours until he mastered it. Spent over an hour reading a book. | Reads for two hours before sleeping. Does homework carefully. |
| | Short | Gives up easily if a toy is hard to use. Asks for help immediately if undressing becomes difficult. | Still cannot tie his shoes because he gives up when he is not successful. Fidgets when parents read to him. | Gets up frequently from homework for a snack. Never finishes a book. |
| Intensity of reaction | Intense | Yells if he feels excitement or delight. Cries loudly if a toy is taken away. | Rushes to greet father. Gets hiccups from laughing hard. | Tears up an entire page of homework if one mistake is made. Slams door of room when teased by younger brother. |
| | Mild | When another child hit her, she looked surprised, did not hit back. | Drops eyes and remains silent when given a firm parental "No." Does not laugh much. | When a mistake is made on a model airplane, corrects it quietly. Does not comment when reprimanded. |
| Threshold of responsiveness | Low | Runs to door when father comes home. Must always be tucked tightly into bed. | Always notices when mother puts new dress on for first time. Refuses milk if it is not ice-cold. | Rejects fatty foods. Adjusts shower until water is at exactly the right temperature. |
| | High | Can be left with anyone. Falls to sleep easily on either back or stomach. | Does not hear loud, sudden noises when reading. Does not object to injections. | Never complains when sick. Eats all foods. |
| Quality of mood | Positive | Plays with sister; laughs and giggles. Smiles when he succeeds in putting shoes on. | Laughs loudly while watching television cartoons. Smiles at everyone. | Enjoys new accomplishments. Laughs when reading a funny passage aloud. |
| | Negative | Cries and squirms when given haircut. Cries when mother leaves. | Objects to putting boots on. Cries when frustrated. | Cries when he cannot solve a homework problem. Very "weepy" if he does not get enough sleep. |

Source: A. Thomas, S. Chess, and H. G. Birch, "The Origin of Personality," *Scientific American* **223** (1970). Copyright © 1970 by Scientific American, Inc. All rights reserved.

the NYLS children had this temperamental type. As infants they ate and slept irregularly, took a long time to adjust to new situations, and were characterized by a great deal of crying. To say the least, such a child would be difficult for a parent to train. Such a child would be difficult even just to interact with. Parents would have to show both tolerance and patience in order to have favorable interactions with such children.

3. *The slow-to-warm-up child.* Here we find a child who has a low activity level, a withdrawal orientation, slow adaptability, a somewhat negative mood, and relatively low reaction intensities. Such children comprised 15 percent of the NYLS sample (Thomas, *et al.,* 1970). These children would also present interaction difficulties and problems for their parents and teachers. It would take some time to get such a child involved in new activities and situations, and similarly, the child's slow adaptability and somewhat negative mood would suggest that the slow-to-warm-up child would not interact favorably with new people. Clearly, the temperamental characteristics of this type of child would provide a basis for parental and teacher interactions different from that of easy children.

One indication of the significant differences in interaction patterns that may be involved in these three types of temperamental styles is found in the proportion of children in each temperamental group who eventually developed behavioral problems severe enough to call for psychiatric attention. Of the total number of children in the Thomas *et al.* project, 42 percent eventually developed such problems. About 70 percent of the difficult children developed such difficulties, only 18 percent of the easy children did so, and the proportion of slow-to-warm-up children who developed such problems was between these two groups. Thus, although only 65 percent of the NYLS sample children had temperamental types falling into one of these three distinct clusters, each of these types was suggestive of differential child-parent interactions.

Other evidence indicates that such different temperamental types are associated with differential reactions on the part of others in the child's environment. Gordon and Thomas (1967) found that kindergarten teachers were able to rate their students in respect to their temperamental styles. The teachers were also asked to estimate the intelligence of these students, and independently, Gordon and Thomas measured these children's intelligence. It was found that teachers distorted the students' intelligence; that is, the teacher ratings of intelligence were biased by the temperamental styles of the students. For instance, children who had temperaments similar to that of the easy child were rated as more intelligent than children who had temperamental styles similar to the slow-to-warm-up child. Yet, these estimates tended to represent an overestimation of the easy children's intelligence and an underestimation of the slow-to-warm-up children's intelligence. Thus, it is reasonable to assume that teachers will interact differently with children they believe to be brighter than with children they believe to be duller. For example, they may attempt to provide remedial work for these "duller" children and might leave the "brighter" children alone to work by themselves more often. These distortions suggest that different children, possessing different temperamental types, will experience different interactions with their teachers over the course of their educational development.

The various temperamental attribute scores of the easy, difficult, and slow-to-warm-up child are presented in Table 9.2. From this table and from our above discussion we can see some important implications not only of these three

**Table 9.2** Temperamental attributes of the easy, difficult, and slow-to-warm-up child.

| | Activity level | Rhythmicity | Distractibility | Approach/ Withdrawal | Adaptability |
|---|---|---|---|---|---|
| Type of child | The proportion of active periods to inactive ones. | Regularity of hunger, excretion, sleep, and wakefulness. | The degree to which extraneous stimuli alter behavior. | The response to a new object or person. | The ease with which a child adapts to changes in his environment. |
| "Easy" | Varies | Very regular | Varies | Positive approach | Very adaptable |
| "Slow to warm up" | Low to moderate | Varies | Varies | Initial withdrawal | Slowly adaptable |
| "Difficult" | Varies | Irregular | Varies | Withdrawal | Slowly adaptable |

Table 9.2 (continued)

| Type of child | Attention span and persistence | Intensity of reaction | Threshold of responsiveness | Quality of mood |
|---|---|---|---|---|
| | The amount of time devoted to an activity, and the effect of distraction on the activity. | The energy of response, regardless of its quality or direction. | The intensity of stimulation required to evoke a discernible response. | The amount of friendly, pleasant, joyful behavior as contrasted with unpleasant, unfriendly behavior. |
| "Easy" | High or low | Low or mild | High or low | Positive |
| "Slow to warm up" | High or low | Mild | High or low | Slightly negative |
| "Difficult" | High or low | Intense | High or low | Negative |

*Source:* A. Thomas, S. Chess, and H. G. Birch, "The Origin of Personality: *Scientific American* **223** (1970). Copyright © 1970 by Scientific American, Inc. All rights reserved.

temperamental types but of temperamental style in general for practical issues in child rearing and for other parental practices. However, before we turn to the practical implications of the results of the NYLS, let us first consider the theoretical implications of this important ipsative longitudinal study of child development.

## Theoretical Implications of the NYLS

The results of the Thomas *et al.* project strongly indicate that children have present at birth characteristically individual, or unique, attributes of reactivity. They tend to show stylistically different reactive repertoires to the stimuli and situations they interact with. This individual pattern of reactivity is presumed to arise out of both the intrinsic and extrinsic variables that provide a source of the child's development and, too, out of an interaction between these variables. In other words, on the basis on the child's individual maturational-experiential interaction the child develops characteristics of individuality, which become furthered on the basis of interactions between this individually different child and his circularly functioning environment. In fact, we have seen that because the child does have such characteristically different attributes of reactivity, he will react to environmental situations differently than will another individually different child who may experience the same environmental situation. Thus, because different children can be expected to react differently to the same environmental situation, these differential reactions will differentially affect significant other persons in their respective environments. These different reactions in significant others will then feed back on the child and provide a further experiential source of his own development.

Thus, even if parents attempt to provide the same child-rearing environment for their different children and even if such parents possess markedly similar personalities, such parental similarities will not have the same effect on different children. Because a child's temperament is largely unrelated to his parents' personality and to child-rearing practices (Thomas, *et al.,* 1970), this suggests (1) that such parental-environmental variables cannot be viewed as the only source of a child's temperament and (2) that the same environment will have a different effect on different children. One may not appropriately focus solely on either hereditary or experiential sources of influences if one wants to accurately deal with the actual source of individuality and development. Rather, one must study hereditary sources, prenatal and paranatal sources and influences, and early life experiences, all of which may interact to contribute to the development of the individual (Thomas, *et al.,* 1963, p. 81).

In sum, the results of the Thomas group's NYLS indicate the following:
1.    Extremely early in their lives children appear to possess, and to maintain characteristically different patterns of reactivity, or temperament, and this individuality finds its source in the interactions of the intrinsic and the extrinsic factors affecting the development of organisms.
2.    Because of this interactively based individuality, different children will react differently even to the same environmental influences. Thus, the same stimulus will not have the same effect on different children, and any analysis of behavioral development that attempts to account for development simply by reference to stimulatory factors is inappropriate, naive, and destined to remain incomplete.

3.    On the basis of the child's individuality and the circular feedback functions that arise out of this individuality (Schneirla, 1957), the child must be viewed as playing an active, participatory role in his own development.

Thus, the ipsative study of the Thomas group has found results consistent with the organismic, interactionist developmental position we have been stressing throughout this book. Consistent with the views of other such organismic theorists (e.g., Schneirla, Piaget, Kohlberg), the child's development is seen by the Thomas group as finding its source in an interaction between the child's organismic characteristics and the characteristics of experience; hence the organism itself plays an active, contributory role in its own development. With these theoretical implications specified, let us now consider the important practical implications of the Thomas group's study.

## Practical Implications of the NYLS

Many parents consult various "how to" books about child rearing in order to gain information about how to raise their children. Often such books tell the parent what a child is like at a particular age period and what child-rearing practices to employ. One important practical implication of the NYLS is that such cookbook approaches to child rearing are inappropriate.

Because children are individually different, because they possess characteristically different and stable attributes of reactivity, one may not appropriately make generalized statements about what a child at a particular age level is like. One may not imply that a given type of rearing procedure will work equally well with all children. Although children do share general, age-related characteristics, they also possess important characteristics of individuality. Thus, a child-rearing book must help parents understand that to an important extent their child is an individual person (see Chess, *et al.,* 1965). Moreover, the cookbook approach to child rearing is also inappropriate because, again, one cannot accurately specify how a general method of child rearing will affect all children. Since children have individually different temperamental repertoires, they will not react in the same way to the same rearing procedure. Different children will react differently to the same exact child-training procedure. For instance, adoption by the parents of a fixed schedule of feeding may work well for an easy child but might prove unfavorable for either a difficult child or a slow-to-warm-up child.

Another practical implication of the Thomas group's study relates to parental responses to children's development. If emotional or behavioral problems arise in a child, the typical response in a parent is guilt. Perhaps because the parents believe the environmentalist doctrine—that anything a child becomes is solely an outcome of his environmental experiences—the parents feel that they are responsible for the child's problems. They feel guilt because they believe that they are responsible for their child not only in a moral sense—which of course one may maintain that they are—but also in a behavioral-determinancy sense. They believe that they are the major environmental determinants of their child's behavior, and in turn they believe that it is the environment that essentially provides a source of their child's behavioral development. Such parents are not aware of the fact that the child plays an active, contributory role in his own development. Thus, their guilt is misdirected because they do not understand that a child's behavioral or emotional problems arise in part from an interaction between his temperament and conflicting environmental demands. While it is easy to imagine that almost any environmental circumstance would be adapted to by an easy child, a difficult child would probably have interactional difficulties with almost any environment.

Thus, parents should not feel guilty. Rather, they should be made aware of the importance of understanding the implications of their child's individuality, and they should attempt to alter their procedures to achieve a more favorable interaction between the child's temperamental characteristics and their child-rearing practices.

In summarizing the implications of their work for both theory and practice in psychiatry, the authors of the study have said:

> Theory and practice in psychiatry must take into full account the individual and his uniqueness: how children differ and how these differences act to influence their psychological growth. A given environment will not have the identical functional meaning for all children. Much will depend on the temperamental makeup of the child. As we learn more about how specific parental attitudes and practices and other specific factors in the environment of the child interact with specific temperamental, mental and physical attributes of individual children, it should become considerably easier to foster the child's healthy development. (Quoted from "The Origin of Personality," *Scientific American* **2** (1970), p. 109, by A. Thomas, S. Chess, and H. G. Birch. Copyright © 1970 by Scientific American, Inc. All rights reserved.)

## Some Concluding Comments

With this specification of the practical implications of the NYLS we have concluded our assessment of how an ipsative orientation to the study of child development may be used to understand the complexities of psychological development. Although this approach, as represented in the work of the Thomas group, is quite different in its procedural orientation from either the stage or the differential approaches, we have seen that the Thomas *et al.* ipsative approach addresses similar issues of development. Thus, consistent with the general organismic, interactionist theoretical positions found in the ideas of stage theorists (e.g., Piaget, Kohlberg), the Thomas group's ipsative approach provides evidence for the interactive basis of psychological development and supports interactionist, organismic notions about the important role that the organism itself plays in its own development.

To this point in this book we have been emphasizing the implications and contributions of organismic developmental theory for the understanding of various aspects of psychological development. Yet, at various points we have also indicated that there exists another dominant, important theoretical perspective in developmental theory. This approach—termed here the *learning approach*—is underlain by the mechanistic, unity-of-science philosophy of science and is represented in the theoretical approaches of such people as Bijou and Baer (1961), Mischel (1971), and of course Skinner. Accordingly, after summarizing the major points made in this chapter, we will turn to a consideration and evaluation of the learning approach to the study of child development.

## Summary

The ipsative approach to developmental psychology assesses intraindividual consistencies and changes in the attribute repertoire and attribute interrelation of a person over the course of life. Hence, a basic and necessary orientation of the ipsative approach is an assessment of the role of the organism's own characteristics in its own development. Thus, consistent with organismic views of development, it is held that an organism's lawful, systematic characteristics of individuality provide an important source of its own development. This belief was the orientational basis of the New York Longitudinal Study, conducted by Thomas, Chess, Birch, Hertzig, and Korn.

Consistent with other organismic conceptions of development—for example, as presented by Schneirla—the Thomas group took an interactionist view of the basis of children's characteristics of individuality. Moreover, a consequence of such interactionally based individuality is that children will be involved in differential circular reactions with their environment; hence, such individuality will provide a basis of the child's future development.

Such individuality suggests that different reactions in different children will occur in response to the same environmental stimulus. Moreover, because of such individual differences in reactivity characteristics, it can be expected that the same environmental event (e.g., a particular parental child-rearing practice) will have a different effectiveness for different children.

In order to translate their theoretical conceptions into empirical facts, the Thomas group had to: (1) develop some measure of individual characteristics of reactivity; (2) ascertain the extent to which children's individuality remains stable; and (3) ascertain the way in which such individuality contributes to the child's development over the course of life.

To accomplish these objectives the Thomas group studied a group of children longitudinally. Measures of individual style of behavioral reactivity—or temperament— were derived from analyses of anterospective parental interviews pertaining to the "how" of a child's behavior (rather than the "what" of behavior). Parents were required to describe, rather than interpret, their child's behavior. An inductive content analysis of these behavioral descriptions indicated nine categories of temperament: activity level, adaptability, rhythmicity, approach-withdrawal, threshold of responsivity, intensity of reaction, quality of mood, distractibility, and attention span-persistence.

Results of the study indicated that marked individual differences in temperamental repertoires were evident in the children over the course of the first ten years of their lives, and that this individuality was not systematically related to either the parents' method of child rearing or to the parents' own personality styles. Moreover, the individually different temperamental repertoires of the children tended to remain stable over the first ten years of life.

The potential significance of such stability was highlighted by the fact that different temperamental types were discernible among the subjects. That is, there were persistent clusters of temperamental characteristics among some subjects, which allowed them to be depicted as easy, difficult, or slow-to-warm-up children; such different types could evoke differential reactions in those people in the child's environment and hence provide differential feedback for the child.

These findings, consistent with the theoretical conceptualizations of the Thomas group, also have practical implications for child-rearing practices. Because children have lawful, stable characteristics of individuality, they cannot be expected to respond in the same way to a given child-rearing practice; hence, a cookbook approach to child rearing is inappropriate. Such general prescriptions do not consider children's systematic individuality. Moreover, since the results of the Thomas group's study indicate that the child is a central source of his own behavior, independent of the parents' behavior, then parents may not be the sole determinant of any neurotic or undesirable child behavior. Recognition of this point might serve to reduce parental guilt about aspects of the child-rearing process.

# 10

## The Learning Approach

In the preceding chapters we have focused predominantly on organismic conceptions of development. These theoretical formulations view a person's psychological development as arising out of an interaction between the intrinsic (nature) and the extrinsic (nurture) variables involved in development. Moreover, such organismic, interactionist viewpoints imply that qualitative discontinuity in part characterizes psychological development, although—because of adherence to the orthogenetic principle—they also view aspects of development as being continuous in nature. Thus, to differing extents, organismic developmentalists believe that development arises out of an interaction between the organism (and/or the characteristics of the organism) and its environment; furthermore, to different extents, they represent such development as proceeding through qualitatively different stages.

Although such organismic conceptions have been given most attention in our presentation, we have also at points indicated that an important opposing point of view exists. This approach may be termed the *learning approach* because of the fact that adherents of it consider the laws of learning invariantly and inextricably involved in psychological development. In Chapter 5, in our discussion of the continuity-discontinuity controversy, we introduced some of the basic components of this point of view and considered some of the ideas of perhaps the most famous contributor to the formulation of the learning approach, B. F. Skinner. We saw that Skinner views the laws of learning as being invariantly involved not only in the behavior of humans but, moreover, in the behavior of all animals. Thus, Skinner maintains that the laws of learning—those involved in either *classical* or *operant* conditioning—are universal; that is, they are continuously applicable to the behavior of all organisms. After one "corrects for" the (seemingly trivial) differences among animals in their anatomical or morphological makeup, one can use the same set of laws of learning to account for the behavior and the development of all animals. Skinner suggests that some animals learn to behave in a certain way, for example by pressing a bar with their paw; other types of animals might have to use their beak, and still others might use a hand. Yet, after such differences are accounted for, one sees that all animals learn in accordance with the very same set of laws, those of classical and operant learning. We may surmise, then, that as opposed to organismic theorists, learning-approach developmentalists stress the continuities of behavioral development. They stress the view that the continuous applicability of the laws of learning accounts for the development of behavior.

Thus, in order to adequately understand the learning approach to psychological development, it is obvious that we must first understand something about the nature of learning and the laws, or variables, involved in the learning process. Accordingly, we will now turn to a consideration of what learning is; after this discussion we will be able to interrelate our knowledge of learning psychology with our previous understanding of the philosophical basis of this approach, the unity-of-science philosophy of science. Finally, we will present some representative positions within the learning-approach theoretical framework and, of course, evaluate and contrast them with organismic developmental positions.

## What Is Learning?

As with any complex psychological phenomenon, there is no general theoretical agreement about what constitutes learning. Although it is fair to say that in general more

B. F. Skinner

attention has been paid by psychologists to learning than to any other psychological process, different workers in this area maintain markedly different conceptualizations about what variables are actually involved in learning and what, in fact, constitutes learning (see, for example, Gewirtz and Stingle, 1968; Bolles, 1972). Despite this controversy there is, to some extent, a general agreement about the *empirical* components of learning. Even though we must recognize that even this empirical analysis might raise some controversial points, we are making a relative choice; that is, there is relatively more agreement about the empirical components of the learning process than there is about its theoretical characteristics.

Accordingly, we may focus on an empirical definition of learning offered by Kimble (1961). *Learning* is a relatively permanent change in behavior potentiality which occurs as a result of reinforced practice, excluding changes due to maturation, fatigue, and/or injury to the nervous system. This is obviously a complex definition, including many important component concepts. In order to understand this empirical definition, let us consider the various key words in this definition.

1. *Relatively permanent.* Learning is defined as a relatively permanent change in behavior. By this we mean that the changes that comprise learning are changes that tend to remain with the person. When a person learns he acquires a behavior; that is, the behavior in the person's repertoire has been changed, and this addition tends to remain. Although you might question this component of the definition, there is considerable empirical support for it. Let us take an extreme example for the purposes of illustration. Many people study a particular subject early in their educational careers (e.g., a foreign language). As adults, they may believe that they no longer remember anything they learned. Yet, if they attempt to relearn the foreign language, they might find that it takes them a shorter time to reach their previous level of competence. Such a *savings*

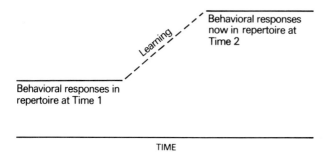

**Fig. 10.1** Learning involves a change in the behavioral-response repertoire of an organism.

*effect,* which has frequently been experimentally verified, indicates that previously acquired changes in the person tend to remain relatively permanent. Although the person did not retain everything he had previously acquired when he began relearning, the fact that he relearned the material more easily than he originally learned it suggests that some of the learning had been saved; it was relatively permanent.

2.    *Change.* Learning constitutes a modification of behavior. The person has a repertoire of behavioral responses. With learning, however, this repertoire is altered. More responses are added to the repertoire, and thus a change has occurred. This is illustrated in Fig. 10.1.

3.    *Behavioral potentiality.* This term refers to a most important concept we must deal with when attempting to understand learning. One never actually sees learning; learning is not a directly observable phenomenon. Rather, what one typically sees when studying learning is performance. One sees an animal perform a task. Thus, on the basis of relatively permanent changes in such performance one may infer that learning has taken place. In other words, the term learning may be used as a summary term, describing an empirical process involving changes in performance. Hence the term behavior potentiality refers to the *learning-performance distinction.* We do not see learning per se; rather, we see performance changes and we summarize these changes by the term learning.

For example, a student may be given a pretest in mathematics. After a certain score on that pretest is achieved, the student is exposed to a given type of instruction designed to improve his score (performance) on a posttest. If the student's score increases, if his performance is enhanced through exposure to this instructional technique, we say that the student has learned. Yet, we do not actually see this phenomenon called learning. We only see an alteration in performance. Still, we infer that learning has taken place on the basis of the observed change in performance. Simply, then, learning is not a variable we directly observe. It has the status of an *intervening variable* in psychology; that is, it summarizes observed changes in performance.

4.    *Reinforced practice.* This term, too, is particularly important for our understanding of learning. Practice per se of a behavior might lead only to fatigue. Yet most learning psychologists would agree that if practice is combined with reinforcement, learning will

occur. In other words, when a behavior is reinforced, a relatively permanent change in behavior potentiality will be obtained. Reinforcement, then, is an essential component in our empirical conceptualization of the learning process. The application of reinforcement will make the acquisition of a relatively permanent change in behavior potentiality more probable. The exclusion of reinforcement, on the other hand, will not lead to such incremental changes.

What, then, is reinforcement? A *reinforcement,* or a reinforcing stimulus, may be defined as any stimulus that produces or maintains behavior. For instance, salivation is a form of behavior. Given the appropriate stimulus conditions, our salivary glands will excrete a liquid substance termed saliva. One way of eliciting this salivary behavior is to show a hungry person his favorite food. The person will probably salivate, and the production of this salivary behavior is under the control of the food stimulus. In other words, the food is a reinforcing stimulus because it produces the salivary behavior.

Another form of behavior involves the muscular responses involved in digging a ditch. It is obvious that each time we shovel dirt up from the ground we are behaving. Now, if someone comes up to us and simply gives us a shovel and tells us to start digging, we might readily decline this request. However, if the person says that for each shovel of dirt we dig we will be given one dollar, most of us will now engage in shovelling behavior quite readily. What leads to the emission of shovelling behavior in this instance? Clearly, it is that the attainment of the money is made contingent upon our performing the behavior. The money that follows our behavior maintains it. If no money were to follow the behavior, we would probably not shovel. Yet, since our attainment of the money is contingent upon our performance, the money maintains our behavior. Hence in this example money is a reinforcing stimulus; it leads us to emit an appropriate response. Our response emission is maintained because a reinforcing stimulus follows (is contingent upon) our behavior.

In sum, a reinforcing stimulus is a stimulus that will lead either to the elicitation of a response (as in the case of the food producing the salivation) or to the emission of a response in order to obtain the reinforcing stimulus (as in the case of digging). In either case the relation between behavior and reinforcement is that a reinforcing stimulus makes a behavior more probable. It is more likely that behavior will occur when it is reinforced. In general, reinforcement is needed for learning because a reinforcing stimulus is a stimulus that increases the probability of a behavior.

5. *Excluding changes due to maturation, fatigue, and/or injury to the nervous system.* Not all changes in behavior involve alterations due to the learning process. Only those relatively permanent changes in behavioral potentiality that occur as a result of reinforced practice may be attributable to the learning process. Changes that may not be reasonably attributed to learning are accounted for by variables involved in such things as maturation, fatigue, or nervous system injury. We may have learned, for example, that cookies are kept in a jar on top of the refrigerator. Yet, because we are not tall enough (and because there are no chairs around), we will not perform the behavior of reaching into the cookie jar. However, when the appropriate maturation has occurred (e.g., we have grown ten inches) such behavior may now be very typical. Fatigue may also lead to changes in behavior. Even if we are digging a ditch for one dollar per shovelful of dirt, our rate of shovelling will, after a time, decrease. Although our behavior might still be maintained by the monetary reward, it will change; it will slow down simply

because we experience muscular fatigue. Finally, it is obvious that after some injury to our nervous system (e.g., serious brain damage following a car accident) our behavior will change, but such changes are attributable to the injury rather than to learning.

## Types of Learning

We have seen some of the essential components of an empirical conceptualization of the learning process, but we have not considered the ways in which these components may interrelate in order to produce learning. What is the way, or ways in which learning takes place? How does learning occur? How do reinforcing stimuli interrelate with behavior to produce learning? Generally, learning psychologists maintain that two types of relations between stimuli and responses account for learning. These two types of learning—*classical and operant learning*—represent the paradigms (models) of the learning process. That is, the classical and the operant learning paradigms are thought to represent (e.g., by Bijou and Baer, 1961) the two ways in which stimuli and responses may interrelate to produce learning. As we will see, classical conditioning involves behavior that is elicited by preceding reinforcing stimuli, while operant conditioning involves behavior that is controlled by succeeding reinforcing stimuli (Bijou and Baer, 1961). Accordingly, we will now consider the essential components of each of these two models.

### The Classical Paradigm

Many of us are probably familiar with what we have here termed the *classical learning paradigm* through knowledge of the work of Ivan P. Pavlov, the Russian physiologist who discovered this type of learning. We know that through happenstance Pavlov discovered that the dogs he was using as experimental subjects would salivate to stimuli other than food (e.g., his white lab coat, a bell). His studies of the variables involved in such associations led to an understanding of the nature of one of the two basic types of learning we have noted, classical learning (or conditioning).

To understand the functioning of the classical paradigm we must first focus on initial associations the organism enters the learning situation with. Let us first posit that there exists a stimulus that reliably (i.e., regularly) elicits a response of strong magnitude. For example, we may assume that food is a stimulus that will reliably elicit a salivary response. Now, if we further assume that no prior association, or learning, is necessary to establish this relation between the stimulus and the response, between the food and the salivation, then we may assume that food is a stimulus that will reliably elicit a salivary response. Given this assumption, we may term the food stimulus an *unconditional,* or *unconditioned, stimulus (UCS).* A *UCS,* then, is a stimulus that reliably elicits a response of strong magnitude without previous learning. Hence, a *UCS* is an unlearned stimulus. Moreover, since no previous association, or learning, is necessary in order for the *UCS* to elicit the salivation, this salivation response is an *unconditioned response (UCR),* an unlearned response. Thus, to begin with, the classical paradigm may be represented as:

(1)   (food) *UCS→UCR* (salivation).

Now, there exist numerous stimuli in the organism's environment which of course do not elicit this particular *UCR*. That is, they are neutral in respect to the above *UCS*→*UCR* relation; such neutral stimuli do *not* elicit the *UCR*. However, if one takes such a neutral stimulus (for example, a bell) and repeatedly pairs this stimulus with the *UCS*, then a different state of affairs will soon exist. For instance, suppose one rings the bell (that is, presents this neutral stimulus) and then presents the *UCS;* after such repeated pairings the previously neutral stimulus will come to elicit a response markedly similar to the *UCR*. Because of the repeated pairings of the bell and the food, the bell begins to acquire some of the properties of the food: it, too, leads to salivation. We say, then, that the bell, previously a neutral stimulus, has become a conditioned stimulus (*CS*), a learned stimulus. Through the repeated pairings of the bell and the food, the bell becomes a *CS* and comes to elicit a learned, or a *conditioned response (CR)*. In this case the bell comes to elicit salivation. However, this salivation is not a *UCR;* rather, it is a response to a stimulus that obtained its control over behavior through its association with another stimulus. Since the organism learned this *CS*—*UCS* association, the response to the *CS* is a learned, or a conditioned, response. Hence, because of:

(2)    (bell) *CS*—*UCS* (food),

a learned response is acquired. A learned association, one that did not previously exist, between a previously neutral stimulus and a response to this stimulus, is acquired. This association may be represented as:

(3)    (bell) *CS*→*CR* (salivation).

This is the classical conditioning, or learning, paradigm. A previously neutral stimulus precedes an unconditioned stimulus, and after repeated pairings of this *CS* and *UCS,* the *CS* comes to elicit a response markedly similar to the original unconditioned response. A summary of this paradigm may be represented as:

(4)    *CS*—*UCS*→*UCR*—*CR*
       (bell)—(food)→(salivation) (salivation).

**Characteristics of Classical Conditioning.**   We see that in classical learning, or conditioning, the *CS* or the *UCS* is said to elicit the response. The term *elicit* is used to signify the fact that classical conditioning involves the autonomic nervous system and the body's involuntary musculature. Hence, we do not have to learn to salivate to food. We do not have to learn to blink in response to a puff of air to our eye. Rather, such responses are reflexive in nature. They are involuntary responses. Hence, classical conditioning involves the conditioning of our involuntary, reflexive responses. Such responses are almost literally pulled out of us by the stimulus in question (e.g., the food or the puff of air). Thus, we say that classical responses are elicited. Moreover, since classical conditioning involves our involuntary nervous system, many of our emotional responses are acquired through classical conditioning. For example, a rat will show unconditioned emotional behavior in response to a strong electrical shock delivered to the floor of its cage. The shock is a *UCS* and the emotional response is a *UCR*. If a buzzer is always sounded two seconds before the shock begins, however, then after some time the rat will show a similar emotional response to the buzzer. The buzzer will become a CS and the emotional response will be a *CR, a conditioned emotional response (CER).* Similarly, if a human pedestrian witnesses a particularly bloody auto accident at a certain street corner, then he or she might experience unpleasant emotional reactions in response to such a sight (e.g., nausea). The sight of the blood will be a *UCS* and the emotional response will be a *UCR.* If at some later time, however, the person is walking by that same street corner and is again overcome with nausea, this might indicate that the particular corner was established, in just one trial, as a *CS* and the emotional response was a *CR.*

Thus, we see that classically learned responses can be considered reflexive in nature and that emotional responses are particularly susceptible to classical learning. Reinforcement, of course, plays an essential role in both of these characteristics of classical learning. In the case of classical conditioning the role of the reinforcing stimulus is to *produce* behavior. That is, classical responses are elicited, they are produced, by the *UCS.* Thus, since the *UCS* (e.g., food) produces the response (e.g., salivation), it provides, or represents, the reinforcing stimulus within the classical conditioning paradigm. In classical conditioning, then, the *UCS,* the reinforcement, elicits (produces) the response, and thus we see that in this paradigm reinforcement produces the response. However, after classical learning has been accomplished, that is, after the *CS* has become able to produce (elicit) the *CR,* there is obviously another stimulus that now produces responding. Obviously, the *CS* also produces a response. However, because the *CS* obtained its reinforcing power (or efficacy) through its association with the *UCS,* we must distinguish between these two levels of reinforcers. Accordingly, we may term the *UCS* a *primary* reinforcing stimulus and the *CS* a *secondary* reinforcing stimulus. However, in the case of both the *UCS* and the *CS,* reinforcement always produces a response within the classical conditioning paradigm. In classical conditioning the reinforcing stimulus always leads to the response.

Finally, we may note that although we have termed this type of learning classical conditioning, other names are used by learning psychologists to represent this process. For example, some psychologists refer to classical learning, or conditioning, as *Pavlovian conditioning.* Others refer to it as *associative shifting,* in recognition of the shift in association between the *UCS* and the response to the *CS* and the response, while other psychologists use the term *stimulus substitution,* for similar reasons. Lastly, another major term representing this type of learning is *respondent conditioning;* this term is used to highlight the fact that this type of learning involves responses to previous stimulation (Bijou and Baer, 1961; Skinner, 1938). However, all terms refer to a type of learning involving responses elicited by preceding, reinforcing stimulation. On the other hand, the other major type of learning that exists—operant learning—works in quite another way. Let us now turn our attention to a consideration of the operant learning paradigm.

### The Operant Paradigm

Many of us have had the experience of being in a bus or subway station on a hot day. Suppose we are in such a situation and that we are hot and tired. Looking around the station we might see two machines, a telephone on the wall and a soda pop machine.

Being hot, tired, and perhaps a bit thirsty, we might put a coin in the soda pop machine and get a glass of soda pop. Certainly, however, we would not put the coin in the phone if we wanted something to drink. Such a response would not be followed by the appropriate (needed) stimulus—soda pop. In other words, only if we emit the appropriate response (putting a coin in a slot) in the presence of the correct stimulus (the soda machine) will we get the "needed" stimulus. If in the presence of certain stimuli we emit a certain response, this response will be followed by an appropriate stimulus. Emission of the same response, but in the presence of an inappropriate stimulus (in this case the telephone), will not be followed by the appropriate stimulus (the soda pop).

The above description represents an analogy of the *operant conditioning paradigm*. Certain stimuli in the environment are *discriminated* (responded to differentially) from other stimuli in the environment on the basis of the fact that responses emitted in the presence of some stimuli are followed by a reinforcing stimulus, while responses in the presence of other stimuli are not followed by a reinforcement. We know from our above discussion of reinforcement that if a response is followed by a reinforcing stimulus, the future occurrence of that response will be more probable. That is, if the occurrence of a reinforcing stimulus is made contingent upon the emission of a response, then the probability of that response occurring will increase. A response of putting a coin into a slot will be followed by a reinforcing stimulus (soda pop) if that slot works the dispensing mechanism of a soda pop machine. Since a response to that stimulus (the soda pop machine) will be followed by a reinforcement (soda pop), while responses to another stimulus (e.g., the telephone) will not be followed by the reinforcement, a discrimination between these two stimuli is established; responses in the presence of the soda machine are quite probable and responses in the presence of the telephone are not. This is the case because the former responses are reinforced while the latter are not. Thus, stimuli are discriminated on the basis of the consequences of responses made in their presence.

Hence, operant conditioning involves learning to emit a response ($R$) in the presence of an appropriate, i.e., discriminative, stimulus ($S^D$); responses in the presence of such discriminative stimuli are followed by a reinforcing stimulus ($S^R$). Simply, in terms of the above analogy, the presence of soda pop is contingent upon the emission of a correct response—a response to a soda pop machine and not a telephone.

A discriminative stimulus ($S^D$), then, is a stimulus that cues the occasion for a response. This is the case because a response ($R$) in the presence of an $S^D$ will lead to the attainment of a reinforcing stimulus ($S^R$). Thus, since the attainment of reinforcement is contingent upon the emission of responses in the presence of only certain stimuli, operant learning involves the acquisition of responses in the presence of $S^D$'s and the absence of responses in the absence of $S^D$'s. We may represent the operant paradigm as:

(5) $S^D—R{\rightarrow}S^R$.

The work of Skinner is, of course, most associated with operant conditioning. Most of his work has dealt with animals, and an example of operant conditioning with animals may be used to further illustrate this paradigm. Suppose you place a rat into a small experimental chamber (what has been termed by some a "Skinner box") containing a small lever (or bar) protruding from the wall and a magazine capable of delivering food into a cup also protruding from the wall. The animal when placed in the chamber will assuredly move around in it and eventually press the bar. If, when this happens, food is delivered, the animal will continue to press the bar if and as long as it is hungry. That is, if the animal has been deprived of food and if the bar press leads to food, the animal will bar press until satiated. However, if there is also a light in the experimental chamber which can be turned on or off by the experimenter, this light could soon be established as an $S^D$. As long as the rat is not satiated it will continue to bar press. However, if the light is turned on and off at random intervals, and bar presses occurring only when the light is on are followed by food, then responses when the light is off will soon diminish (or drop out entirely). Responses only in the presence of the light will remain. This example of operant conditioning may be represented as:

(6)    (light on) $S^D$—$R$ (bar press)$\rightarrow$$S^R$ (food).

Thus, operant conditioning involves the acquisition of responses in the presence of certain (i.e., discriminative) stimuli, stimuli cueing the occasion for a response to be followed by a reinforcement. Responses emitted in the presence of such stimuli will be followed by a reinforcement; responses emitted when such stimuli are not present will not be followed by a reinforcement. The attainment of reinforcement is contingent upon the emission of a response in the presence of a discriminative stimulus.

**Characteristics of Operant Conditioning.**  We see that within the operant conditioning paradigm, responses are emitted in the presence of a discriminative stimulus, and in fact a discriminative stimulus is established as such because such responses are followed by a reinforcing stimulus. An organism emits a response in the presence of an $S^D$ because such responses are associated with succeeding reinforcement. In other words, responses are *maintained* in the presence of an $S^D$, and an $S^D$ is in turn established as such because the occurrence of a reinforcement is contingent upon such responses. Thus, responses are maintained because they are followed by reinforcing stimuli, or conversely, the stimulus following the response in the operant conditioning paradigm maintains the production of that response.

In operant conditioning, the response produces the reinforcement (as opposed to classical conditioning, wherein the reinforcement produces the response). The organism must respond—in the presence of the appropriate stimulus (the $S^D$)—in order to obtain reinforcement. In other words, the organism is instrumental in obtaining reinforcement; it must operate in its environment in order to obtain reinforcement. In the presence of the appropriate, cueing, discriminative stimulus, the organism must itself respond (through pressing a bar, pecking a key, turning a handle, putting a foot on a peddle, etc.) in order for a reinforcement to be obtained. The organism itself must operate on its environment, it must be instrumental itself, in obtaining reinforcement. As opposed to classical learning, wherein responses are elicited by the *UCS* (the reinforcing stimulus), the organism must learn to emit the appropriate response, the response that will lead to the production of an $S^R$ in the presence of an $S^D$. The animal must behave in order to obtain a reinforcement. Thus, since the organism itself is instrumental in obtaining an $S^R$, another name typically applied to operant conditioning is *instrumental learning*.

The term *emit* is used within the context of this paradigm to signify the fact that operant responses involve the body's voluntary musculature. Thus, operant conditioning involves learning to use the voluntary musculature to emit a response that will be followed by a reinforcement. However, this is not to say that operant responses are not controlled. Rather, such responses are under the complete control of the stimulus environment. Since operant responses are maintained by succeeding, reinforcing stimuli, their probability of occurrence is determined by the degree of absence or presence of reinforcing stimuli; operant responses are also set by discriminative stimuli, since such responses are reinforced only when emitted in the presence of the appropriate discriminative stimuli. We see, then, that although operant learning involves the voluntary musculature, such responses are in the final analysis maintained and controlled by the reinforcing stimuli following them.

However, because operant responses do involve the voluntary muscles of the body, the major portion of motor behavior is thought to be acquired through operant conditioning. Such broad involvement in the majority of behaviors emitted by organisms may be illustrated by various kinds of seemingly disparate motor behaviors. If, while driving our car, we see a stop sign at the end of the road, we take our foot off the accelerator pedal and place it on the brake pedal. Soon after this response our car comes to a halt. This motor behavior series may be interpreted as an instance of an operant sequence. The stop sign represents an $S^D$, cueing the occasion for a motor response ($R$) of lifting the foot off one pedal and placing it on another. The $S^R$ in this instance is the halting of the car. Another example may be seen in learning a foreign language. If our teacher shows us the word *garçon* and we respond *boy,* some sort of approval or indication of correctness is offered by the teacher. In this case the French word *garçon* may be seen as an $S^D$, the emission of the word *boy* is the $R$, and the approval is the $S^R$. Operant conditioning may also be involved in the exploratory behavior of young children. A young child may be exploring the kitchen of his home while a roast is cooking in the oven. He puts his hand on the oven and then, of course, rapidly removes it. In further explorations he continues to move away from the oven. Here we may say that the oven is an $S^D$, which is associated with the $R$ of moving away. The reinforcing stimulus in this instance is represented by the heat from the oven, and as we will soon see, this heat represents a negatively reinforcing stimulus. The point now is that the occurrence of most motor behaviors may be construed as being consistent with the operant paradigm.

Yet, it is obvious that most of our daily motor behavior is much more involved than the behaviors described above. People typically emit long sequences, or *chains,* of behaviors mediated by the voluntary musculature, rather than single, discrete responses. Still, in principle, such complex chains of responses can be completely accounted for within the operant conditioning paradigm. However, such an accounting requires reference again to the principle of secondary reinforcement.

## Secondary Reinforcement and Chaining

In our discussion of classical conditioning we saw that after repeated pairing with the *UCS,* the *CS* too obtains reinforcing power. Through its association with the primary reinforcing *UCS,* the *CS* thus becomes a secondary reinforcement—that is, a stimulus that acquires its ability to reinforce behavior through association with another reinforcer. Similarly, within the operant conditioning paradigm the $S^D$, through its association with the $S^R$, becomes a secondary reinforcing stimulus ($S^r$). The $S^D$ cues the occasion when an $R$ will be followed by an $S^R$, and this predictability between the occurrence of the discriminative stimulus and that of the reinforcing stimulus establishes the $S^D$ as a secondary reinforcement. Because of the nature of its association with the $S^R$, reinforcing efficacy accrues to the $S^D$, establishing it as an $S^r$—a secondary reinforcement. Thus, simply,

(7)  $S^D = S^r$.

Because the $S^D$ is also an $S^r$, this means that other responses may be acquired with the $S^D$ used as the stimulus maintaining those responses. In turn, another $S^D$, which may be used to signal the occasion in which a certain response will now lead to the occurrence of the first $S^D$, will also, through its association with the latter discriminative stimulus, acquire reinforcing properties. In turn then this new $S^D$ may now be used to reinforce yet another response. In this way, long sequences of behaviors (chains) may be established. Let us consider an illustration.

On page 262 we considered an example in which a rat learned to press a bar ($R$) when a light was on ($S^D$) to obtain food ($S^R$). The stimulus that maintained bar-pressing behavior in this example was the food, and on the basis of our above analysis we now know that the light's being on represented both a discriminative stimulus and a secondary reinforcement. Accordingly, if the light's being on is, in fact, a secondary reinforcing stimulus (an $S^r$), then this stimulus should be able to maintain another response, say a hook pull. That is, let us create a state of affairs in which the light will only go on when the rat pulls a hook protruding from the side of the chamber. The light going on is contingent upon a hook pull. However, let us further specify that a hook pull will cause the light to go on only when the pull occurs during the sound of a buzzer. After some training with these contingencies present, we would have a situation like this:

(8)  $S^D—R—S^D—R—S^R$
     (buzzer on)—(hook pull)—(light on)—(bar press)—(food).

Thus, the rat's hook-pulling behavior is maintained by the light's going on, and in turn, when the light goes on the rat's bar-pressing behavior is maintained by the consequent food.

Let us continue this chain. Let us now specify that the buzzer will go on only when the rat jumps in the air and, further, that a jump will lead to the occurrence of the buzzer only when a bell rings. After some training with such contingencies the rat will respond in accordance with the following sequence:

(9)  $S^D—R—S^D—R—S^D—R—S^R$
     (bell ring)—(jump)—(buzzer on)—(hook pull)—(light on)—(bar press)—(food).

Thus, in the presence of a bell ring the rat jumps up, which leads to a buzzer going on, which cues the occasion for a hook pull, which is followed by a light going on, which allows a bar to be pressed and food to be obtained.

Obviously, we could continue this chain almost indefinitely, linking one response to another through the use of secondary reinforcement. Since an $S^D$ is also an $S^r$, each response in a chain is maintained by the succeeding stimulus event. In this way, a complex series of behaviors may be built up. Yet, each unit (link) of the chain is basically composed ot the same operant unit: $S^D$—$R$—$S^R$. In other words, even complex behavior series may be broken down (reduced) to the same constituent elements. All portions of the chain are composed of the same basic stimulus-response elements. Although the content of a particular segment of the chain may be different from the content of another component (for example, in one case a bar press may be involved, while in another case a hook pull is necessary), all segments are just basically the same discriminative stimulus-response-reinforcing stimulus unit, linked together on the basis of an $S^D$ being equivalent to an $S^r$.

Hence, even complex adult behavior may be interpreted consistent with this chaining model. Our alarm clock going off in the morning is an $S^D$, which "allows us" to get out of bed to "obtain" the bathroom, which in turn allows us to wash, which in turn allows us to dress, which in turn allows us to eat breakfast, leave the house, get in our car, drive to work, earn our salary, and buy food. One may tear this series of behaviors apart attempting to find the various discriminative stimuli, serving to link the secondary reinforcing function, which chain these discrete, voluntary musculature behaviors into a seemingly complex behavioral series.

With this model, then, complex human behavior is only apparently complex. In actuality, complicated series of motor behaviors are really comprised of the building up of a series of links on a chain. All behavior is comprised of the same constituent elements, the $S^D$—$R$—$S^R$ connections.

At this point some important conceptual implications of this chaining model may be pointed out. Our presentation of this model enables us to see certain basic similarities between it and the reductionistic, unity-of-science position discussed in Chapter 2. The notion of chaining implies that to understand complex (e.g., adult) behavior all one must do is *reduce* this behavior to its constituent elements, these stimulus-response-stimulus connections. Hence, the development of behavior only involves building up these chains; as the child develops, he continually adds more of these identically constituted links. Moreover, since these chaining units are comprised of the same type of elements, all that behavioral development thus involves is the addition of more of the similarly comprised units. Although there have been some arguments to the contrary (see Gagné, 1968), this position implies that development is composed of the continuous addition of qualitatively identical chaining units; hence the only difference between different points in development is in the *quantity* of these units that exist; and since all levels of development are therefore comprised of these similarly constituted units, any and all behavior can be reduced to these common elements.

Thus, one interpretation of the operant conditioning paradigm places it within the context of the unity-of-science philosophy of science (Harris, 1957) discussed in Chapter 2. Since this interrelation is a most crucial one, we will provide further clarification and expansion of it. However, we should first consider one last important component of learning phenomena. To this point we have considered aspects of both the classical and the operant conditioning paradigm. Central to our discussion has been the concept of reinforcement. It is clear that this concept is the core principle in the phenomena of learning, and in fact, many psychologists refer to contemporary learning theory as *rein-*

*forcement theory.* Hence, we should consider in some greater detail other important aspects of the phenomenon of reinforcement.

## Positive and Negative Reinforcement

We have defined a reinforcing stimulus as any stimulus that produces or maintains behavior. In classical conditioning the reinforcement precedes the response, while in operant conditioning reinforcement follows the response. In either case, however, the reinforcing stimulus increases the probability of a response. In our previous discussion we indicated a distinction between primary and secondary reinforcers. Another clarification, that between positive and negative reinforcement, should be mentioned.

In the example of the rat pressing the bar (in the presence of a light's being on) to obtain food, we have an instance of positive reinforcement. That is, food in this example is a positively reinforcing stimulus. We saw that the food maintained the rat's bar-pressing behavior; in other words, bar-pressing behavior was maintained because this behavior produced a stimulus. If an organism behaves (i.e., emits a response) in order to produce a stimulus, then that stimulus may be termed a positive reinforcement. We may define a *positive-reinforcing stimulus* as a stimulus that maintains behavior through its production. We will behave to produce such stimuli as food, water, or money. We will emit responses in order to produce a positive reinforcement, an $S^{+R}$. Hence, such $S^{+R}$'s maintain behavior (as do all $S^R$'s of course) because they are produced by that behavior. Thus, one way that behavior may be maintained is through the production of such positively reinforcing stimuli. One thing that a behavior may result in is the production of an $S^{+R}$.

However, behavior may result in something else. There is another type of reinforcing stimulus that may follow (be produced by) a behavior, a *negative-reinforcing stimulus*. If we are placed in a situation in which a painful electric shock will continue to be delivered to us if we do not press a bar, we will soon press the bar to terminate (turn off) the electric shock. If we are sitting by a very bright light shining in our eyes, we will emit a behavior (turning off the light) that will terminate the light stimulus. What maintains the bar-pressing or light-turning-off behaviors in these examples? Clearly, these behaviors are maintained by the stimulus events following them—the termination of the shock and the bright light, respectively. Thus, these behaviors are also maintained by consequent stimulus events, but in these instances the behaviors lead to a termination of the stimulus. Responses are emitted in order to terminate a stimulus. We may term the stimulus in such an instance a negative reinforcement, an $S^{-R}$. If an organism behaves in order to terminate a stimulus, we say the behavior is maintained through negative reinforcement. Hence, we may define an $S^{-R}$ as a stimulus that maintains behavior through its termination.

Hence a given response may be followed by one of two types of stimuli, an $S^{+R}$ or an $S^{-R}$ (excluding responses that are followed by neutral stimuli, which in any event would not maintain the emitted response). In other words, responses are maintained by either a positive reinforcement ( a stimulus that maintains behavior through its production) or a negative reinforcement (a stimulus that maintains behavior through its termination).

One may view behavioral functioning, then, in terms of only two categories, responses and succeeding stimuli. A given behavioral response may either produce a stimulus or terminate a stimulus, and the stimulus that is either produced or terminated may be either an $S^{+R}$ or an $S^{-R}$. That is, sometimes we emit a behavior that produces an $S^{+R}$ (for example, doing our chores and earning, or producing, our allowance), while at other times we emit a response that terminates an $S^{+R}$ (for example, hitting our brother and losing, or terminating, our allowance). On the other hand, sometimes we emit a behavior that produces an $S^{-R}$ (for example, hitting our brother, which is followed by, or produces, a reprimand by our parent), while at other times we emit a behavior that terminates an $S^{-R}$ (for example, saying—with sobbing sincerity—that we are sorry, which terminates, or ends, our parent's spanking). Thus, any given behavior may be conceptualized in terms of simply whether or not it produces or terminates an $S^{+R}$ or an $S^{-R}$.

Since any and all behavior may be conceptualized in this manner, we may attempt to represent the phenomena resulting from these combinations of responses and stimuli. When our responses either produce a positive reinforcement or terminate a negative reinforcement, our responses become strengthened. Thus, our behavior results in a *reward.* In other words, it is rewarding to produce a positive reinforcement or to eliminate a negative reinforcement, and responses that do these things tend to remain in our behavioral repertoire, and are said to be strengthened. Moreover, responses that terminate an $S^{-R}$, such as a shock, may be labeled as a special type of reward. In ending the presence of such a noxious stimulus state, we may say that the response allows the organism to *escape* from it. Hence, the state of reward comprised of an $R$ terminating an $S^{-R}$ is termed escape.

However, when our responses either terminate a positive reinforcement or produce a negative reinforcement our responses become weakened. That is, behavior that terminates an $S^{+R}$ or produces an $S^{-R}$ constitutes *punishment,* and such behavior tends to drop out of our behavioral repertoire. Because they are punished, such responses tend to be seen with decreasing frequency and are said to be weakened.

Simply, then, the responses that exist in the behavioral repertoire of a person at any time in development may be accounted for in the past history of rewards and punishments that the person has experienced. Hence, a person's behavioral repertoire may be understood simply by reference to the nature of the stimulus-response relationships the person has experienced. A person's behavioral repertoire may be conceptualized, or reduced to, the sum total of the strengthened and weakened responses that have resulted from the stimulus consequences of the responses. Following the presentation of Bijou and Baer (1961, p. 37), we may represent these relations between responses and consequent stimulus events, which lead to the establishment of rewards and punishments, as in Table 10.1.

The notion of secondary reinforcement may also be included in this discussion. Obviously, not all stimuli that maintain responses are either primary positive reinforcers ($S^{+R}$'s), such as food or water, or primary negative reinforcers ($S^{-R}$'s), such as shock. As we have seen, stimuli can acquire either positive or negative reinforcing characteristics through their association with other stimuli. Yet, responses that either produce or terminate such secondary positive reinforcing stimuli ($S^{+r}$'s) or secondary negative reinforcing stimuli ($S^{-r}$'s) similarly result in either reward or punishment. Thus, a response that either produces an $S^{-r}$ or terminates an $S^{+r}$ would be a weakened, punished response, while a response that either produced an $S^{+r}$ or terminated an $S^{-r}$ would be a strengthened, rewarded response. Moreover, since responses that terminate the pre-

**Table 10.1** The establishment of rewards and punishments resulting from the primary reinforcement consequences of responses.

|                     | $S^{+R}$    | $S^{-R}$          |
| ------------------- | ----------- | ----------------- |
| Response produces   | Reward      | Punishment        |
| Response terminates | Punishment  | Reward (escape)   |

*Source:* Adapted from S. W. Bijou and D. M. Baer, *Child Development, Vol. I: A Systematic and Empirical Theory,* New York: Appleton-Century-Crofts, 1961. Copyright © 1961, Prentice-Hall, Inc.

sence of $S^{-r}$'s constitute a case in which a stimulus associated with (or leading to) an $S^{-R}$ is terminated, such responses may be seen as eliminating the eventual presence of this primary negative reinforcement. Thus, by terminating the secondary negative reinforcement the organism is *avoiding* the eventual presentation of the primary negative reinforcer. Hence, this situation constitutes a special case of reward—avoidance. These relations between responses and secondary reinforcing stimulus events, which lead also to the establishment of rewards and punishments, are represented as in Table 10.2.

## Conclusions

In this section we have reviewed the two major types of learning, or conditioning, paradigms that are basically used by those adopting the learning approach to child development study. We have seen that classical conditioning involves the autonomic nervous sytem and our involuntary musculature and can be used to account for the acquisition of reflexive and emotional responses. Operant conditioning, on the other hand, involves our central nervous system and our voluntary musculature and can be used to account for the majority of our "voluntary" motor behavior. Moreover, we saw in our discussions of the concepts of secondary reinforcement, changing, and positive and negative reinforcement that even seemingly complex human behavior can be understood on the basis of these basic conditioning paradigms.

The notions of secondary reinforcement and chaining allow one to reduce seemingly complex series of behaviors into identically constituted constituent elements. If the developing behavior of a person is just regarded "as a cluster of interrelated responses interacting with stimuli" (Bijou and Baer, 1961, pp. 14–15), then one may reduce these

**Table 10.2** The establishment of rewards and punishments resulting from the secondary reinforcement stimulus consequences of responses.

|                     | $S^{+r}$    | $S^{-r}$              |
| ------------------- | ----------- | -------------------- |
| Response produces   | Reward      | Punishment           |
| Response terminates | Punishment  | Reward (avoidance)   |

*Source:* Adapted from Bijou and Baer, 1961.

clusters to their constituent stimulus-response connections, connections that may be acquired only on the basis of either of two processes: classical or operant conditioning. These two paradigms may be continually used to represent the acquisition of any and all behavior because it is assumed that all behavior is learned behavior (White, 1970, p. 662) and that these two paradigms represent the two types of learning that exist. Thus, the same laws of learning are continually applicable to a person's behavior, despite that person's level of development. This is the case because any level of behavioral development can be reduced to the stimulus-response clusters, formed on the basis of the same laws of learning.

Thus, all that behavioral development amounts to is the quantitative addition of similarly acquired stimulus-response associations. The behavior seen in a person's repertoire at any time in development is present as a result of the stimulus consequences of that person's responses. That is, stimulus-response associations are strengthened or weakened on the basis of whether or not a response produces or terminates a positive or negative reinforcement. The number of responses and the content of the responses a person has in his repertoire, and how many responses will be added to this repertoire, are totally dependent on the stimulation the environment provides (Bijou and Baer, 1961).

In sum, we see that behavior at any level of development may be understood by reduction of the behavior into its constituent elements. These elements, lawfully identical stimulus-response associations, are continually quantitatively added to the person's developing response repertoire as a result of the stimulus consequences of the person's responses. Hence, if all behavior is learned behavior, and if such learning proceeds on the basis of the simple stimulus-response mechanisms involved in the laws of learning, then all that is involved in the study of behavioral development is the analysis of two types of events in the natural environment: responses and the environmental stimuli that control them.

It is clear that this position, with its concepts of reduction, mechanism, continuity, and quantitative addition, is consistent with the unity-of-science philosophy of science discussed in Chapter 2. The reductionism and mechanism of the unity-of-science philosophical position (Harris, 1957) may be seen to have been translated into the mechanistic, reductionistic theoretical orientation of those adhering to the learning approach. In order to better understand this interrelation we will now consider the basic assumptions and characteristics of the learning approach. Although we will draw upon the work of several learning-approach developmentalists, we will focus on the work of Bijou and Baer (1961). Although it is clear, as White (1970) has indicated, that it is impossible to use the work of just one (or even a few) learning-approach developmentalists to represent the precise position of all such psychologists, the work of Bijou and Baer will be emphasized because it represents a generally agreeable statement of the learning approach to developmental psychology.

## Characteristics of the Learning Approach

Learning is a function of the organism which obviously has fundamental biological significance. If the organism's behavior were unalterable in the face of environmental changes, then the chances of that organism's survival would be severely diminished. Accordingly, stimuli in the organism's environment that promote such modifications of

Sidney W. Bijou

behavior have primary adaptive significance. Such reinforcing stimuli function to modify the organism's behavior in its environment and thus allow the organism to survive.

If psychology is to be an objective, empirical science, it has to study the observable sources of behavior. Such reasoning led psychologists to adopt the learning approach as the framework within which to conduct psychological investigations, because the essence of this approach is a scrutiny of the interrelations among observable stimuli and responses. Then, to offer a rationale for this emphasis, psychologists emphasized the biologically adaptive role that reinforcement plays in organism survival. As we have

Donald M. Baer

noted, such environmental stimuli serve to naturally select those behaviors that will be strengthened or weakened as the organism's responses interrelate with the stimulus world. Hence the study of learning allows one to assess the processes by which organisms acquire the essential functional characteristics—behaviors—allowing them to survive. Thus, early followers of the learning approach believed that the study of learning allows psychology to be an objective, empirical discipline within the tradition of natural science. As White put it: "There was a vision of reinforcement as a natural selection process in the environment which could select out adaptive animal behaviors—hence the justification for an intensive examination of learning as a reinforcement process" (1970, p. 661). Current learning-approach psychologists have retained this initial orientation and, implicitly, this underlying rationale. Hence, in describing their work, Bijou and Baer assert: "We present here an approach to the understanding of human psychological development from the natural science point of view" (1961, p. 1.)

Accordingly, Bijou and Baer stress that this point of view focuses on observable events—responses and environmental stimuli—and the theory they advance merely represents "generalized summaries and explanation of observable interactions between behavior and environment" (1961, p. 5). However, their use of the term *interaction* must be contrasted with the use of this term by organismically oriented psychologists. To Bijou and Baer this term is tied solely to environmental stimulation: "An *interaction* between behavior and environment means simply that a given response may be expected to occur or not, depending on the stimulation the environment provides" (1961, p. 1). Thus, Bijou and Baer's theory looks at all behavior as ultimately controlled by environmental stimulus events. Whether or not an organism will respond is dependent just on the stimulation in the environmental situation the organism is in. Such situational dependency implies that the organism is a passive recipient of environmental stimulation. Behavior is equated with responses, and whether or not a response will be given is dependent on the stimuli in the organism's environment. Hence, responses (or behaviors) are not dependent on the organism itself. In contrast to the organismic point of view— which holds that the organism plays an active participatory role in its own behavior— this view asserts that the source of all behavior lies merely in the effects that environmental stimulation has on the passive, nonparticipatory organism. Thus, psychological development consists only of "progressive changes in the way an organism's behavior interacts with the environment" (Bijou and Baer, 1961, p. 1). All that a child's development is comprised of is the ongoing accumulation of responses-in-control-by-environmental-stimulation.

The behavior of the developing child is thought of as "being made up of two basic kinds of responses—*respondents and operants*" (Bijou and Baer, 1961, p. 15). Hence, all one must actually know about in order to understand, predict, and control a child's development are the laws of classical and operant conditioning. These learning processes are inextricably linked to observable responses and stimuli present in the child's environmental situation and thus an account of a child's behavior and development may be made merely through an analysis of the stimuli and responses in a particular situation (Bowers, 1973).

We see, then, that this situationalist, learning approach to the development of behavior assumes the following.

1. All human behavior is learned behavior, that is, all behavior is the product of re-sponses controlled by situation-specific environmental stimuli (White, 1970, p. 662).
2. These stimuli exert their control over behavior in accordance with the laws of classi-cal and operant conditioning. Human beings are passive, and they function essentially as a machine; their ouputs (responses) are evoked or maintained by antecedent or con-sequent conditioning mechanisms. Thus, as White has pointed out (1970, p. 662), all human behavior is seen merely as a simple mechanical contrivance.
3. Since all human behavior is comprised of mechanical stimulus-response respon-dents or operants, then stimuli are the cause of human behavior and responses are the effect of these causes (Bowers, 1973; White, 1970).

Although, as White has noted, "No learning theory has ever been constructed from studies of children or been specifically directed toward them" (1970, p. 667), psychologists working from the learning point of view have tended to generalize the re-sults of some studies with nonhuman animals as well as with children into a general ac-count of the behavior of all humans at all ages and even in some cases of all animals of all phylogenetic levels (see our discussion of this point in Chapter 5, and White, 1970, p. 681). This integration is done on the basis of the assumption that behavior at any level of analysis may be reduced to the objectively verifiable operants and respondents that comprise any and all behavior, and only in this way may the study of behavior remain within the objective framework of natural science (White, 1970, p. 666).

In sum, the learning approach to developmental psychology—as represented by Bijou and Baer—views psychological development as merely the accumulated acquisi-tion of operant and respondent behaviors, responses acquired by situationally specific environmental stimulation. The laws of learning involved in classical and operant condi-tioning, and the phenomena involved in these processes (secondary reinforcement, positive and negative reinforcement, chaining), may be used to account for the be-havioral functioning of a person at any level of psychological development. That is, be-havior at any of these levels may be similarly analyzed as being comprised of operants and respondents. Because of this identical comprisal there is continuity in the variables involved in psychological functioning and development. Behavior at any level of de-velopment is qualitatively the same as behavior at any other level, and thus the only difference between levels of development lies in the quantity of these similarly acquired elements.

Before turning to a critical evaluation of the learning-approach viewpoint, we will offer a final summary of its assumptions as specified by Sheldon White, one of the lead-ing authorities on the learning approach. White noted:

What is often called the "learning theory point of view" would seem to amount to these assumptions:
1. The environment may be unambiguously characterized in terms of stimuli.
2. Behavior may be unambiguously characterized in terms of responses.
3. A class of stimuli exist which, applied contingently and immediately following a re-sponse, increase it or decrease it in some measurable fashion. These stimuli may be treated as reinforcers.
4. Learning may be completely characterized in terms of various possible couplings among stimuli, responses, and reinforcers.
5. Unless there is definite evidence to the contrary, classes of behavior may be as-sumed to be learned, manipulable by the environment, extinguishable, and trainable (White, 1970, pp. 665-66).

## An Evaluation of the Learning Approach

In turning to our evaluation of the learning approach we will continue to consider the comments provided by White (1970), as well as another, particularly lucid critique written by Kenneth Bowers (1973). The learning approach clearly attempts to place developmental psychology within an objective, empirical natural-science framework. In fact, proponents of this view contend that "the preservation of objectivity in psychology depends upon the observability of truly causal variables" (Bowers, 1973, p. 308). By focusing on stimuli and responses, it is believed that such causal observations are made. Simply, it is believed that stimuli in an organism's environment cause the organism's responses.

Thus, adherents of this approach appeal to situational stimuli as the cause of all behavior. Accordingly, it is believed that this orientation not only makes developmental psychology an objective natural science, but provides other important assets too. For instance, in discussing the advantages of their theoretical orientation, Bijou and Baer assert: "We can point out as advantages the simplicity of this approach, its frequent fruitfulness, and its freedom from logical tangles which ultimately turn out to be illusory rather than real" (1961, p. 4).

Admittedly, the learning approach is a simple one. Yet the belief that in the stimulus situation lies the cause of behavior raises serious problems. First, it is clear that the exclusive regard of the stimulus situation is associated with an almost complete disregard of the organism, organismic factors, and the active role these variables may play in behavioral functioning and development. Clearly, there is an organism in any stimulus situation. It is the organism upon which the stimuli act, and it is the organism that behaves in any situation. Yet, the learning approach essentially ignores the possibility that the organism may play an active, participatory, and potentially unique role in its own behavior and development. In fact, individual behavioral differences among organisms in seemingly identical situations are held to be, in principle, merely reducible to potential empirical stimulus differences in the situation. Thus, the reliance on the stimulus situation as the cause of the behavior of any organism and as the basis for any differences among organisms in their behavior "is limited by the tendency either to ignore organismic factors, or to regard them as . . . subsidiary to the primary impact of the external stimulus" (Harré and Secord, 1972, p. 27).

Second, the appeal to the stimulus situation as the cause of all behavior raises the very sort of logical problems that Bijou and Baer (1961) claim are obviated by the learning approach. Let us see how.

The core notion in the learning approach is that a stimulus causes a response, whatever characteristics the organism might possess. Simply, it is held that one may essentially disregard the organism and focus just on the stimulus in the situation, because the stimulus is the cause of behavior. However, as White has noted: "The problem is that one cannot seem to find a part of the environment which in and of itself, disregarding the subject, is always a stimulus for behavior" (1970, p. 669). Thus, the learning-approach appeal to the stimulus as a source of all behavior seems to be limited by the fact that a stimulus simply cannot be found in every situation to account for every behavior.

We saw in Chapter 5 and again indicated in this chapter that one of the problems with the learning approach is overgeneralization. We saw that though one might be able to manipulate some behaviors of some animals in some situations and make these animals perform markedly similarly, one is not therefore justified in assuming that one can manipulate all behaviors in all animals in all situations to produce similar performance. In the present discussion we see another instance of such overgeneralization. Although in some situations there may exist stimuli that provide a source of some behaviors, this does not mean that in all situations there exist stimuli that provide a source of all behaviors!

Despite these problems, the learning approach continues to appeal to a stimulus in any account of a behavioral response. If this appeal were not maintained, then according to this position an objective, natural-science orientation could similarly not be maintained (Bowers, 1973, p. 317).

Yet, as Bowers (1973) has lucidly pointed out, many experiments done by those testing the learning approach do not show changes in behavior as a function of situational stimulus alterations. Learning-approach psychologists do experiments in which differing stimulus situations are presented to subjects in an attempt to assess the effect of these altered situations on subjects' behaviors. Thus, the experiment is done to see how differing situations affect behavior. However, the researcher often finds that the differing situations used in the experiment do not result in differing subject behaviors. This is true even though the situations were not randomly selected; that is, they were in fact selected because they were thought to be capable of differentially affecting behavior. Most active researchers know that even the best designed experiments often do not work out—that is, the subjects behave in the same way in different situations.

When such results occur the researcher may often consider the experiment a failure. After all, is it not the case that different situational stimulus conditions cause different responses? Since this assumption may be treated by the researcher as if it were a fact, then when different situations do not effect different responses in subjects, the researcher may view the results as negative and the study as a failure. As pointed out by Bowers (1973), many editors of scientific journals might agree with the researcher's appraisal of the study, since the results from such studies typically are not accepted for publication.

Yet it is possible to offer a different interpretation of such findings. If we assume that all of an organism's behavior is *not* determined just by the situationally specific stimuli impinging upon it, then we may view the results as supportive of another idea. If we assert that organisms possess characteristics that continue to characterize the organism and play an active, contributory role in its behavior apart from any specific situation, then when we see the failure of differing situations to differentially affect the organism's behavior we may take this "as evidence regarding the relative stability of behavior across situations" (Bowers, 1973, p. 317). We may view such experimental results as supportive of the assumption that in addition to specific situational stimulus determinants of behavior, there exist organismic (situational general) determinants of behavior.

Of course, the researcher who believes in the situational determinancy of behavior could always argue that the experiment failed to show situational differences because the study inadvertently used stimulus situations that were not *really* different. However, Bowers (1973, p. 317) points out that such an argument raises serious logical problems. If one hypothesizes that behavior is situation specific, then it must in some way be possible to also show that it is *not* situation specific. If one hypothesizes that A is the case, then in order for this assertion to be scientifically verified one must be able to subject this assertion to a test, one possible result of which is the conclusion that A is *not* the case. If one makes hypotheses that in no way can be proven incorrect, then those hypotheses are useless for science. To fairly test one's assertions one must offer them in a way in which they can be tested for their truth or falsity. Hence, Bowers notes that if a researcher finds that situational manipulations fail to effect behavioral change and then *always* concludes that this only means that the situations were thus not really different, rather than taking such findings as evidence of the cross-situational generalizability of behavior, then the researcher is advancing a nonfalsifiable and scientifically useless assertion. Thus, Bowers concludes that "if (truly) changed environments can only be inferred from changed behavior, then the potential circularity of the situationalist model becomes actual and vicious" (1973, p. 317). To illustrate his argument, Bowers notes a statement by a leading proponent of the learning approach, Walter Mischel: "When the eliciting and evoking conditions that maintain behavior change—as they generally do across settings—then behavior will surely change also" (1969, p. 1016). Bowers views this assertion as constituting a completely circular argument: "When does behavior change? When the situation does. How do you know when the eliciting and evoking conditions change? When the behavior does. Viewed in this way, behavior becomes situation specific because it is impossible for it not to be situation specific" (1973, p. 317).

We see, then, that in addition to the specific problems introduced into the learning position by its disregard of organismic characteristics and its overreliance on the stimulus situation as *the* cause of behavior, some logical problems are involved in a complete adherence to this approach. Some other logical problems may still be noted, however.

We know from our earlier presentations in this chapter that if a response is reinforced it will be maintained, because, by definition, a reinforcing stimulus is a stimulus that increases the probability of a behavior. Thus, as Bowers points out, the assertion that behavior that is reinforced is accordingly maintained is necessarily true because it follows logically from the definition of what a reinforcing stimulus is. However, Bowers argues that learning-approach psychologists often "glide noiselessly from this initial assertion to a more problematic one that is *not* true by definition, nor does it follow logically from the definition of reinforcement, namely, behavior which is acquired and maintained is reinforced" (1973, p. 311).

We may see that this second assertion involves the notion that any behavior that occurs must occur on the basis of reinforcement. Here, then, is the assumption that all behavior is learned behavior and the idea that reinforcement (in accordance with classical or operant conditioning) is the mechanism by which behavior is learned. In other words, while it is true, by definition, that one may shape an animal's behavior by reinforcement, it does not follow that therefore whenever an animal shows behavior it does so because it was reinforced.

Here we see another instance of overgeneralization as well as of circular reasoning. To rephrase some of Bowers' earlier arguments: What does reinforcement do? It increases the probability of behavior occurrence. When a behavior increases in probability of occurrence, what causes this? Reinforcement!

Let us illustrate the overgeneralized, fallacious arguments. From knowing that one can increase the probability of a rat's bar-pressing response by making food reinforcement contingent on that response, learning-approach psychologists have moved toward arguing that when one sees any behavior whatsoever one may account for its presence simply by asserting that its basis lies in reinforcement. Why does one paint a picture, sew a dress, write a book, vote for a particular political candidate, or love a certain person and not another? One does any and all these things because one is reinforced. People show love behavior, political behavior, artistic behavior or moral behavior because there exist stimuli in their environment which reinforce (shape) these behaviors. Thus, because all such human behaviors are merely caused, and therefore controlled by, the external stimulus situations people find themselves in, and these situations exist apart from people in the sense that they themselves do not have controlling influence on situational characteristics, people themselves have no "freedom or dignity." Such concepts as freedom and dignity are fictitious and fallacious, put forth by those who do not "know" that every aspect of human behavior is controlled by situation-specific reinforcing stimuli.

This view suggests that the human organism (or any organism for that matter) has no integrity in that it plays no active, contributory role in its own development. Humans are merely passive machines, malleable balls of clay, waiting to be shaped and controlled by the stimulus environment, which provides the cause of all behavior.

But where are the stimuli that reinforce these behaviors? As pointed out by White (1970) and by Bowers (1973), such controlling stimuli cannot readily be found for these situations. Thus, the appeal to situation-specific, controlling stimuli as the cause for all behavior becomes an overgeneralized, logically circular, and objectively and empirically unverifiable assertion. On the basis of circular reasoning and thus the seemingly unfounded belief that all behavior is reinforced behavior, learning-approach developmentalists attempt to fit all behavior into a learning paradigm. Yet, since in many cases the presence of reinforcement is not seen but only inferred on the basis of the fact that behavior has occurred, the learning appeal loses its status as an objective account of behavior. It becomes at least as unempirical and as unobjective as it claims the theoretical viewpoints counter to it are. In other words, adherents of the learning approach may often criticize organismic approaches to psychological development as being unobjective since the latter use such concepts as cognition, reasoning, personality structure, and individual traits. Yet our analysis of the learning-approach position indicates that its reliance on the stimulus situation does not make it any more objective than these other approaches. As long as the "situational stimulus source of all human behavior" remains as just another elusive, unverified assumption, it seems that people may continue to have the freedom to believe that they have dignity.

## Conclusions

Our analysis of the learning approach leads us to conclude that while this viewpoint does indeed offer a simple formula for the understanding of behavior and development, it is also characterized by rather severe limitations of an empirical and a logical nature. Although adherents of this approach would have us believe that all human behavior is merely situation specific—that is, completely controlled by the stimuli present in a specific environmental situation (e.g., see Mischel, 1968, 1971)—we have seen that it is just as reasonable to infer that in many cases a human possesses traits, or individual characteristics, that lead to behavioral consistency across different situations. For instance, it is clear that most of us behave differently when we are studying in a library than when we are rooting for our favorite football team. Learning-approach psychologists would point to such instances as evidence for the situational control of behavior. On the other hand, we may also observe that when a person is characterized by the trait of hostility or high intensity of reaction, such a trait may be manifested in various situations the person interacts in (e.g., in school, at play, waiting on a line, at a party). Trait theorists would take such evidence as supportive of the notion of cross-situational consistency (i.e., situational independency) of behavior.

Thus, as recognized by Bowers (1973), while learning-approach theorists would predict that a person's behavior should change from situation to situation, trait-oriented psychologists would contend that a person's behavior should be relatively consistent from one situation to another. Put in other words, what is the source of variations among people in their behaviors? The learning-approach psychologist predicts that behavioral variation is a function of situational characteristics. The trait-oriented, or person-oriented, psychologist predicts that a person's individual characteristics are the major source of variation among people.

Of course, another possibility exists. It may be that a third potential source of variation is most important. That is, it is obvious that one cannot treat situations and persons as independent phenomena. Rather, it is always the case that a person *interacts* in specific situations. A person, with presumably individual characteristics, is continually entering into situations, which have their own presumably special characteristics. From our discussions in previous chapters (especially Chapter 9) we know that people with different individual characteristics may be expected to interact differently in the same stimulus situation and that people with even very dissimilar characteristics may be led to similar behaviors as a consequence of their interactions in different situations. Thus, the interaction of a person in a situation may account for behavioral variation. This possibility is, of course, consistent with the organismic, interactionist notions we have been emphasizing throughout this book. Behavior is not a function merely of either intrinsic or extrinsic factors but is an outcome of an interaction between such influences. Hence, while the learning approach would expect the situation to be the major source of behavioral variation and the trait approach would expect the person to be the major source of this variation, we might expect the *Person × Situation interaction* to provide the major source of behavioral variation.

Which of these expectations is borne out by empirical evidence? What percentage of the variation in human behavior is attributable to situational variation, to person variation, and to person × situation variation? Although only a few studies have been done that may be used to address this issue, Bowers (1973) analyzed and reviewed these in an attempt to determine whether situation, person, or interaction accounts for the major percentage of variation in human behavior. As a way of concluding our review of the learning approach, let us turn to Bowers' (1973) analysis.

## Bowers' Analysis of Situations, Persons, and Interactions

As noted above, Bowers (1973) was able to locate a few (i.e., eleven) studies in the psychological literature which could be used to address the issue of whether situations, persons, or interactions contribute the major percentage of variation in human behavior.

Since some of these had more than one set of measurements, Bowers was able to address this issue through reference to nineteen sets of measurements, ranging in form from actual behavioral observation measurements to self-rating measurements made by subjects.

It was found that the percentage of variation due to the situation was greater than the percentage of variation due to the person in eight of the nineteen measurement sets. Thus, the percentage of variation due to the person was greater than the percentage of variation due to the situation in the other eleven measurement sets. However, in all sets the percentage of variation for either the situation or person sources was relatively small. The average percentage of variation due to the person in these measurements was 12.7 percent, while the average percentage of variation due to the situation in these measurements was only 10.2 percent.

What, then, accounted for the most variation in behavior in most of these measurement sets? Consistent with our organismic, interactionist-based expectations, the interaction of persons and situations accounted for a higher percentage of variation than either situation or person alone in fourteen of the eighteen measurement sets (in one measurement set it was not possible to calculate the interaction percentage). Moreover, in eight of these eighteen sets the percentage of variation due to the person × situation interaction was greater than the sum total of the percentage variation due to situation alone and person alone; and the average percentage variation due to this interaction, 20.8 percent, was greater than the average percentage for either the situation alone or the person alone.

In sum, we see that neither the situation nor the person alone suffices in accounting for behavioral functioning. Bowers' analysis allows us to conclude that variation in human behavior and development is not a function of just the external stimulus environment or just the person's intrinsic characteristics. Rather, in most cases behavior seems to be a product of the interaction between such intrinsic and extrinsic variables. The person plays an active, participatory role in his or her own development; this means that just as much as environment serves to actively shape the person, the person in turn acts to continually shape his environment. Thus, behavioral development involves the continual interactions between the person and the environment, and only by analyzing the complex nature of these interactions may one come to understand the major source of behavioral development.

Over the course of this book we have presented and hopefully supported this interactionist, organismic conception of psychological development. After summarizing the major points made in this chapter, we will attempt to offer some of the research and social implications of the issues in developmental psychology.

## Summary

Adherents of the learning approach to the study of development consider the laws of learning invariantly and inextricably involved in psychological development. Consistent with the unity-of-science philosophy of science, those adopting this view believe that all behavior may be reduced to the continuously applicable laws of learning. The laws, or the variables, involved in classical and operant conditioning are seen to be invariantly involved in the behavior of all organisms.

Although there is no agreement about the theoretical meaning of the term *learning,* there is relatively more agreement about the empirical components of the learning process. Thus, after Kimble (1961), learning was defined as a relatively permanent change in behavior potentiality which occurs as a result of reinforced practice, excluding changes due to maturation, fatigue, and/or injury to the nervous system. In detailing the meaning of this definition, we saw the central role of the concept of reinforcement. Reinforcing stimuli provide the bases of both of the two types of learning: classical and operant conditioning. A reinforcement was defined as a stimulus that produces and/or maintains behavior, i.e., a stimulus that increases the probability of a behavior. Essential differences between classical and operant learning relate to whether reinforcement precedes or follows the behavior it makes more probable.

In classical conditioning a reinforcing stimulus (UCS) elicits an unlearned response (UCR); however, a previously neutral stimulus is placed before the UCS, and after repeated pairings of this stimulus with the UCS, this new stimulus becomes a conditioned stimulus (CS); it will elicit a conditioned (learned) response (CR). Classical conditioning typically involves our autonomic nervous system and our involuntary musculature. Hence, emotions are often classically conditioned. Moreover, since the CS has acquired reinforcing properties—through its association with the UCS—it too becomes a reinforcing stimulus, i.e., a secondary reinforcement.

In operant conditioning there exist certain stimuli in the environment which cue the occasion for a response; that is, responses in the presence of such stimuli lead to reinforcement. If in the presence of such a stimulus (an $S^D$) an appropriate response (R) is made, then this response will be followed by a reinforcement (an $S^R$). Thus, organisms learn to emit responses in the presence of certain stimuli and not in others, because reinforcement is contingent on such responses. Such learning typically involves our central nervous system and our voluntary musculature; hence, most of the motor behavior typically engaged in by people as they instrumentally deal with their environment is seen as such operantly learned behavior. Moreover, the $S^D$, too, acquires secondary reinforcing characteristics (through its association with the $S^R$), and in turn, responses may be acquired if the production of such a secondary reinforcement is made contingent on response occurrence. Through such chaining, complex sequences of behavior may be acquired. Yet, all units of the chain are reducible to these identically lawfully constituted stimulus-response units. Hence, behavior at any level of occurrence may be reduced in similar ways to the same constituent elements.

Any behavior may be reduced to stimulus-response connections, acquired from either of the above two paradigms. Thus, because it is assumed that all behavior is learned behavior, those taking a learning approach to the study of development believe that the same laws of learning are continually applicable to a person's behavior, despite the level of development of that person.

Hence, because all behavior is seen to be controlled by either or both of these two types of learning processes, and since these processes involve the application of reinforcing stimuli in the person's environmental situation, all behavior comes to be viewed as responses that are controlled by situation-specific environmental stimuli. Human beings are thus seen as passive; to behave, they must be stimulated. Hence, as opposed to organismic conceptions of developmental functioning, the person is not seen as playing an active, contributory role in his or her own development.

Problems exist, however, in attempting to use these ideas to account for all behavioral functioning and development. Although the learning approach appeals to the stimulus as a source for all behavior, this orientation is limited by the fact that there does not seem to be a stimulus that can be found in every situation to account for every behavior. Moreover, there are many logical, as well as empirical, problems with this approach. For instance, the assumption that all behavior is learned is related to a logical problem. That is, while it is the case, by definition, that an organism's behavior may be shaped by reinforcement, it does not follow that therefore whenever an animal shows behavior it does so because it was reinforced. Other conceptual problems relate to overgeneralization and circular reasoning. For instance, while it is the case, by definition, that the function of reinforcement is to increase the probability of behavior occurrence, it is not necessarily the case that when any behavior increases in probability of occurrence this increase is caused by reinforcement.

Because of these problems, the view that the organism is passive and merely controlled by the laws of classical and operant conditioning, and hence makes no contribution to its own development, is not at all compelling. Rather, an alternative belief, that the organism possesses situation-independent characteristics (or traits) that play an active contributory role in its own development, appears just as viable.

Thus, as much as the situation contributes to variation in human behavior, the individual's own traits may similarly contribute to such variation. Moreover, the interaction between the person and the situation may also be expected to be a source of this variation. Evidence bearing on these expectations was reviewed; the majority of studies reviewed indicate that person-variation is greater than situation-variation; that is, in most studies the amount of variability attributable to the former source was greater than that attributable to the latter source. Yet, in almost all of the studies the amount of variation attributable to the interaction of persons and situations was greater than that associated with either factor alone. Hence, rather than supporting a learning-approach interpretation of the source of behavioral development and functioning, such information was seen as supportive of the view that organism-environment interactions provide the major source of development.

# 11
## Research and Social Implications

In this last chapter we will consider some of the research and social implications of the concepts and theories we have been discussing throughout this book. The primary focus of this book has been a presentation of the basic conceptual issues of developmental psychology, a treatment of the major types of theories in the field, and a consideration of representative examples of each of these formulations. Yet, while we now have some appreciation of the problems and issues that must be dealt with in any attempt to present a systematic theoretical view of development, we must also recognize the vital necessity for an active research commitment on the part of developmental psychologists.

Theory is necessary for the integration of existing facts; yet, this is only part of the role of theory. To be useful, theory must also lead to the generation of new facts. As indicated in Chapter 1, hypotheses must be derived from theories and put to empirical test. Without such research endeavors, without the continual interrelation of empirical investigations and theory construction and revision, theoretical arguments become useless, armchair exercises. Thus, we must recognize that research and theory are both necessary in order for the science of developmental psychology to prosper.

However, theory and its related research do not exist in a social vacuum. A developmental psychologist clearly exists in a specific society at a specific point in time. Thus, as is often the case with much of psychological research, developmental psychological research and theory often have important social relevance to the issues and problems confronting the people living in this society. The student of developmental psychology should be aware of these social implications of the discipline, if only to know what developmental psychology can, and cannot, contribute to a clarification of these issues. Accordingly, as a conclusion to this chapter we will consider some of the social implications of some theory-related developmental research.

We see, then, that as much as research needs theory (to organize and understand knowledge and to lead to the generation of new knowledge), theory needs research (to provide tests, substantiations, and revisions of theory). Moreover, this vital interrelation may become all the more important in light of the possibility that developmental research and theory may have important social implications. Because of its importance, the student of developmental psychology should be familiar with the dimensions of developmental research, the problems and issues of such research, and in turn, the problems that may exist in attempting to interrelate these empirical concerns with theoretical issues. Needless to say, these facets of the research endeavor are complex. Yet, their understanding is necessary for a complete appreciation of the discipline, as well as for an elucidation of some of the theoretical issues we have considered in our previous chapters. Because of their complexity, we will attempt to present the dimensions of developmental research within a framework that may facilitate their comprehension—the developmental research dimensions described by McCandless (1967, 1970).

## Facets of Research

### McCandless' Dimensions of Developmental Research
For many years Boyd McCandless has been an active contributor to the literature of developmental psychology; he has contributed both theoretical and research papers and has also spoken to the issues, problems, and aspects of developmental research per se. It is this last portion of McCandless' writings that concerns us here.

Boyd R. McCandless

McCandless has described (1967, 1970) four dimensions of developmental research. That is, it is possible to place any developmental study on a particular location along each of four continua. In Chapters 6 and 8 we saw that the differential approach to developmental psychology defines individuality as a person's location in multidimensional space. As will be recalled, this definition means that any particular person occupies his or her own individual space on each of a number of bipolar attribute dimensions. Similarly, a given developmental study possesses its own location along each of four dimensions. These four dimensions—or attributes—of developmental research describe the various continua along which any developmental study may vary. Thus, by describing and understanding the characteristics of each of these research attribute dimensions, one will be able to see where any given developmental study fits into the total scheme of possible developmental research.

**The Normative-Explanatory Dimension.** The first of the four dimensions that McCandless describes is termed normative-explanatory. The normative end of this continuum refers to studies that attempt to ascertain the average, or modal, behavior occurring at particular age levels for a specified population of people. As noted in Chapter 1, most of the early research work in developmental psychology takes the form of normative research. Such research supplies important descriptive information for the developmental psychologist. For example, normative research might be aimed at describing the average reading levels from the first through the sixth grades for white, middle-class boys and girls living in the Midwest. Or such research might be aimed at compiling such information about black ghetto children in an eastern city. However, whatever type of norm is sought, the objective of any normative study is to specify and describe average behaviors expected to occur at particular times of development for specific groups of people. Hence, in describing what is expected to occur, normative research gives the developmental psychologist an appreciation of the developmental sequence of the behavioral phenomena he or she may be interested in.

However, such research does not explain why behavior unfolds in this normative manner. Such explanation is the goal of studies that lie toward the alternative end of this first dimension, the explanatory end. Thus, explanatory studies attempt to account for the why of behavioral development. Such studies, however, clearly rest on the collection of norms. After all, if psychologists do not have any idea about how to describe the average occurrence of the behavior under study, they will be at pains to explain it. Thus, while norms are in this way necessary for explanatory research, we may also see that they are not sufficient; in and of themselves they just present a catalogue of descriptions, a collection of unaccounted-for facts. However, when psychologists attempt to account for the presence of these facts, they move toward explanatory research.

But where do such explanations come from? As discussed in Chapter 1 and as also pointed out by McCandless (1970), explanations are often derived from theory. Psychologists may attempt to integrate the facts, or norms, of development within the context of a particular theoretical formulation. Accordingly, they devise an empirical test of their integrations, carry out this test, and in this way ascertain the tenability of their explanation. Thus, theory is useful in that it allows the developmentalist to have an integrative conceptual orientation toward the facts of the discipline and thus a basis for doing the type of research that will allow for an accounting of these facts. In this regard McCandless has stated:

> Norms, while essential and of interest to all, are concerns for the pragmatist. Developmental psychologists . . . are likely to be pragmatists and empiricists. This may be why there are so many facts—and of them there are many about which thoughtful scholars are skeptical—and so few explanations. It is for this reason that . . . an attempt is made to maintain a conceptual orientation. It seems more promising to depend on theory for explanation than on mere collection of facts (1970, p. 42).

Thus, we see that this first continuum describes a dimension that sorts research on the basis of its relative emphasis on either normative description or theoretically derived explanation.

**The Ahistorical-Historical Dimension.** The second dimension described by McCandless is termed by him the ahistorical-historical. This continuum sorts studies on the basis of their relative concern with a temporal parameter. In other words, some developmental studies are concerned with behavior as it exists at one particular time in a person's ontogeny. In such studies there may be no interest whatsoever in how the behavior at this point in development came to take the form that it does or in what form this behavior may take later. Thus, such studies are termed ahistorical because behavior is studied at only one point in time. For instance, a particular study might be concerned with the effects of a certain type of reinforcement on verbal learning in five-year-olds. If the study is ahistorical in its orientation, it will not be concerned about how the child's ontogeny contributed to this relation or about the future status of this relation.

However, as research becomes more concerned with the origins (McCandless, 1970) and the future course of behavior, it moves closer to the historical end of the second continuum. Thus, historical research is concerned not only with the status of a relation between two or more variables at a particular point in development, but also with a determination of the ontogenetic basis of that relation, as well as the future status of that relation. Historical research wants to know what variables in the five-year old's developmental history provided a basis for the relation between reinforcement and verbal learning and what implication the relation at age five has on future relations between reinforcement and verbal learning. In sum, then, the ahistorical-historical continuum sorts research on the basis of its relative emphasis on the temporal sequence of behavior.

The historical type of research study appears best suited for developmental inquiry. Without such historical investigation, core conceptual issues of development would not be able to be empirically addressed. The developmental psychologist would be unable to ascertain either the continuity-discontinuity and/or the stability-instability of behavior. Thus, while the ahistorical study allows us to know the relations among the variables of sex, social class, race, and IQ, at a given age, for example, it in no way allows us to know anything about the previous or the eventual interrelations among these variables. To gain such knowledge the historical type of research study is necessary.

In Chapter 8 we saw that there are several ways to design such historical research: the longitudinal and cross-sectional methods, as well as the relatively recent sequential methods described by Schaie (1965), Baltes and Nesselroade (1970), and Nesselroade and Baltes (1974). We need not reiterate the characteristics, assets, and deficits of these various historical research strategies. Yet, it is clear that while all these methods allow the developmental psychologist to deal with the issues of ontogenetic change, these last sets of methods—the sequential ones—provide the most refined way, in that they allow the developmental researcher to ascertain the various possible components of change, including both ontogenetic (developmental) variables and specific generational background variables.

**The Naturalistic-Manipulative Dimension.**  All scientific inquiry rests on observation. Yet there are many different ways in which scientists may obtain their observations. The third dimension that McCandless describes, the naturalistic-manipulative dimension, sorts studies on the basis of the types of observations they employ.

One way of observing development is to go out into the real world and attempt to observe behavior as it exists and develops. Such observational recourse to behavior as it occurs in its natural setting is termed *naturalistic observation*. In such an observational technique, the researcher in no way intervenes with, or attempts to manipulate, the ongoing behavior. Rather, after deciding what to observe, the researcher attempts to find such behavior as it naturally exists.

Although it is clear that such an observational technique gives the researcher an excellent chance of discovering how behavior really exists and develops in its ecologically valid, or natural, real-life setting, such research also has some limitations. The behavior of interest may occur at infrequent or irregular intervals, the researcher may not be readily able to attend to everything that is possible to observe—even with the help of such apparatus as cameras—and, in any event, such observations are usually difficult to use as a basis for explanations. For example, suppose a psychologist is interested in the development of aggression in five-, six-, and seven-year olds. If the psychologist chooses to study such development with the use of naturalistic observations he or she would simply go out and find an appropriate sample of children and then sit down and watch them, for example, at play in a school yard. Of course, a good deal of behavior might be occurring at a very rapid pace, and to try to cope with such an enormous input of information, the researcher might look at the children for only thirty seconds at a time in five-minute intervals. Moreover, a wide-angle-lensed camera might be used to record these observations. However, despite these techniques the researcher does not in any way intervene or attempt to manipulate the behavior of the subjects. Thus, it is possible that after days of such observations the researcher may have few, if any, observations relevant to the behavior of interest. Although this instance is unlikely in the case of aggressive responses, one may easily think of behaviors that do not occur frequently or regularly. For instance, to use a somewhat unusual topic for developmental inquiry but nonetheless a legitimate one, suppose the researcher is interested in observing masturbatory behaviors among these children. Even after days of intense naturalistic observation, the occurrences of such behaviors among this age group of children, and within the free-play situation, would be expected to be extremely low.

In any event, the researcher using this technique would be unable to make any statements about the variables in the children's development which provided a source of whatever behavior he or she was attempting to observe. Rather, the researcher would be able to describe only a particular sequence of events. Although such a description has the virtue of having ecological validity, because of the lack of control over the observations the data obtained by the researcher may be unsystematic, of a frequency limiting the potential generalizability of any findings, and of a sort that militates against other than descriptive appraisals of the developing behavior.

Because of the limitations of the naturalistic observation technique, researchers often opt for techniques that allow greater control over their observations. Thus, the more control that researchers exercise over their observations, the more these observations conform to manipulative research. For example, if we want to observe aggression in young children with greater control over our observations than that provided through naturalistic observations, we might set up a laboratory playroom. This room might contain only one attractive toy in it, although for the purposes of our observations we would always place two children in the room at a time. Although we would not actually be manipulating the children's behaviors, we would be controlling the situation within which they would be interacting. Thus, we would be using *controlled observation*.

However, if we want to exert maximal control over our observations we would employ the most controlled form of manipulative technique available, the controlled experiment. Rather than allowing all, or even just some, facets of behavior to vary naturally, we would exercise as much control over behavior as possible. We would manipulate conditions such that only the variables whose effects on behavior we want to ascertain would vary, and this variation itself would also be controlled. Everything else that could possibly affect the behavior of interest would be either held constant in all conditions or balanced across the research conditions. In other words, we would control any variable in the situation that could influence the behavior of interest, while manipulating the type or level of variation associated with only certain variables.

For example, suppose we want to ascertain the extent to which each of three types of instructional techniques facilitates learning in children ages five through seven years. Since variables such as the sex, social class, IQ, race, religion, and type of school could all be related to any effects the instructional techniques might have on learning, we would want to control these variables. Thus, subjects might all be five through seven years old, white middle-class males of average IQ, attending a public elementary school in the South. Thus, the only variables that would be different would be the type of instruction the children were exposed to and, of course, the age of the subjects. Thus, the precise effects of age and instruction techniques on a particular type of learning would be known through these manipulations. However, this information would be known only under the conditions of assessment. The effects of such instructional techniques on males or females of different racial and social class backgrounds, attending private schools in different sections of the country, would be unknown. Moreover, the known effects of age and instructional technique even on the assessed subjects would be limited. In the real world, the variables controlled for in the study are not controlled, but vary naturally. The reason such variables are controlled for in the first place is that they are expected to affect learning. Thus, how the experimental results of a controlled, manipulated experiment reflect what actually happens in the real world remains unknown. To find out we would have to ascertain the ecological generalizability of our results. We might have to return to the real classroom situation to see how the instructional techniques of interest to us affect learning in children of the age range of interest when such children are actually learning in real-life settings.

We see, then, that observational techniques always involve a trade-off. One trades precise control over behavior for ecological validity when one uses the naturalistic observational method; on the other hand, one loses such validity when one gains control through manipulation in the context of controlled experimental observations. However, we should also see that both types of observational techniques are needed. The researcher who begins with manipulated, controlled observations may recognize the necessity of seeing if and how the results may actually occur in the natural world. The naturalistic observer, on the other hand, may find it necessary to move into the laboratory and make controlled observations in order to verify the impressions of behavior gained in the field setting and to attempt to understand the independent effects of particular variables on specific behaviors.

**The Atheoretical-Theoretical Dimension.** This last dimension of developmental research sorts studies on the basis of their relative emphasis on theory as the basis of the research. As we discussed in Chapter 1, there may be various reasons that lead a researcher to conduct a particular developmental study. Some research may be initiated simply on the basis of the researchers' interest in some particular behavioral phenomenon. The researchers may be curious about the way something develops, they have a hunch about some aspect of development, or they may simply want to see what happens when something is manipulated or assessed. In addition, research may be used as a way to solve a practical problem (McCandless, 1970). In these cases research is not being conducted from a theoretical origin. The initiative for the research does not derive from hypothetical statements drawn from a theory, and the research ideas, when tested, will not necessarily serve to provide support, clarification, or refutation for the theory. Rather, research of an atheoretical nature is, by definition, initiated on a theory-independent basis. Hence, while such research may be found to have some relevance to theory after the fact, such potential applicability is certainly not intended. In fact, the data from such an atheoretical study may end up being just a piece of scientific data that is without a home. That is, the meaning and relevance of the data to any given theoretical formulation may remain unknown.

Because of such potential limitations, theoretical research has been stressed in this book. As indicated in Chapter 1 and as illustrated in the following chapters, studies initiated on the basis of some theoretical conceptions of development are most useful in

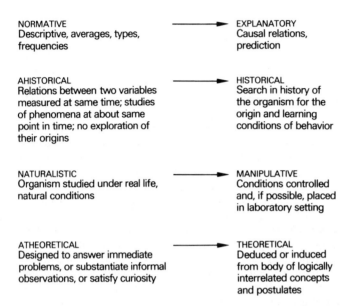

NORMATIVE
Descriptive, averages, types,
frequencies

⟶ EXPLANATORY
Causal relations,
prediction

AHISTORICAL
Relations between two variables
measured at same time; studies
of phenomena at about same
point in time; no exploration of
their origins

⟶ HISTORICAL
Search in history of
the organism for the
origin and learning
conditions of behavior

NATURALISTIC
Organism studied under real life,
natural conditions

⟶ MANIPULATIVE
Conditions controlled
and, if possible, placed
in laboratory setting

ATHEORETICAL
Designed to answer immediate
problems, or substantiate informal
observations, or satisfy curiosity

⟶ THEORETICAL
Deduced or induced
from body of logically
interrelated concepts
and postulates

**Fig. 11.1** Four dimensions of research studies in developmental psychology. *Source:* Boyd R. McCandless, *Children: Behavior and Development,* 2nd edition. Copyright © 1967 by Holt, Rinehart and Winston, Publishers. Reprinted by permission of The Dryden Press.

advancing the science. The resulting data from such research will necessarily have some direct relevance to our understanding of development. Such data will be readily articulated with an already existing set of information, bearing on a particular theoretical formulation, and will thus serve to clarify and/or expand this theoretical understanding of development. The purpose of theory is to integrate existing knowledge and to lead to the generation of new knowledge. This generation of new knowledge is obtained from the tests of hypotheses derived from such theories. Thus, theory-related research always has the promise of providing information expanding our understanding of the attributes and meanings of development.

**Conclusions.** McCandless' framework for describing the possible dimensions of developmental research allows us to see the ways that such research may vary. Developmental research is thus multifaceted; there are several dimensions along which a given study may vary, and thus the developmental researcher has available a large array of techniques and approaches with which to obtain information about psychological development. The usefulness of McCandless' dimensions of research, then, is to allow us to appreciate the many forms that developmental research may take, the many research emphases that may be stressed in such research, and the assets and limitations of each of these approaches to the study of psychological development. As a summary of these dimensions, then, Fig. 11.1 presents the end points of each of these four dimensions of developmental research, along with some brief descriptions of their meaning.

We see that developmental studies have relevance to at least four dimensions of research. Although any given study may be located on any portion of each of these four continua, all developmental studies face certain common methodological problems. Any developmental researcher must recognize that all developmental studies have the danger of being biased or faulty if certain issues of method are not confronted and dealt with. Methodological problems of research are those problems involved in how the actual data of the study are obtained. While certain data collection procedures may be appropriate, others may yield data with serious problems of interpretation. If one collects data in the wrong or in biased ways, little confidence may be placed in such data, and thus such data will be of little use to science. Hence, although all research has methodological problems that must be recognized and dealt with, there are some methodological issues of particular relevance to developmental psychological research.

These methodological problems of developmental research—also reviewed by McCandless (1970)—caution the researcher about the many safeguards that must be taken to ensure that the data give as accurate a representation as possible of the facts of development. If these potential methodological problems are recognized and successful steps are taken, the researcher will have confidence not only in the accuracy of the data but also in the interpretations drawn from it. Let us turn, then, to some of the important methodological problems of developmental research.

## Methodological Problems

**Contamination.** Following McCandless (1970), the first type of methodological problem we will mention is contamination. When data are contaminated, they are influenced by variables extraneous to the empirical study per se. That is, the results of the study are not pure; they are not due to only the actual, or true, relations among the investigated variables. Contamination may occur in several ways. Perhaps we are all familiar with safeguards taken by teachers to ensure that students' responses on tests are not contaminated (or influenced) by the responses of their classmates. Thus, for example, the teacher makes sure that no student has access to the work of any other student during the test. Analogous safeguards against contamination of responses must be taken in experiments.

In some studies subjects are tested successively. If a subject reveals the true intent of the study to a succeeding subject or in some way tells this later subject what to expect, this revelation might influence the second subject's responses. If this second subject's behavior is thus influenced by this extraneous (to the research situation, that is) information, then obviously the second subject's responses are not due solely to the research assessments. Such an instance would represent contamination of responses.

Researchers also may contaminate their own data. Suppose a researcher believes that there is a relationship between the type of body a person has and that person's personality or temperament. To test this belief the researcher might develop means to rate body type and temperament. However, it is possible that if the researcher does both of these ratings for all the subjects, any discovered relation between body type and temperament may be contaminated by the researcher's hypothesis about this relation. To illustrate this possibility let us consider the work of William Sheldon (1940, 1942). Sheldon developed a theory relating a person's physique type to that person's temperament. He specified that there are three essential components of body build and that it is possible to characterize a person's body in terms of the relative contribution of these three components. Moreover, he believed that some people's bodies are comprised of a major contribution by one of these components and of relatively minor contributions by the other two components. Thus, some people are predominantly fat—their bodies are comprised essentially of the contribution of adipose (fat) tissue. Other people's bodies are comprised mainly of the contributions of muscle and bone tissue—they have an athletic-looking body type. Finally, other people's bodies are comprised essentially of neither fat nor muscle tissue but of nervous-system tissue; such a body build would appear thin and linear.

Sheldon also specified that certain types of temperament go along with each of these three body types. He then devised ways to measure the body builds and temperaments of his subjects (4000 Harvard University male undergraduates). However, Sheldon himself performed both of these sets of measurements. He rated body build and then, even though he knew the hypothesized relation between body build and temperament, he rated temperament. Thus, there is the strong possibility that the high relation Sheldon found between these two sets of ratings is due not to the fact that such a strong relation actually exists in nature but to the fact that the ratings were contaminated because the person who did both sets of ratings knew the hypothesized relation between the ratings. Of course, Sheldon did not set out to intentionally contaminate his ratings. We are using this actual instance to illustrate the fact that such errors may often occur among well-trained, but perhaps unvigilant, researchers. Hence, researchers must take precautions to ensure that their subjects' responses are not affected by anything extraneous to the research situation and that the relations found among their data are not influenced by their own hypotheses. In science, asking a question should not determine the answer.

**Researcher Effects on Subject Responses.** Another, related type of methodological problem involving the researcher occurs when the investigator (unintentionally) affects the responses of his or her subjects. These researcher effects have been investigated by Rosenthal (1966), who suggests that such errors may play an important part of much research.

Suppose I want to conduct a study of the racial attitudes of white kindergarten-through-sixth-grade children toward black people and I choose to use a method wherein I individually interview each child. Each child and I sit alone in a small cubicle while I conduct the interview. Now, if I were a black psychologist doing this study I might get verbal responses from the subjects different from what I obtain as a white psychologist. White children may be more candid about expressing any pejorative racial attitudes when interviewed by a white person than when interviewed by a black person. Thus, in this example the race of the researcher might affect the attitudinal responses of the subjects.

Another, perhaps more subtle, example of the researcher affecting subjects' responses may be seen in the following illustration. Suppose a researcher wants to study the differential effects of a particular type of instructional technique on students who do below-average work and students who do above-average work. Obviously, the researcher would want to control everything in the research situation that might conceivably affect the subjects' responses. Thus, other than the fact that one group is slow and the other fast, all other things between the groups should be equivalent. Yet it is possible that the researcher may unknowingly interact with the two groups in different ways. For instance, the researcher may spend more time presenting the instructional technique to one group than the other, or might be warmer with one group than with the other. Such actions would mean that the conditions between the two groups are not in fact identical and that if differences between the groups are found, they might reasonably be due to the differential effects of the researcher's different behaviors toward the two groups.

Although it is difficult to determine when such researcher effects enter into the subjects' responses, the developmental researcher should always be aware of the potential of such bias and design the method of the study with safeguards. For instance, in the example of the racial attitude study, the researcher might want to use two interviewers, one black and one white, in order to control and test for any possible biasing effects introduced by the race of the researcher. In the second example, a standardized presentation of the instructional techniques might be given, perhaps through the use of a videotape recording device.

**Reconstruction Through Retrospection.**   There are many ways to obtain information about the events that characterize people's development. In Chapter 7 we saw the method used by Freud. By asking his adult neurotic patients to recall the events of their early childhood, Freud reconstructed their developmental histories. However, we saw that such a method has a strong potential of introducing serious problems into one's data. Such events may be misrecalled, partially forgotten, distorted, or even lied about. However, there is usually no way to check on these problems. The actual behavioral events and person interactions are not being empirically observed with the retrospective method but are merely being reconstructed through use of a subjective verbal account. Thus, when one reconstructs the past developmental history of a subject through retrospection—by having the subjects look back upon their life and recall previous events—one is using an unempirical, subjective, and perhaps severely distorted and inaccurate account of this developmental history. Hence, the reconstruction through retrospection method is an unacceptable way of obtaining information about the events that characterize people's development. Because the data collected through this method may be severely inaccurate, and because there usually is no way to ascertain whatever level of inaccuracy does in fact exist in the data, any theory devised or inferences drawn on the basis of such information is suspect.

However, in Chapter 9 we saw an example of another way of obtaining information about the events that characterize people's development, the anterospective reconstruction method used by Thomas, Chess, Birch, Hertzig, and Korn (1963) in their longitudinal study of the development of temperament. In this method, behavior is measured at or about the very time that it occurs. Hence, any reconstructions or representations of the course of development are based on actual, empirical observations of behavior as it develops. This anterospective method thus offers usable, empirical data, the accuracy of which may be objectively verified.

**Faulty Logic.**   Another important problem is presented in developmental research when the investigator uses faulty reasoning techniques in interpreting data. In fact, such faulty reasoning may actually influence the design of the study itself and thus, of course, the method used to collect data.

Although faulty logic is by no means unique to developmental research, such problems do play an all too prominent role in such investigations. Let us illustrate the potential problem by offering the following syllogism:

1.   Boats float on water.
2.   X is floating on water.
3.   Therefore X is a boat.

Obviously this is an example of faulty logic. On the basis of the initial premise we cannot exclude the possibility that things other than boats float on water; thus, it is not logical to conclude that just because X floats on water, X is a boat. However, if we assert that boats *and only* boats float on water, then it *would* follow from this premise that if X is floating on water, X is a boat. Although it is clear that the first syllogism is not logical, it is possible to just alter the words of the syllogism (i.e., the content) and leave the logic there intact. Thus, a second syllogism might be:

1.   Infants deprived of their mother's nipple in the first year of their life suck their thumbs as five-year-old children.
2.   John, a five-year-old, sucks his thumb.
3.   Therefore, John was deprived of his mother's nipple during the first year of his life.

Clearly, this conclusion also does not follow from the premise. There may be sources of thumb-sucking among five-year-olds other than nipple deprivation. Yet, when this logically faulty syllogism is cast in terms of developmental events between mother and child, it somehow all too often acquires an air of believability. Yet, the assertion that John's thumb sucking is due to (unseen) nipple deprivation in the first year of life is as lacking in logic as the syllogism concerning X being a boat.

Perhaps one reason for such faulty logic in developmental research is that development per se deals with sequential events. There may be the belief that *post hoc, ergo propter hoc,* "after the fact, therefore because of the fact." That is, when events occur sequentially there may be a tendency to infer that if B happens after A, then A must be a source of B. However, such inferences also rest on faulty logic. If a traumatic event occurs early in a person's development, and years later some neurotic disorder emerges, it is simply not logical to assert that the trauma was *the* source—or even *a* source—of the later neuroticism. Although such a relation might actually exist, the mere fact that the trauma was followed by the neuroticism does not represent a logically necessary reason for the conclusion that the trauma is a source of the neuroticism. The neuroticism's emergence may have occurred in any event, and so in general it is merely an instance of faulty logic to assert that when one event follows another in development, the former is a source of the latter. Clearly, no one would assert that if one rises at 4:00 A.M. every day, and then with astonishing predictability the sun rises just a few hours later, then one's personal rising is the source of the sun's rising. Yet, when such faulty reasoning is couched in terms of sequential events that occur over the course of development, such lack of logic may all too often slip by unnoticed.

As noted above, such faulty logic in interpretation of results may find its way into the methodological design of developmental research. A researcher may wish to ascertain the developmental source of a particular behavior. Thus, the researcher might collect data about events that occurred during the first few years of a child's life and then relate this information to data collected at a later time in the child's life. If a relation between these early and later measures is found—perhaps expressed in terms of a correlation coefficient—the researcher might infer that the early behavior provided a source of the later behavior. Yet, we have seen that simply through the use of the method of data collection, sufficient information was not obtained to make this inference logically necessary.

Throughout this book we have pointed out instances of faulty logic used in relation to the concepts and theories of development we have been discussing. Our discussions of the concept of heritability (in Chapter 3), the notion of instinct (in Chapter 4), and the continuity-discontinuity issue (in Chapter 5) indicated how some psychologists often use faulty logic in their discussions of these concepts and issues. Moreover, in Chapter 10 we saw how the learning approach to development bases its notion that reinforcement may account for all behavior upon faulty, circular reasoning. Thus, it is apparent that faulty logic often finds its way into the developmental literature. Accordingly, the reader of this literature must be aware of this problem and be ready to recognize such faulty logic when it occurs.

**Inadequate Concept Definition.** Another problem of both methodology and interpretation has been noted by McCandless (1970). This problem pertains to how researchers define the concepts they are investigating and thus how they attempt to measure these concepts. A concept is a term used to represent some aspect of the stimulus, response, or behavioral world. Concepts, of course, may be more or less abstract. Thus, a concept used to represent such things as cars, wagons, and trains—i.e., the concept of vehicle—might be considered relatively concrete. The empirical referents of the concept are generally understood. Other relatively concrete concepts might be animal, body, or height. Yet, not all concepts are similarly concrete. Some concepts do not have commonly understood empirical referents. Thus, when psychologists use concepts such as aggression, learning, or personality, it is absolutely necessary that they precisely specify what they are referring to. Then, anyone interested in the researcher's work will know exactly what is meant by the use of a term. If such operational definitions are not used, however, considerable problems of communication may result. Two different researchers may be studying the same phenomenon, but if they define and measure it differently their results may not be comparable. Moreover, if they do not communicate these different meanings clearly, this lack of comparability may never be recognized.

For example, suppose a researcher is interested in studying the "generation gap." What exactly does the term mean? On a simple level one may suppose that it refers to a set of differences that allegedly exist between adolescents and their parents. But this definition will not suffice in making the empirical referents of this concept clear. Adolescents and their parents may differ from each other in many ways. Are the differences referred to by use of the term differences in the physical appearances of the generational groups—for example, in their respective styles of dress and hair lengths? Or does one mean divisions between the generations in their respective behavioral support for radical political causes? Or does one mean differences between the generations in attitudes about such issues of contemporary concern as drug use, sex, and racism?

If researchers do anchor their concepts in precise, empirical terms, considerable confusion may be avoided. For example, several recent studies of the generation gap (Lerner, Karson, Meisels, and Knapp, 1975; Lerner, Pendorf, and Emery, 1971; Lerner, Schroeder, Rewitzer, and Weinstock, 1972; Weinstock and Lerner, 1972) have defined this division in terms of attitude differences between adolescents and their parents.

Specifically, members of each of these generational groups were given a list of 36 statements dealing with such issues as sex, war, and drugs. Subjects were asked to indicate their agreement or disagreement with each statement through use of a seven-point rating scale, with 1 indicating strong agreement and 7 indicating strong dis-agreement. Thus, a generation gap may have occurred on any item wherein the average responses of each group were located at statistically significant different points along the rating scale continuum. In most of these studies it was found that an attitudinal generation gap did exist between the sampled adolescents and their parents. But the authors attempted to be precise about limiting their interpretation to the specific definition they employed (Lerner, 1975). Thus, conclusions were limited to the particular samples of people tested, the specific measure of the generation gap used (i.e., attitude measures), and, even more, the specific instances of attitude statements assessed (Lerner, et al., 1975). These authors recognized the fact that if other attitudes were sampled, if another type of attitude scale were used, or if other possible domains of intergenerational divisions were evaluated (e.g., the physical appearance or the behavioral domains), their findings may not have been relevant. In other words, if someone else used a different definition of the generation gap, the comparability of findings between this other study and those noted above would not be direct.

However, so long as researchers take pains to clearly define what they mean by their use of any concept and design their study with such clear definitions in mind, any confusion about the use of the same term to represent different things may be eliminated. To a great extent researchers may define things as they wish, so long as they anchor their definitions in understandable, empirical referents. Once this is done any possible differences in what is meant by a particular concept may be recognized and understood.

**Sampling.** A sixth type of methodological problem noted by McCandless (1970) deals with the problems involved in obtaining subjects for developmental research and, accordingly, in making inferences about development based on results derived from the particular sample of subjects. Let us say that I want to do a study of the racial attitudes of white and black five-year-old children. Obviously I need a group of black and a group of white five-year-olds to study. The procedures I follow in obtaining such samples will critically affect the conclusions I am appropriately able to make on data derived from these samples.

Ideally I would like to measure such attitudes in all such children. However, this is clearly an economic and practical impossibility. Therefore, researchers must often draw a sample from the larger population—that is, a group of subjects from this population that may feasibly be studied. Through the study of this sample the researcher would hope to obtain results that could be generalized to the entire population: data from the sample would be inferred to represent what the results with the entire population would have been had that population actually been tested.

Thus, the researcher must be sure that the sample that is used is representative of the entire population. If the sample is not representative, if it is *biased,* then the researcher may not appropriately infer that results obtained with the sample may be generalized to the entire population. For example, if the researcher conducting a study of racial attitudes among five-year-old blacks and whites chooses as his sample white children from a large eastern city and black children from a small southern city, then it would be inappropriate to infer that such children are representative of all white children or of all black children living everywhere. The sample would be biased in the direction of children living in cities in two specific geographical locations.

Standard procedures are of course known for obtaining unbiased samples. For instance, all researchers know that a random sample is needed in order to appropriately make inferences from sample to population. In a random sample of a population each subject within the population has an equal chance of being selected for the sample. To ensure this equal likelihood, every time a subject is drawn from a population to become part of the sample, the subject is again put back into the population so that when the next subject is selected there exists the same number of subjects in the population to "compete" against for selection. Thus, instead of mere random selection, a researcher would use random selection with replacement. Moreover, the researcher would want to know that the sample used in the research actually was representative of all possible social strata that existed in the population. If 70 percent of all five-year-old whites were in the socioeconomic middle class, 10 percent in the upper class, and 20 percent in the lower class, the researcher would want the proportions of children in the sample from these socioeconomic classes to correspond to the proportions in the population. Thus, the researcher would randomly sample with replacement within each of these socioeconomic levels to differing degrees in order to obtain proportions of subjects within the sample corresponding to the proportions within the population. Hence, stratified random sampling with replacement would be the preferred procedure for obtaining a representative, unbiased sample.

However, although such procedures are well known to all researchers, it is still often the case that studies are done with knowingly biased, unrepresentative samples. Why? To answer this question we must recognize that there are often ethical, economic, and practical problems that interfere with the researcher's desire to obtain a truly representative, unbiased sample. For example, it should be obvious that not all five-year-old black and white children are available for the researcher to sample from. The researcher is located in a particular part of the country, and only children living in that area are usually potentially available for study. Even then, however, not all these children may be available. Schools may not want or be able to allow a researcher to enter to study the children there. And even if a school does cooperate, all the appropriately aged children in that school may not be available for study. In any psychological study, the researcher is ethically bound to obtain the informed consent of those responsible for the child to study the child. Usually, then, the parents will have to be fully informed of the intent of the study in terms that they are capable of understanding (i.e., the psychologist may not relate the purpose of the study in highly technical and complex terms, incomprehensible to the average layman), and they must give their consent for their child's participation. In this way the researcher is taking one necessary step to ensure that the rights and safety of the subjects are not being violated. Of course, while other such steps must be taken (e.g., the researcher may not do a study that he or she even suspects will in any way harm the child), the fact that only volunteer subjects may be used limits the representativeness of any sample. In other words, only some population strata will be even potentially available for any researcher to study; only some groups of children will be potentially available within that strata; and only some children will be available within those groups.

Of course, a good researcher will still apply appropriate sampling techniques even within such an unrepresentative sample. Yet, because of the seemingly inescapable sampling problems involved in developmental research, any researcher must be aware that any inferences made on the basis of results obtained with such samples are limited. We saw that there were serious sampling problems in the Kagan and Moss (1962) longitudinal study (Chapter 8) and in the Thomas, et al. (1963) New York Longitudinal Study (Chapter 9), which limited the generalizations that could be made from the data.

Thus, sampling is always a problem in any developmental research study. The investigator must always be aware of these problems of sampling, and in fact, because of absolutely necessary ethical restrictions (imposed on developmental researchers by themselves), more sampling problems are introduced. Hence, the results of any developmental study are limited to the extent that biased sampling procedures interfere with obtaining a representative sample. Accordingly, the results of any such study may be generalized to such broader populations only with extreme caution. Thus, because of methodological problems of sampling, the researcher always encounters a related problem, that of generalization.

**Overgeneralization.** We have seen that if limitations imposed on developmental research by sampling problems are not recognized, the researcher may try to interpret the study's results as being more representative than they actually are. That is, the researcher may attempt to generalize such results to broader populations. However, such overgeneralization is unsound in light of the limitations imposed on the data by the sampling problems. Thus, we see that one source of unsound generalization is the lack of recognition of limitations imposed by sampling inadequacies.

However, as noted by McCandless (1970, p. 55), there are other types, or sources, of overgeneralization. The results of a particular study might indicate that there exist small, but reliable, differences between two groups of children. Yet the researcher may speak of these differences as if they were reflective of wide disparities between the groups. If such statements occur, we may also term this overgeneralization. Let us say that a particular researcher is interested in the attitudes that adolescent males and females maintain about their own bodies. To study such body concepts, the researcher might ask a large group of adolescent males and females to rate several body characteristics (e.g., arms, legs, face, body build, height, general appearance) in terms of how important each is in determining the person's satisfaction with his or her body's appearance (see Lerner, Karabenick, and Stuart, 1973). Now, suppose that female adolescents have a mean importance rating for the face of 4.20 (on a five-point scale, with 5.0 being extremely important), and the corresponding rating for the male adolescents is 3.95. Because of the fact that many adolescent responses went into the calculation of these means and thus only small differences are needed for statistically significant differences to occur, the researcher might find that such a small difference between males and females is statistically significant (i.e., the chances of this difference occurring just by chance were very slight). However, such statistical significance may not correspond to psychological significance. Can one say that on the basis of only a 0.25 point difference (out of a possible 5.0 point difference) that the importance of the face for adolescent females' body concepts is considerably greater than the importance of this body part for adolescent males' body concepts? Probably not, and in fact, if such an assertion were made, it might be seen as an instance of overgeneralization.

Other types of overgeneralization also exist. Suppose that in the above study of body concept, the researcher is also interested in finding out what parts of the male body are most important to females in deciding that the male is attractive and what parts of the female body are most important to males in deciding that the female is attractive. The researcher might again ask the adolescent males and females to rate each of the body parts, but this time in terms of the attractiveness of the opposite sex. Now suppose that it is found that females rate general appearance as the most important characteristic of the male's body in determining male attractiveness, while males rate face as the most important part of the female's body in determining a female's attractiveness. Would the researcher be justified in concluding that when adolescent males go about choosing a female for a dating partner they are most concerned about the female's face, and that when females choose a male dating partner they are most concerned about the male's general appearance? May these ratings be generalized to choice of partners in dating situations? Since the findings of the study pertain to ratings obtained about females and males in general, not about choices of dating partners, such generalization would appear unwarranted. As McCandless has clearly indicated, "applying findings gathered in one situation to circumstances different in essential characteristics" is an instance of unsound generalization (1970, p. 55).

Over the course of this book we have seen several instances of such overgeneralization. In Chapter 5 we saw that Skinner (1956) generalizes findings involving some responses of some animals in some situations, to all responses of all animals in all situations. Similarly, in Chapter 10 we saw that other learning-approach psychologists also overgeneralize in reference to their use of the concept of reinforcement. Whenever one applies one's specific results found with particular measures in particular situations to situations that may be considered to be different in important ways, one is guilty of overgeneralization.

To avoid unsound overgeneralization, researchers must be wary of attempting to (1) extend their results to situations different from those their data actually bear on; (2) attribute more meaning, clarity, or significance to their results than are actually indicated; and (3) apply their findings to groups of people not actually represented in their sample (McCandless, 1970). The developmental psychologist must also recognize that because of sampling, situational, and thus interpretational problems, the body of existing knowledge in the discipline may not be applicable to many groups of people. The "facts" of development, obtained through considerable research work, may in any event not be reflective of the "facts" for all people.

For example, due to both an intense interest in studying child development and the difficulty of readily obtaining samples of children to study, many university and other research institutions set up laboratory schools in earlier decades of this century. Many of the "facts" of development (at that time mostly "normative facts") were obtained through the study of children at these schools. Yet, these children were often the children of the university or institutional people. Hence, they were primarily white, middle-class children of highly educated parents. Certainly, while the "facts" of development of such children are important, these "facts" may not be generalizable to all other children. Most children do not have parents who are professors or researchers. Many children are not white, and many children do not come from middle-class backgrounds. Thus, the "facts" of development derived from such samples may be highly biased and unrepresentative.

In recognition of this problem, research in developmental psychology over the last several years has focused on other populations. Hence, developmental psychology today is moving away from being a psychology of the development of only white, middle-class children of highly educated parents. Studies of the poor, of blacks, of Chicanos, and of minority groups in general are being conducted in an attempt to broaden the basis of our knowledge of development in all strata of society. Moreover, the increase of scope has not been limited to disenfranchised, culturally deprived, or minority groups within our own country; there has been the recognition for the need for study of other societal and cultural settings. The facts of development found in this country may not be generalizable to the development of people in all countries, and hence there is a need for and a growing concern with cross-cultural studies of development. Finally, but by no means least importantly, there has been the recognition that some people—although they may even be white and middle class—possess characteristics that may make their development considerably different from other people's. These people are women, and until relatively recently there has not been considerable concern with the possibly unique phenomena that might be encountered by growing up as a woman in our society. Thus, a major recent extension of developmental research and theory has been the concern with women's psychological development (e.g., see Bacon and Lerner, 1975; Block, 1973; Marshall and Karabenick, 1975; Mednick and Tangri, 1972; Sarason, 1973). In sum, as research broadens, developmental psychology will move toward providing a body of knowledge about the development of all people.

## Conclusions

To this point we have considered some of the dimensions and problems of developmental research, using McCandless (1970) as a framework for our presentation. We have seen that a theory is useful if it fulfills its function as an integrator of facts *and* serves as a basis for the generation of new facts. Thus, this chapter has considered the problems of doing developmental research that will allow theory to fulfill its second role. If these problems are not dealt with correctly in developmental research, then such research will not provide an appropriate test of any given theoretical formulation. Yet, if such theoretically relevant, appropriate research is done, it will also potentially have another use—it may provide evidence for the clarification of, or have implications for, some important practical problem of society. In this sense then it has often been said that there is nothing so practical as a good theory. A good theory will well integrate existing knowledge, lead to the generation of appropriately researched new knowledge, and thus provide meaningful, accurate information that may be useful for solving the practical problems and issues of society. Developmental research often has such theory-relevant, practical implications. Let us turn, then, to a consideration of some of these practical implications.

## Some Social Implications

Throughout our discussions of the various theoretical positions presented in this book, we have indicated that there exist some societal implications of the positions. The research done in support of these formulations has often both supported and clarified these formulations and suggested social extensions of the theory. Let us consider some instances of these occurrences.

## Stages in the Development of Moral Reasoning

In Chapter 7 we saw that Kohlberg proposes a stage theory of the development of moral reasoning. Six stages exist in the development of moral thinking, and consistent with all stage formulations, all people (if they develop) pass through these stages in an invariant sequence. Moreover, people at different times in their development may be modally at one stage or another. We saw in both Chapters 6 and 7 that saying that a person is at one or another stage is a modal attribution; it is a designation based on the most frequent type of structure revealed by the person. Thus, people maintain moral reasoning structures of more than one developmental level at a given time in their development, but they are said to be at a certain level in their reasoning because modally most of their structures are at this level.

Research by Kohlberg and his colleagues indicates that although six possible stages of modal moral reasoning exist, most adult Americans do not function at the more advanced stages (stages 5 and 6) of development (Turiel, 1969). Rather, most adult Americans seem to modally function at no higher than stage 4, the "authority and social order maintaining" moral orientation, although many public moral statements— for example, by our national leaders—are at the postconventional, higher levels of reasoning (Turiel, 1969). What may be a consequence of this interrelation between the moral level manifested by national leaders and the moral level of reasoning modally maintained by the average American listener? Turiel suggests that one consequence may be that "social leaders expressing moral statements at a level higher than that of their audience may elicit a positive attitude toward the content endorsed. However, the structural level of thought used by the leaders may be assimilated by the listener to his own level" (1969, p. 131).

For example, suppose the president were giving a speech on a national policy decision and, as might be typical, this speech was couched in level 5 or 6 terms. However, the average American listening to this speech maintains a level 4 orientation, which means that institutions of society are seen as ends in and of themselves. Acts that maintain such institutions and that thus perserve the social order are seen as moral. Since the presidency is seen as such a societal institution, acts that support or maintain the presidency are seen as moral; acts that do not are seen as immoral. Such a moral orientation would lead the stage 4 listener to view the presidential speech in a positive light. Stage 4 listeners would tend to agree with the speech because the president is maintaining the positions reflected in the speech, the president is the embodiment of a primary national institution—the presidency—and one must support and maintain such national institutions in order to be moral. But notice, however, that in this process the structural level of thought represented in the president's speech is not evaluated on its own level. Rather, the stage 4 reasoners view the speech within the context of their social order and institutional-maintenance morality; they assimilate the higher level content into the terms of this developmentally lower level of reasoning.

Evidence for such an assimilational distortion process was found in research by Kohlberg and his colleagues (cf. Turiel, 1969), and such "findings help explain why the majority of people in the society do not themselves attain the moral level contained in public statements, such as those expressed by social leaders and in documents such as the Constitution" (Turiel, 1969). Moreover, such findings suggest a hypothesis about the source of possible intergenerational divisions over the policies advanced by public leaders. If it is the case that the modal level of moral reasoning among college youth, as a group, is at a higher level than that maintained in the general adult population, then while college youth may more often evaluate statements by national leaders at the statement's own level of moral reasoning, adults in the general population may more often assimilatorily distort such statements toward their social order and institutional-maintaining moral reasoning level. Thus, if college youth disagree with these statements made by national leaders, adults in the general population may often view such disagreement as counter to the maintenance of a basic national institution and thus view such disagreement as immoral.

However, since we know that such assimilatory distortion can be countered through the establishment of cognitive conflict (see our discussion of this point in Chapter 7), a procedure may be offered to both allow people to move toward the evaluation of such statements at their own level and possibly reduce such hypothesized intergenerational and interpersonal conflict. If higher-level statements induced disequilibrium, they would not be as readily distorted (Turiel, 1969). To induce such disequilibrium those interested in such social change might initiate a program of offering statements to the public at a level that would induce cognitive conflict—for example, statements presenting a cognitive discrepancy between the objectives of maintaining two equally important societal institutions (e.g., the presidency and Congress). Such conflict would tend to move the person toward increased utilization of higher, though not previously modally used, reasoning structures and hence decrease the chances of assimilatory distortion (Turiel, 1969).

## The Rearing of Individually Different Children

In Chapter 9 we reviewed the Thomas, et al. (1963) ipsative study of temperamental development in children. The results of the New York Longitudinal Study indicate that children possess different temperamental attribute repertoires, identifiable within the first few months of life, and that this individual uniqueness tends to remain relatively stable throughout the first decade of the child's life. Since temperament was conceptualized as behavioral style, or reactivity patterns, we saw that the results of the NYLS strongly suggested that such individually different children would interact with even identical environmental situations in different ways. Hence, we concluded that even if the very same environmental situations could be presented to different children—a highly improbable occurrence—we would still expect different children to develop differently as a function of their individually characteristic interactive patterns. In other words, we concluded that similar—or even identical—child-rearing patterns cannot be expected to result in similar behaviors in all children.

These conclusions were bolstered by the research of Bowers (1973). In Chapter 10 we saw that Bowers analyzed the results of studies that compared the relative effects of traits, situations, and interactions between them on variation in human behavior. Although in some cases traits contributed more to such variation than did situations, while in other cases the reverse was true, in the preponderant majority of cases the *interaction* accounted for the major share of variation in human behavior.

These results have important implications for parents, who are inevitably faced with decisions about the appropriate rearing procedures to use with their children. Any approach to child rearing that dictates the invariant applicability of a procedure with children of a specific stage or age is apt to be misleading, since it implies that all such children will react similarly to this procedure. Thus, statements taking the form of, "Two year-olds are like this, and thus should be treated like this," will mislead parents because they ignore the characteristically unique repertoire of attributes that children seem to possess and that lead children to interact differently with even the same prescribed procedure. On the other hand, we also know that children do possess stage-specific attributes (i.e., general developmental attributes, for example, as specified by Piaget and Kohlberg), and we also know that the situation the child is in does contribute—in interaction with the child's characteristics—to the child's development. Thus, any statement about preferred techniques of child rearing which stresses only the essential uniqueness of children is misleading also, in that it ignores the general developmental characteristics shared by all children and the interactive significance of specific situational determinants of behavior.

Thus, the implications of both the Thomas, *et al.* (1963) study and the research by Bowers (1973) for parental child-rearing practices are similar. Both indicate that parents should be made aware that the sources of their children's development are many, and that these sources interrelate in a complex way to provide a basis of a child's development. If this is done, parents will not be misled to think that all one must know about child rearing is certain standard procedural formulas that may be applied to their child in order to produce certain behaviors. When such information is conveyed, parents will be better informed about current scientific understanding of the actual state of affairs involved in their child's development and, moreover, will be less prone to feel guilty when a particular child-rearing procedure does not result in the specified behavioral outcome. After all, if parents understand that the child-rearing procedures they choose provide only a portion of the source of their child's behavioral development, they will understand the limitations on the extent to which they themselves may influence their child's development. Behavioral development is interactive in nature, and only a portion of the basis of this interaction is provided by parents and their chosen child-rearing procedures.

## Racial Social Stereotypes

In Chapter 3 we reviewed Anastasi's (1958) conceptualization of the interactive contributions of heredity and environment to behavioral development. We saw that the effects of environment on behavioral development may be conceptualized as making contributions along a continuum of breadth and that the effects of heredity on behavioral development may be thought of as making contributions along a continuum of indirectness. The effects of heredity are seen as always being indirect; that is, they always contribute with the moderating context of particular environmental characteristics. We also saw that one can specify various points along this hypothetical continuum of indirectness representing increasingly more indirect influences of heredity. Thus, we learned that social stereotypes may be thought of as the most indirect, though still hereditary, contribution to behavioral development which exists along this continuum.

On the basis of *least* indirectly inherited physical characteristics, people are placed into categories. That is, physical characteristics are used as stimulus cues for categorizing people in groups. This categorization results from a basic, seemingly biologically adaptive orientation to be economical in our perceptions of the world. Certain behavioral expectations are maintained and certain personality attributions are afforded people on the basis of their categorization. This categorization-attribution process is maintained because of the need to reduce the vast amount of stimulus information that exists in the environment and thus to be able to efficiently interrelate with the stimulus world. Moreover, once such attributions are contained in a category, they are held as generally applicable. To maintain economical perceptions, all people in a category are seen to possess these characteristics. Thus, attributions become overgeneralized beliefs; they take the form of *social stereotypes*.

We noted that people who possess chubby body builds are put into one category, people who possess average body builds put into another category, and people who possess thin body builds put into yet another category. Not only are different personality/behavior expectations and attributions similarly maintained toward these differently categorized people, but different social interactive patterns have been found to exist in responses to these differently built people. Moreover, the attributions made toward those with a chubby physique are negative, while the attributions made toward those with an average physique are positive, and these differential social stereotypes have been found to be related to unfavorable personality developments among chubby children and favorable personality developments among average build children (Lerner and Korn, 1972). Hence, this body of research indicates that important personality and social implications exist in relation to the social stereotypes maintained toward the physical cue of body type.

However, in Chapter 3 we also discussed the possibility that similar social and personality implications may exist in our society in relation to another physical cue: skin color. Similar to those possessing a chubby physique, those possessing a black skin color may be unfavorably categorized in ways that are associated with unfavorable personality developments and negative social interactions. While considerable research has been devoted to ascertaining the parameters of such pejorative racial stereotypes (see Brigham, 1971), relatively little developmental research has been devoted to attempts to alter such categorizations. Although of course a value judgment, it would seem that if the effects of negative categorizations on the basis of skin color may be as severe as those found in respect to body build, then research efforts attempting to ameliorate such categorizations are most needed. Such racial social stereotypes can have only the most pernicious effects on our society, and it thus may be argued that researchers should increase their attempts to find ways to alter such categorizations.

However, such a suggestion clearly represents a value judgment. Science is devoted to a search for truth, and in our society any scientist may choose whatever aspect of empirical reality he or she is interested in as a topic for study. Yet, one may wonder whether the scientist has a duty to society to study those things that have some chance of bettering society rather than seemingly esoteric phenomena. This question raises the issue of the scientist's dual role as a scientist and as a citizen. Let us turn to a consideration of this issue as a conclusion to this chapter.

## The Scientist as Citizen

In attempting to ascertain the sources and characteristics of development, the developmental psychologist is necessarily concerned with the essential variables involved in behavior. As scientists gain greater understanding of the functioning of these variables, as they further specify the ways in which such variables exert their influence on behavioral development, a certain type of power accrues to them. That is, with increased understanding may come increased control over the functioning of these variables. Thus, because of their technological and intellectual training, scientists have power not typically possessed by the other, nonscientist citizens of society.

This special status of the citizen scientist may create special moral and ethical problems. To illustrate these, let us use a hypothetical, and *extremely improbable, if not impossible,* example. Suppose that a developmental psychologist discovers the variable that controls intelligence; the scientist has found a means of controlling the variable such that any level of intelligence can be developed in any child. As a scientist, committed to the search for truth within a scientific community, the scientist has an obligation to communicate such a finding. Yet, it is also clear that such knowledge could be used for unacceptable social purposes—for example, some groups of people could have produced in them low levels of intelligence. Thus, because of the potentiality for misuse of such a finding, should the scientist suppress the finding? Although this specific dilemma is unlikely to ever occur, one may see that those who were associated with the discovery of atomic energy might have been confronted with a similar dilemma. The issue is, does the scientist have a social obligation to suppress or ignore findings that either may be misused by society or that may show the truth of a socially unacceptable doctrine?

Unfortunately, there is no ready answer to this dilemma. Scientists as scientists have an obligation to communicate their findings; yet, as citizens they may feel the obligation to avoid promoting social unrest. The scientist must walk a line between complete commitment to the search for truth—no matter how unpleasant that truth may be—and a commitment to better society. Thus, although not an answer to this dilemma, the scientist does have an option. The scientist may use his or her technological and intellectual powers in an attempt to study developmental variables that have some applied, practical relevance. Although having a finite amount of time to devote to research, the developmental psychologist may opt to devote some of this time to an assessment of the variables that may be involved in processes that do have such social relevancy. For instance, we have noted the need to study how unfavorable categorization of people on the basis of their skin color may be ameliorated. Although it is clear that such socially relevant research may also be misused, it would then become necessary for the scientist as citizen to work for the proper application of the knowledge. In this way the scientist may fulfill his or her dual role as a scientist and as a citizen. The scientist may work for an increased understanding of the sources and characteristics of psychological development. Then the scientist, as citizen, may work for what he or she feels is the proper social application of this knowledge. In this way the science of developmental psychology may advance, and the status of the psychological development of the children in our society may similarly be favorably enhanced.

## Summary

While theory is necessary for a full understanding of developmental psychology, research represents a necessary, vital component of the science. This chapter was devoted to a specification of the dimensions of developmental research, an indication of common methodological problems of such research, a clarification of the interrelation of theory and research in development, and finally, a suggestion about some of the social implications of developmental research.

The dimensions of developmental research specified by McCandless were used as a framework within which to describe attributes of such research. McCandless suggests that developmental research may be characterized as varying along four dimensions. The first dimension of such research is termed *normative-explanatory*. The former end of the continuum refers to studies that attempt to ascertain average, or modal, behavior occurring at particular ages within specified populations; the latter end represents studies that offer explanations for why behavior appears as it does. The second dimension of developmental research is termed *ahistorical-historical*. Studies representative of the former end of the dimension are not concerned with temporal parameters; behavior is depicted as it exists at one point in time. Studies typical of the latter end are concerned with the antecedent and consequent events involved in depicting behavior at any time in life, that is, with similarities and/or differences in behavior across at least some portion of the life span. Several designs exist for historical developmental research; while the longitudinal and cross-sectional designs have been traditional, arguments favoring the relatively recently developed sequential research design strategies—advanced by Schaie, Baltes, and Nesselroade—were presented.

The third dimension of developmental research is termed *naturalistic-manipulative*. Here we see a contrast between studies designed to assess behavior as it occurs in its ecologically valid niche and studies that attempt to exert maximum control over the observational situation and the variables therein. The last dimension of developmental research—the *atheoretical-theoretical* dimension—attempts to sort studies on the basis of the relative emphasis on theory as the basis of the research. Research relatively more related to the latter end of this final continuum was stressed in the present text.

In addition to providing a framework for the dimensionalization of developmental research, McCandless also offers a framework for considering methodological problems often encountered in developmental studies. The first problem is one of contamination—influences on the data of the study derived from variables extraneous to the study. For example, contamination may result from one child in a study indicating to another in the study what to expect from the experimenter.

A second problem deals with possible influences on subjects' behaviors which may be derived from the experimenter's behavior—for example, as might be derived from differential behavior on the part of the researcher toward subjects in various observational conditions. A third problem of developmental research involves distortions and inaccuracies that may be introduced into developmental data by reconstructing the events in the life span through retrospection. A fourth problem involves faulty logic. An instance of such faulty logic is the argument that because event A developmentally preceded event B, then A provided a source of B. A fifth problem of developmental method is inadequate concept definition—omission of appropriate operational definitions of the concepts used in developmental research.

Finally, two related problems of developmental research were considered: the problems involved in obtaining a representative sample of subjects (e.g., ethical problems) and problems involved in making generalizations from data derived from the typically biased samples used in developmental research. Types of overgeneralizations were reviewed, and the inability of developmental psychology to make fully informed generalizations to important segments of our population (e.g., the aged, women, various minority groups) was indicated.

Several potential applications of developmental research and theory to important societal issues were discussed. Some extensions of the work of Kohlberg and of Turiel, on the development of moral reasoning, to social change were evaluated. Thus, on the basis of theoretical understandings associated with the concepts of stage mixture, disequilibrium, and cognitive conflict, means to induce modal shifts in moral reasoning levels characteristic of the general population were suggested.

The implications of the Thomas, *et al.* (1963) New York Longitudinal Study for parental child-rearing practices were indicated. On the basis of the findings of this study, it may be said that children possess lawful characteristics of individuality which remain stable throughout their lives. The relevance of such facts for parents interested in applying general "rules" of child guidance and for the emotional reaction of parents upon viewing the outcome of their rearing practices were specified.

The implications of racial social stereotypes, both for people whose behavior may be canalized as a consequence of being the target of such overgeneralizations and for the people who may maintain such stereotypes, were specified. While we depicted the cognitive basis of such stereotypes and the possible role of such stereotypes in increasing the level of racial tension and conflict in our society, we also indicated that major, systematic efforts to attenuate such overgeneralizations are lacking.

Thus, we raised the issue of whether the scientist has a duty to society to study those things that have some chance of bettering society rather than just those things that are of mere esoteric interest. Hence, we discussed the issues involved in the scientist's dual role as both a person committed to the search for empirical truth and a person who functions as a citizen in society.

# References

Abravanel, E. (1968). *The Development of Intersensory Patterning with Regard to Selected Spatial Dimensions*. Monographs of the Society for Research in Child Development 33, No. 2.

Adelson, J. (1970). "What Generation Gap?" *New York Times Magazine,* 18 January, pp. 10–45.

Anastasi, A. (1958). "Heredity, Environment, and the Question 'How?' " *Psychological Review* 65:197-208.

Anderson, P. W. (1972). "More Is Different." *Science* 177: 393-96. Quoted by permission. Copyright 1972 by the American Association for the Advancement of Science.

Atz, J. W. (1970). "The Application of the Idea of Homology to Behavior." In L. R. Aronson, E. Tobach, D. S. Lehrman, and J. S. Rosenblatt (eds.), *Development and Evolution of Behavior: Essays in Memory of T. C. Schneirla*. San Francisco: W. H. Freeman.

Bacon, C., and R. M. Lerner (1975). "Effects of Maternal Employment Status on the Development of Vocational Role Perception in Females." *Journal of Genetic Psychology* 126: 187–193.

Baltes, P. B. (1967). "Langsschnitt-und Querschnittsequenzen zur Erfassung von Altersund Generationseffekten." Ph.D. dissertation, University of Saar.

——— (1968). "Longitudinal and Cross-sectional Sequences in the Study of Age and Generation Effects." *Human Development* 11:145–71.

Baltes, P. B., and J. R. Nesselroade (1970). "Multivariate Longitudinal and Cross-sectional Sequences for Analyzing Ontogenetic and Generational Change: A Methodological Note." *Developmental Psychology* 2:163–68.

——— (1972). "Cultural Change and Adolescent Personality Development: An Application of Longitudinal Sequences." *Developmental Psychology* 7:244–56.

Bandura, A., and F. J. McDonald (1963). "Influence of Social Reinforcement and the Behavior of Models in Shaping Children's Moral Judgment." *Journal of Abnormal and Social Psychology* 67:274–81.

Bandura, A., and R. Walters (1963). *Social Learning and Personality Development*. New York: Holt, Rinehart and Winston.

Bayley, N., and M. H. Oden (1955). "The Maintenance of Intellectual Ability in Gifted Adults." *Journal of Gerontology* 10:91–107.

Bell, R. Q. (1968). "A Reinterpretation of the Direction of Effects in Studies of Socialization." *Psychological Review* 75:81–95.

Bertalanffy, L. (1933). *Modern Theories of Development*. London: Oxford University Press.

Bijou, S. W., and D. M. Baer (1961). *Child Development. Vol. 1: A Systematic and Empirical Theory.* New York: Appleton-Century-Crofts © 1961, Prentice-Hall, Inc., Englewood Cliffs, N.J.

Birch, H. G., and A. Lefford (1963). *Intersensory Development in Children*. Monographs of the Society for Research in Child Development 28, No. 5.

——— (1967). *Visual Differentiation, Intersensory Integration, and Voluntary Motor Control*. Monographs of the Society for Research in Child Development 32, No. 2.

Bitterman, M. E. (1960). "Toward a Comparative Psychology of Learning." *American Psychologist* 15:704–12.

——— (1965). "Phyletic Differences in Learning." *American Psychologist* 20:396–410.

——— (1975). "The Comparative Analysis of Learning." *Science* 188:699–709.

Block, J. H. (1973). "Conceptions of Sex Role: Some Cross-Cultural and Longitudinal Perspectives." *American Psychologist* 28:512–26.

Bloom, B. B. (1964). *Stability and Change in Human Characteristics*. New York: Wiley.

Bolles, R. C. (1967). *Theory of Motivation*. New York: Harper & Row.

———— (1972). "Reinforcement, Expectancy, and Learning." *Psychological Review* 79:394–409.

Boring, E. G. (1950). *A History of Experimental Psychology*. 2d ed. New York: Appleton-Century-Crofts.

Bower, T. G. R. (1966). "The Visual World of Infants." *Scientific American* 215:80–92.

Bowers, K. S. (1973). "Situationalism in Psychology." *Psychological Review* 80:307–36.

Breland, K., and M. Breland (1961). "The Misbehavior of Organisms." *American Psychologist* 16:681–684.

Brigham, J. C. (1971). "Ethnic Stereotypes." *Psychological Bulletin* 76:15–38.

Bronfenbrenner, U. (1960). "Freudian Theories of Identification and Their Derivatives." *Child Development* 31:15–40.

———— (1963). "Developmental Theory in Transition." In H. W. Stevenson (ed.), *Child Psychology*. Sixty-second Yearbook of the National Society for the Study of Education, Part 1. Chicago: University of Chicago Press.

Buss, A. R. (1973). "An Extension of Developmental Models That Separate Ontogenetic Changes and Cohort Differences." *Psychological Bulletin* 80:466–79.

Cattell, R. B. (1957). *Personality and Motivation Structure and Measurement*. New York: World.

———— (1965). *The Scientific Analysis of Personality*. Baltimore: Penguin.

———— (1966). "Psychological Theory and Scientific Method." In R. B. Cattell (ed.), *Handbook of Multivariate Experimental Psychology*. Chicago: Rand McNally.

Cattell, R. B., H. W. Eber, and M. M. Tatsuoka (1970). *Handbook for the Sixteen Personality Factor Questionnaire (16 PF)*. Champaign, Ill.: Institute for Personality and Ability Testing.

Chess, S., A. Thomas, and H. G. Birch (1965). *Your Child Is a Person*. New York: Viking.

Dion, K. K. (1972). "Physical Attractiveness and Evaluations of Children's Transgressions." *Journal of Personality and Social Psychology* 24:207–13.

Dollard, J., and N. E. Miller (1950). *Personality and Psychotherapy*. New York: McGraw-Hill.

Douvan, E., and J. Adelson (1966). *The Adolescent Experience*. New York: Wiley.

DuBois, C. (1944). *The People of Alor*. Minneapolis: University of Minnesota Press.

Dunn, L. C. (1965). *A Short History of Genetics*. New York: McGraw-Hill.

Eacker, J. N. (1972). "On Some Elementary Philosophical Problems of Psychology." *American Psychologist* 27:553–65.

Elkind, D. (1967). "Egocentrism in Adolescence." *Child Development* 38:1025–34.

Emmerich, W. (1968). "Personality Development and Concepts of Structure." *Child Development* 39:671–90.

Erikson, E. H. (1959). "Identity and the Life Cycle." *Psychological Issues* 1:18–164.

————(1963). *Childhood and Society*. Rev ed. New York: Norton.

————, ed. (1964). *Insight and Responsibility*. New York: Norton.

————, ed. (1965). *The Challenge of Youth*. New York: Doubleday, Anchor.

———— (1968). *Identity, Youth and Crisis*. New York: Norton.

Esposito, N. J. (1975). "Review of Discrimination Shift Learning in Young Children." *Psychological Bulletin* 82:432–55.

Eysenck, H. J. (1960). *The Structure of Human Personality*. 2d ed. London: Methuen.

———— (1971). *The IQ Argument: Race, Intelligence and Education*. New York: Library Press.

Fantz, R. L. (1958). "Pattern Vision in Young Infants." *Psychological Record* 8:43–47.

Fantz, R. L., J. M. Ordy, and M. S. Udelf (1962). "Maturation of Pattern Vision in Infants During the First Six Months." *Journal of Comparative and Physiological Psychology* 55:907–17.

Flavell, J. H. (1963). *The Developmental Psychology of Jean Piaget.* Princeton, N.J.: Van Nostrand.

Freud, A. (1969). "Adolescence as a Developmental Disturbance." In G. Caplan and S. Lebovici (eds.), *Adolescence.* New York: Basic Books.

Freud, S. (1923). *The Ego and the Id.* London: Hogarth.

——— (1949). *Outline of Psychoanalysis.* New York: Norton.

——— (1950). "Some Psychological Consequences of the Anatomical Distinction Between the Sexes." In *Collected Papers,* Vol. 5. London: Hogarth.

Gagné, R. M. (1968). "Contributions of Learning to Human Development." *Psychological Review* 75:177–91.

Gesell, A. L. (1929). "Maturation and Infant Behavior Pattern." *Psychological Review* 36:307–19.

——— (1946). "The Ontogenesis of Infant Behavior." In L. Carmichael (ed.), *Manual of Child Psychology.* New York: Wiley.

Gesell, A. L., and H. Thompson (1941). "Twins T and C from Infancy to Adolescence: A Biogenetic Study of Individual Differences by the Method of Co-Twin Control." *Genetic Psychology Monographs* 24:3–121.

Gewirtz, J. L. (1961). "A Learning Analysis of the Effects of Normal Stimulation, Privation and Deprivation on the Acquisition of Social Motivation and Attachment." In B. M. Foss (ed.), *Determinants of Infant Behavior.* New York: Wiley.

Gewirtz, J. L., and K. G. Stingle (1968). "Learning of Generalized Imitation as the Basis for Identification." *Psychological Review* 75:374–97.

Ghiselli, E. E. (1974). "Some Perspectives for Industrial Psychology." *American Psychologist* 29:80–87.

Gordon, E. M., and A. Thomas (1967). "Children's Behavioral Style and the Teacher's Appraisal of Their Intelligence." *Journal of School Psychology* 5:292–300.

Gottlieb, G. (1970). "Conceptions of Prenatal Behavior." In L. R. Aronson, E. Tobach, D. S. Lehrman, and J. S. Rosenblatt (eds.), *Development and Evolution of Behavior: Essays in Memory of T. C. Schneirla.* San Francisco: W. H. Freeman.

Hall, C. S. (1954). *A Primer of Freudian Psychology.* New York: World.

Hamburger, V. (1957). "The Concept of 'Development' in Biology." In D. B. Harris (ed.), *The Concept of Development.* Minneapolis: University of Minnesota Press.

Harré, R., and P. F. Secord (1972). *The Explanation of Social Behaviour.* Oxford: Basil Blackwell & Mott.

Harris, D. B., ed. (1957). *The Concept of Development.* Minneapolis, Minn.: University of Minnesota Press.

Hebb, D. O. (1949). *The Organization of Behavior.* New York: Wiley.

——— (1970). "A Return to Jensen and His Social Critics." *American Psychologist* 25:568.

Held, R., and A. Hein (1963). "Movement-Produced Stimulation in the Development of Visually Guided Behavior." *Journal of Comparative and Physiological Psychology* 56:872–76.

Herrnstein, R. J. (1971) *"IQ." Atlantic Monthly* 228:43–64.

——— (1973). *"IQ in the Meritocracy."* Boston: Little, Brown.

Hempel, C. G. (1966). *Philosophy of Natural Science.* Englewood Cliffs, N.J.: Prentice-Hall.

Hirsch, J. (1963). "Behavior Genetics and Individuality Understood." *Science* 142:1436–42.

—— (1970). "Behavior-Genetic Analysis and its Biosocial Consequences." *Seminars in Psychiatry* 2:89–105.

Horn, J. L. (1970). "Organization of Data on Life-Span Development of Human Abilities." In L. R. Goulet and P. B. Baltes (eds.), *Life-Span Developmental Psychology: Research and Theory.* New York: Academic Press.

Horn, J. L., and R. B. Cattell (1966). "Age Differences in Primary Mental Ability Factors." *Journal of Gerontology* 21:210–20.

Jensen, A. R. (1969). "How Much Can We Boost IQ and Scholastic Achievement?" *Harvard Educational Review* 39:1–123. Quoted by permission. Copyright © 1969 by President and Fellows of Harvard College.

—— (1973). *Educability and Group Differences.* New York: Harper & Row.

Jones, H. E. (1959). "Intelligence and Problem Solving." In J. E. Birren (ed.), *Handbook of Aging and the Individual.* Chicago: University of Chicago Press.

Kagan, J. (1969). "Inadequate Evidence and Illogical Conclusions." *Harvard Educational Review* 39:274–77.

Kagan, J., and H. A. Moss (1962). *Birth to Maturity.* New York: Wiley.

Kaufmann, H. (1968). *Introduction to the Study of Human Behavior.* Philadelphia: Saunders.

Kellogg, W. N., and L. A. Kellogg (1933). *The Ape and the Child.* New York: McGraw-Hill.

Kendler, H. H., and T. S. Kendler (1962). "Vertical and Horizontal Processes in Problem Solving." *Psychological Review* 69:1–16.

Kimble, G. A. (1961). *Hilgard and Marguis' Conditioning and Learning.* New York: Appleton-Century-Crofts.

Kohlberg, L. (1958). The Development of Modes of Moral Thinking and Choice in the Years 10-16." Ph.D, dissertation, University of Chicago.

—— (1963a). "The Development of Children's Orientations Toward a Moral Order: 1. Sequence in the Development of Moral Thought." *Vita Humana,* 6:11–33.

—— (1963b). "Moral Development and Identification." In H. W. Stevenson (ed.), *Child Psychology.* Sixty-second Yearbook of the National Society for the Study of Education, Part 1. Chicago: University of Chicago Press.

—— (1966). "A Cognitive-Developmental Analysis of Children's Sex-Role Concepts and Attitudes." In E. E. Maccoby (ed.), *The Development of Sex Differences.* Stanford, Calif.: Stanford University Press.

Kurtines, W., and E. B. Greif (1974). "The Development of Moral Thought: Review and Evaluation of Kohlberg's Approach." *Psychological Bulletin* 81:453–70.

Kuo, Z. Y. (1967). *The Dynamics of Behavior Development.* New York: Random House.

Langer, J. (1969). *Theories of Development.* New York: Holt, Rinehart and Winston.

—— (1970). "Werner's Comparative Organismic Theory." In P. H. Mussen (ed.), *Carmichael's Manual of Child Psychology,* Vol. 1. New York: Wiley.

Layzer, D. (1974). "Heritability Analyses of IQ Scores: Science or Numerology?" *Science* 183:1259–66. Quoted by permission. Copyright 1974 by the American Association for the Advancement of Science.

Lehrman, D. S. (1953). "A Critique of Konrad Lorenz's Theory of Instinctive Behavior." *Quarterly Review of Biology* 28:337–63.

—— (1970). "Semantic and Conceptual Issues in the Nature-Nurture Problem." In L. R. Aronson, E. Tobach, D. S. Lehrman, and J. S. Rosenblatt (eds.), *Development and Evolution of Behavior: Essays in Memory of T. C. Schneirla.* San Francisco: W. H. Freeman.

Lerner, R. M. (1969). "The Development of Stereotyped Expectancies of Body Build–Behavior Relations." *Child Development,* 40:137–41.

―――― (1972). " 'Richness' Analyses of Body Build Stereotype Development." *Developmental Psychology* 7:219.

―――― (1973). "The Development of Personal Space Schemata Toward Body Build." *Journal of Psychology* 84:229–35.

―――― (1975). "Showdown at Generation Gap: Attitudes of Adolescents and Their Parents toward Contemporary Issues." In H. D. Thornburg (ed.), *Contemporary Adolescence.* 2d ed. Belmont, Calif.: Brooks/Cole.

Lerner, R. M., and E. Gellert (1969). "Body Build Identification, Preference, and Aversion in Children." *Developmental Psychology* 1:456–62.

Lerner, R. M., S. A. Karabenick, and M. Meisels (1975). "Effects of Age and Sex on the Development of Personal Space Schemata toward Body Build." *Journal of Genetic Psychology* 127: 91–101.

―――― (1975). "One-Year Stability of Children's Personal Space Schemata towards Body Build." *Journal of Genetic Psychology* 127: 151–152.

Lerner, R. M., S. A. Karabenick, and J. L. Stuart (1973). "Relations among Physical Attractiveness, Body Attitudes, and Self-Concept in Male and Female College Students." *Journal of Psychology* 85:119–29.

Lerner, R. M., M. Karson, M. Meisels, and J. R. Knapp (1975). "Actual and Perceived Attitudes of Late Adolescents and Their Parents: The Phenomenon of the Generation Gaps." *Journal of Genetic Psychology* 126: 195–207.

Lerner, R. M., and J. R. Knapp (1975). "Actual and Perceived Intrafamilial Attitudes of Late Adolescents and Their Parents." *Journal of Youth and Adolescence* 4:17–36.

Lerner, R. M., J. R. Knapp, and K. B. Pool (1974). "The Structure of Body Build Stereotypes: A Methodological Analysis." *Perceptual and Motor Skills* 39:19–29.

Lerner, R. M., and S. J. Korn (1972). "The Development of Body Build Stereotypes in Males." *Child Development* 43:912–20.

Lerner, R. M., J. Pendorf, and A. Emery (1971). "Attitudes of Adolescents and Adults toward Contemporary Issues." *Psychological Reports* 28:139–45.

Lerner, R. M., and C. Schroeder (1971a). "Kindergarten Children's Active Vocabulary about Body Build." *Developmental Psychology* 5:179.

―――― (1971b). "Physique Identification, Preference, and Aversion in Kindergarten Children." *Developmental Psychology* 5:538.

Lerner, R. M., C. Schroeder, M. Rewitzer, and A. Weinstock (1972). "Attitudes of High School Students and Their Parents toward Contemporary Issues." *Psychological Reports* 31:255–58.

Looft, W. R. (1972). "The Evolution of Developmental Psychology." *Human Development* 15:187–201.

Lorenz, K. (1965). *Evolution and Modification of Behavior.* Chicago: University of Chicago Press.

Marshall, J. M., and S. A. Karabenick (1975). "Self-Esteem, Fear of Success, and Occupational Choice in Female Adolescents." Eastern Michigan University.

McCandless, B. R. (1967). *Children.* New York: Holt, Rinehart and Winston.

―――― (1970). *Adolescents.* Hinsdale, Ill.: Dryden Press.

McGill, T. E., ed. (1965). *Readings in Animal Behavior.* New York: Holt, Rinehart and Winston.

Mednick, M. S., and S. S. Tangri (1972). "New Social Psychological Perspectives on Women." *Social Issues* 28:1–16.

Mischel, W. (1968). *Personality and Assessment.* New York: Wiley.

————— (1971). *Introduction to Personality.* New York: Holt, Rinehart and Winston.

Misiak, H. (1961). *The Philosophical Roots of Scientific Psychology.* New York: Fordham University Press.

Moltz, H., and L. J. Stettner (1961). "The Influence of Patterned-Light Deprivation on the Critical Period for Imprinting." *Journal of Comparative and Physiological Psychology* 54:279–83.

Mussen, P. H. (1970). "Preface." In P. H. Mussen (ed.), *Carmichael's Manual of Child Psychology, Vol. 1.* New York: Wiley.

Nagel, E. (1957). "Determinism and Development." In D. B. Harris (ed.), *The Concept of Development.* Minneapolis: University of Minnesota Press.

Nesselroade, J. R., and P. B. Baltes (1974). *Adolescent Personality Development and Historical Change: 1970–1972.* Monographs of the Society for Research in Child Development 39, No. 1.

Nesselroade, J. R., K. W. Schaie, and P. B. Baltes (1972). "Ontogenetic and Generational Components of Structural and Quantitative Change in Adult Cognitive Behavior." *Journal of Gerontology* 27:222–28.

Piaget, J. (1950). *The Psychology of Intelligence.* London: Routledge & Kegan Paul.

————— (1952). *The Origins of Intelligence in Children.* New York: International Universities Press.

————— (1965). *The Moral Judgment of the Child.* New York: The Free Press.

————— (1970). "Piaget's Theory." In P. H. Mussen (ed.), *Carmichael's Manual of Child Psychology, Vol. 1.* New York: Wiley.

Rosenthal, R. (1966). *Experimenter Effects in Behavioral Research.* New York: Appleton-Century-Crofts.

Sarason, S. B. (1973). "Jewishness, Blackishness, and the Nature-Nurture Controversy." *American Psychologist* 28:962–71.

Scarr-Salapatek, S. (1971a). "Unknowns in the IQ Equation." *Science* 174:1223–28.

————— (1971b). "Race, Social Class, and IQ." *Science* 174:1285–95.

Schaie, K. W. (1959). "Cross-sectional Methods in the Study of Psychological Aspects of Aging." *Journal of Gerontology* 14:208–15.

————— (1965). "A General Model for the Study of Developmental Problems." *Psychological Bulletin* 64:92–107.

————— (1967). "Age Changes and Age Differences." *The Gerontologist* 7:128–32.

————— (1970). "A Reinterpretation of Age-Related Changes in Cognitive Structure and Functioning." In L. R. Goulet and P. B. Baltes (eds.), *Life-Span Developmental Psychology: Research and Theory.* New York: Academic Press.

————— (1973). "Methodological Problems in Descriptive Developmental Research on Adulthood and Aging." In J. R. Nesselroade and H. W. Reese (eds.), *Life-Span Developmental Psychology: Methodological Issues.* New York: Academic Press.

Schaie, K. W., G. V. Labouvie, and B. U. Buech (1973). "Generational and Cohort-Specific Differences in Adult Cognitive Functioning: A Fourteen-Year Study of Independent Samples." *Developmental Psychology* 9:151–66.

Schaie, K. W., and C. R. Strother (1968). "A Cross-sequential Study of Age Changes in Cognitive Behavior." *Psychological Bulletin* 70:671–80.

Schneirla, T. C. (1956). "Interrelationships of the 'Innate' and the 'Acquired' in Instinctive Behavior." In *L'instinct dans le Comportement des Animaux et de l'Homme.* Paris: Masson & Cie.

—— (1957). "The Concept of Development in Comparative Psychology." In D. B. Harris (ed.), *The Concept of Development*. Minneapolis: University of Minnesota Press.

Schneirla, T. C., and J. S. Rosenblatt (1961). "Behavioral Organization and Genesis of the Social Bond in Insects and Mammals." *The American Journal of Orthopsychiatry* 31:223–53.

—— (1963). " 'Critical Periods' in Behavioral Development." *Science* 139:1110–14. Excerpted by permission. Copyright 1963 by the American Association of the Advancement of Science.

Scott, J. P. (1963). "Critical Periods in Behavioral Development." *Science* 138: 949–58.

Sears, R. (1957). "Identification as a Form of Behavioral Development." In D. B. Harris (ed.), *The Concept of Development*. Minneapolis: University of Minnesota Press.

Secord, P. F., and C. W. Backman (1969). *Social Psychology*. New York: McGraw-Hill.

Sheldon, W. H. (1940). *The Varieties of Human Physique*. New York: Harper & Row.

—— (1942). *The Varieties of Temperament*. New York: Harper & Row.

Sherrington, C. S. (1951). *Man On His Nature*. London: Cambridge University Press.

Simpson, E. L. (1974). "Moral Development Research. A Case Study of Scientific Cultural Bias." *Human Development* 17:81–106.

Skinner, B. F. (1938). *The Behavior of Organisms*. New York: Appleton.

—— (1950). "Are Theories of Learning Necessary?" *Psychological Review* 57:211–20.

—— (1956). "A Case History in Scientific Method." *American Psychologist* 11:221–33.

Sluckin, W. (1965). *Imprinting and Early Experience*. Chicago: Aldine.

Thomas, A., and S. Chess (1970). "Behavioral Individuality in Early Childhood." In L. R. Aronson, E. Tobach, D. S. Lehrman, and J. S. Rosenblatt (eds.), *Development and Evolution of Behavior: Essays in Memory of T. C. Schneirla*. San Francisco: W. H. Freeman.

Thomas, A., S. Chess, and H. G. Birch (1968). *Temperament and Behavior Disorders in Children*. New York: New York University Press.

—— (1970). "The Origin of Personality." *Scientific American* 223:102–9.

Thomas, A., S. Chess, H. G. Birch, M. Hertzig, and S. Korn (1963). *Behavioral Individuality in Early Childhood*. New York: New York University Press.

Turiel, E. (1969). "Developmental Processes in the Child's Moral Thinking." In P. H. Mussen, J. Langer, and M. Covington (eds.), *Trends and Issues in Developmental Psychology*. New York: Holt, Rinehart and Winston.

Walker, R. N. (1962). *Body Build and Behavior in Young Children: I. Body Build and Nursery School Teachers' Ratings*. Monographs of the Society for Research in Child Development 27, No. 3.

Watson, J. B. (1914). *Behavior: An Introduction to Comparative Psychology*. New York: Holt.

Weinstock: A., and R. M. Lerner (1972). "Attitudes of Late Adolescents and Their Parents Toward Contemporary Issues." *Psychological Reports* 30:239–44.

Werner, H. (1957). "The Concept of Development from a Comparative and Organismic Point of View." In D. B. Harris (ed.), *The Concept of Development*. Minneapolis: University of Minnesota Press.

White, S. (1970). "The Learning Theory Approach." In P. H. Mussen (ed.), *Carmichael's Manual of Child Psychology, Vol. 1*. New York: Wiley.

# index

Abravanel, E., 107
Abruptness, 114
Accommodation, 161–162
Acquired schema, 165
Action and knowledge, 161
Activity level (as a temperamental attribute), 236
Adaptability (as a temperamental attribute), 236
Adaptation, and assimilation and accommodation, 160
    in Piaget's theory, 160
Adelson, J., 4, 162
Adolescence, and the generation gap, 4
    and personality differences with adults, 20
    and saliency of the peer group, 8
    and storm and stress, 4, 120
Adolescent egocentrism, 172
    and imaginary audience, 172
    and personal fable, 173
Adulthood (as Stage 7 in Erikson's theory), 207–208
Ahistorical studies, 284
Ahistorical-historical dimension of developmental research, 284–285
American Psychological Association, 50
Anal stage (in Freud's theory), 188
Anal-musculature stage (as Stage 2 in Erikson's theory), 202
Anastasi, A., 22, 50, 51, 55, 58, 60–64, 76, 301
    interactionist position of, 50–63
Anterospective reconstruction method, 291
Aristotle, 48
A/S ratio, definition of, 92
    and sense domination, 92
    and stereotypy-plasticity, 92–94
Assimilation, 160–161
Association cortex, 91
Atheoretical studies, 287
Atheoretical-theoretical dimension of developmental research, 287–288
Attention span and persistence (as temperamental attributes), 237
Atz, J. W., 86
Approach/withdrawal (as a temperamental attribute), 236
Attribution and social stereotypes, 302
Autonomy versus shame and doubt (as Stage 2 crisis in Erikson's theory), 203
Avoidance, 268

Backman, C. W., 58
Bacon, C., 298
Baer, D. M., 11, 16, 26, 27, 35, 153, 249, 258, 260, 267–269, 271 –273
Bain, A., 49
Baltes, P. B., 3, 196, 217, 218, 221, 285
Bandura, A., 174, 182, 183
Bayley, N., 216
Behavior potentiality, 256
Behavioral reactivity, 230
Bell, R. Q., 16
Bertalanffy, L. V., 4, 23, 25, 30, 33
Biased samples, 294–295
Bijou, S. W., 11, 16, 26, 27, 35, 153, 249, 258, 260, 267–269, 271–273
Birch, H. G., 16, 37, 86, 105–107, 152, 153, 226, 231–239, 244, 247–249, 291, 296, 300, 301
Bitterman, M. E., 122–127
    and implications of tests of assumption of phyletic continuity, 125–127
Block, J. H., 298
Bloom, B. B., 64
Body build, components of, 290
    and temperament, 22, 34
Bolles, R. C., 24, 255
Boring, E. G., 184
Bower, T. G. R., 96
Bowers, K. S., 271–278, 300, 301
    and analysis of situations, persons, and interactions, 277–278
Breland, K., 124
Breland, M., 124
Breuer, J., 184
Brigham, J. C., 302
British School of Empiricism, 49
Bronfenbrenner, U., 5, 6, 189
Buech, B. U., 3
Buss, A. R., 218

Calvinism, 49
Castration anxiety, 188–189
Categorization, and person perception, 58, 302
    and social stereotypes, 58–59, 301–302
Catharsis, 184
Cattell, R. B., 12–15, 20, 21, 145, 216
    and inductive-hypothetico-deductive model, 12–15
Chess, S., 16, 37, 152, 153, 226, 231–239, 244, 247–249, 291, 296, 300, 301

Child rearing, cookbook approach to, 248
  of individually different children, 300–301
Chromosomal anomalies, 55
Circular functions, definition of, 102–103
  and self-stimulation in development, 102–104
Circular reactions, 165–166
Classical conditioning, 7, 258–260
  characteristics of, 259–260
  and reinforcement, 266
  synonyms of, 260
Cognition, and action, 161
  as a biological system, 160
  synonyms of in Piaget's theory, 160
Cognitive development, 159
  as an active, self-generated process, 173
  and disequilibration, 173
Cohort, 216
Concept, 293
Conditioned emotional response (CER), 260
Conditioned response (CR), 259
Conditioned stimulus (CS), 259
Concrete operational stage (in Piaget's theory),
  170–171
Conscience, 189
Conservation, 168
Constructionist hypothesis, and emergence,
  29–30
  and problems of scale and complexity, 29
Contamination, 289
Continuity-discontinuity issue, 22, 112–133
  as an empirical issue, 113
  influence of theory on, 120
  and nature-nurture issue, 112
  and phylogeny of learning, 122–126
  and study of problem solving in ontogeny,
    127
Controlled experiments, 286–287
Controlled observation, 286
Critical or crucial tests, 8
  and hypothesis testing, 8
Critical period hypothesis, 98–100
  in Erikson's theory, 201
Cross-sectional method, 210, 285
  confoundings in, 216–217
  limitations of, 210

Darwin, C., 112–123
  and phyletic continuity assumption, 122
Davis, A., 120

Décalage, 174
Deductive reasoning, 9
Descartes, R., 49
Development, core concepts of, 21–23
  as a dialectical process, 120
  and orthogenesis, 117
  Schneirla's definition of, 94
  as a self-generated phenomenon, 104
Developmental change, 113–116
  and continuity-discontinuity, stability-
    instability issues, 131
Developmental psychology, 20
  and advances in factual knowledge, 2–5
  goal of, 20
  history of, 5–6
Developmental research, and cross-sectional
    method, 210
  dimensions of, 282–288
  and longitudinal method, 209–210
  methodological problems of, 289–298
  and sequential methods, 218, 285
  some social implications of, 298–303
Dialectical development, 120
Differential approach, 141–148, 196–223
  and core concepts of development,
    146–148
  and individual differences, 144
  and nomothetic laws, 144
Differentiation, 94
Difficult child, 239, 244
Dion, K. K., 37
Discontinuity, 112
Discriminative stimulus ($S^D$), 261
Distractibility (as a temperamental attribute),
    236–237
Dobzhansky, T., 63
Dollard, J., 123
Douvan, E., 4
Down's syndrome, 55
DuBois, C., 199
Dunn, L. C., 63
Dylan, B., 4

Eacker, J. N., 30
Easy child, 239
Eber, H. W., 20
Ecological validity, 285
Ego, 7, 198
  function of, 198
  and Id, 197–198

Ego *(continued)*
   implications of, 198–199
   and society, 198–199
Ego development, 200
Ego integrity versus despair (as crisis in Stage
   8 of Erikson's theory), 208
Ego-ideal, 189
Elkind, D., 159, 166–168, 171, 172
Emergence, 30–31
   and constructionist hypothesis, 29–30
   and epigenesis, 31–32
Emery, A., 62, 293
Emmerich, W., 129, 136–141, 144, 147, 149,
   151
Environmental differences hypothesis, 67, 69
Environmentalist viewpoint and empirical
   philosophy, 7
Environmental effects along continuum of
   breadth, 61
Environmental stimulus effects, 62
Epigenesis, 31–32
   and emergence, 30–31
   and nature-nurture controversy, 35
   and predeterministic position, 35
Epistemology, 159
Equilibration, 162
Erikson, E., 8, 11, 16, 99, 140, 141, 144, 148,
   153, 191, 196–209
   epigenetic principle in theory of, 199–201
   notion of critical periods in theory of, 201
   notion of maturational ground plan in theory
    of, 140
   stage and differential theory of psychosocial
    development, 196–209
Erogenous zone, 186
Escape, 267
Esposito, N. J., 41
Ethical considerations in developmental re-
   search, 295–296
Ethologists, 34
Experience, 95
   in Schneirla's theory, 95
   interactions with maturation, 96
Explanatory studies, 284
Eysenck, H. J., 70, 177

Factor analysis, 20
Fantz, R. L., 2–3
   and study of neonate vision, 3
Faulty logic, 291–293

   examples of, 292
Fels Research Institute, 211
Fidelity (as virtue in Stage 5 of Erikson's theory),
   206
Fixation, 187
Flavell, J. H., 158, 159, 163, 166, 174
Formal operational stage (in Piaget's theory),
   172–173
Free association, 184
   and repressed memories, 184–185
Freud, A., 8, 115, 120, 197, 199
Freud, S., 8, 11, 15, 42, 43, 136, 140, 141, 153,
   158, 159, 174, 177, 184–191, 196–199,
   201, 203, 204, 234, 291
   notions about personality structures, 197
   and psychoanalysis, 201
   and retrospective method, 234
   stage theory of psychosexual development,
    43, 184–191
Frustration, 187
Functional invariants, 160
Functional orders, 88, 94
Functional (reproductive) assimilation, 163–164

Gagné, R. M., 50, 120, 265
Gappiness, 114–115
Gellert, E., 60
General and specific laws compromise, 42
General developmental model, features of,
   218–220
Generalization problems, 296–297
   and sampling, 296
Generation gap, 62
   and adolescence, 4
   definition of, 293
Generativity versus stagnation (as crisis in
   Stage 7 of Erikson's theory), 207
Genetic differences hypothesis, 69–71, 79
   and A. R. Jensen, 70
   and IQ heritability, 70
Genetic inheritance, 63
Genital-locomotor stage (as Stage 3 in Erik-
   son's theory), 203–204
Genotype, 63
Gesell, A. L., 5, 50
Gestalt psychology, 32, 50
   and nativist view of perception, 22
Gewirtz, J. L., 26, 27, 153, 255
Ghiselli, E. E., 2
Gordon, E. M., 244

Gottlieb, G., 31
Gradual change, 114
Greek philosophy, 48
Greif, E. B., 184
Growth, 94

Hall, C. S., 184, 186–188
Hamburger, V., 35, 86
Harré, R., 273
Harris, D. B., 23, 265, 269
Hartley, D., 49
Hartman, H., 199
Hebb, D. O., 16, 22, 50, 51, 60, 64, 71, 76–78,
    91–93
    and the A/S ratio, 91–92
Hein, A., 107
Held, R., 107
Hempel, C. G., 8, 9, 12, 16
Hereditary effects along continuum of indirect-
    ness, 53–57
Heritability, 69, 72, 78
    environmental influences on, 77–80
    formula for, 73
    and genetic determination, 74
    of IQ, 69, 80
    measurement reliability, 74–75
    and norm of reaction, 78–79
    uses and misuses of, 72–75, 76
Herrnstein, R. J., 60, 70
Hertzig, M., 16, 37, 152, 153, 226, 231–239,
    244, 247–249, 291, 296, 300, 301
Hirsch, J., 63–67, 71, 73–77, 80
Historical developmental research, 284
    and continuity-discontinuity, stability-
        instability issues, 285
    designs for, 285
History of developmental psychology, 5–6
Hobbes, T., 49
Homology, 86–88, 177
Homunculus, 49
Horizontal décalage, 174
Horn, J. L., 3, 216
Hume, D., 49

Id, 197–198
    and the ego, 197–198
Identification, 189
    and castration anxiety, 188–189
Identity crisis, 205
Identity versus role confusion (or identity diffu-
sion) (as crisis in Stage 5 of Erikson's
    theory), 206
Ideology, 205
Idiographic laws, 148
Inadequate concept definition, 293–294
Inductive reasoning, 10, 12
Industry versus inferiority (as crisis in Stage 4 of
    Erikson's theory), 204
Initiative versus guilt (as crisis in Stage 3 of
    Erikson's theory), 204
Innate schema, 164
    examples of, 165
Instability, 128
Instinct, 34, 98, 100–102
Instinctive behavior (as defined by Lorenz), 100
Intellectual development, across the life span,
    3–4
Intelligence, and nature-nurture controversy,
    22, 67–80
Intelligence A, 64
Intelligence B, 64
Intensity of reaction (as a temperamental attri-
    bute), 236
Interaction in learning approach to develop-
    ment, 271
Interactionist critique of position of Lorenz, 101
Intersensory integration, 105
    as a developmental phenomenon, 106–107
    and ontogeny, 106
    and phyletic development, 105
    and role of child's exploratory behavior, 107
Intimacy versus isolation (as crisis in Stage 6 of
    Erikson's theory), 207
Ipsative approach, 148–153, 226–251
    and continuity-discontinuity issue, 151–152
    versus environmentalist view of individuality,
        230
    and idiographic orientation, 148
    and nature-nurture issue, 152–153
    and the organismic probabilistic epigenetic
        view of individuality, 230
    and the organism's contribution to own
        development, 152, 226
    and orthogenetic principle, 151
    versus preformationist views of individuality,
        229–230
IQ, 67, 68
    black-white score differences, 67, 70, 79–80
    culture-free and culture-bound tests of, 79
    and heritability estimates of, 69, 80

Jensen, A. R., 22, 50, 60, 66–71, 74, 77, 78
    and genetic differences hypothesis, 68–70
    and social reactions to the genetic differ-
        ences hypothesis, 70–71
Jones, H. E., 216

Kagan, J., 50, 148, 153, 196, 209–215, 296
Kagan and Moss study of Birth to Maturity,
        209–215
    method of, 210–211
    results with status variables of age period
        and sex, 212–213
    sources of data in, 211–212
Karabenick, S. A., 16, 60, 296, 298
Karson, M., 4, 62, 293, 294
Kaufmann, H., 20, 21
Keller, H., 57
Kellog, L. A., 93
Kellog, W. N., 93
Kendler, H. H., 39–41, 126–127
Kendler, T.S., 39–41, 126–127
Kimble, G.A., 122, 255
Knapp, J. R., 4, 60, 62, 293, 294
Kohlberg, L., 10, 15, 16, 88, 139, 140, 153, 158,
        176, 178, 181, 183, 184, 191, 248, 249,
        299, 301
    stage theory of development of moral reason-
        ing, 174–184
Korn, S. J., 16, 22, 37, 58, 60, 152, 153, 213,
        226, 231–239, 244, 247–249, 291, 296,
        300, 301, 302
Kris, E., 199
Kuo, Z. Y., 50
Kurtines, W., 184

Labouvie, G. V., 3
Langer, J., 22, 27, 113, 117
Latency stage (as Stage 4 in Erikson's theory),
        204
Latency stage (in Freud's theory), 190
Law, 16
Law of conservation of energy, 185–186
Laws of learning, and assumption of phyletic
        continuity, 122, 123
    and universality in the learning approach,
        245
Layzer, D., 60, 64, 65, 79, 80
Learning, 122, 255
    empirical definition of, 255
    as an intervening variable, 256

    phyletic differences in, 122
    types of, 258–268
Learning approach to development, 127,
        254–280
    characteristics of, 269–272
    and definition of behavior, 271
    evaluation of, 273–276
    and notion of interaction, 271
    as translation of unity of science philosophy,
        269
Learning-performance distinction, 256
Lefford, A., 105–107
Lehrman, D. S., 50, 51, 78, 79, 86, 100, 101
    and critique of "instinct" concept, 101
    his view versus that of Lorenz on what is
        innate, 100–101
Leipzig, Germany, 50
Lerner, R. M., 4, 16, 22, 58, 60, 62, 213, 293,
        294, 296, 298, 302
Level of analysis, 23
Levels of organization hypothesis, 38
Libido, 185–187
Locke, J., 49
Longitudinal method, 209–210, 285
    compared to cross-sectional method, 216–
        217
    and cross-sectional method depiction of age
        changes, 215–216
Looft, W. R., 5, 6
Lorenz, K., 34, 35, 50, 100, 101
    his use of the term "innate," 101

Marshall, J. M., 298
Maturation, 94
    as defined in Schneirla's theory, 94
    and interactions with experience, 95–98
Maturity (as Stage 8 in Erikson's theory), 208
McCandless, B. R., 22, 50, 282–285, 287–289,
        293, 294, 296–298
    and dimensions of developmental research,
        282–288
McDonald, F. T., 183
McGill, T. E., 73
Mechanism, 25
Medieval Christian religious philosophy, 49
Mednick, M. S., 298
Meisels, M., 4, 16, 60, 62, 293, 294
Mental energy, and erogenous zones, 43
    and psychosexual stages, 42
Mesoderm, 94

Methods of scientific reasoning, 11
Mill, J., 49
Mill, J. S., 49
Miller, N. E., 123
Mischel, W., 249, 275, 276
Misiak, H., 49
Moltz, H., 86, 99
Moral development, learning and psychoanalytic views of, 176–178
    and moral responses versus moral reasonings, 177
    and theory of Kohlberg, 10, 179–181
Moral dilemmas, 178–179
Moral reasoning development, and cognitive conflict, 300
    and stage mixture, 182
    stages of, 179–181, 299–300
    transitions between stages of, 181–183
Moss, H. A., 148, 153, 196, 209–215, 296
Motor cortex, 91
Mussen, P. H., 6

Nagel, E., 23, 38
Naturalistic-manipulative dimension of developmental research, 285–287
Naturalistic observation, 285–286
Nature-nurture issue, definitions of, 21, 48
    and independent, additive action assumption, 51
    and independent, isolated action assumption, 51
    and intelligence, 67–80
    and interactive action assumption, 52
    and nature continuum of indirectness, 53
    and nurture continuum of breadth, 60
    and organismic position, 52
    and the question "how," 48–83
    and Schneirla's theory, 85–109
    synonyms of, 21, 48
Nazi Germany, 71
Negative identity formation, 206
Nesselroade, J. R., 3, 217, 218, 221, 285
New York Longitudinal Study (NYLS), 228–249
    and attributes of temperament found in, 235–237
    as example of ipsative developmental research, 226–227
    method of, 232–235
    practical implications of, 248–249
    results of, 238–247

theoretical implications of, 247–248
Nomothetic laws, 137
Nonreversal shifts, 41, 126
Normative data, role in history of developmental psychology, 5
Normative-explanatory dimension of developmental research, 283–284
Normative studies, 283
Norm of reaction, 63–67
    and genotypic uniqueness, 66
    and heritability, 78–79
    limitations of concept of, 65–67
Norms, 97
    and individual differences, 98
Nurture continuum of breadth, 60

Objective moral judgments, 176
Oden, M. H., 216
Oedipus complex, 188–190, 197, 204
    and castration anxiety, 188–189
Ontogeny of learning, 127
Operant conditioning, 260–268
    characteristics of, 262–263
    and position of reinforcement in, 266
    synonyms of, 262
Operations (in Piaget's theory), 170
Oral-sensory stage (as Stage 1 in Erikson's theory), 201–203
Oral stage (in Freud's theory), 187–188
Ordy, J. M., 2
Organic environmental effects, 61–62
Organism, as source of its own development, 102
Organismic philosophy, 30–33
    assumptions of, 32–34
    and unity of science philosophy compromises, 38–44
Organismic theory, 15–17
    and development as a self-generated process, 38
Organization (in Piaget's theory), 160
Orthogenetic principle, 116–117, 151
    and continuity-discontinuity issue, 117–120
    and general and specific laws compromise, 120
Original sin, 49
Overgeneralization, 296–298

Pavlov, I. P., 258
Pendorf, J., 62, 293

Penis envy, 189
  effects of, 189–190
Perception, 104
  development of, 104–108
  and organism's own activity, 107
Person perception, and categorization-
    attribution process, 302
  cues in, 58
  efficiency and economy in, 58
Phallic stage (in Freud's theory), 188–190
  female phallic stage, 189–190
  male phallic stage, 188–189
Phenotype, 63
Philosophy of science, 7, 19–45
Phyletic continuity assumption, 124–127
  ontogenetic implications of, 126–127
  overgeneralizations involved in, 124
  tests of, 125
Physical attractiveness, 37
Physique-behavior relations, 22
Piaget, J., 5, 11, 15, 16, 42, 88, 113, 120, 139,
    140, 153, 158–160, 162–166, 173, 174,
    176, 181, 182, 184, 191, 205, 226, 230,
    248, 249, 301
  and general and specific laws compromise,
    174
  organismic developmental theory of cogni-
    tion of, 158–164
  stage-dependent conceptions, 164–173
  stage-independent concepts, 159–164
  views about moral development, 174
Plasticity, 89
Plasticity versus stereotypy, 89–90
  and A/S ratio, 92–94
  ontogenetic implications of, 92–94
Plato, 48, 49
  and innate ideas, 48
  and mind-body problem, 48
Pleasure principle, 198
Pool, K. B., 60
Predetermined epigenesis, 35
Preoperational stage (in Piaget's theory), 167–
    170
Primary process, 198
Probabilistic epigenesis, 35
  characteristics of, 36–37
  and role of organism's own action, 37–38
Problem solving, 39, 41, 127
  and reversal and nonreversal shifts, 126
Project Head Start, 68, 70

Psychoanalysis, as a theory of development, 8,
    185
  therapeutic methods of, 185
  as a treatment method, 185
Psychological levels, 88, 94
Psychosexual stages (in Freud's theory), 42,
    187–190
Psychosocial stages (in Erikson's theory),
    201–208
Puberty, 190
  changes of, 204–205
  mental changes occurring at, 205
  and secondary sexual characteristics, 205
  and sex drive at adolescence, 115
Puberty and adolescence (as Stage 5 in
    Erikson's theory), 204–206
Punishment, 267
Puritanism, 49

Qualitative change, 115
Qualitative discontinuity, 115
Quality of mood (as a temperamental attribute),
    236
Quantitative change, 114

Racial social stereotypes, 301–302
Rapaport, D., 199
Reality principle, 198
Reconstruction through retrospection, 291
Reductionism, 24
  and constructionism, 28
  and finite regression, 30
  and unity of science continuity assumption,
    24–25
Reinforcement, 257
  and biological adaptation, 269–271
  as a natural selection process, 270–271
  positive and negative, 266–288
Reproductive (functional) assimilation, 163–
    164
Research, reasons for doing, 8–10
Research effects on subject's responses, 290 –
    291
Retrospective methods, 7, 291
  in Freud's work, 185
Reversal shifts, 40–41, 126
Reward, 267
Rewitzer, M., 293
Rhythmicity (as a temperamental attribute), 236
Rosenblatt, J. S., 98–99

Rosenthal, R., 290
Rousseau, J. J., 49

Sampling, 294–296
    ethical considerations in, 295–296
    and generalization problems, 296
Sarason, S. B., 298
Savings effect, 255–256
Scarr-Salapatek, S., 67, 69, 76
Schaie, K. W., 3, 4, 196, 210, 215–218, 221,
    285
    general developmental model of, 215–222
Schema, 164
    characteristics of, 164–165
Schema of object permanency, 166
Schneirla, T. C., 16, 30, 35, 37, 38, 43, 50, 51,
    64, 78, 80, 86–89, 92–99, 102–105, 107,
    113, 124, 152, 177, 226, 230, 248
    and critical periods in development, 99
    interactionist position of, 86–108
    and levels of organization compromise, 88
    and probabilistic epigenetic position, 97–98
Schroeder, C., 60, 293
Scientist as citizen, 302–303
Scott, J. P., 99
Sears, R., 174, 177
Secondary process, 198
Secondary reinforcement, 260
    and chaining, 264–265
Secord, P. F., 58, 273
Self-fulfilling prophecy, 59
    as basis of black-white intellectual differ-
        ences, 60
    and black Americans, 59–60
    and social stereotypes, 59
Sensation, 104
Sense of trust, 7, 202
Sensorimotor stage (in Piaget's theory), 164–
    166
Sensory cortex, 91
Sequential methods, 218, 285
Sheldon, W. H., 22, 34, 50, 233, 289, 290
Sherrington, C. S., 105
Sixteen P. F. Test, 20
Skinner, B. F., 16, 26, 27, 30, 123, 124, 153,
    249, 254, 260, 261, 297
Skinner's position, contrasted with Schneirla's
        position, 124
    as example of position of phyletic continuity,
        123

and use of phyletic continuity assumption,
    123–124
Simpson, E. L., 184
Sleeper effect, 213–215
Slow-to-warm-up child, 244
Sluckin, W., 99
Social psychology, 4
Social stereotypes, 57–60
    and attribution, 302
    and categorization, 301–302
    and physical characteristics, 57, 302
    and race, 301–302
Socialized anxiety, 120
Soul, 48
Stability-instability issue, 127–129
    relations to continuity-discontinuity issue,
        129–132
Stage mixture, 140
    and cognitive conflict, 183
    and disequilibration, 183
Stage theories of development, 136–141,
    158–194
    and continuity-discontinuity issue, 136, 140,
        158
    and critical periods issue, 140–141
    and development as a dialectical process,
        158
    and disequilibration versus libido as sources
        of stage progression, 191
    and general and specific laws compromise,
        140
    and individual differences, 137–138, 158
    and nature-nurture issue, 140, 158
    and nomothetic laws, 137
    and stage attribution, 138–139
    and stage transition, 138–140
    synonyms of, 136
Stettner, L. J., 99
Stereotypy versus plasticity, 89–90
    and A/S ratio, 92–94
    ontogenetic implications of, 92–94
Stingle, K. G., 27, 255
Strother, C. R., 3, 215–217, 221
Stuart, J. L., 296
Subjective moral judgments, 176
Superego, 7, 189, 197

Tabula rasa, 49
Talking cure, 184
Tangri, S. S., 298

Tatsuoka, M. M., 20
Temperament, 233
  attributes of (in New York Longitudinal Study), 235–237
Theories of development in overview, 136–155
Theory, and deductive reasoning, 12
  definition of, 12, 288
  and empirical tests of hypotheses, 12
  its function in science, 4–6, 288
  interrelations with philosophy and research, 6–8, 282
Third source of development (in Schneirla's theory), 102
Thomas, A., 16, 37, 104, 152, 153, 226, 230–239, 244, 247–249, 291, 296, 300, 301
Thompson, H., 50
Threshold of responsivity (as a temperamental attribute), 236
Tobach, E., 86
Trace effects, 95
  and experience, 95
  and maturation interactions, 96
  and perception, 105
Trust versus mistrust (as crisis in Stage 1 of Erikson's theory), 202
Turiel, E., 88, 140, 177–179, 181, 183, 299, 300
Twain, M., 77

Udelf, M. S., 2
Unconditioned response (UCR), 258
Unconditioned stimulus (UCS), 258

Unconscious, 185
Unity of science philosophy, 23–28
  assumptions of, 23–26
  and compromises with organismic philosophy, 38–44
  and continuity-discontinuity issue, 33
  and learning theory, 27, 34
  and nature-nurture issue, 34
  problems of, 28–30
  synonyms for, 17
  and translation into psychological theory, 26–27

Variance, 72
Vertical décalage, 174
Vision in the neonate, 2, 3

Walker, R. N., 22
Walters, R., 174
Wapner, S., 113
Warren, Justice E., 181
Watson, J. B., 123
Weinstock, A., 4, 62, 293
Werner, H., 22, 42, 88, 113, 114, 116, 117, 120, 151, 158, 174
  and definitions of quantitative and qualitative change, 115
White, S., 153, 269, 271–273, 276
Wundt, W., 50

Young adulthood (as Stage 6 in Erikson's theory), 206–207